American Multinationals in Europe

American Multinationals in Europe: Managing Employment Relations across National Borders

Edited by

Phil Almond and Anthony Ferner

with contributions by

Phil Almond, Peter Butler, Ian Clark, Trevor Colling, David Collings, Tony Edwards, Anthony Ferner, Paddy Gunnigle, Michael Morley, Michael Muller-Camen, René Peters, Javier Quintanilla, Lourdes Susaeta, Anne Tempel, and Hartmut Wächter

OXFORD
UNIVERSITY PRESS

OXFORD
UNIVERSITY PRESS

Great Clarendon Street, Oxford ox2 6DP
Oxford University Press is a department of the University of Oxford.
It furthers the University's objective of excellence in research, scholarship,
and education by publishing worldwide in

Oxford New York

Auckland Cape Town Dar es Salaam Hong Kong Karachi
Kuala Lumpur Madrid Melbourne Mexico City Nairobi
New Delhi Shanghai Taipei Toronto with offices in

Argentina Austria Brazil Chile Czech Republic France Greece
Guatemala Hungary Italy Japan Poland Portugal Singapore
South Korea Switzerland Thailand Turkey Ukraine Vietnam

Oxford is a registered trade mark of Oxford University Press
in the UK and in certain other countries

Published in the United States
by Oxford University Press Inc., New York

© Oxford University Press 2006

British Library Cataloguing in Publication Data available
Library of Congress Cataloging in Publication
American multinationals in Europe: managing employment relations
across national broders / edited by Phil Almond and Anthony Ferner;
with contributions by Phil Almond ... [et al.].
p. cm.
1. International business enterprises—Europe. 2. International
business enterprises—United States. 3. Corporations, American–Europe.
I. Almond, Phil. II. Ferner, Anthony.
HD62. 4. A435 2006
338.8′897304—dc22   2006007423

Typeset by SPI Publisher Services, Pondicherry, India

Printed in Great Britain
on acid-free paper by
Biddles Ltd., King's Lynn, Norfolk

ISBN 0–19–927463–0   978–0–19–927463–5
1 3 5 7 9 10 8 6 4 2

Preface

This book is about employment relations in American multinationals. These companies are the dominant corporate actors of the international economy, representatives of the most powerful business system the world has seen. How they manage their 'human resources' is of considerable practical interest, not least since in the eyes of many observers they represent a model of international organization on which the multinationals of other nations are likely to converge. Yet they originate from a national economy that, however dominant it may be, is in many ways distinctive, and certainly still very different in many respects from the economies of the countries in which its international firms operate—even from those, such as the UK, which have a generic affinity with the US 'model'. The book asks how human resources are managed across these different national 'terrains'. In what way do the employment policies and practices of US multinationals bear the imprint of their origins in the American business system? How do they transfer these practices to other business systems with other 'rules of the game'? And how are the practices shaped by the specific conditions of the varied host environments in which these companies operate? In exploring these questions, the volume engages with a range of theoretical debates about the nature of 'globalization' and about the enduring specificity of different national models of business organization.

The genesis of the project on which this book is based lies in a range of work, influenced by comparative institutional research of Lane and other authors, carried out by members of the project team in the 1990s. This earlier work included, notably, two parallel projects (by Anthony Ferner and Matthias Varul, and by Javier Quintanilla, respectively) exploring the extent to which German companies in the UK and in Spain were influenced in their employment practices by the defining characteristics of the German system. At the same time, Anne Tempel was also examining similar issues in the UK and Germany, while Michael Muller-Camen was looking at US and British firms in Germany. Tony Edwards was researching the way in which employment relations practices were diffused from subsidiaries to headquarters within British multinationals. In Ireland, Paddy Gunnigle and his colleagues were carrying out research in the 1990s on the impact of foreign capital, particularly US firms, on industrial relations in Ireland.

The present project grew out of these earlier studies, particularly those on the 'country-of-origin' influence on employment relations in multi-nationals. But its focus is broader, explicitly encompassing the *interaction* between influences of parent and host business systems; hence the inclusion of a range of host-country environments against which to measure the variable impact, if any, of 'Americanness'. It is more concerned than was perhaps the case in earlier research with the *dynamics* of national business systems, taking a more sceptical view of their homogeneity and stability, and exploring in particular the dynamic interplay of multi-nationals and national institutional contexts. Finally, it attempts to combine a macro-level focus on comparative institutional analysis, a meso-level attention to the cross-cutting influence of *sector*, and a more micro-level consideration of cross-national organizational dynamics. This last focuses in particular on the explanatory value of the power and interests of organizational actors, in different locations and at various hierarchical levels within the multinational, for an understanding of the management of employment relations in these firms; and it asks how actors' power and interests are anchored in the institutional specifics of different national business systems.

The comparative research design involved detailed fieldwork in five countries: the USA, and four European hosts—Germany, Ireland, Spain, and the UK. This ambitious design posed significant challenges of research organization and management. These were addressed by means of a 'consortium' approach, bringing together under the coordination of the UK team a number of collaborating institutions in the four host countries. The academic teams involved in the project come from Leicester Business School and King's College, London in the UK; from the Universities of Trier and Erfurt in Germany; from the University of Limerick in Ireland; and from IESE Business School in Spain. As the project evolved and as 'bilateral relations' flourished, the consortium developed more into a self-sustaining network—a quality we were able to exploit in developing this volume.

Project coordination 'across national borders' was based primarily on email contact, and on a number of meetings over the lifetime of the project. In addition, at least one member of each of the country teams participated in the fieldwork in one or more of the other countries, helping to promote a common understanding of the issues. While differences in resources among the teams inevitably led to some unevenness in the research effort across countries, the relations of trust between the participants, built up over many years, enabled a coordinated and generally consistent approach to the research question, research methods, and to data analysis. Over the lifetime of the project, no fewer than eighteen researchers were involved; fifteen of them have contributed to the present volume.

Orchestrating the contributions of such a large number of people to what was conceived as a multi-authored monograph rather than an edited collection has posed a daunting editorial challenge. We approached it in the following way. In 2003, we proposed to our colleagues in the four national teams an outline for a book based on the research. Following discussion and amendment, we then asked individuals to take the lead role for the main data chapters. Each lead author took responsibility for establishing a group of co-authors from the different countries and for coordinating their inputs into a coherent whole. In short, the process of writing each chapter was something of a microcosm of the volume as a whole. We are extremely grateful to our colleagues for the professional and timely way in which they responded to sometimes radical suggestions for change through several successive drafts as we attempted to ensure the overall coherence and logical flow of the argument through the volume.

Such a project incurs many intellectual debts, and these will become clearer in the course of the book. Here, however, we would like to record our thanks to the participants in two international conferences, organized by Anthony Ferner and Javier Quintanilla, the first at Leicester Business School in July 2001 and the second in IESE Business School, Barcelona, in July 2004. The contributions and discussions at both conferences helped us to formulate and refine our own arguments as these gradually emerged over the course of the project. Important contributions were made, too, by participants at a workshop in December 2003, at which we provided detailed feedback to practitioners and academics on the early findings of project. We would particularly like to thank Bob Scott, Peter Blackwell, Paul Edwards, and Janet Walsh for their role as panel members at the workshop.

On behalf of the project team, the editors would like to acknowledge the role of a number of individuals and organizations in the research. Dr Len Holden, formerly of the Department of Human Resource Management, De Montfort University, made an important contribution to the early development of the project. He was instrumental in securing access at one of our most important case-study companies, and he carried out a significant proportion of the fieldwork there. Len retired before the end of the project and decided not to take part in writing the book, but we would like to record our gratitude here for his valuable contribution. Marta Portillo, formerly of IESE, and Bob Pattinson, formerly of the University of Limerick, were also involved in fieldwork as researchers. We are grateful to Harry Katz for reading and commenting on an early working paper that forms the foundation of the arguments of Chapter 3 on the nature of the US business system. Mike Emmott of the CIPD provided early backing for the research and gave formal CIPD support to a successful ESRC funding proposal.

The editors would also like to thank Sue Brown for her secretarial assistance to the project. She transcribed a large number of complex interviews and helped organize project workshops and meetings. Margaret Spence provided additional clerical assistance. We would also like to acknowledge the active support of Leicester Business School, De Montfort University, which was also crucial to the success of the project. The School provided invaluable 'pump-priming' funding to enable us to get the project off the ground in the early stages, paving the way for successful research funding bids. The UK and US legs of the research were funded by the Economic and Social Research Council (grant number R000238350), and the German component by the Anglo-German Foundation for the Study of Industrial Society (grant number 1292). We are very grateful for these bodies for their financial support. We would like to thank OUP for their backing for this book, in particular commissioning editor David Musson, and assistant commissioning editor Matthew Derbyshire.

Finally, we would like to thank those many managers, employees, and union officials who spoke to us at such length and in such depth, and without whose cooperation our research could not have taken place.

Contents

Contents

List of Figures

List of Tables

List of Abbreviations

ACAS   Advisory Conciliation and Arbitration Service

CIP   country institutional profile

CMEs   coordinated market economies

CWU   Communication Workers Union

DGFP   *Deutsche Gesellschaft für Personalführung* (German Society for Personnel Management)

ELM   external labour market

FDI   foreign direct investment

HR   human resources

HRIS   HR information systems

HRM   Human resource management

ICT   information and communication technology

ILM   internal labour market

IR   industrial relations

IRN   *Industrial Relations News*

LMEs   liberal market economies

MNCs   Multinational companies

NBSs   National business systems

NLRB   National Labour Relations Board

PBR   Payment By Results

WTO   World Trade Organization

List of Contributors

Phil Almond is Reader in Human Resource Management at Leicester Business School, De Montfort University. His published research interests include labour management in multinationals, comparative industrial and employment relations, wage determination systems, gender pay inequality, comparative methodology, and the effects of corporate governance regimes on the management of labour.

Peter Butler is lecturer in Industrial Relations at Leicester Business School. Since acquiring his Ph.D. from the University of Warwick he has researched the relationship between systems of high performance working and workplace learning (Centre for Labour Market Studies, University of Leicester) and also published in the area of non-union employee representation.

Ian Clark is Reader in Industrial Relations at the University of Birmingham. Ian has researched and published on economic performance and productivity and the impact of American management techniques in the UK during the post-war period. Ian continues to work on management strategies in multinational firms and is currently researching the impact of shareholder value approaches to management and the implications of this for the management of industrial relations and HRM.

Trevor Colling is Senior Lecturer in Industrial Relations at Warwick Business School. He has researched and published in areas including public sector industrial relations, sex discrimination and collective bargaining, and trade union organization and renewal. His current work focuses on trade union legal strategies and the enforcement of statutory employment rights.

David G. Collings is a member of the Human Resource Management Research Group at the University of Limerick and a Visiting Research Fellow in the Strathclyde International Business Unit, University of Strathclyde,

Glasgow, Scotland. His current research interests centre on human resource management and industrial relations in the multinational firm.

Tony Edwards is a Senior Lecturer in International Human Resource Management in the Department of Management at King's College London. His research focuses on the management of international workforces within multinational companies, particularly the diffusion of employment practices across borders.

Anthony Ferner is Professor of International Human Resource Management at Leicester Business School, De Montfort University, Leicester. His research is concerned with employment relations in multinational companies, focusing in particular on the interaction between multinational behaviour and national employment relations systems.

Patrick Gunnigle is Professor of Business Studies at the University of Limerick, where he is also Director of the Employment Relations Research Unit. His main research interests are in the areas of multinational corporations and human resource management, trade union membership and recognition, and management strategies in industrial relations.

Michael Morley is Assistant Dean (Research) at the University of Limerick. His refereed journal contributions have appeared in sources such as the *International Journal of Human Resource Management, Human Resource Management Journal*, and *Human Resource Management Review*. He is Consulting Editor of the *Journal of Managerial Psychology* and is a member of the Editorial Board of a number of journals including the *International Journal of Cross Cultural Management*.

Michael Muller-Camen is a Reader in Human Resource Management at Middlesex University Business School in London. His work appeared in outlets such as the *British Journal of Management, Journal of Management Studies*, and *Organization Studies*. His main research interests are the comparative study of human resource management, age management, and sustainable human resource management.

René Peters is a doctoral candidate in the department of business studies at the University of Trier. He received his diploma in 2001 and has served as a research associate since then. His current research explores the underlying reasons for the diffusion of stock option plans in the German business system.

Javier Quintanilla is Associate Professor at IESE Business School, University of Navarra (Spain). His current research interests are the management of professional service firms and international human resource management, subjects on which he has published widely.

Lourdes Susaeta is researcher in the Department of Managing People in Organizations at IESE, and Associate Professor of Management in Complutense University of Madrid. She is currently investigating workforce diversity in multinational companies for her doctoral thesis. Her research area is the study of the transfer of the human resource policies in multinationals.

Anne Tempel is Senior Lecturer in Organization Theory and Management at the University of Erfurt in Germany. Her research focuses on the international diffusion of organizational forms and management practices. She is currently involved in research on the transfer of HRM practices in multinational companies and the diffusion of shareholder value practices in Europe.

Hartmut Wächter is Professor of Human Resource Management (HRM) and Organization at the University of Trier, Germany. His research is in the fields of work design, industrial relations, manpower planning, and comparative and international aspects of HRM. He recently published a book on *Managing in a European Context* and edited a series on *Diversity Management*. He co-founded the leading German-speaking academic journal in HRM, *Zeitschrift für Personalforschung*, of which he is currently editor-in-chief.

Part I

Introduction

1

Introduction: American Multinationals and the Cross-National Management of Employment Relations

Anthony Ferner and Phil Almond

INTRODUCTION

This is a book about the way in which American multinationals (MNCs) manage their employees across national borders. It explores to what extent they disseminate 'home-grown' employment relations and human resource management (HRM) structures, policies, and practices to their European subsidiaries, and asks why they do so. It considers how the different host environments in which they operate influence what is disseminated and how it is implemented in the local operations.

The analysis is based on a five-year, international research project that carried out in-depth case studies of around a dozen American MNCs, and less detailed studies of several others. The companies covered a range of sectors from traditional manufacturing, such as engineering and chemicals-pharmaceuticals, to business services such as IT consulting and logistics. Their management of employment relations and HR was explored across four host countries: Germany, Ireland, Spain, and the UK, chosen to represent a range of national-'institutional' arrangements, notably in relation to the management of employment relations. Thus at one end of the spectrum, Germany may be seen as a highly regulated host environment with a distinctive set of labour market and labour relations institutions; at the other end, the UK and Ireland are less regulated, more 'market oriented', and in many respects more similar to America's 'liberal market economy' (Hall and Soskice 2001*b*) from which our case-study companies originate; Spain is in an intermediate position, with a higher degree of labour market regulation than in the UK or Ireland, but with systems less well-entrenched than in Germany. The cross-national transfer of practices was studied by looking in depth at a number of substantive employment relations issues, including pay and performance management, collective representation and employee participation, the management of managerial staff, and employee 'diversity'. These areas were chosen to reflect the distinctiveness of US MNC behaviour, in some cases a priori on the basis of earlier studies of American companies, in others on the basis of themes emerging from the fieldwork. In general the issues were exploited to uncover and explore the typical patterns of behaviour, structural mechanisms, and organizational processes whereby policies were formulated, transferred across borders, and implemented in subsidiaries. More details of the research design are given in the Appendix. It stresses our multilevel approach to fieldwork, based on the collection of empirical data from respondents both within foreign subsidiaries and at higher organizational levels, and from employees as well as from managers.

The book engages with a variety of debates in international business. Its principal theoretical contribution is twofold. First, it presents a comparative institutionalist approach that develops existing work in a number of ways. For example, building on the work of such writers as Streeck and Thelen (2005) and Djelic and Quack (2003a), it explores the way MNCs exploit the indeterminate 'spaces' found within even the most highly regulated national business systems (NBS) in which these companies operate. Moreover, the book contributes to the emerging conceptualization of business systems as fluid, evolving institutional arrangements by examining the way in which MNCs 'inhabit' and shape to their own ends existing institutions such as systems of employee representation.

Second, the volume constructs an image of the MNC as a complex micropolitical system of actors and interests at different organizational levels. Organizational principles, strategies, and practices do not necessarily (or even routinely) flow smoothly down through the company from a lofty elite tier of senior strategists but evolve through the interplay of the interests and strategies of a variety of groups with differential access to power resources. This strand of theoretical development stands in contrast to the 'top-down', rationalistic assumptions of much of the international business literature, and builds on work of writers, such as Birkinshaw (2000) and Kristensen and Zeitlin (2005), who take seriously the strategies of subsidiary actors. In addition, however, it is argued that what makes the MNC distinctive is that its organizational levels extend across national-institutional domains. As a result, the interaction between different organizational groups and interests—managers and employees, headquarters officials and subsidiary actors, cross-cutting functional groupings, regional or international business division functionaries, and so on—is complicated by the interaction of different national-institutional configurations. To put it another way, the tensions and incompatibilities between different national-institutional domains are acted out by the various groups that constitute the MNC as they struggle to pursue their agendas and impose their meanings and interpretations of strategies and objectives. In particular, local actors' access to institutional resources allows them some room to bargain over the role they occupy within the overall MNC. The implications for how MNCs disseminate and implement policies in the field of employment relations are far-reaching. These themes are laid out in greater depth in Chapter 2 and thread their way through much of the empirical detail of the book.

WHY STUDY AMERICAN MULTINATIONALS?

It is curious to recall that only a few years ago US MNCs were seen as 'dinosaurs', under threat from better adapted Japanese rivals (e.g. Locke 1996). They have proved not only remarkably resilient as the 'Japanese challenge' faded but have been the standard-bearers of America's global economic hegemony. In Western Europe as well as in many other parts of the world the subsidiaries of US MNCs form a major, long-standing part of the economic fabric. In 2003, 24 of the top 100 non-financial 'transnational' companies identified by the UN annual review were American (compared with 26 in 1990) (UNCTAD 1993: 6–7; 2005: 267–9). Increasingly, these firms are internationalized: for the 13 US MNCs in the top 100 in both 1990 and 2003, the proportion of their global workforce outside the US grew from 39 per cent in 1990 to 50 per cent in 2003 (calculated from UNCTAD 1993, 2005).

In the four host countries studied in this book—Germany, Ireland, Spain, and the UK—they are by far the most important foreign investors, in terms of the volume of investment, the number of companies and employees, and dominance of industrial sectors (see Chapter 4). Engineering, electronics and computing, a variety of business services, chemicals and pharmaceuticals, and other industries are, to varying degrees in different countries, dominated and shaped by the presence of American firms.

But it is not just the weight of their presence that justifies a focus on US companies. They raise fundamental questions about what it means to compete in the international economy. Much research has certainly shown that US companies are in many ways distinctive. For example, compared to equivalent companies from other national systems, they are relatively centralized and formalized, and 'short-termist'.[1] US MNCs have been depicted as pioneers, a source of innovation in HR and other areas (on the UK, see, e.g. Enderwick 1985; Flanders 1964). Their continuing vitality and indeed dominance raise important questions about this innovativeness as an element in international competitiveness.

Broadly speaking, the international business literature has two contrasting responses to American MNCs. On the one hand, the implicit assumption of much of the literature appears to be that the distinctive modus operandi of US MNCs constitutes a vision of the future, a model of how to operate in the international economy, and a template on which MNCs from other countries will inevitably converge.

But such assumptions of globalization *à la américaine* sit uneasily with the evidence of continuing difference. The predominant mode of explanation of such difference in the international business literature has until recently fallen back on inherent, long-lasting variations in national 'cultural values'. Creaking under the weight of criticism in recent years, and challenged by more sophisticated comparative institutionalist analysis (see Chapter 2), cultural values perspectives cannot deal adequately with the fact that MNCs compete in the global economy on the basis of differences in resource endowments, competitive advantages, and patterns of behaviour that are distinctively rooted in the nature of their domestic economies (Doremus et al. 1998; Porter 1990).

It is a basic premise of this study that US MNCs are embedded in an American business system—which Chandler (1990) designates as 'competitive managerial capitalism', in contrast to German and Japanese 'co-operative managerial capitalism'—that is distinctive on a number of dimensions: for example, in its model of corporate governance and associated control systems; in the structure, strategy, and evolution of firms; in the nature of labour and product markets; in its business culture and ideology; in the role of state intervention in industrial relations (IR) and more generally; in the organization within the firm of different management functions, including personnel; and in the evolution of workplace relations and the division of labour.

Yet consideration of the twin themes identified earlier—of the complications of operating across national-institutional domains, and of the complex internal micropolitical structuring of MNCs—suggests that the international deployment by US MNCs of nationally embedded HR practices as a source of international competitive advantage is unlikely to be straightforward or 'uncontested'. The resulting tensions form the substance of much of the analysis in this volume.

THE STRUCTURE OF THE BOOK

Part I elaborates on the conceptual underpinnings and methodology of the study. Chapter 2 presents an analytical framework that offers a modified version of comparative institutionalism as the basis for understanding the behaviour of US MNCs. It locates institutional differences between countries within the overarching dynamics of the global economy and the pressures that this exerts. But it is through national differences that the dynamics of the global system are characteristically expressed—for example, through the way in which MNCs 'leverage' differences between NBSs in pursuit of international competitive advantage. The chapter also emphasizes the importance of understanding the MNC not only as a powerful actor that shapes its own institutional environment to some degree, but also as a complex, differentiated structure in which efforts at cross-border integration and coherence are continually challenged by the disparate nature of organizational actors and of their interests and power resources. The analysis borrows from currents in institutionalist approaches to understand MNCs. In a modified way, it draws on the insights of the 'new institutionalism' into the importance of cognitive and normative frameworks of action. From comparative institutionalism, it takes the need for a detailed understanding of the specific institutional arrangements characterizing business systems in different countries; such understanding allows comparison along a range of conceptual dimensions, such as the extent of regulation through statutory frameworks and other formal arrangements, the relationship between economic actors within markets, the role of the state in setting the framework of economic activity, the mechanisms through which different sub-systems are integrated, and so on.

Part II sets out the empirical context for the study. Chapters 3 and 4 examine in detail the institutional arrangements of the parent business system and of the four host business systems across which US MNCs operate. Chapter 3 identifies the core defining features of the American business system and the way in which it has provided an institutional terrain on which companies have evolved with specific ways of doing business and of managing their employees. It also suggests ways in which this context may influence the behaviour of American countries abroad. Chapter 4 looks at the four host countries, focusing in particular on the institutional arrangements underpinning their IR systems, in order to identify possible points of sympathy or antagonism towards the assumptions and practices of US firms. Chapter 5 provides pen portraits of the case-study companies.

Parts III and IV present and analyse the empirical findings of the study. Part III focuses on four substantive areas of human resources and employment relations HR/ER: collective employee relations, employee participation, and the role of unions (Chapter 6); the management of pay and performance (Chapter 7); the management of workforce 'diversity' as a mechanism for achieving business advantage (Chapter 8); and the management of managerial careers (Chapter 9). In each case, the theme has been chosen because it illuminates the policies and practices of US MNCs. Thus, pay and performance, diversity, and managerial careers are all areas on which earlier research has pointed both to the innovativeness of American companies and to their desire to transfer their practices across borders; while collective employee relations is one which highlights a distinctively American concern with the preservation of management's direct relationship with its workforce—a predominant theme of our exploration of the US business system in Chapter 3. In each of these chapters, our approach is, fundamentally, the same: to identify the practices and policies adopted by US MNCs; to understand to what extent and in what ways such practices are embedded in features of the US institutional context; to assess the mechanisms of transfer; and to analyse the way in which transferred practices are assimilated by the range of host countries with their different institutional constraints and opportunities.

Part IV draws together the substantive issues by looking at some crosscutting themes of process and structure. Chapter 10 explores the relationship between headquarters and subsidiaries reflected in oscillating patterns of centralization, decentralization, and recentralization. It thus provides an important qualification to accounts in the literature that stress the broadly centralized nature of US MNCs and their management of HR. In doing so it picks up a theme common to many of the substantive chapters: the importance of *micropolitics* in determining the structures and relationships that emerge, and the processes whereby they evolve. Chapter 11 scrutinizes a key issue in the literature on US MNCs—their innovativeness. It relates innovation in HR/ER to current debates on organizational learning, asking whether innovation in US MNCs involves multilateral learning between different parts of the organization, or whether it is predominantly a 'top-down' exercise. It finds strong evidence to support the view of these companies as 'ethnocentric' organizations. In Chapter 12, the structure of the personnel function itself is considered. It looks at the ways in which American traditions of personnel management have shaped the international HRM function in US MNCs. The chapter explores the contrasts between the American heritage and the distinctive ways in which the profession is institutionally shaped in the host countries. It sees the evolving international structure of the function as responding both to efficiency and cost-saving pressures generated by international competition and to a dynamic process of interest negotiation between organizational actors at different levels.

Chapter 13 focuses on some underlying themes by way of conclusion. It assesses the sources of variety across companies. It finds to be important not only national-institutional factors, such as the features of the host environment, but such factors as the nature of the sector and the kinds of international integration to which it gives rise, and the strategies adopted within the individual company, both at the level of the global firm and within subsidiaries with strategic capabilities of their own. It also reflects critically on the notion of national-institutional effects, arguing that a variety of forms of 'Americanness' are generated within the US business system and that these themselves are undergoing dynamic evolution in response to changes in international competition, technology, industrial structure, and institutional regulation.

Note

1. For example, on centralization and formalization, see, e.g. Harzing 1999; Negandhi 1986; Young, Hood, and Hamill 1985; Yuen and Kee 1993. On short-termism, see, e.g. Child et al. 2000; Coates et al. 1992.

2

Multinationals and National Business Systems: A 'Power and Institutions' Perspective

Anthony Ferner and Anne Tempel

INTRODUCTION[1]

This chapter discusses some elements of a conceptual framework for viewing employment relations in MNCs. The starting point for the analysis is the notion that US MNCs are embedded within a distinctive 'institutional domain', that of their parent NBS. This complex of institutional features shapes the way these companies operate. When they go abroad, they do so, to varying degrees that need to be empirically determined, on the basis of competences, cognitive frameworks, and modes of operating developed in their parent business system. However, at the same time their foreign operations take place within a distinct institutional domain, that of the host country. This host domain may differ in significant ways from that of the US NBS. Institutional arrangements, such as the way actors relate to each other in labour or product markets, or the framework of regulation provided by the state, may encourage or impede the transfer and implementation of parent-country ways of doing things in the host country. In order to understand the extent of transfer, its mechanisms and outcomes, it is necessary to develop a conceptual framework that allows exploration of the interactions—at the level of the MNC—of distinct institutional domains.

The framework borrows from two broad strands of contemporary institutional theory: the comparative institutionalism that explores 'varieties of capitalism', 'NBSs' and 'societal effects'; and the so-called 'new institutionalism' in sociology that seeks to understand how social action is structured by institutional pressures into patterns that persist over time. However, the chapter argues that both these broad approaches have significant flaws. First, comparative institutionalism has failed to take sufficient account of how the national-institutional level relates to both sub-national and supranational institutional arrangements within the emerging 'global political economy'. Moreover, the way in which the 'macro-institutional' features of an NBS and the 'micro-institutional' features at the level of the organization interrelate with each other is insufficiently conceptualized. The new institutionalism, while offering useful insights into the integration of micro-institutional, organizational-level effects with comparative macro-institutional analysis (e.g. Kostova 1999), has neglected the role of power and actors' interests in shaping and responding to institutional constraints.

The chapter first briefly outlines the broad institutionalist approaches as context within which to consider actors that operate across institutional domains. It then explores some of the theoretical gaps. In particular, it considers how institutional and power perspectives may be integrated, paying attention to the interaction between power and institutions at multiple levels, notably at the micro-organizational level of MNCs and at the macro-level of nation states. It also discusses the dynamics of institutional domains, and the role of MNCs themselves in driving institutional change. Finally, it relates this 'power and institutions' approach to the question of the cross-national transfer of employment relations practices within MNCs.

OPERATING ACROSS BORDERS: AN INSTITUTIONALIST APPROACH

Comparative Institutionalism

The comparative institutionalist approach explores persistent differences in business organization and behaviour deriving from the national development paths pursued by different countries, and by the institutions that have been generated out of the interaction of social groups and classes (e.g. Hall and Soskice 2001a; Lane 1989; Whitley 1999). Varieties of capitalist economic organizations, based in nation states, are seen as providing alternative and often competing modes of operating in the global economy. Though competition between national systems at the international level leads to much borrowing and diffusion of practices, it does not necessarily promote convergence, since borrowings are integrated into pre-existing, nationally distinctive complexes of business practice (e.g. Berger and Dore 1996; Crouch and Streeck 1997; Djelic and Quack 2003c; Doremus et al. 1998; Hollingsworth and Boyer 1997a). Moreover, as Cox (2000: 27) argues, the dynamic of globalization is as likely to lead to new differentiations as economic actors exploit the 'territorial divisions of the international economy, playing off one territorial jurisdiction against another' in their search to minimize costs, avoid constraining regulation, and secure political stability and favour. Nonetheless, with the growing integration of the international economy in recent decades, national systems have become increasingly intertwined, resulting in more systematic mutual influence. As a consequence, as Djelic argues in her account of the influence of the American 'system of industrial production' on other western economies, there are complex patterns of both 'convergence and persistent differentiation' (1998: 1).

Despite many variants of terminology, the underlying notion of the comparative institutionalist approach is that NBSs comprise interlocking structures and institutions that fundamentally shape the nature of markets, competition, and business activity in general. Institutions may be defined simply and broadly, following Hall and Soskice (2001b: 10) as 'a set of rules . . . that actors generally follow'. Writers have explored from a comparative perspective the specific characteristics of a variety of national-institutional structures, including: training, education, and skills systems; the division of labour within productive activity; the employment relations system; the structure and governance of firms; the interrelationship of firms, employees, and other actors in markets; and the role of the state in constituting and regulating markets. Beyond that, in the words of Hollingsworth and Boyer (1997b: 2), writers have explored national differences in 'a society's idiosyncratic customs and traditions as well as norms, moral principles, rules, laws, and recipes for action'.

A number of writers have attempted to group NBSs into broad categories, based on generic differences in mechanisms governing economic activity: for example, the relative weight in the governance of economic relationships of markets, hierarchies, and networks of economic actors such as business associations (e.g. Hollingsworth, Schmitter, and Streeck 1994). Chandler (1990) uses the dimensions of 'competitive' versus 'collaborative' and 'personal' versus 'managerial' capitalism to establish broad classifications of different types of business system. Hall and Soskice (2001b) have contrasted 'liberal market economies' (LMEs), such as Britain and the United States, with 'coordinated market economies' (CMEs), such as Germany or Japan. In the former, market relations are predominant. Firms relate to other economic actors, including other firms and the labour force, primarily through arm's-length contracts in markets. In Whitley's words (2001: 42), companies 'operate as isolated islands of order in a sea of market disorder'. The 'CME' depends much more on non-market mechanisms such as business associations, government involvement, and networking among firms for the development of the 'core competences' whereby firms can profitably compete. Economic actors are often bound together in long-term relationships in which arm's-length contracting plays a relatively small part. Such systems generate what Hall and Soskice (2001*b*) call 'institutional complementarities' whereby one institution complements or enhances the efficiency of others so that the elements within institutional complexes are locked together to a significant extent. Needless to say, there are important differences, particularly with regard to HR and employment practices, within both the CME and LME groups, as well as between them.

NBSs have profound implications for the behaviour of firms. Since firms gravitate towards strategies that take advantage of the opportunities provided by the system of economic coordination and institutional arrangements of a particular business system, Hall and Soskice (2001*b*: 15) predict that there will be 'systematic differences in corporate strategy across nations'. For example, firms in LMEs such as the USA, are more likely to invest in 'switchable assets' that can be diverted to other purposes as external circumstances change; while in CMEs where institutions encourage a longer-term approach to investments, firms are more likely to invest in assets that cannot be switched to other uses.

It has been argued (Ferner 1997; Whitley 2001) that national institutional distinctiveness has implications for the behaviour of MNCs. First, these firms are likely to be influenced in their international operations by the strategies, structures, ways of doing things, and shared understandings as to appropriate behaviour that they have developed in response to the institutional constraints and opportunities of their home business system. Thus in Chapter 3 we argue that US MNCs are likely to be influenced in the management of their international operations by their rootedness in the distinctive American business environment. Second, if the originating NBS exhibits distinctive patterns of economic organization and institutional arrangements, the same is logically the case in the host countries in which MNCs operate. Our research examines the behaviour of US MNCs in four distinct national-institutional environments (see Chapter 4).

The manner in which these various institutional domains interact, and how their mutual interaction shapes employment practice within MNCs, is one of the prime concerns of this research.

Institutions, Change, and Power

Some strands of comparative institutionalism have been criticized for their inadequate treatment of system dynamics, in other words the way in which change occurs within business systems. Nonetheless, a key tenet of the comparative institutional approach is that institutional arrangements reflect a 'path-dependent' historical dynamic: the system's evolution over time shapes future choices (e.g. Mahoney 2001). Key historical influences include the nature of the transition from feudal to capitalist production systems, and the timing of industrialization in relation to such developments as the political organization of social classes, as well as more contingent and short-term events such as war or economic crisis.

Path dependency means that choices made at a critical point in time make it 'progressively more difficult to return to the initial point where multiple alternatives were still available' (Mahoney 2001: 113; see also Katznelson 2003). Path dependency exists because of the creation of structures, routines, and interests that 'crystallize' relations in a form that persists over time. One implication of this is that NBSs whose paths diverge at one point in time are likely to continue to be divergent, sometimes over long historical time periods. Crouch (1993), for example, explores the way in which features of modern industry, such as the German system of vocational training, reflect aspects of a pre-capitalist legacy of guild organization that survived industrialization. Another implication is that the order in which causal events occur matters: an event at time A may have different consequences from the same event occurring at time B, given that particular choices are ruled in or out as an institutional arrangement proceeds along a given path. In short, periodization is important.

The concept of path dependency is generally applied to the macro-level of national systems, but equally it could be applied to the micro-level of organizations (see also Morgan 2005). For example, Ortiz's detailed historical account (2002) of the evolution of teamworking at the Spanish subsidiary of vehicle manufacturer FASA-Renault shows how management–union relationships became progressively institutionalized as management responded to local labour market opportunities and constraints. Subsequently, when management attempted to introduce Japanese-style teamworking, it found itself tightly constrained by this 'micro-institutionalization'. Ortiz's study is also indicative of the way in which the macro- and micro-levels interact—a point taken up in more detail in a later section.

The underlying model of institutional change posited by path-dependency arguments has been labelled as one of 'punctuated equilibrium' (e.g. Thelen 2003; see also Djelic and Quack 2003*a*; Streeck and Thelen 2005), in which periods of institutional creation, typically sparked by external shocks, alternate with periods of relative institutional stasis during which institutions exert strong constraints over actors. Recent literature, however, has attempted to provide a more complex account of system dynamics. First, writers have theorized about the sources of system dynamics in a context of greater globalization (e.g. Morgan et al. 2005). Djelic and Quack (2003*a*, 2003*b*) argue that institutional change is likely 'to emerge at the interface of national and transnational rule systems' (2003*a*: 29) through the interaction of national actors, such as states, and transnational actors, such as MNCs and supranational agencies. On this analysis, 'globalization' is about setting 'the rules of the economic game' both at the level of NBSs and at lower- and higher-institutional levels, including those rules that regulate the economic space between NBSs (Djelic and Quack 2003*b*). One implication of this for the arguments of this volume is that cross-national actors, such as MNCs, should not be conceptualized as 'exogenous shocks' to preexisting national-institutional systems but as one element in a constant interaction between institutional levels. Moreover, Djelic and Quack's formulation emphasizes the role of MNCs as active participants in the shaping of institutional rules within and across borders. This point is returned to the following section.

Second, a number of writers have probed the nature of causal phenomenon. The punctuated equilibrium model is built on the assumption that systemic change is initiated by sudden drastic events—such as war or economic crisis. But other causal models are possible. Pierson (2003) points out that 'big, slow-moving' macro-social processes, such as the emergence of new industries and their associated social groups, may take a long time to reach a critical point that triggers institutional change. Likewise, institutional *outcomes* may also be slow moving rather than sudden, as when change is dependent on generational replacement. Similar points could be made about the nature of micro-institutional change at the organizational level—for example, institutional change may depend on the replacement of a long-serving tier of senior managers.

Third, both Streeck and Thelen (2005; see also Thelen 2003) and Djelic and Quack (2003*b*) argue that the punctuated equilibrium model ignores the scope for the cumulative impact of small incremental changes that may transform the way in which NBSs operate even in the absence of radical challenges. For Streeck and Thelen (2005), existing institutions designed for one purpose may be converted to other ends, or supplemented by additional institutional arrangements in processes they call 'institutional conversion' and 'institutional layering'. Thus a picture may be developed of NBSs as composed of institutional 'sediments', with older, slower-changing layers of institutional arrangements upon which are superimposed successive strata of more transient or volatile elements. Moreover, the *role* of different elements may evolve over time even while the institutional form remains the same. Streeck and Thelen (2005: 19–20) also point out that 'displacement' of existing institutional forms occurs as new models emerge and slowly diffuse, calling into question existing taken-for-granted forms and practices.

As a result of such processes, there may never be a single coherent institutional framework, even though one set of arrangements may impose a dominant 'logic of action' within a national system. This internal differentiation and fragmentation of institutional logics, in conjunction with sub-national sources of variation within NBSs (see later), provides considerable 'space' for alternative paths of action in an NBS, and multiple entry points for the transfer of practices from different national-institutional domains. At the same time, MNCs may be seen as one of the most important sources of incremental institutional layering, conversion, and displacement.

Views of change in the comparative institutionalist literature are closely bound up with views of power. Punctuated equilibrium and path dependency approaches often turn on the assumption that institutions are fundamentally shaped by the influence of powerful actors at critical junctures (e.g. Mahoney 2001). Mahoney also suggests that the exercise of power is manifest during an initial phase of 'institutionalization' during which contending actors struggle to define the path taken: 'power conflicts between actors with different endowments of resources, and thus different interests are crucial to explain trajectories of political development' (2001: 135). The end point of such struggles is a situation of relative institutional equilibrium reflecting a pattern of stable dominance and subordination among social groups. Such notions of path dependency promoted by power relations at a particular point in time are implicit in some historical studies in the field of employment relations. A notable example is Sisson's comparative analysis (1987) of the critical moments in the foundation of national collective bargaining systems. The balance of power at critical junctures becomes 'locked in', as instanced by the 1938

Saltsjöbaden agreement between Swedish employers and unions. The institutions that result serve as dampers on ebbs and flows in the 'raw' balance of power between social groups because they change only with a lag and with considerable resource investment

Other scholars (especially Streeck and Thelen 2005; Thelen 2003; see also Katznelson 2003) challenge the view that the overt exercise of power is important mainly at critical moments. Streeck and Thelen assert that the agency of powerful actors is important in driving system change also during periods of institutional consolidation. Notions of institutional 'conversion' and 'layering' imply the partial re-negotiation of institutional elements. Reappraisal of institutional arrangements is an ongoing process, reflecting (Thelen 2003: 231) the continual 'political contestation over the form and functions of institutions forged at ... critical junctures'. Similarly, Djelic and Quack (2003*b*) see globalization as involving the 'contested negotiation and renegotiation' of rules regulating the international economic space.

But clearly, these views are not the polar opposite of those of path dependency theorists. Institutions may at the same time 'lock in' the power balance pertaining at critical junctures, and be the site of ongoing political mobilization as social actors wage constant battle to colonize and exploit institutional spaces for their own ends. Moreover, institutions may give rise to new sets of interests and constituents through the allocation and reallocation of resources. The key point is the use of power not only to establish but also to maintain and incrementally to redefine institutions.

The focus of the NBS approach and other strands of the comparative institutionalist literature has naturally been on the *national* level. This is justified on the grounds that 'many of the most important institutional structures—notably systems of labour market regulation, of education and training, and of corporate governance—depend on the presence of regulatory regimes that are the preserve of the nation state' (Hall and Soskice 2001*b*: 4). First, however, within a single NBS there are major sources of variation. In many countries regional variations are important, for reasons of historical patterns of economic development, as in Italy, or because of the importance of political structures at sub-national level, notably in federal structures, as in the USA, where states have considerable freedom to set the framework of business. In some instances—and this is true of the American system as we argue in Chapter 3—the institutional arrangements that govern economic behaviour are flexible enough to allow actors considerable freedom to deploy a range of strategies, their choices being determined by a variety of contingent factors. As a result, business systems may tend to generate clusters of outcomes, rather than a single model of organization and behaviour. This has important implications for our arguments in later chapters on how MNCs transfer practices between institutional domains; notably, how they find 'institutional space' within even highly regulated NBSs. It could be argued that even the most coherent and 'tightly coupled' institutional systems still exhibit a degree of internal differentiation, not least as a result of the system dynamics (see earlier section) that drive institutional change.

Second, economic organization is not solely influenced by national economic structures and institutions. Katz and Darbishire (2000) argue that economic organization increasingly has a strong sectoral dynamics that crosses national borders. Industries, such as automobiles and industrial chemicals, for which production is highly integrated internationally and which serve increasingly global markets, are likely to generate different patterns of behaviour, including in the field of HR/ER, from less-integrated sectors serving primarily domestic markets (even though there may be considerable international learning and borrowing in these sectors). Moreover, international sectors often generate border-spanning institutional complexes that regulate and shape relations between actors within them. One important issue that arises from this is how sectoral governance regimes interact with institutional arrangements at the level of the NBS (e.g. Colling and Clark 2002; Hollingsworth, Schmitter, and Streeck 1994).

Third, the primacy of the nation state as the arena for defining institutional arrangements is being challenged by the growth of supranational regulation, through regional economic communities, such as the European Union (EU), and through the growth in global regulatory instruments such as the World Trade Organization (WTO). These developments raise significant questions about the interaction between nation states and institutions of economic globalization—a key theme of recent 'international political economy' literature (e.g. Michie 2003; Palan 2000; Stubbs and Underhill 2000). In the words of Cox (2000: 29), the 'old state system is resolving itself into a complex of political-economic entities: micro-regions, traditional states, and macro-regions with institutions of greater or lesser functional scope and formal authority'. With the intensification of globalization, the ability of nation states to insulate NBSs from global forces has been compromised (Ó Riain 2000), and the focus of activity of the national polity has increasingly been to increase the international competitiveness of national economic activity: the so-called 'competition state' (Cerny 2000). However, this has been more problematic for social-market systems, such as the German CME, than for the Anglo-Saxon 'liberal states' (Ó Riain 2000) that under the post-war framework of 'embedded liberalism' promoted the predominance of markets relative to non-market solutions. In short, the conceptual integrity of the NBS as a level of analysis, and hence as a primary level influencing the parameters of MNC behaviour, is under considerable pressure. This suggests the need to understand US MNCs' institutional influences not only in terms of the US NBS but also of a variety of other sub-national-, supranational-, and international-sectoral institutional arrangements.

New Institutionalism

A separate strand of institutionalism relevant for understanding the behaviour of MNCs in different national contexts is the influential 'new institutionalism' (e.g. DiMaggio and Powell 1983; Scott 2001; Zucker 1988; for an incisive critical analysis, see Oliver 1991; also Clemens and Cook 1999). This approach focuses on the modes of rationality, beliefs, and value systems that shape actors' behaviour. It is concerned with the mechanisms by which institutional effects are diffused within 'organizational fields': the sets of organizations that 'in the aggregate, constitute a recognized area of institutional life: key suppliers, resource and product consumers, regulatory agencies, and other organizations that produce similar services or products' (DiMaggio and Powell 1983: 143). DiMaggio and Powell emphasize pressures within organizational fields that tend to generate institutional 'isomorphism'—the tendency for organizations to adopt similar practices and perspectives in the search for 'legitimacy'. Isomorphism occurs, it is argued, as a result of different kinds of institutional pressure.

The new institutionalists acknowledge the importance of 'coercive' or 'regulative' pressures (DiMaggio and Powell 1983; Scott 2001) for institutional compliance. These comprise explicit systems of rules in the form of laws or regulations, together with monitoring and enforcement procedures, that force organizations to comply with certain behaviours. However, the primary emphasis of this body of literature has been on two further institutional mechanisms: the normative and the cognitive. The first of these includes *values* (normative rules about what is preferred or desirable) and *norms* (judgements as to the legitimate means whereby things should be done). Actors conform to normative pressures because of social expectations and obligations on them to do so. Cognitive pressures concern shared understandings about what 'constitute[s] the nature of reality and the frames through which meaning is made'—what Scott refers to as 'internalized symbolic representations of the world' (2001: 40). In other words, institutional pressures for isomorphism occur because of shared modes of rationality and ways of doing things among organizational actors.

As Tempel and Walgenbach (forthcoming) have argued, while this approach has not been primarily comparative in nature, it has significant implications for understanding organizations such as MNCs that operate across national 'institutional domains'. They stress the need to regard organizational fields as increasingly extending across national borders, reflecting the global activities, not just of MNCs but of other organizational actors such as consulting firms and professional associations. In particular, the question arises of how MNCs deal with tensions between conflicting pressures for isomorphism arising in two domains—the parent and host NBSs—with different cognitive, normative, and regulatory frameworks.

In recent years, new institutionalists have begun to apply the approach to the study of MNCs (e.g. Kostova 1999; Kostova and Roth 2002; Kostova and Zaheer 1999; Rosenzweig and Nohria 1994; Westney 1993). The most developed work in this area is that of Kostova, who focuses on the struggle by MNCs to achieve legitimacy in different and sometimes conflicting institutional environments. She has formulated the concept of 'institutional' distance (by approximate analogy with the notion of 'cultural distance' in comparative cultural value studies). This is the difference between the 'country institutional profile' (CIP) of an MNC's country of origin and country of operation, respectively. The CIP is constructed from the regulative, normative, and cognitive institutions of a country (Kostova 1999). Kostova argues that where transferred practices do not accord with the cognitive frameworks of the host institutional environment, subsidiary employees are likely to struggle to interpret and evaluate the practices. As a result, practices may be implemented but not *internalized*, that is to say assimilated to the employees' cognitive and normative systems.

Thus new institutionalist insights potentially provide a useful adjunct to comparative institutionalism, in particular through an emphasis on the potential tensions between regulative, cognitive, and normative pressures in different national-institutional domains. As we argue later, their insights provide a way of integrating the micro-institutional organizational level into a comparative institutionalist perspective.

However, in order for this to be done, the shortcomings of the approach need to be addressed. First, issues of power are under-theorized. While, comparative institutionalism has been relatively sensitive to issues of power in shaping institutions (see especially Mahoney and Rueschemeyer 2003), this is not the case, with the new institutionalism. Indeed, it exhibits an almost wilful lack of concern for power and interests of actors.

Second, and partly as a result, it provides an inadequate account of institutional dynamics, that is change in institutions over time (cf. Clemens and Cook 1999).

As DiMaggio (1988) has argued, the 'defocalizing' of power in new institutionalism reflects the concern with factors that stop actors from recognizing and acting on their interests, in particular their taken-for-granted assumptions and the limits on cognition that make it hard for actors to appreciate means–ends relationships. In general, institutionalism has tended to emphasize organizations as passive subjects of institutional pressures. But organizations do not merely respond to institutions; powerful organizational actors, pursuing their particular interests, also play an active role in constructing institutions and in determining how they operate. Thus organizations may influence government and other bodies that construct institutional norms, and they may have important roles in shaping and disseminating cognitive and normative schemas. In the case of MNCs, there is much evidence of the way in which they make the institutional weather, at the level of the global institutional system (e.g. Djelic and Quack 2003c; Sell 2000), within NBSs (e.g. DeVos 1981) and within their specific organizational field (e.g. Levy and Egan 2003).

Even where they do not shape institutions, organizations actively develop a range of strategies for responding to—and sometimes resisting—institutional forces, as Oliver (1991) compellingly argues. Such strategies vary according to the dependence of the organization on the source of institutional norms; the perceived legitimacy of the norm; the impact of conformity on efficiency; and the multiplicity and coherence of sources of institutional pressure. Tempel et al. (2004) apply Oliver's approach specifically to the case of MNC subsidiaries as they respond to corporate pressures regarding policy and practice on collective representation. Moreover, as discussed earlier in relation to comparative institutionalism, institutions are the subject of *ongoing* contestation in which actors battle for control over their meaning and impact. In the words of Katznelson (2003: 288), it is necessary to invite 'power into the house of institutions'. The following section considers how this might be done.

POWER, INTERESTS, AND MNCs

In principle, it is possible to combine insights from the new institutionalism with a power and interests perspective (see Ferner and Edwards 1995; Ferner et al. 2005b; Levy and Egan 2003). This section proposes a way of integrating the 'three pillars' framework of new institutionalism (Scott 2001) with a power perspective, and again draws out the implications for understanding the behaviour of firms operating across national borders.

New Institutionalism and Power

An important strand in the literature on power, notably in the work of Lukes (1974), has been the analysis of the so-called 'third face of power'. This focuses on the ability of powerful actors and structures to shape the way in which groups and individuals construct their interests. Similarly, Clemens and Cook (1999: 446) argue that despite the apolitical bias of institutional analysis, 'the processual question of how social arrangements and beliefs come to be taken for granted resonates with political theorists' articulation of the "third level of power" '. At the societal level, the notion of 'hegemony' in the classic analysis of Gramsci (1971) refers to structures of power that are rooted not merely in overt economic domination and the coercive powers of the state, but also in ideological ascendancy whereby the perceptions and values even of disaffected groups are shaped by prevailing dominant norms.

Analogous arguments may be made at the level of the organizational field and of the individual organization, rather than of society as a whole. For example, Levy and Egan (2003) explore the way in which oil MNCs shaped their 'organizational field' through a contested political process of assembling a coalition of forces to establish a hegemonic position on the issue of climate change. They conclude (p. 824) that organizational fields are characterized by 'multiple social actors competing for influence over the rules, institutions, norms, and policies that structure markets and economic relations'. At the micro-level of the organization, similar preoccupations are evident in the analysis of the 'mobilization of bias' (Schattschneider 1960) and in the study of rhetorics and symbolic systems deployed by interest groups within organizations to 'manage meaning' and to legitimate some courses of action while delegitimating others (Pettigrew 1973, 1985). Bachrach and Baratz (1970: 43–4) explore the way in which corporate 'culture' is imbued with the influence of powerful groups, defining the 'mobilization of bias' as 'a set of predominant values, beliefs, rituals, and institutional procedures ("rules of the game") that operate systematically and consistently to the benefit of certain persons and groups at the expense of others'.

Such issues are particularly pertinent for the analysis of organizational actors operating across national institutional domains, as will be argued in the following section.

Power and MNCs

Although mainstream business literature tends to have a unitarist conception of the firm as comprising a set of complementary actors, a powerful tradition insists on the essentially 'contested' nature of the firm. Amoore (2000) argues that the internationalization of the economy increases the points of tensions between the 'competing social forces' (p. 183) that compose the firm. Such considerations are likely to apply to MNCs as firms that by their nature operate across international socio-economic spaces. In the words of Kristensen and Zeitlin (2005: 11) MNCs are 'an arena for internecine rivalries in which the normal opportunism of the market [is] compounded by ongoing political struggles over the allocation of resources and responsibility for success or failure'.

Tensions are particularly likely to arise in situations where institutional rules derive from a multiplicity of sources and where there is a lack of consistency among the pressures being exerted (Clemens and Cook 1999: 449–50; Oliver 1991). This is quintessentially the case with the operations of MNCs, which can be conceptualized as bringing into interaction two distinct institutional domains: that of the parent NBS and of the host NBS, each with significantly different cognitive, normative, and regulative frameworks. One of the defining characteristics of cognitive systems is that they shape taken-for-granted ways of thinking that are not necessarily accessible to organizational actors. But at the junction of two different institutional domains, previously 'invisible' cognitive schemas may be revealed through juxtaposition. As a result, these systems may become more open to contestation and change by different groups of actors operating within MNCs.

These arguments have clear echoes of Weberian analyses of 'authority' as legitimated power (see Pfeffer 1981: 4–5). Authority reduces costs of exercising power because fewer resources need to be invested in overcoming resistance: authority is 'taken for granted', maintained by the social norms that sanction existing power distributions. But where organizations operate across national boundaries, authority may be challenged by rival claims to legitimacy in different national-institutional domains, leading to conflicts of legitimacy. In such situations, the legitimation of power may be problematic and contested (cf. Pfeffer 1981: 6).

Such contestation involves two parties—those whose interests are bound up with the propagation of a given set of institutional rules, and those whose interests are shaped and constrained by such rules (or what Streeck and Thelen (2005) refer to as 'rule makers' and 'rule takers'). Where the propagators of rules come from a different institutional domain, as in the case of MNCs, the underlying cognitive assumptions may become more transparent as a result of their difference from prevailing schemas, and hence open to challenge. Moreover, challenge may be facilitated by the resources that actors in the host NBS derive from the macro-institutional rules of the host. For example, managers in an MNC subsidiary may resist global corporate policies on the grounds that they contravene local institutional rules such as legislation on employee representation. Alternatively, subsidiary actors may present themselves as 'interpreters' to corporate HQ of the precise meaning and implication of complex and opaque local rules; this again provides them with leverage. Thus what appear to be constraints on actors in the local institutional domain may in fact provide them with a power resource vis-à-vis actors from the parent-country institutional domain.

Local actors can draw on institutional resources from the host NBS to negotiate over the terms of their insertion into the global firm. Kristensen and Zeitlin (2005: Chapter 3), for instance, show how employee representatives and managers at the Danish subsidiary of a UK MNC used their linkages with local training institutions to upskill the workforce, and created alliances within traditional networks of local suppliers, as part of their campaign for the subsidiary to play a strategic role within the wider MNC. In short, local actors can use host-country institutional resources to lever a degree of freedom of manoeuvre vis-à-vis the 'institutional pulls' coming from corporate HQ.

The fractioning of the firm in general into 'competing social forces' (Amoore 2000) of management, investors, employees is cross-cut in MNCs by a fractioning into organizational interest groups according to different national-institutional spaces. A subsidiary, while itself composed of competing interest groups, may in some respects define itself as a collective interest group vis-à-vis another subsidiary or corporate HQ. From this follows the need to take seriously the subsidiary's scope for intentional 'strategizing' and pursuit of its specific interests (Birkinshaw 2000; Kristensen and Zeitlin 2005). In the words of Birkinshaw and Fry (1998: 52), subsidiaries engage in a political process, based on 'proactive, pushy, and sometimes Machiavellian tactics'. The scope for local subsidiary alliances between, for instance, managers, employees, and suppliers will depend on the opportunities provided by the local institutional domain for conflict and cooperation, as Amoore (2000) suggests in her analysis of the impact of globalization on intra-firm relationships in the contrasting cases of Germany and the UK.

The conception of power used here goes beyond the conventional emphasis on 'resource dependency' (e.g. Ghoshal and Nohria 1993) in the business literature, in two ways. First, power depends not only on the pool of 'resources' available to be actively wielded by groups and individuals in pursuit of their interests. Rather, power may be structural. There may be structured imbalances in the availability of resources between different groups, and such imbalances may be systematically embodied in ways of organizing socio-economic activity at different levels. Partly such structuring occurs through the way in which power is 'wired in' to institutional rules, including cognitive and normative frameworks, reflecting to some degree the crystallization of power relations at critical historical junctures into persistent institutional arrangements. Such arguments apply both at the macro-systemic level and at the micro-organizational level.

Second, the exercise of power is dynamic. It does not depend simply on what resources groups and individuals have at a point in time. A key question neglected in most of the business literature (for an exception, see the work of Birkinshaw 2000) concerns the processes whereby MNC actors acquire and build on resources and how they deploy them dynamically in pursuit of their interests. As Levy and Egan (2003) argue, actors can create advantages through the skill and timing with which they deploy their available resources, allowing protagonists relatively weak in resources to exploit the poor strategizing of their opponents.

Power and Institutional Levels

One of the most complex issues in analysing the behaviour of MNCs is the relationship between the different conceptual levels. The importance of multilevel analysis has been stressed by new institutionalists such as Kostova (1999) in her study of the transfer of practices within MNCs. Our own analysis is driven by the need to integrate power and system dynamics at different conceptual levels. Drawing on the global political economy literature discussed earlier, the global, national, and micro-organizational levels may be identified as the key tiers of our conceptual framework. Other overlapping or composite levels—such as global-sectoral and national-sectoral—are also important components of the analysis at various points.

'Globalization' is heavily contested, as a concept and as a reality, and there has been fierce debate, for example, over how far the scope of action is merely regional rather than 'global' (e.g. Rugman 2005). But there is general agreement that in some respects it makes sense to talk of a global system in which actors—notably states and corporations—conduct operations that are international in scope (e.g. Dicken 2002). Rationalization and restructuring of industries and production chains are increasingly taking place at the level of the global economy or within important subsets of it.

The global political economy approach (e.g. Cox 1987; Stubbs and Underhill 2000; Palan 2000) stresses the importance of an understanding of power relations within the global system. At the global system level, power manifests itself in a hierarchical relationship between NBSs according to their degree of dominance within the world economy. Such 'dominance effects' (Smith and Meisksins 1995) mean that dominant NBSs invite emulation from those that are in a weaker position. NBSs lower in the hierarchy, and firms embedded in those NBSs, may see it as in their interest to adopt practices from more dominant economies. Dominance relations depend not only on raw power but also on hegemonic control of ideas and cognitive schema for 'legitimizing and maintaining the fundamentally conflictual socio-economic structures of global capitalism' (Underhill 2000: 16). Hegemony in the global system includes the generation of cognitive assumptions about the superiority of practices from dominant countries and their companies as sources of international competitive advantage. As Elger and Smith (2006: p.53) put it, 'practices that have been developed in leading national economies, industrial sectors or indeed firms have the potential to exert a distinctive influence on key actors in a wide range of business enterprises situated in different societies, by virtue of their claimed efficacy'. Power at the global system level is partly maintained through the actions of hegemonic national states such as the USA, including their deployment of political and military as well as economic power, and this in turn partly reflects the interests of dominant economic actors such as powerful MNCs based in the USA. Sell (2000), for example, shows how powerful private sector actors led by US MNCs helped drive the introduction of a new global regulatory framework for trade in services and for intellectual property rights.

In short, therefore, analysis of the interaction of the institutional domains of different NBSs through the actions of MNCs needs to take account of the location of NBSs in a power and dominance hierarchy of states within the global political economy. Moreover, the institutional frameworks that govern the operations of MNCs, both at the level of NBSs and globally, arise from a complex process of interaction between national states and supranational and cross-national actors, both state and non-state, including MNCs themselves (e.g. Djelic and Quack 2003*c*). The rules result from what Cerny (2000: 300) calls 'complex aggregation of multi-level games played on multilayered institutional playing fields, *above* and *across*, as well as *within*, state boundaries'.

As Ó Riain (2000) argues, it is increasingly difficult to insulate the level of the national system from the global political economy. Nonetheless, the NBS can still be seen as an analytically distinct level with its own specific scope for setting institutional rules that apply within its territory. Such rules both reflect and shape power relations and group interests within the NBS, even though they increasingly embody power influences arising outside national borders. The reasons are, first, that the nation state has sovereign jurisdiction over important areas of economic life; second, that there are national path dependencies which reflect past choices and that have generated, for example, economic specialisms and the accompanying national-institutional arrangements that persist over time; and third, that there is a continuing dynamism of the global economic system whereby new economic activities, competences, and sources of competitive advantage are continually being generated at a local or national rather than a global level, giving rise to specific institutional arrangements that may well be at the level of the NBS rather than global.

Similarly, as argued earlier, the MNC itself can be seen as a *sui generis* institutional level, characterized by power struggles over the institutional framework for action between different organizational actors located within and across different national-level institutional domains. In the work of the new institutionalists (notably Rosenzweig and Nohria 1994), the MNC is seen as a key source of institutional norms structuring the behaviour of subsidiary actors and demanding responses that are 'iso-morphic' with corporate systems. In reality, the situation is more complex, since in MNCs there are multiple interactions between different subsidiaries as well as between subsidiaries and the corporate centre. Moreover, there are often intermediate organizational levels occupying ambiguous institutional spaces. An example is the regional office; this structure may mediate relations between HQ and subsidiaries in the region, while itself being influenced by the national-institutional context of the NBS in which it is located, and by the national origins of the managers who staff it (cf. Pulignano 2006).

However, the *interaction* between different institutional levels is problematic. What is the relationship, for example, between the institutional tier of the MNC and that of the NBS (both of the parent country and of the host country)? Is the former straightforwardly 'nested' within the latter, or may there be zones within the micro-level institutional domain that are distinct from and at odds with the macro-level domain? How far can the MNC's institutional arrangements be insulated from that of the wider NBS? A full exploration of this issue is beyond the scope of this volume, although pointers to it emerge in the exploration of empirical themes in Part II. But some general points may be made.

First, the micro-level is not a 'microcosm' of the NBS institutional domain. It may have characteristics that reflect sub-national (e.g. sectoral) organizational fields or local factors, such as labour markets, union traditions, and so on, that are only partly shaped by national-institutional arrangements. Or it may have *sui generis* organizational features reflecting strategic choices by actors within the company, both management and employees and their representatives. Such choices may be embodied in management systems, corporate cultures, and so on, and exert strong cognitive and normative pressures on organizational actors (but not routinely on the broader NBS). Where its norms conflict with those of the host NBS, the MNC's norms may prevail if it has the power resources to overcome pressures for isomorphism to the host environment—for example, if it is willing to bear the cost of legal sanction and the associated detriment to the legitimacy of the organization, as in Royle's study (2000) of McDonald's evasion of NBS institutional rules in Germany. In other words, powerful MNCs may break the institutional rules—even regulative ones for which sanctions are explicit and enforced.[2]

Second, as writers from different institutionalist traditions have stressed (e.g. Clemens and Cook 1999; Oliver 1991; Streeck and Thelen 2005), institutional domains may be heterogeneous and generate multiple and inconsistent institutional rules. NBSs are rarely monolithic, undifferentiated fields, but may operate differently at various sub-national levels, or indeed may generate a range of incompatible institutional rules; or, institutional arrangements may operate differently for historical reasons or because of local power balances, or be enforced more or less strongly, in different sub-areas of the system. MNCs are able to exploit such 'niches' within the NBS so that they may be able without penalty to operate significantly different institutional regimes from those of the host environment (or indeed of the parent NBS). An example would be the location of MNCs in former East Germany, where the institutions of labour regulation did not have the same historical embeddedness as identical institutions in West Germany. Another example, which we discuss in depth in Chapter 6, is the tendency of US MNCs in Germany to move between different sectoral bargaining systems. Such behaviour does not necessarily contravene institutional rules in the NBS but exploits the flexibility in the system. Different NBSs are likely to have different degrees of variability and scope for 'niche' behaviour, depending on the dominance, coherence, and degree of enforcement of institutional rules.

Finally, MNCs are themselves powerful actors who may intervene directly to shape the arrangements of the macro-level institutional domain, for example, by lobbying for change in the system, or by introducing new practices that diffuse into local firms and create pressures for isomorphism to imported institutional norms.

TRANSFER OF EMPLOYMENT PRACTICES BETWEEN NATIONAL-INSTITUTIONAL DOMAINS IN US MNCs

The final step in the argument is to link the conceptual elements sketched earlier to the specific issue of cross-national transfer of practices within MNCs (see Edwards 2004; Ferner, Almond, and Colling 2005a). In conventional approaches, based on the rationalistic assumptions of the 'resource-based view' of the firm, transfer is seen as taking place where central corporate policymakers see the international competitive advantage of doing so (e.g. Taylor, Beechler, and Napier 1996). Given competitive advantage, transfer will depend on such factors as the degree to which a practice is 'codified' and hence capable of being implemented successfully in a new environment; and on 'causal ambiguity' where the specific elements responsible for the effectiveness of a complex practice are unclear (Szulanski 1996: 31). Other explanations of transfer tend to be rooted in structural features of MNCs, such as the degree of functional integration of units in different countries (e.g. Bartlett and Ghoshal 1998; Gupta and Govindarajan 1991).

The implication of our argument earlier, however, is that transfer needs to be seen as the movement of practices between different national-institutional domains, under conditions in which actors may have divergent interests in transfer and differential power resources with which to effect—or to hinder—it. It is a fundamental premise of our approach that transfer is a political and contested process (cf. Edwards 2004) and cannot be understood simply as a rational response to efficiency considerations by senior corporate decision-makers.

The institutionalist approach argues that there are differences in how business is organized in different NBSs. Practices have to be seen in the context of the 'institutional complementarities' (Hall and Soskice 2001b) of the system in which they operate. As a result, practices that operate efficiently in one NBS may not do so in another, or they may operate differently. As Lam's work (1997) indicates, national-institutional properties interact with the properties of individual practices such as their degree of codification and causal ambiguity: work systems in Japan, for example, tend to be more tacit than their counterparts in the UK and thus less amenable to transfer from Japan.

Similarly, the new institutionalists have drawn attention to the problematic nature of transfer between national-institutional domains whose cognitive and normative systems differ, an approach formalized by Kostova (1999) in the concept of 'institutional distance' and in her construct of the 'country institutional profile'. As noted earlier, Kostova (see also Saka 2003) contributes to the transfer literature with her distinction between implementation and 'internalization'; in the former, practices are implemented but do not have the same significance or function in the same way as in the national-institutional domain in which they originate because they do not conform to the cognitive (or normative) schemas of employees in the host domain.

Our modified institutionalist approach takes these arguments a step further by exploring the power relations that underlie transfer at different conceptual levels. First, transfer is shaped by power relations at the level of the global system, in that flows of practices are more likely to take place from dominant to subordinate systems in the hierarchy of NBSs, and within MNCs from dominant parent countries. This is both because MNCs from dominant countries are likely to perceive that their practices are superior, and because subsidiary actors in recipient countries are likely to have an interest in adopting practices from successful systems and that are perceived to be sources of competitive advantage.

Second, political struggles may take place at the level of the NBS over transfer. States may put pressure on other states to revise their regulatory frameworks, and as argued earlier MNCs may take an active role in the political networks that result in such pressure; or may exert pressure directly on host or parent states. An example in the field of employment practices is the attempt of US MNCs and the American Chamber of Commerce (AmCham) in Germany to put pressure on the federal government in 1973–4 to tone down its proposed extension of the codetermination system, with the implicit threat of the loss of planned investment (DeVos 1981: 174–8).

Third, the nature of MNCs as agglomerations of contending interests extending across national borders raises the question of the internal organizational power relations that exist in situations of transfer, both between different organizational groups and across the different national-institutional terrains in which the MNC operates. Considered in this way, the transfer process within the MNC is determined not so much by the rational decision-making of senior corporate executives but by the interplay of interests and the possession and deployment of power resources by a variety of actors at different organizational levels. For example, functional management groups at HQ may resist the transfer of practices to subsidiaries because their monopoly of organizational expertise may be threatened. Managers in the subsidiary may resist the transfer from the MNC of practices that disrupt stable relations with other local stakeholders such as unions and employee representatives. As discussed earlier, actors may draw on resources from the national-institutional domain to exert influence over the transfer process. For example, employee representatives may use the threat of a statutory right of veto (e.g. under codetermination legislation) in order to bargain for control over the conditions under which a practice is imported. They may also use their superior knowledge of the institutional complexities of the local environment to 'interpret' the constraints and possibilities for corporate managers, and thereby negotiate the terms under which practices are transferred. But subsidiaries may also actively drive the transfer process, seeing an interest in acquiring competences located in the corporate centre, even in situations where transfer is not actively promulgated by HQ. Meardi and Tóth (2006) illustrate this process, which they term 'pull' or 'attraction' transfer, in relation to work organization practices in west European MNCs operating in Hungary and Poland.

One outcome of the exercise of power in the transfer of practices is that transfer is not an 'either-or' matter. The power of subsidiary actors can be used to divert a practice from its original function through their control over how it is implemented; or a practice may be implemented ritualistically without the commitment necessary to make it function effectively (cf. Oliver 1991). The growing literature on the 'hybridization' of practices transferred by MNCs (Boyer et al. 1998; Doeringer et al. 2003; Ferner and Varul 2000; Meardi and Tóth 2006) suggests that the reshaping that routinely occurs can be partly explained through the contestation that takes place between organizational actors over the interpretation of the practice's meaning and function. In short, transfer is a negotiated process.

CONCLUSION

This chapter has drawn on two important traditions in institutional analysis: comparative analysis of NBSs and the emphasis of 'new institutionalists' on the three institutional pillars—cognitive, normative, and regulative—that pressurize actors towards conformity with institutional rules. It has qualified the insights of these perspectives by incorporating a more explicit focus on the power and interests of actors, and how these both determine and are determined by institutional arrangements. Institutions are not objective givens but embody and perpetuate power relations pertaining at critical moments in institutional development. At the same time they serve to define and constrain the interests and resources of those subject to them. Our approach emphasizes the importance of a dynamic view of institutional formation and maintenance, and of the varying weight of structure and agency (Thelen 2003), at different moments in the institutionalization process. However, it is an underlying premise that institutions are subject to contestation, amendment, and defence by actors whose interests they engage. This approach can be applied in specific ways to MNCs as actors that routinely cross institutional domains and that are themselves composed of actors with different institutional interests and power resources.

As well as proposing the incorporation of a more explicit power perspective into institutionalist concerns, the chapter has also explored a multi-level conceptual approach that permits analysis of the complex interactions between institutional processes at macro-systemic (both global and NBS), meso-sectoral, and micro-organizational levels. MNCs deploy their power to influence institutional rule formation at supra-national, national, and sectoral levels as well as within their own micro-institutional domain. At the same time, their contending internal interest groups, including employees and managers, pursue their organizational interests at the intersection of the micro-institutional level of the MNC and the macro-institutional domain of the NBS in which they operate. Part II will explore how such ideas can be operationalized in relation to substantive themes of employment relations in US MNCs.

Notes

1. The arguments of this chapter take forward ideas and analysis developed by the authors and by other team members in a number of earlier papers. These include

notably Edwards 2004; Edwards et al. 1999 Ferner and P. Edwards 1995; Ferner et al. 2004, 2005a, 2005b, Tempel and Walgenbach forthcoming; Tempel et al. 2004.

2. In principle, the same argument about the ability of the MNC to enforce its own institutional rules with respect to the NBS, applies also to its relationship to its parent NBS.

Part II
The Context

3

Overview of the US Business System

Ian Clark and Phil Almond

INTRODUCTION[1]

This study investigates the extent and nature of the 'Americanness' of American MNCs. In other words, it analyses which characteristics of their management practice can be traced back to their 'embeddedness' within the US NBS. In order to do this, it is necessary to establish both *how* and *why* the American business system is different from its international competitors.

This chapter therefore examines the distinctive and evolving characteristics of the American model of capitalism. It will follow comparative institutionalist methodologies (see Chapter 2) in emphasizing the linkages between embedded features of the US NBS through a review of its historical development. Finally, it briefly examines which embedded features of the operation of US firms are most likely to be transferred to their foreign subsidiaries.

As Chapter 2 reflects, the US business system, like its British counterpart, is generally characterized within the comparative institutionalist literature as a 'compartmentalized' system, or 'LME' (Hall and Soskice 2001*a*; Whitley 1999). The 'arm's-length' coordination between economic actors in such economies is associated, in the employment sphere, with the predominance of flexible external labour markets (ELMs), weak public training systems, occupational trade unionism, and decentralized collective bargaining.

The dichotomy between CME and LME may well be of utility in analysing the different ways in which firms in different types of institutional systems seek to achieve competitive advantage. For the purposes of this study, however, it is necessary to go beyond a typology that simply places countries such as the USA and the UK together. In particular, given the current study's focus on the management of HR, it is worth asking why the particular pattern of 'compartmentalization' in the American business system has created such embedded features as a deep-seated anti-unionism among most of the capitalist class, a very weak societal attachment to notions of collective or individual labour rights, and a strong role for unitarist paradigms of management such as 'welfare capitalism' (Jacoby 1997). Such characteristics are not replicated to the same extent, or in the same ways, in other 'compartmentalized' business systems. In other words, while the USA is widely seen as the epitome of the 'LME', in which economic activity is predominantly coordinated *within* firms, and regulated by markets, it follows a distinctive model of economic organization within this general group of economies.

DISTINCTIVE FEATURES OF AMERICAN CAPITALISM

In investigating how and why American capitalism is distinctive, it is necessary to understand how its historical development has shaped the nature of the most important institutional features of a capitalist economy, namely the organization of firms, the state, and markets for products, labour, and capital. Given that this book is focussed on the management of the Human resource, the structure of the capital–labour relationship will be treated in more detail below.

American History and the American Firm

The development of American industrial capitalism took place against a social and demographic background quite different from the context in which industrialism occurred in European countries. Most notably, as a colony, and later as a virgin country, the USA did not have to dismantle a complex and well-established feudal society on its route to industrial capitalism. Indeed, both in the colonial period and beyond, immigrants flocked to America precisely to escape European forms of class control. Values of individualism, self-reliance and liberty, echoing those of the original Puritan colonists, were thus strongly embedded among the white American communities from a very early stage.

The socio-economic profile of the immigrants therefore pointed towards a form of individualism. This was, at least initially, a threat to the establishment of industrial capitalism. Long after the USA had become a recognizably capitalist economy, settlers sought to establish their own small-holdings and/or craft workshops, rather than to engage in 'wage slavery'. In particular, the supply of skilled workers prepared to work under an employment relationship was insufficient for the rate of expansion of the economy. This enhanced the incentive for small-holders and local manufacturers to substitute capital for labour, and to pursue technical innovation (Habakkuk 1960; Landes 1998).

Following the War of Independence, the lack of an embedded class structure among the colonists and immigrants also had decisive effects on the nature of product markets. As the American colonies were freed from British control over the manufacture of goods and taxation, a single political state of continental dimensions was formed. This state defined the boundaries of a market which was relatively free not only of the effects of status differentials, but also of local and regional preferences. In other words, patterns of demand for products were relatively homogeneous, as consumers in American markets were more ready to accept standardized products than their European counterparts (Hollingsworth 1997; Landes 1998). These features were confirmed decisively by the Northern Civil War victory and the consequent formal abolition of slavery.

American industrialists, then, were faced with product and labour market characteristics which were not mirrored in the other early-industrializing countries. On the one hand, there was the potential to develop mass markets for standardized products. On the other, labour, particularly skilled labour, was scarce relative to materials and factor endowments such as ores, wood, oil, coal, and water power. In a labour-scarce economy, standardization was—and was to remain—a way of substantially enhancing productivity by reducing unit labour costs. In major areas of manufacturing, American capitalism was a pioneer, combining production strategies and innovations to combat the scarcity of labour, for example, through the use of interchangeable parts developed within the machine tool industry (Landes 1998).

Later, the techniques of mass production would be successfully extended from consumer goods such as food, drink, and cosmetics, to goods of affluence such as domestic appliances, bicycles, and automobiles. Indeed, the economies of scale developed within mass production were essential to the establishment of mass markets for such luxury products. In the early twentieth century, Henry Ford, for instance, combined the armoury industry's use of interchangeable parts with the benefits of machine tooling, in order to produce standardized cars at the lowest possible price in order to stimulate demand. Ford added a new dimension to the American system—the moving assembly line—which, given the huge number of interchangeable parts and special-purpose machine tools used, was necessary in order to cut throughput times and unit labour costs. These production principles were later extended by General Motors to allow interchangeability between models, creating a flexible form of mass production, and allowing mass production to sit alongside niche marketing techniques.

A further consequence of the establishment of large firms serving mass markets and employing mass production methods was the early emergence of formalized management hierarchies—the use of the famous 'visible hand' (Chandler 1977) to coordinate and control operations. This promoted the professionalization and specialization of American management into distinct functions such as production, marketing, finance, and eventually personnel. It also encouraged the development of a specialized infrastructure of management education (cf. Locke 1996). The emergence of multidivisional firms as the dominant organizational form led to further differentiation, between the 'strategic' functions of the head office and the operational role of business divisions. This stimulated the development of forms of management control, such as planning and budgeting disciplines and the scrutiny of returns on capital invested, in companies such as DuPont and General Motors (Chandler 1962, 1977; Locke 1996: Chapter 1; Sloan 1986). In the post-war period, the strengthening role of financial markets and hence of external investor scrutiny of bottom-line performance (see later) gave a further push to the introduction of sophisticated forms of control and evaluation of the financial performance of operational units

In summary, American firms before, during, and after the emergence of the American system of manufactures were not embedded within a set of institutional arrangements in civil society such as those found in European business systems. Rather, the modern business enterprise and the emergence of managerial capitalism was an institutional response to rapidly changing technology and consequent innovation during a period of sustained growth in consumer demand. The managerial capitalist enterprise, characterized by distinct operating units managed through a hierarchy of salaried managers, had become the dominant business institution in the American economy by 1914. By the 1960s, multidivisional firms employed thousands of managers, supervising the work of business units that in some cases employed tens of thousands of workers. The class of managerial capitalists had become arguably the most influential group of decision-makers in the American business system and civil society (Galbraith 1967).

As Chandler (1990) and Djelic (1998) emphasize, there was considerable diffusion of these models—particularly of multidivisional or 'M-form' structures—to European systems after 1945. The evidence suggests, however, that the diffused models were significantly modified in practice by the nature of the national-institutional environments into which they were incorporated (Clark 2000; Djelic 1998). Moreover, however widely such organizational models were diffused, the *timing* of their adoption is also important: it remains the case that the American business system was characterized by their *early* emergence and consolidation, at a time when more traditional forms of competition, ownership patterns, and organizational structures predominated in Europe. Their impact in the US business system was therefore distinctive compared with their role within European economies.

Chandler argues (1990) that the dynamic created by the early development of mass markets in the USA also enabled large American firms to build 'organizational capabilities'—in production, marketing, and distribution as well as in areas such as financial control—that in turn provided the foundation both for diversification and for international expansion. As a result, US firms became pioneers of internationalization in sectors such as engineering, food and—along with German firms—chemicals, some as early as the last decades of the nineteenth century, with a major outflow of direct investment in the early decades of the twentieth (see also Dunning 1998: Chapter 1). The experience of managing foreign operations then enabled these firms to develop yet further their existing organizational capabilities. The effects of the formalization of managerial hierarchies in US MNCs on the process of decision-making in HR management are an important theme of the current study, and are investigated specifically in Chapters 9 and 10.

The State and Interest Associations

The predominance of economic coordination through markets and hierarchies in the USA partly reflects the relative underdevelopment both of the state and of inter-organizational mechanisms of governance such as networks and business associations. Historically, the US business system has been characterized by the weakness of the state as an economic actor. According to Jacoby (1991: 176) 'Before the New Deal, the United States had the weakest government in the western World', small in size and lacking in cohesion as a result of its fragmented, federal structure. Again, the weakness of the state can partly be explained by the 'virgin' nature of the country, and the ideological or religious values around individualism, liberty, and self-reliance on which the country was founded.

The state's main role, therefore, has been to set parameters for the behaviour of other economic actors, in particular to create a favourable climate for private sector investment, and it generally refrained from intervening to coordinate and plan economic activity in contrast, say to the Japanese state, or to make up for a late start to industrialization as in continental European states, such as Germany and France in the nineteenth and twentieth centuries. Decisions on investment, production, and distribution have generally been left to private companies, and there is no explicit 'industrial policy'.

The weakness of business associations can partly be attributed to the weakness of organized labour (see later), but has also been seen as related to the much larger number of large firms and the diversity of their economic interests (Hollingsworth 1997b: 135). This has restrained inter-firm networks on the German or Japanese model, as has the short-termism of market-driven relations (see later), although important networks have emerged in high-tech areas, including defence, IT, and pharmaceuticals, often coordinated by the federal or state government and involving close links with university researchers (Hollingsworth 1997b: 141–3; O'Sullivan 2000: 122–44). However, attempts to strengthen networks in the market-driven mass-production industries, such as automobiles—for instance, through longer-term relationships with suppliers—have generally foundered as short-termist market pressures assert themselves (Harrison 1997: Ch. 8).

The embedded individualist values cited earlier may also inform the strong statutory bias against cartels and trusts, as manifested in the Sherman Act of 1890. More fundamentally, however, in the absence of aristocratic or feudal institutions, the process of industrialization in the USA did not require business to define itself collectively in reaction to a strong pre-existing state or civil society. This allowed capitalists to use the ideology of individualism and liberty to their own ends (Sutton et al. 1956); the societal emphasis on individual progress through effort, self-reliance, and enterprise could easily be used to defend the interests of liberal capitalism (e.g. Hollingsworth 1997b), and to extol the virtues of private employers, who 'developed an especially strong belief in the virtues of free enterprise and apotheosized themselves as self-made men' (Jacoby 1991: 177).

These features meant that the market—and intra-organizational hierarchy—assumed prime importance as the means of economic coordination, with a resulting emphasis on atomistic, arms-length, contractually driven relationships between firms rather than trust-based long-term networks, as found in the German or Japanese business systems. Similarly, a market logic prevailed in the supply of both capital and labour. Long-term, stable relationships between firms and suppliers of financial capital or of labour, were discouraged by the logic of the system.

Capital Markets

The most striking characteristics of the American financial system are, first, the absence of long-term relationships between financial organizations and industrial firms; and second (and relatedly), the development of a strong 'market for corporate control' particularly from the 1980s onwards (O'Sullivan 2000: Chapter 5). The consequences of this model of 'shareholder capitalism' for corporate behaviour generally and for the management of HR/IR in particular have been profound.

Historically, banks were important providers of investment finance to the railways and other industries. But anti-trust legislation and government intervention to impose a clear distinction between commercial and investment banking worked against their assuming the role of their German or Japanese counterparts (Doremus et al. 1998: Ch. 3; Hollingsworth 1997a: 292–6; Kester 1996). The relatively weak role of banking in corporate finance encouraged the early development of equity markets. Stock market capitalization as a percentage of GDP continues to be very much higher in the USA than in Germany or France (Fukao 1995: Chapter 2; International Federation of Exchanges 2005).

Shareholdings in large US corporations have been highly fragmented, with few individuals or institutions holding large blocks of shares. The role of bank and insurance company shareholding, for the reasons discussed earlier, has been minimal (less than 1 per cent in the early 1990s) compared with some 20 per cent in Germany and 43 per cent in Japan (Fukao 1995: 27; Pauly and Reich 1997: 8–12). The equity markets' traditional importance in financing new firms and the consequent concern for small investors led to much tighter restrictions on 'insider trading' compared with other major countries, inhibiting effective communication between large shareholders and management (Fukao 1995: 36). 'Exit' rather than 'voice' was the primary action open to shareholders (Appelbaum and Berg 1996: 203–7; Fukao 1995; Kester 1996; Nooteboom 1999). This relative lack of voice available to the direct owners of capital was a crucial factor in the emergence of a managerial class, and of managerial capitalism. The frequent exercise of the 'exit' option by shareholders further perpetuated the division between ownership and control.

In recent decades, major changes have taken place in the financial system resulting from factors, such as the growth of international product and financial market competition; the shift of share ownership from individuals to institutions, such as pension funds and mutual funds, with statutory obligations to maximize their gains; and financial deregulation (O'Sullivan 2000: Chapter 5). The 1980s saw the growth of a strong 'market for corporate control'. In sharp contrast to Japan or Germany, the threat of hostile corporate takeovers became a key mechanism for disciplining 'underperforming' management. Together, these factors have sharpened investor short-termism, driven companies' focus on 'shareholder value', and increased pressures for higher returns at the expense of investor commitment to a particular company. The average length of time for which shares are held has declined steeply, rising percentage of profits distributed as dividends, and the size of transactions sharply increased.

The evolution of the US financial market has reinforced a systematic bias against firms 'that set strategic goals, designed to ensure the survival of the organization, but that do not lend themselves easily to present-value calculations' (Appelbaum and Berg 1996: 200). Under pressure from the unwanted attentions of corporate raiders, even more strategically minded companies came under increasing pressure to take a short-term approach to investment in such intangible areas as training and R&D that are not capitalized under US accounting rules (Appelbaum and Berg 1996: 200; Blair and Kochan 2000; Dertouzos et al. 1989: Chapter 4; Konzelmann, Forrant, and Wilkinson 2004). At the same time, the traditional distance between shareholders and corporate managers diminished as executives' remuneration became increasingly tied to share price through performance-related pay and stock options (Appelbaum and Berg 1996: 208–9; O'Sullivan 2000: 196–204).

One notable consequence of these developments was that many companies used 'downsizing'—severe, rapid reductions in workforce numbers—as a short-cut to maintaining investor confidence and share prices (O'Sullivan 2000: Chapter 6). The extent and breadth of downsizing in the 1980s and 1990s was unparalleled, affecting professional and white-collar employees as well as blue-collars, and older and more educated workers, in all economic sectors (Cappelli et al. 1997: Chapter 2).

Nonetheless, observers see the structure of US financial markets as advantageous to the development of new business by funding small firm start-ups with venture capital, particularly in comparison to the risk-averse Japanese or German financial systems (e.g. Fukao 1995; Hall and Gingerich 2004; Hall and Soskice 2001*b*: Chapter 1; Hollingsworth 1997*b*). As a result, the US system has tended to excel in the development of new products and industries, although the short-termist logic has arguably often prevented consolidation and innovation in established industries where potential returns are less enticing to risk-taking investors.

Labour Markets

US labour markets have been characterized as extremely flexible. Standardized mass production helped create ELMs based on the transfer between companies of workers with simple, standardized skills. This has been further encouraged by the short-termism of financial markets, since labour is seen as a cost to be minimized; the burden of adjustments in times of market difficulties is generally borne by employment levels through downsizing—or traditionally in cyclical industries by lay-offs and rehirings—rather than by working hours as would be the case in Japan (Fukao 1995: 43–4) or by employee earnings.

There are few of the institutional—and indeed cultural—constraints on 'numerical flexibility' to be found in systems such as the Japanese or the German. As a result, employees stay in jobs for significantly shorter periods in the USA compared with other major economies. Osterman (1999: Chapter 2) argues that job tenure became significantly less secure in the 1990s, particularly for men. Flexible ELMs have been seen (e.g. Hollingsworth 1997*b*) as a factor in the emergence and rapid growth of new business sectors in the USA, by providing a ready supply of mobile workers in mid-career.

The prominence of the ELM applies not just to rank-and-file employees but to managerial employees as well. Career structures in US corporations have been characterized by much greater mobility between firms than would be the case in, say, German or Japanese companies (Evans, Lank, and Farquhar 1989; Jackall 1988). This has been greatly intensified in recent decades by the strengthening grip of 'shareholder value' and consequent downsizing and 'delayering' that has affected whole strata of middle management. As a result, a labour market ideology of 'employability' has emerged, with an emphasis on the acquisition of a portfolio of portable management skills.

Flexible ELMs have traditionally combined with highly rigid internal ones, at least in the unionized sector, in which jobs were very tightly delineated through detailed job descriptions; there were sharp horizontal and vertical demarcations between jobs, and the criteria (usually seniority-based) for progression up job ladders were clearly defined (e.g. Kochan, Katz, and McKersie 1994: Chapter 2).

Compared with continental European or Japanese labour markets, the US labour market has traditionally been relatively untrammelled by institutional constraints. Notably, the legal doctrine of 'employment at will' (see Chapter 7) generally allows employers to dismiss workers for any reason, such that the employer is not bound in law to demonstrate that a dismissal is 'fair'. Therefore, with some recent exceptions in the area of government regulation on issues such as equality of employment opportunity (see Chapter 8), the labour market has been 'a place where anything goes' (Kochan, Katz, and McKersie 1994: xiii). This absence of regulation has permitted one of the most notable recent features of the US labour market—its increasing turbulence. This has been a response to such inter-related factors as 'shareholder value', corporate restructuring, and international competition and has been manifested in the devaluing of ILMs, growing insecurity of tenure, increasingly polarized earnings, and a trend to 'contingent' forms of employment such as temporary, agency, and contract work (Osterman 1999: Chapter 2).

Industrial Relations

The interlocking components of the American business system detailed earlier have had a profound impact on American industrial relations (IR) and the management of HR. The recurrent theme of individualism has stimulated a strong and persistent anti-state and anti-union ideology and a corresponding union weakness. This weakness is often explained by arguments that American labour never had to coalesce in a struggle for political rights, as was the case in Europe, and that it was weakened by ethnic and cultural diversity and comparatively high rates of social mobility. However, as argued in Chapter 6, we must add the fervent union suppression pursued by employers, aided by state agencies, at the start of the twentieth century and at various subsequent points in US labour history. A further factor may be the emergence of centralized management control over job regulation that left trade unions continually on the defensive when responding to the deskilling inherent in the predominant system of manufacturing.

What is beyond dispute is that unionization has been low, and the role of the state in encouraging collectivism shallow, except during the crisis of the American business system that resulted in the New Deal reforms of the 1930s. The National Labor Relations Act of 1935 (commonly known as the Wagner Act) established legal mechanisms for unions to gain formal recognition where they were able to demonstrate sufficient support, employers with obliged to bargain in good faith. However, it is important to point out that the commitment of the US state to IR pluralism was never particularly strong, and its level of embeddedness within the wider American business system remained shallow.

Contemporary evidence suggests that unless compelled to do so by the courts many American employers exhibited little or no good faith, and failed to comply with rulings passed by the National Labor Relations Board (NLRB). Indeed, in 1939 only 20 per cent of corporate executives expressed support for the provisions in the Wagner Act. Moreover, challenges to the constitutionality of the New Deal and the Wagner Act in particular delayed and eroded its full legal impact (Bernstein 1970). From 1938, a powerful coalition of conservative Republicans and individualist southern Democrats attacked the New Deal as 'un-American', that is, against individualism, further arguing that the New Deal administration and the labour movement was infested with communists. Post-war, the McCarthy committee continued and formalized this attack on the labour movement (Auerbach 1966). Such tactics, alongside the 1947 Taft–Hartley amendments to the National Labor Relations Act, diluted and undermined the New Deal, and provided support for more established individualistic patterns of non-unionism.

Despite these attacks, in many large American manufacturing companies, unions organized successfully, and workplace IR revolved around legally enforceable contracts and highly codified collective agreements that set detailed grading structures and procedures for grievance and discipline (Kochan, Katz, and McKersie 1994; see also Chapter 6, this volume). But from the 1960s, the declining significance of domestic mass production and consequent shifts in the labour force towards white-collar and professional occupations, combined with greater international competition, reduced employers' preference for stability in IR, with more rapid speed of reaction and flexibility of production gradually becoming the main focus. Employers turned towards non-union strategies, relocating operations to greenfield sites in employer-friendly states, generally in the south, beyond the eastern seaboard and mid-western states where New Deal IR were more developed (Kochan, Katz, and McKersie 1994).

Non-Unionism and Welfare Capitalism

Even when full employment and relative trade union strength meant that the New Deal system was accepted as the official IR system of US managerial capitalism, and the system promoted abroad as the model on which industrial societies would eventually converge (Kerr et al. 1960), wide swathes of the American economy sustained anti-collectivism and non-unionism. This assumed a variety of forms, from the low road exploitation of peripheral labour in agriculture, cotton and retailing, through to the more sophisticated techniques associated with post-New Deal 'welfare capitalism' (Jacoby 1997).

Historically, welfare capitalism was a sophisticated version of non-union paternalism, often incorporated within the 'company town' philosophy. Sustained by a belief that the firm rather than unions or the state should provide for the security and welfare of employees, welfare capitalism was characterized by an ideological and philosophical opposition to collective relations in the workplace (see Foulkes 1980). As the New Deal led to wage increases and improved terms and conditions of employment in unionized workplaces, welfare capitalist firms matched or exceeded wage increases and introduced innovative personnel management policies in areas such as pensions, health care, and unemployment insurance. Welfare capitalist firms, which included major names, such as Kodak, Polaroid, Sears Roebuck, Thompson Products, DuPont, Eli Lilly, IBM, Standard Oil, and Proctor & Gamble, are credited with pioneering systems of individual performance-related pay, profit-sharing, team working, and worker appraisal (Jacoby 1997). They attempted to build on the individual psychological commitment of employees by promoting a strong, explicit, and inclusive corporate culture. This included the use of social science techniques such as employee attitude surveys to maintain a dialogue with employee opinion (Foulkes 1980: Chapter 13). Equally, when necessary, welfare capitalists were prepared to suppress attempts by trade unions to organize in the workplace (Jacoby 1997). Essentially, this group of employers elicited individual employee commitment, built on a cornerstone of long-term employment security, as a strategy to avoid trade union or state 'interference' in their management of the employment relationship.

Welfare capitalism, like the New Deal system, was supported by structural factors, in particular the long period of stable product market growth following the Second World War. During this period, welfare capitalist employers could sustain enlightened personnel policies as a form of efficiency wage because, to a large extent, they were able to externalize low-skill and more volatile activities to peripheral firms, where lower road variants of non-unionism predominated (Katz and Darbishire 2000: Chapter 2). In the contemporary period, the intensification of international product market competition, technological developments, and changes in the operations of financial markets have eroded the bases of both the New Deal and welfare capitalist approaches. The institutionalized narrow job descriptions of the New Deal system have become increasingly mismatched with market demands for product flexibility and cost controls, while most of the classic welfare capitalist employers have faced competitive and cost crises forcing them to downsize their labour forces quite radically, clearly undermining the 'psychological contract' in such firms. The effects of these changes have to some extent blurred the boundaries between former New Deal firms and the welfare capitalist sector, and created a general trend towards the use of labour management approaches, particularly in the management of the ILM, which are more 'low road' in nature. However, as is reflected later in this volume, significant differences still persist between large firms with a welfare capitalist and those with a New Deal heritage.

The Organization of Work and HR

The application of mass production techniques, which as explained above aimed to substitute capital for (skilled) labour, resulted in an intensive division of labour in which specialized machinery allowed the separation of task conception from execution and the breakdown of production tasks into simple elements capable of being performed by unskilled or semi-skilled labour (e.g. Braverman 1974: Chapter 4). This in turn promoted a tradition of industrial engineering (e.g. Noble 1977) concerned with measuring and scrutinizing the performance of subdivided tasks and with designing the organization of the production process to allow maximum managerial control.

In stark contrast to the models of work organization in Germany, Italy, or Japan (e.g. Lane 1989), American mass production techniques involved a systematic assertion of management control over areas of craft activity. As Lazonick (1998: 206) argues, 'what made US industrial corporations unique among their counterparts in the advanced economies was their dedication to a strategy of taking skills, and hence the possibilities for craft learning—much less corporate learning—off the shop floor.' This model of 'hierarchical segmentation' meant that American companies relied almost exclusively on managerial organization for the development of new productive capabilities (p. 207; see also O'Sullivan 2000). The mass production model was reinforced by the upsurge in unionization and bargaining from the New Deal (Kochan, Katz, and McKersie 1994). As Jacoby argues (1997: 44), 'confronted with scientific management as a fait accompli, the new industrial unions pragmatically constructed their regulatory systems around the division of labor wrought by the Taylorists. Hence unionism's contractual restraints reinforced Taylor's unimaginative approach to work design.'

Standardized mass production and scientific management also implied the development of a mass education system turning out potential employees with basic skills and industrial discipline to work in mass production sectors (Dertouzos et al. 1989: Chapter 6). The training of rank-and-file workers was subsequently 'brief, narrow and job specific' (Hollingsworth 1997b: 140), leaving employees vulnerable to rapid obsolescence (Dertouzos et al. 1989: 81). This contrasted with Japan or Germany where on-the-job training was commonly used to expand more general skills, creating a greater adaptability in the face of change. The US model was suited for standardized mass production, but not appropriate for a system of production based on multiple sophisticated skills and flexibility (e.g. Lazonick 1998; Streeck 1997). The pattern of skills reinforced and was reinforced by the role of the ELM. The system was premised on low-skilled, interchangeable workers who could be laid off and rehired according to the phase of the business cycle and whose skills were easily transferable between firms; there was therefore little incentive for companies to make long-term investments in training and complex skills, particularly if other firms were not also doing so, since trained workers could easily be poached by 'free-riders'; nor were workers motivated to invest in long-term firm-specific skill acquisition since companies could or would not offer them the necessary security and continuity of employment.

The mass production model has come under increasing challenge since the 1970s as an outdated strategy no longer appropriate in an era of intensifying international competition (e.g. Dertouzos et al. 1989: Chapter 3). Quality of design and product performance became criteria of commercial success as important as low-cost production. Technological innovation had to be more flexible and more adapted to fragmented and changing consumer demand, rather than to long runs of standardized designs. The reappraisal of standardized mass production was brought to a head by Japanese investment in the USA from the 1970s and particularly by the well-known developments in the automobile industry (Womack,

Jones, and Roos 1990), which exposed US producers to a model of production based on flexible automation, a different organization of work, a radically different approach to quality, the use of teamwork, and close, long-term relationships between producers and suppliers. At the same time, worker and union discontent with the numbing impact of the mass production system (e.g. Fairris 1997: Chapter 5) led to the growing interest from the 1960s in Quality of Working Life (QWL) issues, and to attempts to reform the way work was organized (Kochan, Katz, and McKersie 1994: Chapter 6).

The upshot has been the widespread introduction in recent years of at least some elements of what Appelbaum and Batt (1994) call 'high performance work systems' based on greater worker discretion, more flexible job specifications, and payment systems, a greater commitment to training and organizational learning, and greater worker involvement in decisions affecting the organization of work. Osterman (1999: Chapter 4) presents survey data showing a significant spread during the 1990s of such practices as quality circles, job rotation, and total quality management (TQM) (see also Cappelli et al. 1997: Chapter 3).

There have been some high-profile examples of radical change in work organization in plants, like GM's Saturn facility (e.g. Fairris 1997: Chapter 8), GM's NUMMI joint venture with Toyota, or the Corning plant described by Appelbaum and Batt (1994: 88). Moreover, there is evidence that such work systems outperform the traditional model (Osterman 1999: 101–2). Nonetheless, such exemplar cases have been fairly isolated, due to severe constraints on the adoption of new forms of work organization such as semi-autonomous multiskilled work teams in the American environment (see esp. Lazonick 1998). First, as Kochan, Katz, and McKersie (1994: Chapter 4) suggest in reference to QWL initiatives, the model of New Deal collective bargaining was intimately associated with mass production technologies. These gave rise to ILMs, job categories, career progressions, and so on, that were institutionalized through collective contracts. Managerial and union interests grew up around this pattern of 'shop-floor contractualism' (Fairris 1997). The QWL challenged such arrangements, provoking fears that 'QWL processes would undermine the role of the local union and the sanctity of the collective bargaining contract' (p. 150). Such fears were exacerbated by the fact that many innovative elements of work organization or of participation were pioneered in non-union firms; TRW, for example, was in the vanguard of work organization based on teams (Jacoby 1997: 259; Kochan, Katz, and McKersie 1994: 96–9).

Second, as a result of the skills base of the American workforce, combined with the predominance of semi-skilled production jobs, only a 'select group' of the workforce appeared to have the necessary characteristics to operate teamwork successfully (Kochan, Katz, and McKersie 1994: 99). Indeed, as Turner (1991: 159–62) argues, while teamwork in the German car industry emphasized raising skill across the board, US team experiments in the car industry focused on broadening the skills of the already-skilled. In the typical team, production workers performed repetitive tasks in short cycle times with occasional job rotation.

Third, the wider institutional context in the USA allows firms to pursue the 'low-road' option of using low-skill, low-cost labour to operate standardized production processes (Appelbaum and Berg 1996; Ichniowski et al. 1996; see also Pil and MacDuffie 1996). Financial short-termism militates against the heavy investments in technology, logistical redesign of the work site, and intensive training of workers required to introduce high-performance work systems. Moreover, the trust required by high-performance work systems is extremely difficult to build when the pressures of financial markets and the pursuit of 'shareholder value' have impelled companies to downsize. Trust has also been undermined by the relocation strategies of companies, which have led to the uneasy cohabitation of union and non-union IR in the same firm (Ichniowski et al. 1996: 328).

As a result of such factors, high-profile examples of extensive innovative work organization, such as the Saturn project, have become isolated experiments, whose practices have not widely diffused to similar plants and companies. Moreover, 'lean production' models have been adapted to the US business environment: they are, for example, distinguished from the original Japanese model by the absence of such structural features as employment security and intensive training (Fairris 1997).

The US Business System and the Scope for Strategic Choice

This chapter has explored how the US business system comprises a set of distinctive and interrelated institutions that have emerged from a contingent historical trajectory of development. The earlier discussion has tried to indicate how different elements interact in complex ways to influence the development of HR/IR within the firm. One conclusion is that the American system is marked out at a general level from other business systems, particularly in Europe, by a lesser degree of institutional development in many areas. This feature is seen, first, in the far weaker role of the state in determining many aspects of the business system, including the institutional frameworks of employment relations; and, second, in the absence of the labour and product market constraints that result in countries such as Germany from the strength of business associations and the dense patterns of inter-organizational networks. This can be argued to permit a greater range of strategic choices and outcomes for firms and managers. Turner (1991) argues in his comparative study of the car industry in the USA and west Germany that the greatest difference in IR and work organization between the two countries is that the range of outcomes in Germany is narrow, while in the USA, the range is very wide, 'extending from innovative nonunion to traditional (including both adversarial and cooperative variants) to innovative unionized (including both relative successes and failures)' (p. 154). As a result, one may observe a greater diversity across actors and a higher degree of changeability, even volatility, over time in the strategies and behaviours of firms and other actors than one would expect in many more institutionalized continental European systems.

In other respects, however, American companies may be *more* constrained than their European or Japanese counterparts. Notably, financial markets impose a discipline on managers that militates against long-term and strategic decisions on markets, R&D, and investment. Moreover, the historical pattern of work organization has given rise to institutional constraints at firm level (but also at societal level in terms of vocational education and training) that constrain the adoption of 'high performance' work systems.

International Transfer within MNCs

Another general conclusion from this brief review is that, in contrast to the implicit evolutionary premises of much research and writing on international and comparative HR/IR, the American system does not represent some vision of a universal business model to which other less-developed business systems are tending (if not aspiring). On the contrary, it is *sui generis*. There has clearly been borrowing, and in some areas, convergence, but, equally, NBSs have retained distinctive ways of organizing markets, structuring firms, shaping skills, and so on.

This consideration is of vital importance in considering the transfer of elements of 'HRM', since as discussed earlier, HR practices in the US context have emerged out of an interrelated set of deeply rooted aspects of the American business system, notably the nature of production organization and of managerial 'capabilities', the dynamic interaction between union and non-union firms, the persistence of corporate welfare capitalism, and the distinctive evolution of the personnel function itself.

The sheer variety of US MNCs and their subsidiaries, in terms of structural factors, corporate history, and the forms and meanings attached to specific policies makes generalizations about the extent of transfer, and about the policy areas in which it occurs, a somewhat risky enterprise. This in itself is a strong reason for the use of qualitative research methodologies. From the analysis earlier, however, one might expect US MNCs, which have built competitive advantage through economies of scale, under the aegis of managerial capitalism, to be more likely than their foreign competitors to use standardized, formalized decision-making, and centrally propagated policies. Consequently, they might be anticipated to tend towards cross-national 'isomorphism', that is, to exhibit similar characteristics in their overseas and domestic operations, even where the host country environment is at first glance unpropitious. This strong centralizing tendency might be expected to lead to relatively strong roles for the international HR function.

Beyond these very general comments, the picture arguably becomes less clear. Because of the relatively unconstraining nature of the home business system, US MNCs might also be expected to have large numbers of innovative (from the host-country perspective) HR policies that will be diffused internationally. Yet this might well be contradicted by the (increasingly) short-term time horizons and tight budgetary controls under which US firms have to work, suggesting perhaps that innovation is more likely in those areas where results are fairly clear and quantifiable, and much less likely in areas where returns are long-term or unpredictable.

Equally, the outcomes of the interaction between US MNCs and host-country institutions and traditions are far from clear. On the one hand, one might logically argue that 'Americanness' is more likely to be manifest in institutionally close systems, such as Ireland and the UK, and less manifest in more institutionally distant systems, particularly that of Germany. On the other hand, it is quite possible that US firms are less likely to be tolerant of institutional constraints—particularly, for non-union firms, with regard to collective IR—in institutionally distant countries, where US management views the constraint as a 'problem', than in fellow 'LMEs', where, for example, pluralist arrangements may be tolerated as long as they appear to cause little threat to management prerogative.

CONCLUSION

This chapter has reviewed how distinctive elements of the American NBS are embedded in the historical pattern of development of American industrial capitalism, as well as American society and the US state. In a 'new' country with a lack of pre-existing societal institutions, a combination of factors, ranging from the importance of the founding values of individualism, self-reliance, and egalitarianism (among white men), through to a structural scarcity of labour and the consequent premium on progress in production technology, gave rise to a distinctive form of industrial capitalism. The chapter illustrates the interdependent and interlocking nature of the important characteristics of the American business system as it developed over the course of industrialization. The system's defining features include: the early development of large firms serving large, relatively homogeneous product markets; the associated early evolution of formalized management functions and mechanisms of control and coordination to allocate resources and to evaluate performance in diversified multidivisional companies; the predominance of atomistic arms-length market relations in product, capital, and labour markets, characterized by short-termist considerations; a relatively weak state; and the ability, in the absence of market and institutional constraints, to innovate by moving human and capital resources flexibly and rapidly into the development of new industries.

In the area of labour management, a tradition of large firms, mass markets, and standardized mass production has allowed economies of scale and work organization based on Taylorism, with fragmented work tasks and the separation of conception and execution, further encouraged by chronic shortages of skilled labour. Relatedly, the USA developed a mass basic education system, and a narrow, limited, task-related pattern of on-the-job training. This in turn has generated an uncertain response to the challenge of new models of work organization, particularly 'lean production', with only a partial erosion of the traditional model, reflecting institutional constraints such as short-termism and the external flexibility of labour markets.

Within this system, anti-unionism is deep rooted. A relatively brief period of institutional support for collective bargaining and unionization was never strongly embedded in the NBS. The 'New Deal' in IR was strongly contested at both the societal and firm levels. This gave rise to a differentiated model of HR/IR in large American firms with distinctive patterns of behaviour in unionized and sophisticated non-union firms, although the distinctions between unionized, sophisticated non-union, and lower road non-union firms have probably diminished over recent years. This reflects economic and financial pressures, along with the contemporary weakness of collective labour, leading to a trend away from the protections (employment security, seniority provisions, and so on) once afforded workers. Whether, and how, firms with a welfare capitalist heritage remain distinctive in their HRM policies from unionized firms, particularly in their overseas operations, remains an empirical question, however.

It has been argued that such systemic traits within US capitalism are likely to inform the behaviour of US companies abroad in a number of ways that may be identified as 'Americanness'. Such distinctive behaviour is likely to be quite robust in that it stems from a profound confidence in the universality of American business methods encouraged by economic and political hegemony and from the early development of organizational capabilities, based on the economies of scale made possible by managerial capitalism and mass production, and transferable to operations abroad.

The argument of the chapter also suggests that there is likely to be a pattern of heterogeneity, partly because the American institutional framework is underdetermined, allowing a greater variety of outcomes to arise; partly because of the deep-rooted differences of approach to the management of labour to be found in unionized and non-union firms (and indeed within each of these groupings). It also suggests that manifestations of Americanness are likely to vary according to the constraints imposed by different institutional structures in different host systems.

Note

1. This chapter draws extensively from an earlier project working paper, Ferner 2000.

4

Overview of the Host Business Systems

Tony Edwards, Paddy Gunnigle, Javier Quintanilla, and Hartmut Wächter

INTRODUCTION

This chapter provides a summary of some of the key features of the four host business systems—the UK, Ireland, Germany, and Spain. It begins by establishing the profile of foreign direct investment (FDI) in each country, noting that each is a major base for American MNCs; goes on to review the key aspects of the IR framework in each case, establishing the main institutions in the labour market that may operate as constraints to the transfer of practices by foreign MNCs; and concludes by reviewing the evidence concerning the 'openness' of each system to MNCs. We show that the four countries provide contrasting host systems for American MNCs but that they are characterized by varying degrees of openness.

THE PROFILE OF US FOREIGN DIRECT INVESTMENT

All four countries in our study are major recipients of investments by American MNCs. This section provides data on the scale of FDI in each of the four countries, the extent to which levels of FDI have grown and the relative importance of American FDI compared with that from other countries. The UN defines FDI as 'an investment involving a long term relationship and reflecting a lasting interest and control by a resident entity in one economy in an enterprise resident in an economy other than that of the foreign direct investor' (2003: 231). Two measures of FDI are commonly referred to: the flow of FDI which measures new capital flows in a particular year and the stock which measures the accumulation of capital flows over time.

Table 4.1 provides data for the stock of total FDI, showing that the four countries together are recipients of around 20 per cent of the world's total, with the UK the largest recipient of the four followed by Germany, Spain, and Ireland, respectively. When judged as a percentage of national output, the table shows the remarkably high level of FDI stock in Ireland, comprising nearly 130 per cent of GDP. The figures in Table 4.2 relate to flows of inward FDI and demonstrate the rapid increases into Ireland and Germany over the last decade.

The increase in FDI into the Republic of Ireland has been associated with an extraordinary economic transformation and a decade of rapid growth. It is estimated that in 2002 foreign MNCs accounted for some 50 per cent of manufacturing employment, compared to an average of 19 per cent in 12 other EU countries for which data are available (Barry 2002), with MNCs dominating sectors such as electronics, pharmaceuticals, health care, and software. This reliance on FDI results from a consistent public policy of providing incentives to MNCs to locate in Ireland. The policy has

Table 4.1. Total inward FDI stock at end of 2003

Country	Value ($billion)	% of global FDI stock	% of national GDP
Germany	544.6	6.6	22.6
Ireland	193.4	2.3	129.7
Spain	230.3	2.8	27.4
UK	672.0	8.2	37.4

Source: UN *World Investment Report*, 2004.

Table 4.2. Total FDI inflows 1992–2003 ($million and % of global total)

Country	1992–97 average	1998	1999	2000	2001	2002	2003
Germany	6,042 (1.9%)	24,593 (3.6%)	56,077 (5.2%)	198,276 (14.3%)	21,138 (2.6%)	36,014 (5.3%)	12,866 (2.3%)
Ireland	1,694 (0.5%)	8,579 (1.2%)	18,218 (1.7%)	25,843 (1.9%)	9,659 (1.2%)	24,486 (3.6%)	25,497 (4.6%)
Spain	8,615 (2.8%)	11,797 (1.7%)	15,758 (1.5%)	37,523 (2.7%)	28,005 (3.4%)	35,908 (5.3%)	25,625 (4.6%)
UK	19,527 (6.3%)	74,321 (10.8%)	87,979 (8.1%)	118,764 (8.6%)	52,623 (6.4%)	27,776 (4.1%)	14,515 (2.6%)

Source: UN *World Investment Report*, 2004.

its genesis in the late 1950s when the government abandoned the strategy of protecting indigenous industry and decided to accelerate the industrialization of the country by attracting foreign firms. The most significant incentives were low taxes on profits from exports and financial grants towards fixed assets. The USA is by some way Ireland's largest source of FDI, accounting for just under half of all foreign-owned firms in the country (see Table 4.3). The weight of US FDI is highlighted by *The Economist*'s (1997) finding that FDI stock from US firms amounted to $3,000 per head of population in Ireland, compared with $2,000 in Britain, $500 in Germany and France, and $200 in Spain.

American FDI also features very strongly in Germany. As shown in Figure 4.1, the total inward stock of American FDI increased from DM 0.9 billion in 1962 to more than DM 109 billion in 1998. Figure 4.1 also demonstrates the dominance of American MNCs. They accounted for nearly half of FDI for much of the post-war period, and although this figure has fallen as MNCs of other nationalities have increased their presence in the last two decades or so, US firms still account for around a quarter of total FDI. As Figure 4.2 shows, American subsidiaries comprise only around 15 per cent of all foreign companies. The implication is that US-owned firms tend to be larger than other foreign-owned firms. American firms account for more than a quarter of total employment in foreign-owned firms in Germany, employing 530,000 people (see Figure 4.3) or 1.5 per cent of total employment.

Britain has long been a major recipient of American FDI. The ties between the two countries and similarities in many of the key institutions have encouraged many US firms to use their British operations as a bridgehead into Europe. Thus American MNCs dominated patterns of FDI into the UK in the period immediately following the Second World War

Table 4.3. FDI by ownership in Ireland

Country	Number of Firms
USA	507
Germany	148
UK	132
Rest of Europe	211
Far East	38
Rest of the World	62
Total	1,098

Source: Forfas, *Annual Employment Surveys*, 2001, 2002.

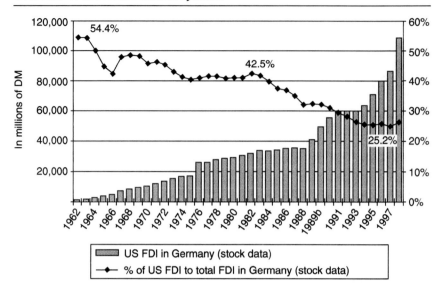

Figure 4.1 FDI of American companies in Germany
Source: **Deutsche Bundesbank (1984, 1989, 1992, 1993, 1995, 1997, 2000); Krägenau (1975: 139); and own calculations.**

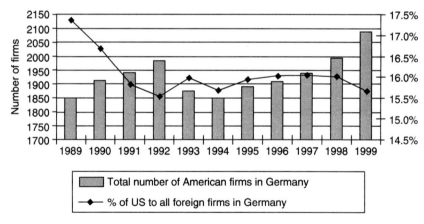

Figure 4.2 American firms in Germany
Source: **Deutsche Bundesbank (1984, 1989, 1992, 1993, 1995, 1997, 2000) and own calculations.**

(Dunning 1998). Table 4.4 demonstrates that American MNCs continue to account for a large proportion of total FDI. With the exception of 2002 when there was net disinvestment by US firms, they have consistently been the largest single source of inward FDI. A recent study found that of

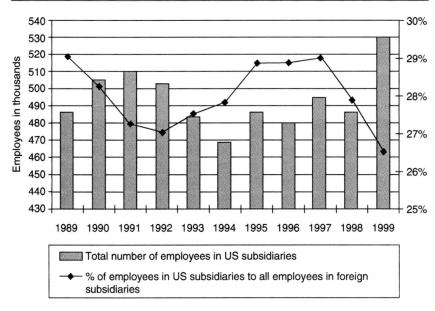

Figure 4.3 Number of people employed in American companies in Germany
Source: **Deutsche Bundesbank (1984, 1989, 1992, 1993, 1995, 1997, 2000) and own calculations.**

Table 4.4. American net FDI flows into the UK 1993–2002

Year	Value (£million)	% of total inward FDI
1993	5,142	52.1
1994	2,138	35.4
1995	9,293	73.4
1996	6,742	43.0
1997	10,045	49.5
1998	18,596	41.4
1999	15,953	29.3
2000	12,741	16.3
2001	15,025	41.1
2002	−3,011	–

NB: Net investment includes unremitted profits. A '–' indicates net disinvestment in the UK.
Source: Office for National Statistics (2004).

over 2,500 overseas-owned firms with at least 100 employees in Britain and at least 500 worldwide, just over a third were of American origin (Arrowsmith 2002).

In Spain, the proportion of industrial output in hands of foreign enterprises is exceptionally high at 42 per cent (Buesa and Molero 1996) and American MNCs account for a high proportion of this inward investment. This was particularly the case during the 1960s and 1970s; the USA was the source of a third of new FDI into Spain between 1960 and 1979 (Elteto 2000). This proportion dropped in the 1980s and 1990s as MNCs from other European countries increased their investments in Spain following its accession to the EU. Despite this trend, the USA remains by some way the largest single source of FDI into Spain. The Invest in Spain Bureau estimates there to be around 600 American companies in the country, accounting for 7 per cent of GDP (Invest in Spain 2004). They are key players in sectors such as IT, consulting, chemicals, pharmaceuticals, and the auto industry—indeed, American firms account for a third of all cars produced in Spain and nearly 40 per cent of all pharmaceutical products—and are concentrated in the conurbations around Madrid and Barcelona.

In sum, given both the significant presence of American MNCs in all four countries and the 'dominance' of the American system more generally, it is reasonable to suppose that they are key players in shaping the nature of HR and IR practice in the four countries. However, the constraints that they face in introducing novel employment practices vary according to the nature of the host system of employment relations. Thus in the next section we turn to examine the main features of these systems.

KEY ASPECTS OF THE IR FRAMEWORK

There is considerable variation across the four countries in the extent to which the key aspects of the IR framework restrict the freedom of American firms to introduce their preferred practices. This variation stems from systematic differences in the key institutions shaping the level and scope of collective bargaining, forms of employee representation at workplace or firm level, and other statutory obligations on employers, such as requirements to consult employees before introducing major organizational changes. Thus despite an emerging common framework of labour regulation at the EU level, covering issues such as working time and parental leave, the IR context differs significantly across countries.

The national system of IR that we might expect to pose the tightest constraints on US MNCs is Germany. There is a highly codified system of employee representation that takes the form both of collective bargaining and workplace-based councils. The primary level of collective bargaining has tended to be the sector, with provisions of these agreements applying across the vast majority of firms within the industry concerned. Although there has been an increase in firm-level agreements in recent years, for most non-managerial employees, labour conditions and basic wages are set by negotiations outside the firm, and even for those firms that are not formally part of sectoral agreements there is a normative pressure to comply with their terms. Collective bargaining is complemented by employee representation at firm and establishment level. In relation to the former, firms employing more than 2,000 people are required to set up an *Aufsichtsrat* (supervisory board), which has equal numbers of management and worker representatives. At establishment level, employee representation is through works councils (*Betriebsrat*), which have powers to negotiate the introduction of significant changes to working practices. Worker representatives on the works councils are commonly union members, giving unions some influence at workplace level (for more details see Jacobi et al. 1998). These characteristics of the German IR system appear to present significant constraints on the freedom with which managers can make substantial changes to employment practices following a merger or acquisition, though this needs to be qualified; works councils have far from universal coverage, for example, and the institutional constraints on employers are not as tight as they once were (Hassel 1999).

The Spanish system also affords employees rights to workplace representation, primarily through workers' committees (*comités de empresa*). While any employee may stand for election, in practice, these committees are normally dominated by union representatives, meaning that unions derive much of their influence at workplace level through this channel. This is significant partly because the workers' committee has the power to negotiate collective agreements at firm level. The importance of union support from employees voting for them in works council elections has led to the term 'voters' unionism' being used to describe the Spanish system (Martínez Lucio 1998). This is related to the prevalence of *simpatizantes*; these are employees who are favourably disposed to unions, tend to vote for union representatives in elections for workers' committees and may even take industrial action, but are not formally union members. Union influence also comes from the existence of sectoral collective bargaining, although the agreements reached at industry level are normally 'provincial' or regional rather than national in their coverage. These agreements provide minimum levels of pay and working conditions that are particularly important in small- and medium-sized firms that have no workers' committee (Aguilera 2004). Among large and state-owned firms, there has been a growth recently in firm-level collective bargaining through which employers have sought to achieve greater flexibility. The ease with which they could achieve this was enhanced by major reforms of the labour market in 1994 and 1997 that swept away many central edicts, known as *ordenanzas laborales*—a legacy of the Franco era governing many aspects of work organization. The labour market reforms also made it much easier and cheaper for firms to lay off staff. Overall, the Spanish system presents a number of significant constraints on management, but these are highly variable in their impact across Spain as large swathes of the country are characterized by very weak patterns of employee representation.

In Britain and Ireland, the regulations and institutions in the labour market appear to present fewer constraints to American firms. In the UK, a series of measures taken by successive Conservative governments in the 1980s and 1990s curtailed the role of unions and, coupled with a harsher economic climate, led to the contraction of collective bargaining (Edwards 2002). Indeed, multi-employer bargaining has almost disappeared over the last thirty years, and so the ability of unions to exert influence through negotiations depends on their organization at firm and workplace level. Despite recent legislation under which firms can be obliged to offer recognition following a ballot of workers, union influence varies markedly across the economy. The absence of strong legal or institutional supports for collective bargaining means that unions are formally recognized by management in less than half of workplaces (Cully et al. 1999). The statutory obligations on employers to operate forms of workplace representation are weaker than in Germany and Spain, and this will change only slightly when the UK introduces legislation obliging employers to engage in information disclosure and consultation with employee representatives as part of the European Directive on Information and Consultation. Overall, many managers appear to have a relatively free hand in implementing changes to employment practice.

The Irish IR system has some similarities but also some differences with the British system. First, there is a higher level of union density in Ireland (43 per cent in 2001 compared with less than 30 per cent in the UK). Second, the Irish IR system is much more centralized in practice. A series of centrally negotiated accords have been agreed by the 'social partners' (principally government, employers, and trade unions but also involving groups representing farming and community/voluntary interests). These agreements, which are voluntary in nature, deal not only with pay but also with a range of economic and social policy issues such as welfare provision, employment creation, and tax reform. They have given the union movement some influence over the nature of economic and social policy (Gunnigle et al. 2002). This contrasts sharply with the marginalization of unions in the UK, even after the Labour victory of 1997. The similarities are also in evidence, however, notably in the tradition of 'voluntarism' whereby the recognition of unions for collective bargaining purposes depends on the available power resources of the union and employer (D'Art and Turner 2003). There is no constitutional or legislative provision which can force an employer to recognize or negotiate with a trade union, except in the case of collective redundancies. Consequently, the pattern of union recognition is highly uneven across the economy.

The differences are summarized in Table 4.5. In sum, in terms of the formal institutions and regulations in the four countries, the German

Table 4.5. Key aspects of the national industrial relations system in each country

Country	Union density and organization	Statutory support for employee representation	Coverage and level of collective bargaining
Germany	Density at 30% Unions organized mainly by sectors with unions covering multiple occupations within firms	Quite strong 'Co-determination' through Works Councils and employee representation on Supervisory Boards in large firms	Coverage at 80% Industry-based bargaining still the dominant form, though some rise in firm-based collective agreements in the last few years
Spain	Density at 15% Two main union groups—one communist, the other more moderate socialist. A third smaller (anarchist) confederation exists	Moderate Workers committees are empowered to reach collective agreements with management. Unions are highly influential on the committees	Coverage at 75% Industry-based bargaining formally the key level, but considerable variation in practice between regions and firms
UK	Density at 30% Unions organized traditionally by craft/occupation—more recently, mergers have created larger general unions	Weak The Employment Relations Act (2000) provides for ballots on recognition. Some additional rights through European Directives	Coverage at 40% Collapse of multi-employer bargaining in last twenty years means that firm and plant bargaining are now the principal levels
Ireland	Density at 43% A small number of general unions	Weak No statutory mechanisms allow trade unions to secure recognition from employers, though emergence of tripartism has strong state support	Coverage at 66% Tripartite negotiations set 'framework' agreements—supplementary firm-level bargaining is important

Source: Various.

system would appear to present the strongest constraints on attempts by American MNCs to introduce novel practices, while the constraints in the other three countries are not as strong or as widespread. In the next section, we consider what the evidence from previous studies of MNCs in each country tells us about the nature of these constraints in practice.

THE 'OPENNESS' OF NATIONAL IR SYSTEMS

This section considers the evidence from each of the four countries concerning the extent to which foreign MNCs have been restricted by the regulations and institutions of the country concerned. In considering the degree of 'openness' of each system to novel employment practices, it demonstrates that the institutions and regulations of each of the countries constrain the actions of MNCs, but it also shows that powerful (sometimes footloose) MNCs possess some scope to introduce novel practices into these distinctive contexts.

Ireland

The sheer scale of US MNCs in Ireland gives them the potential to exert great influence on the national system of employment relations. Their scope to do so is strongly shaped by the nature of collective relations in their Irish operations. Until relatively recently, MNCs in Ireland appeared to accept the country's pluralist traditions in that they were as likely to recognize trade unions as were Irish firms. Much of the early research revealed little difference between larger indigenous firms and MNCs in their IR practices (e.g. Enderwick 1986). These studies formed the basis for what was termed the 'convergence thesis', which saw the IR policies and approach of MNC subsidiaries as largely similar to host-country practice, characterized then by widespread trade union recognition among larger firms and extensive collective bargaining (Kelly and Brannick 1985). Undoubtedly this finding was related to the role played by Ireland's industrial promotion agencies. In the 1960s and 1970s, these agencies advocated union recognition among new inward-investing firms, specifically by arranging introductions to union officials and encouraging MNCs to conclude recognition agreements prior to start-up.

However, more recent evidence has indicated an increasing tendency for MNCs in Ireland to operate on a non-union basis. Union recognition has become an area of significant controversy, largely due to the fall in density and the concomitant rise in union avoidance strategies, particularly among MNCs (McGovern 1989; Gunnigle 1995; Roche and Geary 1995; Turner, D'Art, and Gunnigle 1997a, 1997b). While the decline in union density reflects a confluence of factors, there is a consensus that MNCs have played a significant role. For example, a study of 'greenfield' firms in the manufacturing and internationally traded services sectors found a high incidence of union avoidance—65 per cent of such firms were non-union—especially among US MNCs in the ICT sector (Gunnigle et al. 2002). A change away from a pro-union recognition stance among Ireland's industrial promotions agencies undoubtedly contributed to increased union avoidance among inward-investing firms. Since the 1980s these agencies have adopted a position that is less favourable to unions, indicating to inward-investing firms that they have the freedom to recognize or avoid trade unions (McGovern 1989; Gunnigle, Turner, and D'Art 1997a, 1997b).

MNCs have influenced the Irish IR system not just through their practices but also through lobbying and influencing public policy. For example, the debate on working time legislation, introduced in order that Ireland complied with the EU Working Time Directive, saw the AmCham play an important lobbying role on behalf of US subsidiaries in Ireland. AmCham claims to represent almost 500 US companies in Ireland, including major names such as Intel, Hewlett-Packard, and IBM. Its submission to the government committee dealing with the Organization of Working Time Bill argued that the proposed legislation would limit company flexibility and damage Ireland's efforts to win US investment: 'It is no exaggeration to say that the lack of flexibility in this Bill could represent the single most negative change in Ireland's flexibility to win US direct foreign investment that has happened in the past 20 years . . . ' (from AmCham submission, *Irish Times*, 22 February 1997).

Another difficulty highlighted by AmCham concerns what it saw as an in-built bias in the bill favouring firms which recognized trade unions. It argued that, under the bill, a collective agreement on working hours could only be negotiated by bodies recognized under the Trade Union Acts. However, since many of the MNCs represented by AmCham were non-union, such criteria were unlikely to be met. AmCham's lobbying in this regard has met with some success, prompting the head of IDA Ireland— Ireland's main industrial development agency—to support AmCham's position in stating that the proposed legislation would make it more difficult for that organization to attract international, particularly US, firms to Ireland.

The influence of the US MNC lobby has also played an important role in the ongoing debate on public policy concerning trade union recognition. Under the terms of the Partnership 2000 Accord, a 'High Level Group' was established to address the issue of union recognition, comprising representatives of government, union and employer peak organizations, and IDA Ireland. Their work resulted in the introduction of the Code of Practice on Voluntary Dispute Resolution and the Industrial Relations (Amendment) Act 2001. The influence of lobbying by foreign MNCs is widely seen as a factor in the report of the High Level Group, which rejected any mandatory system of union recognition, apparently on the grounds of its incongruity with Ireland's tradition of voluntary collective bargaining.

This picture of relatively weak employee representation at workplace level in MNCs coupled with the influence of MNCs on labour market regulation appears to afford considerable scope for the transfer of practices to their Irish operations. Accordingly, there is a broad consensus that MNCs, particularly those of US origin, have been an important source of innovation in management practices in Ireland. Illustrations of this include the according of a key role to specialist HR functions, which have tended to have more proactive and strategic roles than has been common in Irish firms (Murray 1984; Gunnigle 1998), and innovations in areas such as the diffusion of 'high performance' work systems (Mooney 1989) and performance related pay (Gunnigle et al. 1998).

Overall, the findings suggest that US MNCs in Ireland have managed to shape the context in which they operate in a way that affords them considerable scope to operate their desired employment approaches, allowing them to introduce a range of novel practices.

Britain

It is also reasonable to expect the British system of employment relations to be open to novel practices by MNCs. The programme of deregulation of the labour market pursued by successive Conservative governments in the 1980s and 1990s and the sharp reduction in union presence and influence in the last quarter of a century have meant that the prerogative of managers is considerably stronger than it was. The literature on Japanese MNCs in the UK demonstrates the scope for innovation that such firms have enjoyed in organizing production and managing workers. There is evidence of significant changes in the organization of work processes being introduced by Japanese firms and also by British emulators, although the nature and extent of innovations varied considerably (Elger and Smith 1994; Elger and Smith 2005).

Moreover, evidence on US-owned multinationals in Britain suggests that they have been able to impart a distinctly American flavour to their employment practices in the UK. One indicator of this was the hostility to multi-employer bargaining evident in the 1970s and 1980s. US MNCs have also been more likely to introduce productivity bargaining, try to narrow the scope of bargaining, and prefer formalized agreements and procedures (Buckley and Enderwick 1985; Innes and Morris 1995; Knox and Mckinlay 1999; Gennard and Steuer 1971). This assessment should be qualified, however, as the evidence also demonstrates the way in which US MNCs have had to adapt to the British system in some respects. This is particularly apparent in terms of union recognition; while many American MNCs are clearly antagonistic to unions, this is not universal. For instance, Guest and Hoque's (1996) evidence revealed that, compared with German and Japanese MNCs, union recognition was lower in US firms, but not significantly so. In a similar vein, Knox and Mckinlay (1999) show how unions in Scotland encountered 'a clear strategy of marginalizing shop-floor trade-unionism from 1945 to the mid-1960s' in many American MNCs, but were nevertheless successful in 'blunting the edge of aggressive American management techniques' (p. 25). Arguably, those US MNCs that set up in the UK in the 1950s and 1960s were more constrained grudgingly to accept unions as an aspect of the host country's IR system, while those that have entered in the last two decades have had more scope to maintain non-union status.

Previous studies of American MNCs in the UK also demonstrate that the US influence is less constrained in areas of employment relations other than collective relations. Thus US MNCs are regularly characterized as HR 'innovators' (e.g. Dunning 1998; Buckley and Enderwick 1985). This is particularly evident in areas, such as pay determination and payments systems—for example, in the use of productivity bargaining, perform-ance-related pay, job evaluation, and employee share ownership—and US MNCs were pioneers in the UK of company-based employment systems (e.g. Gennard and Steuer 1971). A key element of such systems is a clear preference for performance-based pay and associated formalized perform-ance appraisal systems (e.g. Innes and Morris 1995). The practice of single status, in which some aspects of the terms and conditions of blue- and white-collar workers are harmonized, is another element of HRM associ-ated with American MNCs. Gennard and Steuer (1971), for instance, cite IBM as one of the first companies to operate the practice in the UK.

A further HR technique which American MNCs have commonly deployed in their British subsidiaries is direct employee involvement. Thus Innes and Morris (1995) found that US MNCs more commonly used quality circles and team briefings than did MNCs of other nationalities, and Beaumont and Townley (1985) found a high incidence of autonomous work groups and quality circles. Even in the 1950s, US MNCs in Britain were innovative in their use of 'social' policies such as the provision of social amenities and non-contributory pension schemes (Dunning 1998). More recently, they have been in the forefront of the introduction of HR initiatives such as employee 'diversity' policies, performance and development appraisals, and the sounding out of workforce opinion through regular attitude surveys (e.g. Guest and Hoque 1996).

In sum, the influence of American MNCs on the British system of employment relations is readily apparent. Their significant presence in sectors such as IT, business services, pharmaceuticals, and investment banking, has given them the means collectively to establish new norms within the labour market in the UK. The changing nature of the regulations and key institutions in Britain have meant that the scope that they have to introduce novel practices, which was always significant, is greater now than in previous periods.

Spain

Despite the deregulation of the Spanish labour market in the 1990s, it is still characterized by a complex web of legal regulations that ostensibly constrain the ability of MNCs to introduce new practices. One instance of how a multinational in Spain has had to adapt its preferred practices in order for them to be accepted is GM's move to introduce teamworking in its Spanish subsidiary. Managers were faced with overcoming the potential resistance of its trade unions and the workers' committee. Following protracted negotiations, involving a number of management concessions, agreement was reached at the works committee in November 1993. However, at the end of the pilot scheme in November 1994, a majority of workers voted in a workforce ballot to discontinue teamworking, despite a campaign for ratification from all the unions. This outcome reflected workers' concerns about loss of status and mistrust of management's motives. While it is likely that many workers in GM's plants in other countries shared such concerns, the Spanish system of workers' committees and the legal provisions for workforce ballots on major changes to working practices provided a channel through which management's plans could be blocked (Ortiz 1998).

However, the evidence concerning foreign MNCs in Spain more generally also demonstrates that there is a degree of openness to new practices and that these can establish new norms in the host (Dickmann 1999; Ferner et al. 2001; Muller-Camen et al. 2001). Despite the framework of labour market institutions, management styles and traditions in Spain have not gelled into a highly defined business model. On the one hand, Spanish business has been characterized by a large number of small-to-medium domestic firms in which traits, such as conservatism, a lack of professionalization, centralized decision-making, and paternalism under family ownership, predominate (Costa 1996). On the other hand, the driving force of economic development since the 1960s has been foreign capital. One result is that while a Spanish 'national' managerial style may be evident in the small firm sector, the influence of foreign styles of management has been predominant in larger firms and more modern sectors. Consequently, innovations in HRM and IR—in areas such as work organization, payments systems, and management training—have largely originated in this latter category. In parallel, business education is dominated by US-style business schools and their MBA programmes. Many managers in Spanish subsidiaries of US MNCs have had an American-style business education, either in Spanish business schools or in the USA itself (Quintanilla 2001). They also commonly have had active business experience in the USA or have worked in a range of other MNCs in Spain.

Martínez Lucio reviews a range of sources of evidence about the Spanish system and notes that one of the key aspects of collective bargaining in Spain is that the 'bargaining effectiveness of union organization varies widely between provinces and regions' (1998: 445). Indeed, while the sector is the main formal level of bargaining, more than twice as many employees are covered by 'provincial-sectoral' agreements than are covered by 'national-sectoral' agreements. Even among those collective agreements that are national in coverage, the constraints imposed by national bargaining on individual workplaces are often limited (Aguilera 2004; Edwards et al. 2006). The extent to which plants are affected by forms of employee representation, therefore, depends primarily on the ability of unions to exert influence at the level of the workplace. In many small workplaces, particularly those in rural areas, the representative arrangements that are necessary to provide meaningful bargaining at local level have become, in Martínez Lucio's terms (1998: 445), 'inoperative'. In larger workplaces in urban areas, a category in which the majority of those controlled by MNCs fall, the constraints posed by employee representation are more significant.

In summary, the Spanish system of employment relations is highly regulated in many ways but the constraints it imposes on MNCs are variable. In those firms and workplaces where institutions and regulations are influential, such as at GM, there are significant constraints on MNCs, but the partial coverage and variable institutional strength of collective bargaining and workers' committees means that managers in MNCs commonly have considerable freedom. Moreover, the American-style business education that many managers receive, and managers' mobility between multinational subsidiaries of different nationality, have facilitated the spread of American HR techniques. Thus, while Spain is less 'open' to novel employment practices than the UK and Ireland, there is some scope for US MNCs to transfer their desired practices.

Germany

In Germany also the evidence suggests that American management principles, particularly HRM practices, are of great importance because of the high profile of many large American MNCs. Although the American and the German business systems have sometimes been seen as being at opposite ends of the spectrum of modern capitalist systems (e.g. Hall and Soskice 2001b), the influence of US politics on Germany in the twentieth century was strong. This political dominance has eased the way for American companies doing business in Germany (Djelic 1998; Smith and Meiksins 1995), and they face a more hospitable environment than an examination and comparison of the institutional frameworks of the two countries might suggest. The country's political and ideological collapse, which occurred twice during the twentieth century, opened the way for the USA to become the decisive political and economic player within Germany. The demise of the *Kaiserreich* in 1918 and the collapse of the Nazi regime in 1945 also prompted a particular readiness in Germany to change and learn. The Marshall Plan illustrates the importance of the USA for the development of post-war West Germany (for a general discussion see Hogan 1987; Clark 2000), providing a conduit through which the influence of the USA was felt (Herbst 1989: 48).

One instance of this American influence was the role of American trade unions, especially the AFL, in influencing the orientation of their German counterparts. American unions were anxious to persuade German unions to prioritize the goal of maximizing the economic interests of their members, rather than pursuing wider political priorities (see Fichter 1982). Another example concerns how the American government tried to influence, if not obstruct, German legislation on the extension of co-determination in large companies (MitbestG 1976). The inclusion of worker representatives and labour union officials on the supervisory board (*Aufsichtsrat*) of large enterprises (more than 2,000 employees) was claimed to be an illegal restriction of property rights and a breach of the German–American Treaty of Friendship, Commerce, and Navigation of 1954 (DeVos 1981: 175). The American initiative encouraged a number of large German firms to challenge the constitutionality of co-determination legislation. However, these moves had little tangible success. Indeed, unlike the early post-war years, the political climate of the 1970s precluded heavy American intervention and American political influence has, of course, decreased with Germany's increasing economic strength and with European integration.

While the direct political influence of the USA has declined, German unions are evidently concerned by the employment practices of American MNCs. An analysis of trade union journals (*Metall; Der Gewerkschafter*) in the metalworking industry provides some interesting insights. Analysis of four periods (1949–52; 1970–3; 1986–9; 1998–2001) identified a total of eighty-six articles on American companies. GM, Ford, and IBM attract the most attention. In terms of HR and IR practices, these companies are often characterized as 'innovators', with the nature of the innovations ranging from groundbreaking models of managing HR to an open rejection of IR institutions. The most well-known case of the latter is McDonald's (Royle 1998). Royle identified a range of 'avoidance strategies' used by the company, such as discriminating against union members or sympathizers in recruiting workers.

The significance of US MNCs as chief HRM innovators in Germany is also demonstrated by the fact that they are frequently quoted as examples of good HRM practice by German HR practitioners. These MNCs are also prepared, to a greater degree than German employers, to challenge the institutional environment. For instance, many MNCs have left employers' associations and set up company-level bargaining (Muller 1998). Analysis of articles from the personnel practitioner journal *Personalführung*[1] reveals that, in approximately 100 articles focusing on foreign firms, over half the firms covered were American. This far exceeds their share of FDI stock or employment and also dwarfs the attention given to French, Swiss, Dutch, British, and Japanese companies. A few high-profile American firms received a lot of attention; thirteen contributions, more than a quarter of the total number of articles concerning US-owned firms, are about IBM. According to a 1990 survey of 182 senior German HRM managers, in answer to the question 'Which company has implemented the best HRM strategy?', 29 per cent of the respondents suggested IBM and 26 per cent Hewlett-Packard. In comparison, the best-ranking German company, Daimler-Benz, was only cited by 17 per cent (Heidrick and Struggles 1991: 10).

The evidence concerning the employment practice of American MNCs in Germany testifies to there being scope to introduce practices that depart from norms in the host system. For example, many foreign, particularly American, MNCs opt out of sector-level collective bargaining and the vocational training system (Muller 1998). Wever considers the issue of implementing American-style employment practices in Germany and argues that 'there is considerable room for the development of organizational styles that may be inconsistent with local norms and traditions' (1995: 622). More generally, forms of 'variable' pay, such as performance-related pay, profit-related pay, and employee share ownership, have grown in MNCs in Germany. On the basis of these findings, it is reasonable to presume that the growth of FDI in Germany in recent years has contributed to the 'erosion' of the German system of IR (Hassel 1999). This picture needs to be qualified, however; while the constraints imposed on firms by the German system are not always binding, they are nevertheless notable, something that shows up in Schmitt and Sadowski's (2003) survey-based analysis of MNCs in Germany, which pointed to a strong degree of adaptation on the part of foreign MNCs.

CONCLUSION

The four host countries in this study possess a number of important similarities and differences. One key aspect of all four is that they are major recipients of American FDI, meaning that US MNCs have the potential to exert considerable influence over each of the national systems of employment relations. The actions of companies in introducing American norms into host systems is facilitated by other sources of influence from the US business system, such as political pressure, emergent institutions such as employers' associations, and business education.

However, these national systems are quite different from one another in the ways in which labour markets are regulated. One difference is that the British and Irish systems have a voluntarist tradition while Spain and Germany are characterized by greater regulation. Within these two broad categories there are further important differences. For instance, the Irish system has witnessed a modest renewal of tripartite structures in recent years, while employer cooperation for the purposes of bargaining has continued to wane in the UK. Similarly, while both Germany and Spain have a greater degree of active state regulation, the nature of regulation in Spain is less encompassing and more permissive than in Germany.

Variations in the character of labour market institutions mean that the 'openness' of each of the host systems to the introduction of novel employment practices by US MNCs also varies. We have seen that this openness is a feature of all four countries to some extent. Institutional constraints are not as binding as they may appear, and their strength in practice differs between sectors and regions. Moreover, MNCs may be able to find ways around these constraints, either wholly or partially. Nonetheless, the constraints are real ones and vary in their significance across the four countries.

In sum, the four countries are all major hosts for inward investment yet exhibit marked differences in the constraints presented to foreign investors. The varying degree of openness evident across the countries provides a strong rationale for choosing them as suitable national contexts in which to examine US MNCs.

Note

1. This influential practitioner journal is published monthly by the *Deutsche Gesellschaft für Personalführung* (DGFP), which is the most influential German association of HRM professionals and is highly visible and influential on practice. In order to measure the impact of American MNCs on HRM practice in Germany, we analysed the contents of *Personalführung* from 1990 to 2000 and recorded all articles, which described HRM or IR practices of a specific organization; 505 articles fitted these requirements, almost all of which were written by HR managers of the organizations and only a few published in co-authorship with consultants or academics. The selection criteria of the journal are not specified but are obviously a mixture of editorial selection (each edition normally focuses on one topic, e.g. international HRM or working hours, but there are contributions on other aspects as well) and self-selection.

5

The Case Study Companies in Their Organizational Context

Peter Butler, David Collings, René Peters, and Javier Quintanilla

This chapter provides a brief overview of the case-study companies that form the empirical basis of the research. The sketches below are grouped into three categories. The first comprises 'core' case-study companies where it was possible to carry out in-depth research in two or more international subsidiaries. (It also includes one instance, EngCo1, where research was restricted to the UK subsidiary, but where it was nevertheless possible to secure a concise 'view from above', through interviews conducted at the US HQ.) In these companies, interviews were also carried out at the corporate HQ in the USA and/or at international business unit HQ or European regional level. These six core firms cover a diverse range of sectors, including mechanical engineering, logistics, and business services. In a further group of firms, research was generally less in-depth and interviews were conducted in only one or two national subsidiaries; relatively little information was obtained from higher organizational levels. While the empirical coverage of these studies is partial, they nevertheless contribute significantly to the overall analytical purchase of the study. These 'secondary' case-study companies are predominantly in manufacturing: chemicals and pharmaceuticals, computing equipment, health care, consumer products, and beverages, but also include a smaller number of service sector firms. A final group comprises 'minor' case studies in which only a very small number of interviews was conducted, usually in only one country. Data from these minor cases are used to supplement the main sources. Further details on data collection can be found in the Appendix.

CORE CASE-STUDY COMPANIES

ITco *(Germany, Spain, Ireland, UK)*

Deriving originally from an amalgamation of three businesses in the early years of the twentieth century, ITco is a world leader in the field of IT manufacture and services. The reach of the organization now extends to scores of countries. More than half the global workforce is located outside the USA and the bulk of annual revenues is derived from overseas operations. The European presence may be traced back to the founding of the German subsidiary in the early twentieth century.

The company formerly enjoyed a high degree of market dominance in its product market. However, this position was severely eroded in the 1980s and 1990s, triggering a financial crisis and a worldwide reduction in staff. During this period both the UK and German subsidiaries experienced significant cuts in their workforce. Recent expansion into service provision, however, has seen global staffing levels rise to a new high. A major source of growth has been a move into the provision of 'outsourced' IT services for major companies.

Across the subsidiaries the balance of employment has reflected such change, with a reduced manufacturing labour force set against a rapid increase in employees in the business units providing services. The turnaround in corporate fortunes has had a particularly pronounced impact on the Irish subsidiary which currently employs over 4,000 people, making it one of the country's largest private sector employers. The establishment of a subdivision responsible for the worldwide management of ITco's 'chip' business has accounted for most of the recent growth.

Structurally, the company is a matrix of geographical regions and business divisions. The organizational importance of country operations has decreased sharply. Business unit autonomy has been subject to oscillation, with recentralization driven by the financial problems of the 1990s, followed by a certain amount of negotiated autonomy more recently where prudent profit and revenue management has been demonstrated. At the regional level, a strong presence of American expatriate managers helps to consolidate central coordination.

Centralization has been particularly evident in the HR arena, manifest in greater coordination by the European regional headquarters of both specialized functions (such as recruitment) and administrative aspects of HR (e.g. routine advice through a call centre). Likewise, a European HR model has been developed. This seeks to reduce duplication, replacing

Table 5.1. Main case-study companies

	Sector	Employment				
		Global	German	Irish	Spanish	UK
Core companies						
Business Services	Business consultancy and technical services	75,000	4,000	*	6,800	7,000
CPGco	Manufacturing consumer and medical products	75,000	2,000	*	670	3,000
Engco1	Manufacturing: capital engineering equipment	69,000	*	*	*	11,000
Engco2	Manufacturing capital engineering equipment	28,000	100	*	*	5,000
EngServs	Process plant construction services	11,000	*	*	100	2,000
ITco	Manufacturing and servicing of IT equipment	365,000	26,000	4,000	8,800	20,000
Logistico	Logistics services	360,000	14,000	400	*	4,000
Secondary companies						
Bankco	Banking and other financial services	130,000	3,000	*	*	9,000
Chemco	Manufacturing: industrial, consumer, and health care products	72,000	*	*	1,000	4,000
Compuco	Manufacturing of IT equipment	35,000	*	4,000	*	*
Drugco	Manufacturing: pharmaceutical products	43,700	*	*	1,200	2,500
Groomco	Manufacturing of consumer products	29,000	*	*	260	*
HealthCo	Manufacturing: pharmaceutical products	7,100	*	1,800	*	*
Household	Manufacturing: consumer household products	10,000	100	*	*	700
Pharmaco	Manufacturing: pharmaceutical products	120,000	*	1,400	*	4,000
Refresco	Manufacturing and distribution of soft drinks	34,000	*	*	5,000	120

Note: data supplied by the case-study companies.

local HR processes with European operations, while striving to be flexible enough to suit the needs of the different business units. This is supported by three European HR centres located in the UK and eastern Europe—an HR services call centre, a European function for recruitment, and a centre responsible for the management of international assignees. Over the last decade or so, a burgeoning range of global and regional policies have emerged in areas such as pensions and compensation.

The company is staunchly non-union both in its domestic operations and, where local legislation permits, overseas. In Ireland and the UK there is no history of union recognition. In Spain, too, there is little active union presence. In Germany, the company has operated under sectoral collective agreements, but has—as detailed in Chapter 6—sought to find flexibility by moving between sectoral bargaining arrangements.

CPGco (Germany, Spain, UK)

The origins of CPGco and of its initial foray into the European market may be traced back to the late nineteenth century. By the end of the nineteenth century CPGco had already built a manufacturing plant in England, and in the same year a branch office was opened in France. Subsidiaries were opened in Germany and Spain shortly after. The current business focus is on the development, manufacture, and sales of traditional and digital imaging products and services for both consumer and professional markets. Technologically, the business is moving into a more challenging era as a result of the impact of digital technology on its products and services.

Non-US business accounts for around 50 per cent of global revenues. Sales, which peaked in the mid-1990s, have been severely affected by the worldwide economic slump, the aftermath of 9/11, and the shift to digital imaging. This has been reflected in a significant drop in worldwide employment, which currently stands at 75,000. Some 44 per cent of these are based outside the USA. Further large-scale job cuts worldwide are envisaged.

CPGco has major manufacturing sites in the USA, Canada, Mexico, Brazil, Australia, France, and England. Most strategic jobs are located in the USA, although there are major R&D facilities in the USA, the UK, France, China, Japan, and Australia. The company is structured around a matrix of customer-facing product groups and geographical units. The recent trend has been towards increased centralization within international product groups and over the years the autonomy of these business units has increased significantly. This has meant far-reaching changes for local subsidiaries: managers who formerly reported locally now have superiors on a regional level. In addition to the regional and business units dimension, CPGco has several global functions such as finance, HR, marketing, and manufacturing. The US HQ sets directions for those functions and recommends ways of organizing them within countries. However, the heads of the European business units do have some scope to centralize or decentralize certain tasks subject to local needs.

HR policy is driven from the centre, but with regional operationalization of broad principles. European input into policy formation is very much dependent upon the policy under review. Traditionally, CPGco has provided generous benefits to its employees as part of a sophisticated HR approach. CPGco in the USA has always remained union-free and has in many ways behaved as an archetypal welfare capitalist company. Nevertheless, across its three main production sites CPGco UK recognizes three trade unions with local managers reporting a good working relationship. Similarly, CPGco Germany concludes collective agreements with the chemical union IG BCE. In Spain, there is likewise trade union coverage of shop-floor workers.

Logistico *(Germany, Ireland, UK)*

Logistico offers a range of delivery and transport services. Its origins may be traced back to the turn of the nineteenth century. Until relatively recently the company was exclusively a US operator. However, the organization currently serves more than 200 countries with several hundred thousand employees, generating global turnover of tens of billions of dollars. The business has seen rapid growth in recent years, largely through strategic acquisitions of existing companies. Particularly marked has been the expansion of capabilities in Asia. Nevertheless, with 80 per cent of revenues still generated in the USA, it cannot be characterized as highly internationalized. Unusually for a firm of its size, less than 10 per cent of Logistico is owned by institutional investors. A high proportion of shares is held by employees, particularly managers.

Results are reported in three segments: US domestic operations (the principal market segment), international operations, and business outside the core activity (for example, supply chain solutions). The company is marked by a global divisional structure divided into regions. The role of the European HQ in Belgium varies depending on function. There is relatively close coordination in functions such as marketing and technical areas. However, for other functions, including HR, there is far less regional input, as direct corporate influence is very visible, with strict implementation of American standards in areas such as internal promotion, compensation, and working methods.

The first European subsidiary was established in Germany in the mid-1970s, and Germany remains by far the most important market in Europe. There are approximately seventy German package centres and central sorting locations. The UK subsidiary, formed at the beginning of the 1990s, currently employs 4,000, mainly blue-collar workers, predominantly drivers and handlers, based at 23 operating facilities. The main location in Ireland is a call and customer service centre providing a wide range of services to European customers.

Logistico is unusual for a US service-based company in its high union coverage. Reflecting the US position, where a large proportion of Logistico employees are represented by the Teamsters, collective representation exists for operational employees, namely drivers and package handlers, in both Germany (ÖTV) and the UK (T&G). While in Ireland the sites have until recently been non-union, the Communication Workers Union (CWU) is gradually increasing its influence, particularly within a small packaging operation.

Business Services *(Germany, Spain, UK)*

The youngest of our study organizations, Business Services was established as a separate business unit of an accounting firm in the 1980s. The firm obtained a public listing only recently, as a result it has a relatively low-institutional shareholding. Currently, only about 10 per cent of the company's shares are traded. The organization operates globally with one common brand providing consulting and technology outsourcing services to both private and public sector organizations. The nature of the work gives rise to geographically mobile and functionally flexible professional employees. In 2001, around half of net revenues were generated outside the USA. Global employment currently stands at 75,000.

Structurally, there are five global market units overlaid with a regional tier made up of management representatives from the subunits, that is, countries or groups of countries. While geography is becoming increasingly important, the market unit remains the most dominant element of the matrix. There is additionally a European tier superimposed across the majority of the market units. Because of the size and maturity of the company's UK operations, which traced can back to the 1980s, London is the de facto European HQ. The bedrock here is the provision of services to financial institutions. The workforce broadly falls into two streams: consulting staff (4,000) and outsourced services (3,000), in other words, IT or accounting functions transferred from the client organization and run typically by employees transferred from the client.

The HR function has an important status within Business Services, reflected in the high ratio of HR to consulting staff. HR policy is formulated at a global level and is uniform across market units. Corporate policies serve as frameworks with unified terminology and logics, which are adapted nationally according to local market conditions and laws. The global–local balance varies between different substantive areas. For example, HR workflow management is centrally driven by global processes and systems, whereas recruiting is much more local. Given the nature of the workforce—predominantly professionals, with a high degree of career mobility—there is little demand for collective representation, either through unions or works councils. Even in the German subsidiary, the role of the works council is limited to support staff.

Engco1 (UK)

Founded in the 1920s, Engco1 designs and manufactures a range of engineering-based capital equipment. There is a marked degree of internationalization, with a manufacturing presence in twenty countries: almost half of sales are generated outside the USA and 50 per cent of employees are non-US based. Worldwide, the number of employees currently stands at below 70,000—a significant reduction on the six-figure peak of the late 1970s. This fall was triggered by increased international competition, significantly from Japan. There has nevertheless been some expansion through acquisition, notably in the UK where operations commenced in the 1950s. Current UK employment is approximately 2,000, mostly at a Midlands facility. There are a further 9,000 based in recently acquired engineering subsidiaries. Given the nature of the product, technological development is more incremental than cutting-edge, with reliance on steady and thorough improvement.

There are six global business groups, each composed of various product divisions. These, along with their constituent business units, have operational autonomy within a corporate framework set by a centralized review and budgetary process. Strategic planning also remains centralized. With regard to HR, some policy is centrally driven (for example, pay and performance systems), but there remains local flexibility on implementation. Greater leeway is provided within broad framework policies in some fields (such as issues relating to cultural values and teamwork). Recently, there have been moves internationally to centralize HR, particularly routine HR administration, through the concept of shared services.

While the US parent is headquartered in the heavily unionized midwest, the recent trend has been to relocate to states where the union tradition is weak. In consequence US rates of unionization halved during the 1990s. Likewise, managerial and salaried staff in the UK subsidiary have been deunionized and representation is now provided by a joint consultative committee. Around three-quarters of hourly paid employees in the UK, however, are still covered by collective agreements.

Engco2 (Germany, UK)

Employing a total of 28,000 workers, Engco2's core business is the manufacturing of engineering equipment for vehicles and industrial use. Forty per cent of total employment is now located outside the home territory, with 6,000 employees in the 'Central Region' (Europe, Middle East, and Africa), 5,000 of them in the UK. Most of the region's other employees are located at plants in France and Turkey. The remainder are spread across small sales and parts distribution centres in different European countries. Nearly half of total revenues are currently generated outside the USA.

The company has a matrix structure of business units, geographical territories, and support functions. The most important elements of the matrix are the four business units: automotive, industrial, power generation, and filtration. The geographical business organizations supplement the business units through the discussion of territory-specific issues and the customization of corporate policies and processes where necessary.

Traditionally, formal HR policies only rarely covered overseas units. Policies were broad and characteristically non-formalized, allowing overseas subsidiaries latitude in their interpretation. The recent trend, however, has been towards global standardization in a range of areas such as performance management, appraisal, employee development, and diversity. This change was the result of cost-cutting, triggered by difficult market conditions, combined with the desire to generate more coherent global policies as the company became more internationalized.

Engco2 has been strongly influenced by its early family ownership, in particular by the role of the founding father of the company. This actor strongly shaped the principles and philosophies of the organization, instilling it with 'mid-western' and 'small town values'. This extends to the company's attitude to trade unions, seen by the founder as a legitimate check on management. In the USA, unions are recognized, although they are not affiliated to broader federations. The company has latterly evolved into a patchwork of union and non-union operations in the USA. The policy is to work constructively with unions where they are present, and to maintain a collective dimension through employee councils where they are absent—a pattern replicated globally. In the UK there is a long history of trade union representation. However, in Germany, where the corporate presence is limited to a small sales operation, there is no union presence, nor is the subsidiary a member of the employers' association or bound by collective agreements.

EngServs (Spain, UK)

This firm was founded at the turn of the twentieth century. A UK subsidiary was established as early as the 1920s. EngServs is a specialist engineering services company involved in the design and construction of large-scale civil engineering projects across a range of industries. The workforce comprises skilled professionals, who are often graduate engineers.

Globally the company employs over 10,000, nearly half based outside the USA. The bulk of annual revenues are generated overseas. Economic problems in Japan and financial crisis in other export-orientated Asian economies undermined demand in the late 1990s, triggering a reduction in worldwide employment.

The company is structured around two major business streams: the production of heavy equipment for the energy industry and process plant contracting. The latter is the dominant part of the corporation, contributing approximately three-quarters of turnover. Significantly, the UK subsidiary specializes in the process plant business, employing nearly two-thirds of the organization's non-US workforce. The strategic position of the UK subsidiary within the firm has enabled it to lever strong operational independence from the centre in terms of work organization, finance, and human resources. Until recently, relatively few corporate controls were in place. Indeed EngServs UK represents the most decentralized subsidiary amongst our study firms. (The regional level is unimportant as it does not cover the process plant contracting division.) Thus, in terms of HR policy, there is a marked degree of decentralization and subsidiary autonomy. Importantly, in contrast to the USA and most other European operations, EngServs UK is a non-union company. Representation on matters of health and safety and terms and conditions is provided by a consultative forum. EngServs Spain employs 750 workers on two sites, one of which is fully unionized.

SECONDARY CASES

Household *(Germany, UK)*

Founded in the 1880s, Household is primarily a manufacturer of consumer household products with some output additionally aimed at the professional market. Unique amongst our study organizations, the company remains in the (fifth generation) hands of the founding family. Private ownership is reflected in the strong and explicit culture, allied to a long-term approach to business strategy. Currently, the company has a workforce of 10,000 people, spread across dozens of countries worldwide. International business represents an estimated 60 per cent of total sales. There has been considerable growth through acquisition.

While structurally the firm is split into five geographic regions, there has been a recent move to business divisions (consumer and professional), which now dominate the business–region matrix. Country-level autonomy has been diminished as a result of the growing importance of the European region and an increasing emphasis on becoming more global. This is reflected in HR policy: pay and benefits, management development, and succession planning are all globally driven.

The UK, where European HQ is located, is the largest and most mature of the European operations. The workforce of around 700 are mostly employed at one manufacturing plant and are non-unionized—a reflection of the centralized 'welfare capitalist' ethos. The single German site (sales and administration), employing around 100 employees, is similarly non-union.

Bankco *(Germany, UK)*

Founded in New York at the turn of the twentieth century, Bankco is one of the world's leading consumer banks. It was the first bank to create a unified global image, from the design of credit cards to the layout of its branches. Today it employs over 250,000 staff world wide, nearly half outside the USA. The corporation has grown rapidly in recent years both organically and through mergers and acquisitions. The current structure was born of an amalgam of two financial services organizations in the 1990s. Structurally, Bankco is a matrix. The banking and financial services business segments are subdivided into product lines and overlain by four regional structures. Of these, North America is dominant by far, providing approximately 60 per cent of revenues with Europe following at 13 per cent. Current employment within the European region stands at approximately 16,000. The majority (9,000) are based in the UK where the bank has maintained a presence since the early part of the last century. German operations date back to the 1970s.

In terms of HR there is a tiering of policy. Executive compensation, management of high potentials, and stock option policies are formulated at a global level. Other aspects of policy, such as promotion criteria, are more decentralized. Reflecting the divergent requirements of the divisions, there are no written HR policies in such areas. In IR, industry-level collective agreements cover the majority of Bankco's German workers. Works councils have been active in negotiating the introduction of performance-related pay. In the UK, there are no collective agreements. The European Works Council, convening once a year, is the sole joint vehicle for the discussion of corporate strategy and pay.

Drugco *(Spain, UK)*

Established in the late nineteenth century, Drugco develops, manufactures, and sells a range of pharmaceutical products. Globally it is organized into three geographic operating regions dominated by the USA and Europe. Drugco is highly internationalized and has grown significantly recently through acquisition. Over 40 per cent of annual revenues are generated outside the USA, and over 50 per cent of the global workforce of 43,000 are employed in overseas subsidiaries. There are major R&D facilities in nine countries, and clinical trials are conducted in over thirty. The company's presence within the pre-dates the Second World War. The 2,500 workers, split between four locations, are involved in manufacturing, sales and marketing, and research. The Spanish subsidiary, established in the 1950s, houses one of the most modern industrial complexes in the country and is considered a key piece of corporate structure.

Prescriptive global HR policy is generally absent and countries are free to develop their own frameworks. However, some aspects, such as performance management, are centrally formulated. While there is no union recognition in the USA, there is collective representation at the main (acquired) UK manufacturing site. However, at the time of research, collective bargaining was being replaced with an individual merit-based pay system. In the Spanish operations, while unions exist formally, their influence is limited.

Chemco *(Spain, UK)*

Founded at the end of the nineteenth century, Chemco is involved in the manufacture of industrial, consumer, and health care products. Current worldwide employment stands at around 72,000; of these nearly half are employed outside the USA. In 2001, some 54 per cent of sales were made outside the USA. In recent years, in response to economic conditions, the company has eliminated several thousand jobs, including several hundred in the UK.

Structurally, Chemco has six customer facing and one global manufacturing division. There has been a UK subsidiary since the early 1950s, where currently some 4,000 employees are based at four manufacturing locations. The Spanish subsidiary, likewise founded in the 1950s, employs 1,000 workers.

The organization has generally followed fairly paternalistic personnel policies, although a 'harder', more centrally driven, form of HR has been introduced in recent years. Despite a stated corporate philosophy of 'championing individualism', there is nevertheless a history of union representation within the UK where two main unions are recognized: the T&GWU and Amicus. Single-table bargaining has been in place since the mid-1990s. In Spain, there is also extensive trade union coverage and a company-level collective agreement on wages has been in operation since 1979.

Refresco *(Spain, UK)*

Employing 34,000 people around the world, around two-thirds of them outside the USA, Refresco is one of the world's leading manufacturers and distributors of non-alcoholic beverages. Its operating management structure consists of four geographic groups. These have assumed increased significance as markets have matured, and there has been a marked shift from a highly centralized to a highly decentralized managerial style. Within regional units, operations are essentially territorial bottling and distribution franchises. The parent retains responsibility for consumer demand, performing a predominantly marketing and branding function. The Iberian division (Spain and Portugal) is one of the most important in the international system and accounts for a ninth of sales worldwide. Spanish employment, in seven bottling plants, currently stands at 5,000. The UK is a far less significant player: only around 120 people are directly employed by Refresco. In HR, decentralization has been reflected in a great deal of local freedom to design HR policy within European and global policy frameworks. While there is no union representation, a communications forum covers the EU. In Spain, collective representation is additionally afforded via the works council (*comité de empresa*) format.

Compuco (Ireland)

Established in 1984, Compuco manufactures and sells computer hardware products. Roughly half of the current workforce of 35,000 are based outside the USA; 11,000 in the European region. Approximately 70 per cent of total revenues are generated in the Americas, with the European region accounting for 20 per cent. The company is primarily structured by country, with each country reporting to a regional HQ. Corporate strategy is to grow through diversification rather than acquisition. At the time of the research Compuco Ireland remained the company's only European manufacturing site. This subsidiary has grown very rapidly since its opening in the early 1990s and employs one-third of the company's 9,000 European employees. The subsidiary's personnel function traditionally enjoyed significant autonomy. However, with a switch to global HR systems, HR planning and performance management is becoming more centralized and standardized. Mirroring the US situation, there is no history of unionization.

Healthco *(Ireland)*

Healthco was founded in the 1880s. It has evolved into a diversified health care company, with a third of revenues derived from outside the USA. Employing some 71,000 people in 135 countries, it is one of the top 10 health care companies in the world. Healthco acquired one of its major competitors in 2001. The influence of Healthco's founder is claimed to be palpable to the present day. The legacy is said to include: a culture of slow, steady acquisitions; an emphasis on R&D; and a willingness to ride out any storm in the business cycle. Healthco has had a sales and marketing presence in Ireland since the 1940s, and the first manufacturing facility was established in 1974. Currently, there are seven production facilities and a workforce of around 1,800. On HR matters, there is significant autonomy at subsidiary level. With regard to succession planning, for example, there is no higher-level monitoring of the credentials of senior managerial candidates. Similarly, while all of Healthco's US plants are staunchly non-union, the early manufacturing plants established in Ireland were heavily unionized at shop-floor level.

Pharmaco *(Ireland, UK)*

Pharmaco's core business is the development and manufacture of prescription medicines. Established in the USA in the middle of the nineteenth century, the organization has a presence in over 150 countries. There are three business segments: pharmaceutical, consumer health care, and animal health. In 2000, Pharmaco merged with another large pharmaceutical/health care organization, and in recent years has nearly tripled in size. Currently, 120,000 employees generate sales exceeding $45b, with some 40 per cent of revenues realized through overseas operations. An Irish manufacturing base was established in 1969 to provide access to the European market. Since then the size and importance of the Irish operations have grown, to become the most significant in Europe. Most of the 1,400 employees are involved in the manufacture of food chemicals and bulk pharmaceuticals. While there is very little tradition of unionization in the USA, five of the seven Irish plants are unionized.

Groomco *(Spain)*

Groomco, formed at the turn of the last century, is a market leader in consumer products in grooming, oral care, and alkaline batteries. The company has grown significantly over the last few decades, predominantly through the acquisition of related consumer brands. The company has manufacturing operations at thirty-one facilities in fourteen countries. Over 60 per cent of revenues are generated outside North America. The company has a global workforce of around 29,000, over 70 per cent outside the USA. It has five operating segments, each of which operates within five geographic regions. The company has taken an aggressive stance on cost reductions and business process improvements in recent years, with significant workforce reductions and plant closures. Groomco Spain comprises one site employing 260 workers. The personnel function's autonomy depends on the area. Central control over compensation and benefits policy is usually tight. In other areas, HR objectives and guidelines are interpreted with some flexibility through the European HQ. In line with the global template, there is no trade union presence.

MINOR CASES

Healthcare *(Spain, UK)*

Founded as a family concern in the 1880s, Healthcare manufactures a broad range of health care products. While the bulk of business is conducted within the USA, the European region is of increasing importance, accounting for over 20 per cent of revenues. There are currently some

Table 5.2. Minor cases

	Sector	Employment				
		Global	German	Irish	Spanish	UK
Bor-Tec	Machinery equipment	25,000	500	*	*	*
Bulkchem	Manufacturing of chemical products	90,000	12,000	*	*	*
Healthcare	Manufacturing: consumer, medical, and pharmaceutical products	108,000	*	*	1,000	500
Pharma-chem	Manufacturing: chemicals and pharmaceuticals	13,700	*	*	*	150
Silico	Manufacturing and servicing of IT equipment	80,000	5,000	*	*	*
Softco	Manufacturing and servicing of IT products (software)	55,000	*	*	2,400	*

Note: data supplied by the case-study companies.

112,000 employees world wide, half of them outside the USA. The company operates on a decentralized basis with dozens of global affiliates and nearly 200 autonomous operating units in 54 countries. There is significant flexibility on HR issues within a central framework of values. *Healthcare*'s workforce in the UK and in Spain is numbered in several hundreds. UK sites are unionized.

PharmaChem *(Spain, UK)*

Structured into two business streams: agrochemical and pharmaceuticals, PharmaChem has a workforce of nearly 14,000 employees worldwide. Itself the product of a merger, the company was recently absorbed into a larger entity as the result of further consolidation within the industry. In 2002, some 37 per cent of revenues were generated outside the USA. Within the UK, where workers are based at three main sites, employment was approximately 2,000. In HR, a trend to increased centralization was evident following mergers and acquisitions, giving to increasing corporate intervention on such issues as pay. The parental ethos was markedly 'pro-individual', with a broad preference for union avoidance. Nevertheless, a union was recognized at one manufacturing site in the UK, and there was some representation of professional employees.

Bor-Tec *(Germany)*

Bor-Tec, founded in 1900, is an engineering company providing equipment to the oil industry. The corporation has a presence in over 80 countries with some 60 per cent of the 26,000 employees based outside the USA. The European HQ is located in the UK, the largest and most mature European operation. Bor-Tec's presence in Germany dates back to the 1950s. German employment currently stands at around 500. The subsidiary is relatively autonomous, a position sustained owing to the technical competence and competitiveness of German operations. German HR managers were heavily involved in the setting up of the European Works Council, but there is no union presence.

Bulkchem *(Germany)*

Founded in the early nineteenth century, Bulkchem operates in over 70 countries. Its 81,000 employees are active in a range of markets including agriculture, nutrition, electronics, communications, and transportation. The company is structured around a matrix with European senior managers reporting to both the region and to business units (pharmaceuticals, materials, electronics, and communications). Since the late 1980s employee numbers have been radically reduced. Current employment in the German subsidiary is around 2,300. While in the past key positions were filled by US expatriates, the subsidiary and its HR function are fully self-sufficient and independent. Only major decisions have to be approved by the US or European HQ. The subsidiary is covered both by collective bargaining and various works council agreements.

Silico *(Germany)*

Founded in 1939, Silico is one of the world's largest companies, supplying information technology and imaging products to consumers and business customers. The company has a global workforce of 89,000. The first production site outside the USA was established in Germany in the late 1950s and this remains the most important location outside the USA, with 5,000 employees. Europe contributes an important proportion of global revenues. In the 1990s, in a period of global economic downturn, *Silico* was forced to lay off employees for the first time in ten years. The company is divided into three major business segments covering imaging and printing systems, computing, and IT services. While the business is predominantly managed through these units, the company has installed separate sales and marketing functions.

Subsidiary HR policy works in line with globally driven policies and principles, but there is latitude to accommodate local standards and legal requirements. In 1974, Silico Germany left the employers' federation, and is not covered by either sectoral or company agreements. Nevertheless, it adheres strongly to the spirit of the co-determination legislation, manifest in the high number of works agreements concluded with the works council.

Softco *(Spain)*

Softco was formed in the mid-1970s and is a now world leader in the development and licensing of PC operating systems, software products, and servers. The key to the company's growth has been innovation. The company is organized into seven business areas of which the dominant ones are operating systems and servers. It has a workforce of 55,000, of whom 24,000 work in R&D. 20,000 of the total workforce are employed outside the USA. None of the firm's employees is subject to collective bargaining. The Spanish subsidiary, which numbers some 2,500, was established in 1997.

Part III

The Findings: Employment Relations Policies and Practices

6

Collective Representation and Participation

Trevor Colling, Paddy Gunnigle, Javier Quintanilla, and Anne Tempel

INTRODUCTION

As Chapter 3 reflects, the approach of American companies towards workforce representation and participation is a critical issue. The intensity of employer opposition to unions found in America is unparalleled anywhere in the industrial world; unionization has largely been seen as 'unnatural, illegitimate, and un-American, and to be resisted' (Kochan, Katz, and McKersie 1986: 15). Many other aspects of employment policy flow from this orientation, or are influenced by it. Pay and benefits systems are often pitched as a defence against potential unionization, and adjustments to work organization are often made for similar reasons (Voos 1999: 512). This chapter focuses on the ramifications of this orientation at home for the policies and behaviour of the foreign subsidiaries of American companies.

European traditions of workplace regulation differ significantly from the American system. The UK and Ireland share several institutional features with the USA, though union membership and collective bargaining coverage are much higher. Mainland European traditions in Germany and Spain diverge much more strongly from the American model. Legal protections for employee representation and trade union activity are stronger, and collective bargaining coverage is more significant. Given the marked home-country orientations of American managers, and the fact that hostility to unions and social regulation has been a strongly observed feature of American-owned multinationals (Ferner et al. 2005; Gunnigle 1995; Muller 1998; Royle 2004), the adaptation of US multinationals to host environments with different traditions and institutional frameworks poses critical questions.

We begin by examining the animus towards collective employee representation present in the American business system, its sources, and current extent. Critical here are the relatively fragile legislative supports for union organization. We contrast this with the main features of employment regulation in our host countries. From this point, analysis of our case study findings focuses on the issues of collective bargaining and representation, exploring how US companies, many of which emanate from a non-union tradition, adapt to host systems with greater potential to delimit managerial freedoms.

COLLECTIVISM, INDIVIDUALISM, AND THE AMERICAN BUSINESS SYSTEM

The American system of IR is significantly different from most other developed economies (Jacoby 1985: 173). The key differences are manifest in a marked preference for non-collective employee representation. The high-water mark of American collectivism was reached in 1945, shortly after the 'New Deal' legislation of the 1930s legitimized union activity, when just over one-third (36 per cent) of the workforce were union members (French 1997: 93). Long-term falls have been sustained ever since. For every 100 private sector workers in America during 2003, only 8 were union members—a cut in membership of about 50 per cent over the previous 10 years (BLS 2004). Even in the relatively stable public sector, the average density level across occupations was only 37 per cent (ibid.). Moreover, levels of collective bargaining are relatively low; agreements tend to cover companies or business streams and very rarely extend across organizational boundaries to other employers. Consequently, collective bargaining sets the terms and conditions of employment directly for only 15 per cent of the American workforces—the lowest proportion of the leading industrialized economies (EIRO Online 2001a).

Some selected points of American social history help to explain this marginal role for social regulation. First, the American working class, and the union movement that developed to represent it, was deeply divided (Jacoby 1991; Kaufman 2001; Wheeler and McClendon 1998). High rates of labour mobility during the early years of industrialization weakened attempts to establish 'voice' mechanisms such as collective bargaining (Fairris 1997). Functionalist accounts of American IR tend to

jump straight from observation of these social traits to presume an enduring preference amongst American workers for acquisitive individualism.
This is to underplay a second key factor—the powerful influence of American capital and its vehement hostility towards unions (Jacoby 1991). From
the Pittsburgh shootings of 1877, to the Memorial Day massacre of 1937,
where 'uniformed policemen [fired] their revolvers point-blank into a
dense crowd of men, women, and children, then pursuing and clubbing
the survivors unmercifully as they made frantic efforts to escape' (Auerbach 1966: 122–3), it is estimated that 600 people died in strike-related
violence (Babson 1999). The nature of this violence was qualitatively
different from that in other Western capitalist democracies, as it centred
not around macropolitical demands, but rather around workplace issues.

The effectiveness of employer opposition to trade unions was further
facilitated by the political influence wielded by employers in the early
1900s (Jacoby 1991; Wheeler and McClendon 1993). As Vogel notes, 'for
most of the history of capitalism, the large business corporation in the
USA effectively enjoyed a monopoly of political and institutional power
without parallel in the capitalist world' (1978: 63). This takes us to a third
critical factor, the relative weakness of the American state. The early
independence and power enjoyed by employers in the USA has meant
that the relationship between business and government in the USA was
unlike that found in most other countries: American employers enjoyed
an unusually high degree of political power and the government was
dominated by business interests (Jacoby 1991). As Wheeler and McClendon (1998: 70) observe, 'the political strength of capital and its representatives has always been sufficient to preserve broad areas of managerial
discretion from government regulation'.

Following confirmation of the Wagner Act in 1937, the New Deal is
credited with establishing collective bargaining at the heart of US IR.
But, as argued in Chapter 3, US employers never relinquished their
fundamental preference for individualized employment relationships
(Blanchflower and Freeman 1992; Katz and Darbishire 2000), and the
New Deal model of IR was always fragile and weakly embedded.

Three key aspects of New Deal collective bargaining need to be emphasized (Towers 1997). First is the rights and procedures embodied in the
legislation itself. These include majority unionism; representation elections; determination of bargaining units by the NLRB; the duty to bargain;
protections against employer interference during union organizing campaigns; and bans on company unions, closed shops, and secondary boy-
cotts. Second is the range of countervailing rights upheld by the US

Supreme Court. These include rights to replace strikers; distinctions between mandatory and permissive bargaining items; duty of fair representation; written contracts; and implied arbitration and no-strike clauses. Finally is the web of 'workplace contractualism'—a web of jointly determined rules characterized by an emphasis on seniority; detailed job descriptions; narrow jobs; elaborate legalistic and multistage grievance procedures and employer-funded fringe benefits. Since collective agreements are legally enforceable in the USA, workplace contractualism is a common feature of case law wherever collective bargaining exists. In short, the system is profoundly adversarial in nature, founded on the separate and often contending rights of employers and employees. Procedure is also emphasized, tying both unions and employers to established systems of dispute resolution.

As explored in Chapter 3, a significant number of large American firms never tolerated union involvement, and have long implemented 'union substitution' approaches, involving the adoption of HRM policies designed to contain the demand for collective representation amongst employees (see Dundon 2002). Sophisticated HRM procedures—such as fewer job grades, task flexibility, team-working arrangements, and extensive communications and grievance handling systems—restrict the recruitment opportunities of trade unions (Beaumont and Townley 1985*a*; Foulkes 1980; Kochan, Katz, and McKersie 1986).

Conversely, there is a range of anti-union companies that rely on *union suppression* tactics, based on deterring expressed allegiance to unions, rather than *union substitution*. Tactics include dismissals and related sanctions and threats to close or relocate the firm. In her research on employer responses to union organizing drives, Bronfenbrenner (2000: 43–4) found that 67 per cent of employers held supervisor 'one-on-ones' with employees at least weekly; 25 per cent of employers discharged workers for union activity; and 10 per cent used electronic surveillance of union activists. The research focuses, however, on the threat of relocation in the event of a union certification victory. This is found to have occurred in more than half of cases overall, and well over two-thirds of cases in relatively 'mobile' sectors like electronics and apparel (p. v).

It is possible to overdraw distinctions between union substitution and suppression (Dundon 2002; Gall 2001). Jacoby (1997) acknowledges that when faced with particularly determined organizing drives, even large sophisticated companies can revert to unsophisticated union suppression. Katz and Darbishire (2000: 22) note that high-paying, non-union employers have diminished as a proportion of the total and 'sizeable declines have occurred in worker real earnings over the past twenty years, suggesting that the low-wage pattern has been growing'.

REGULATION OF INDUSTRIAL RELATIONS IN THE HOST COUNTRIES

On the face of it, the IR context facing American companies investing in Europe is very different from that in the USA. The average European employee is three times more likely than their American counterpart to be a trade union member and five times more likely to be covered by a collective agreement (EIRO 2001*a*). Though the level at which bargaining is conducted varies across the EU, sectoral level and even inter-sectoral level agreements are much more important than in the USA. This leads to the greater diffusion of collectively negotiated terms and conditions across industries, particularly where principles of *erga omnes* bring non-signatory firms within the enforceable scope of agreements.

This section highlights the main IR provisions affecting subsidiaries in the four countries featuring in this book. Following legal scholars like Barnard, Clark, and Lewis (1995: 5), we distinguish between the *Anglo-Irish* model and the *Roman–Germanic* model evident in countries including Spain and Germany. These labels capture fundamental similarities within the pairings in the extent to which business, and employment particularly, is subject to regulation beyond the firm. Assessments of the density of product market regulation in twenty-one economies, for example, place the UK and Ireland together, as 1st and 2nd, respectively; at the least regulated end of the spectrum, whilst Germany and Spain appear at 10th and 13th, respectively (Nicoletti, Scarpatta, and Boylaud 2000: 34). Extending that analysis to employment protection—measured in terms of regulations governing the freedom to 'hire and fire' workers—the two pairings rank closely once again: the UK and Ireland are the 2nd and 4th least-regulated labour markets, respectively, whilst Germany and Spain are 15th and 18th, respectively (p. 46).

Differences in the extent of regulation between the two pairings stem from differences in its character. Ireland and the UK shared historically a common law model of employment regulation in which voluntary self-regulation by actors in the employment relationship through collective bargaining was given primacy. In Spain and Germany, on the other hand, a civil law model predominated, in which the state played 'a central and active role in industrial relations' and 'constitutional provisions [guaranteed] a core of fundamental rights and freedoms' (Barnard, Clark, and Lewis 1995: 5). Enforcement and extension of these rights depended still on collective bargaining to a large degree but this was buttressed by stronger roles for the state via the court system, epitomized by the endowment of collective agreements with statutory effect (see Kahn-Freund 1965).

These socio-political contexts condition the institutions of IR. Subject to necessary caveats about the content of agreements (see later), bargaining coverage can be taken as one indication of the strength of regulation. On this measure, as illustrated in Table 6.1, Spain and Germany appear similarly and strongly regulated, and lower proportions of the UK and Irish workforces are covered by collective bargaining. As important, this is the case despite relatively low levels of union organization in Germany and Spain. Regulatory norms set by sector-level agreements in these countries are extended to non-signatory companies by inter-firm comparison—complying with the 'going rate' set through collective bargaining—reinforced by formal extension practices. In Spain, *erga omnes* extension is automatic in law and augmented by other regulatory mechanisms. Bargaining parties can apply to the Ministry of Labour, for example, to 'enlarge' sectoral agreements to industries where no bargaining structures exist (EIRO 2002). Automatic extension is also possible in Germany. Such mechanisms are much weaker in Ireland and are absent entirely in the UK (OECD 2004: 147).

It follows that, all other things being equal, the *Roman–Germanic* pairing of Germany and Spain provides the more substantial challenge to the American model. Employment rights are established and monitored by the state directly, and there are stronger supports for regulation through collective bargaining. Of course, this potentially masks nuances and important differences *within* the pairings, and these are explored in the next section.

Table 6.1. Selected industrial relations characteristics by country

Country	Union density	Bargaining coverage	Bargaining level	Bargaining coordination	Extension practice
Germany	30	79	Sect/Comp	Medium–Strong	Moderate
Spain	15	83	Sect/Comp	Medium–Weak	High
Ireland	45	66	Nat/Sect/Comp	Medium–Strong	Moderate
UK	29	39	Sect/Comp	Weak	None

Sources: Adapted from Rubery, Grimshaw, and Figueired (2005: 195); EIRO (2001*a*).

The Roman–Germanic Economies: Germany and Spain

The Spanish and German systems rest on the dual structure of collective representation: collective bargaining at either industry or company level and workers' representation through works councils at workplace level (Aguilera 2004). Formally, these represent two separate arenas with different actors and regulations. However, in reality, there is considerable mutual dependence and an elaborate division of responsibilities between them.

Collective bargaining in Germany is the responsibility of unions and employers' associations at industry level or of unions and single employers at company level. The legal enforceability of collective agreements in Germany gives these actors the status of law-creating institutions, able to socially generate legal norms. Industry-level bargaining has traditionally been the main pattern of collective bargaining, with company-level bargaining being limited primarily to smaller firms. Three different kinds of collective agreements cover a wide range of matters: wage agreements regulate the level of wages; framework agreements specify wage-payment systems; and umbrella agreements regulate all other conditions of employment, including, for example, working time.

These institutional mechanisms interlock with works councils at enterprise level, regulated by the comprehensive and detailed Works Constitution Act (1972). This has the potential to subject all workplaces with more than five employees to uniform regulation of employer–employee relations between works councils and management, through works agreements which are legally binding. Works councils are accorded a range of different representation rights ranging from information and consultation to codetermination rights. Their rights are strongest in the area of social policy, weaker in the case of personnel issues, and weakest in financial and economic matters (Wächter 1983). There are also regulations as to the setting up of company works councils where a company has several plants. Technically, these systems are independent of union organization, but unions often provide training, information, and legal advice to works councillors and the majority of works councillors have traditionally been trade unionists, often actively involved in policy-making and recruitment of union members (Jacobi, Keller, and Muller-Jentsch 1998).

The Spanish system looks very similar, though there are some important differences beneath the surface. Bargaining coverage is extensive and derives from relatively centralized IR structures. Historically, bargaining took place at several levels but the regional-sectoral level has come to predominate. In 1996, 88 per cent of collective agreements were concluded at levels above the workplace, mainly at provincial-sectoral level (Hamann and Martínez Lucio 2003: 66). Both government and unions are committed publicly to further coordinated collective bargaining, as a consequence of the need to manage incomes growth in the context of the single European currency. From 1997, government began to review the operation of workplace regulation and reinforced, 'the power and autonomy of the sectoral federations in collective bargaining' (Romo 2005: 18). The total number of collective agreements has grown since, and provincial-sectoral agreements have multiplied at a faster rate than company-level ones (EIRO 2004).

The legal framework in Spain also specifies a *dual* system, with worker representation at plant level channelled through the *comité de empresa*. As in Germany, unions are closely involved in workplace representation: 'typically 80 per cent of workers participating in works committee elections vote for union candidates' (Rigby and Aledo 2001: 296). But works councils operate differently in the two countries. In Germany, 'no other IR institution is as unquestioned as the works council' (Jacobi et al. 1998: 213). Such a mandate has never been consolidated in Spain and works councils there are subject to 'the micro-politics and alliances that emerge within the workplace' (Hamann and Martinez Lucio 2003: 69). Outside of core manufacturing sectors, and away from the major conurbations, strongly paternalistic management can mould local representation. In part, this is permitted by differing strategies between the main union confederations (UGT and CCOO), and weakness at local level occasioned by competition between them. Whilst workplace elections play important roles in determining the balance of power between the unions at higher levels, they face real resource problems in turning electoral activity into coordinated industrial activism (Martínez Lucio 1998).

Thus IR systems are similarly structured in the two countries; these are strongly regulated systems in which civil and social actors play prominent roles. Both systems have changed recently in response to domestic and international pressures. Whilst there have been attempts to promote coordinated collective bargaining in Spain, parts of the German model are now more loosely integrated than previously (Dörre 1996; Hassel 1999; Jacobi, Keller, and Muller-Jentsch 1998; Kohaut and Schnabel 2001). Important differences, however, stem from the degree of *articulation* between the workplace and higher-level institutions. Quests for bargaining flexibility in Germany have been characterized principally by the legal delegation of the regulation of terms and conditions to plant-level actors

(Bispinck 1997). This can take the form of 'opening clauses', which allow specific deviations at company level from standards laid down in industry-level agreements and which are estimated to be used in one-third of companies across most sectors (EIRO 2003*a*); 'hardship clauses', allowing companies with economic problems to pay their employees below the minimum rates set by the collective agreement for a limited period of time (EIRO 1997); and 'company pacts for employment', whereby employees make concessions on pay or working conditions in exchange for limited job guarantees (EIRO 2003*b*; Bispinck 2003). This degree of coordination is less common in Spain, indeed company-level bargaining often proceeds there without formal reference to developments at higher levels. Sector-level bargaining in Spain tends also to be 'ritualistic' (Martínez Lucio 1998: 429), often producing relatively meagre agreements covering only elementary issues such as pay and working time. At the workplace, bargaining can be more confrontational and unpredictable (Rigby and Aledo 2001). Around half of the total number of strikes called in Spain each year are organized by works committees, rather than by the union confederations.

The Anglo-Irish Economies: The UK and Ireland

By contrast, the UK and Ireland offer the fewest barriers to the transfer of American approaches to IR. Most notably, the state has played relatively minor and indirect roles in facilitating regulation and a similar emphasis on 'single channel' collective relations has displaced workplace representation comparable to the 'dual systems' of mainland Europe. Moreover, social regulation through collective bargaining has weakened in recent years, though the genesis and extent of this process has been different in the two countries.

British IR have been regulated principally through voluntary agreements between employees and trade unions as their representatives. In contrast to Germany and Spain, legal process and the court system were deliberately absented from these processes, giving rise to the notion of 'free collective bargaining' or 'collective laissez-faire'. For most of the twentieth century, there were no labour inspectorates, specialist labour courts, or state bodies actively to oversee the operation of the employment relationship, much less to intervene in it. Law did not prescribe the conduct of bargaining, its level or content and the resultant collective agreements were not enforceable at law. Law did not impinge either upon the scope of collective bargaining and most individual employment rights were determined and enforced solely through collective relations. Moreover, unions were seen as the legitimate representatives of labour; whilst differences between negotiation and consultation were acknowledged, unions were involved in both. This 'single channel' system of representation differed formally from the separate 'dual systems' evident in Germany and Spain.

That collective bargaining spread in the UK is due to the pragmatic orientation of most IR actors. In the context of more or less untrammelled growth in imperial markets, collective bargaining did little to impede the freedoms of employers and became an accepted element of public policy. But this consensus had relatively weak institutional foundations. As Hyman notes (2001: 69):

While workers became free to organize collectively, the employer was equally free to dismiss those who joined a union; while unions were entitled to bargain collectively, employers were equally at liberty to refuse to negotiate or to recognise a union, whatever its level of membership; and while a union could lawfully call a strike [. . .] individual strikers were still in breach of their contracts of employment and might therefore be summarily dismissed.

This voluntarist infrastructure, and the policy consensus it fostered, has been substantially altered over the last twenty years. Collective relations are now regulated more closely by the state, effectively delimiting the autonomy and activity of trade unions (Smith and Morton 1993, 2001). Protections for striking workers were narrowed, making strike activity more difficult; mechanisms to ensure automatic union membership—such as the closed shop and deduction of union fees at source—were abolished or complicated; and controls over the internal decision-making of unions were imposed. Coinciding initially with high rates of unemployment and then deindustrialization of union heartlands, such gambits led to the hollowing out of collective bargaining. As in Germany, bargaining has been decentralized but the process and the extent have led to more radical consequences. Relatively modest extension mechanisms were abolished, including the Fair Wages Resolution and the Wages Councils, and multi-employer bargaining has been practically eradicated (Brown et al. 2000: 614). These processes effectively removed the checks and balances across workplaces apparent in the delegated German system. Bargaining has devolved not just to company level but beyond that to business units, where union organization is weakest and most susceptible to quests for cost savings.

The Irish 'system' of collective bargaining was grounded historically in these same voluntary principles, relying on the moral commitment of the participants to implement agreements achieved through the bargaining process. There is no legal requirement on employers or trade unions to comply with the terms agreed. Differences between the two countries stem principally from the relatively stable policy context (cf. Roche 1997). In the absence of ideological divisions between the main parties on the role of unions, Ireland has avoided dramatic shifts in policy orientation associated with changes in government (Roche 1992, 1997; Turner and Morley 1995). As indicated in Table 6.1 earlier, this has fostered a more prominent role for national and sectoral bargaining and more scope for coordination than exists in the UK.

However, as noted in Chapter 4, evidence that multinational firms are willing to exploit the leeway afforded by voluntarist systems is particularly apparent in Ireland. Since the 1980s, there has been a significant increase in union avoidance in the MNC sector, most particularly among US subsidiaries (Gunnigle 1995; Gunnigle, O'Sullivan, and Kinsella 2002; Roche 2001; McGovern 1989). A number of factors help explain this phenomenon. The high level of US FDI into Ireland, particularly during the 1990s was previously noted (see Chapter 4). Much of this occurred in the information and communication technology (ICT) sector, particularly electronics and software—areas widely seen in the US context as important sources of opposition to union recognition (Foulkes 1980; Kochan, Katz, and McKersie 1986). A change in the policy stance of Ireland's state agencies with responsibility for attracting FDI was also significant. During the 1960s and 1970s, these bodies generally encouraged inward-investing multinationals to recognize trade unions and engage in collective bargaining—a strategy similar to that pertaining in most larger Irish organizations of the period (McGovern 1989). In the face of increased international competition for MNC investment since the early 1980s, these agencies have since adopted a 'union neutral' stance, emphasizing the prerogative of inward-investing firms to recognize or avoid trade unions as they so wish (Gunnigle et al. 2006). In due course, union avoidance has become the preferred approach among US investors in Ireland.

As with Germany and Spain, these differences should not be exaggerated and some recent developments reinforce the fundamentally similar policy orientations. The outright assault on collective relations in the UK have abated with the election of Labour governments since 1997, and some modest supports have been enacted, notably a statutory procedure for trade union recognition which has, 'acted to shift the balance of employer attitudes towards greater approval of trade unions' (Oxenbridge et al. 2003: 331). Key amongst these initiatives was the transposition of the

Information and Consultation Directive, which has also been echoed necessarily in Ireland. Employees wishing to be consulted over a range of workplace issues now have the right to negotiate a structure for consultation, or where negotiations are unsuccessful and workforce support has been demonstrated in a ballot, to have a statutory model inserted within the company. The likely impact of these regulations in practice is difficult to assess in advance (see Hall 2005), but their significance lies in the potential to challenge 'single channel' approaches to collective relations.

FINDINGS

In this section, we review the data on collective employment relations in the four countries. Point-by-point comparison is difficult in the context of the substantial differences just noted in statutory requirements and industry practice. For example, the notion of trade union recognition is pivotal in the UK and Ireland; it is less so in Germany and Spain, where works council representation and extended sectoral bargaining offer indirect avenues of influence for unions. Consequently, we distinguish in broad terms between collective representation and collective bargaining. The former covers consultation on issues including business reorganization and redundancies. Collective bargaining refers to joint regulation of pay and conditions of employment, whether at company or industry level.

Corporate Orientations

First, though, it is necessary to explore policy preferences relevant to IR emanating from American corporate headquarters. Expectations that these would generate non-union stances were predominantly met, but with some important caveats.

Conventional 'New Deal' bargaining was evident in mainstream manufacturing firms such as Engco1. Significantly, though, American managers expressed preferences for non-union arrangements even here. Following bruising confrontations with the UAW through the 1990s, Engco1 had developed new production capacity in 'right to work' states, demonstrating a determination not to reinvest in areas, 'which are controlled by an institution which you know is antithetical to our objectives' (senior American HR manager, Engco1). Apparently more flexible approaches were apparent in Engco2. Bucking the prevailing anti-union sentiment of the early post-war period, the company's founding father had proclaimed that unions were an important check on management. But this did not extend to certification of wholly independent unions—where bargaining took place; it was conducted instead with 'unaffiliated' unions—and this company too had opened non-union facilities.

Traces of welfare capitalism were manifest in CPGco and ITco. Fundamental opposition to unions in these companies extended to collective representation of almost any kind.

We are very careful on not having anything that smacks of one employee representing another. We'll just back right off if it looks like, you know, an employee comes in and says, 'I want to talk to you, the shopfloor has concerns, I want to represent the shopfloor.' No. Let's talk about your concerns but we won't set an employee off at all to talk to or talk about other employees. (US HR manager, CPGCO)

Sophisticated HRM techniques were combined with a robust approach to combating union organizing drives. 'Pulse checks' were conducted randomly by HR departments in American plants, in which employees in particular workgroups were interviewed about their work experience. Grievances highlighted by this process were taken up on behalf of employees by HR managers. Less cordially, plants faced with union organizing drives were subject to swift and intense corporate responses. Groups of specialist managers were sent to galvanize resistance amongst 'leaders', from managers down to supervisory and team leader level. Employee 'leaders', those leading demands for union certification or seen otherwise to be influential, were then identified and their grievances were explored individually: 'so if you've got a list of 10 things that are broad issues across the organization and three of them were the top issues of these people, those were what they picked off first' (ibid.).

Such anti-union approaches were strongly embedded into corporate management culture in a number of our cases. But while the force of American animus towards unions needs to be acknowledged in the assessment of employment practice within European subsidiaries, some qualifications should also be noted. First, though ideological preferences were shared amongst our American respondents, their expression in practice could be focused on experiences at home. Attitudes in Engco1 were conditioned strongly by the aftershocks of the strike activity during the 1990s, for example. In EngServs the objection was quite specific and focused on the lack of flexibility associated with New Deal collective bargaining systems.

The biggest negative of union involvement is seniority because if we had the ability to pick and choose who we kept and didn't keep, *we wouldn't care if somebody was unionized or not.* But you could have the worst performing individual with the highest seniority and it's almost impossible to get rid of that person. (Corporate HR manager, EngServs, emphasis added)

Second, opposition to union presence sometimes applied mainly in practice to American plants. Quite strident views about practice at home could sometimes coexist with pragmatism about approaches within operations in other national contexts. American managers were apt to contrast adversarial relations with 'radical, stronghold type unions' in the USA with more cooperative approaches abroad:

The union's got a much different role in my opinion in the US than they do in the UK. Not good or bad, they play a different role. We have a target for employee engagement, employee leadership and how you get to those points or those levels could be different in the US and the UK because what's necessarily important to an employee in the UK may not run exactly parallel to what's important to somebody in the US, but if here's what our goal is and it's good for the division and the company, the mannerisms in which the US or the UK does it, there could be some differences to achieve the same goal based on their culture or environment. (HR manager, EngCo1, USA)

Thus, managers were able to talk at length about working 'real hard to stay, in keeping non-union' at home, only to acknowledge the potential benefits of unionization within subsidiaries.

The Leaders that I talk to who've had experience of working in the union environment will say they are able to do things like a lay-off or down-sizing, people reduction, much easier in those environments *than what we have in this country.* (US HR manager, CPGco, emphasis added)

In short, ideological preferences for non-unionism were widely apparent and sometimes forcefully expressed but this was rooted explicitly and consciously in experiences in the USA. Whilst clearly carrying the potential to colour attitudes to employment practice abroad, the practical impact could be quite specific, focused on particular adverse features of unionized environments, and pragmatic, allowing for different strategies in contexts where these features could be diminished or eradicated.

Collective Bargaining

We start with the strongest indicator of union influence—formal collective bargaining. Our findings on this issue showed tremendous variation according to particular company and host-country circumstances. To the extent that any particular pattern was evident, intention to avoid union influence appeared strongest in Germany, our archetypal *Roman–Germanic* system, and weakest in the UK, with its *Anglo-Irish* characteristics. The more hybrid features of Spain and Ireland fostered more mixed or indeterminate outcomes.

Despite the relatively strong collective rights conferred on German workers, three of the case-study companies (Business Services, Bor-Tec, and Silico) managed to insulate themselves altogether from collective bargaining. The former two companies did so by paying significantly higher than collective agreements in their respective industries. Silico had formerly been covered by the metalworking agreement but had left the employers' association in 1974 in order to avoid a strike over working time. Since then it had not been covered either by an industry-level or company-level agreement, which in Germany is quite unusual for a company of its size. The three companies had in common that their employees—the majority of whom were very highly qualified—did not have a strong orientation towards unions. This was particularly noticeable in Silico where employees had repeatedly rejected recruitment attempts by IG Metall.

More generally, strategies were aimed at minimizing the influence of multi-employer bargaining, particularly where this constrained the development of ILMs. Only four of the ten case-study companies (BankCo, CPGco, Logistico, and Chemco) were members of their employers' associations and full participants in the bargaining process. Logistico voluntarily joined its employers' association in 1991, apparently in the quest for labour market information that would permit the company to differentiate its pay structures prior to new agreements taking effect. Other companies found industry-level bargaining less congenial and attempted to undermine it in various ways. In the course of downsizing and disposal of most of its production units in Germany in the 1990s, CPGco moved all of its operations from the metalworking industry agreement to a sub-agreement of the chemical industry, in order to increase the degree of pay flexibility (see Chapter 7). Similarly, ITco left the metalworking employers' association and was reorganized into a number of smaller companies, which concluded collective agreements with *DAG* (now part of the services union *Ver.di*), a less militant union than IG Metall.

Such opposition was more muted in Spain, where the paucity of sector-level bargaining left plenty of scope to mould firm-level settlements. Chemco, for example, was a signatory to the sectoral agreement but this did little to prevent the introduction of performance-related remuneration (see Chapter 7). Because of the greater overlap between bargaining and consultation in Spain, union avoidance strategies were more evident at workplace level, and these are discussed later.

Irish subsidiaries exhibited similarly pragmatic approaches; instances of union avoidance here appeared to be explained by sectoral factors and by the age of the subsidiaries. Both Pharmaco and Healthco recognized trade unions and engaged in collective bargaining in all their early plants, and collective bargaining remains the major vehicle for handling IR issues in these facilities. Both Healthco and Pharmaco have a long tradition of conceding pay increases in excess of those provided for under national accords. *Industrial Relations News*[1] (IRN) reports found that unionized workers in Healthco received pay increases which were 'a good deal higher' than that prescribed under the prevailing national pay accord, and concluded that the company agreed the largest number of 'above the norm deals' during a previous accord. The Pharmaco experience was similar. IRN reports found that operator grades in its largest site received pay increases 'well in excess' of the prevailing national accord (IRN Report). It further observed that Pharmaco had a long tradition of paying above the norm set out in national accords. This 'above the norm' phenomenon seems to reflect a strong sectoral effect: IRN reports have for some time identified pharmaceuticals and health care as sectors with consistently the largest numbers of 'above the norm deals', labelling them as 'normally recession-proof' sectors.

Union avoidance had grown recently in both these hitherto heavily unionized companies. This had come about as a result of the use of 'double-breasting' arrangements, whereby multi-establishment organizations opt to recognize trade unions and engage in collective bargaining in some (older) sites but not in other (newer) sites (cf. Beaumont and Harris 1992). This was most evident in Healthco where all three of its more recently established plants were non-union. *Pharmaco's* newest manufacturing plant also operated on a non-union basis.

Both ITco and Compuco, by contrast, could be categorized as staunchly non-union. While the former followed the traditions of union substitution, the latter, which operated on the basis of a low-price competitive strategy, initially pursued a conventional union suppression model. It is instructive that both these companies only established significant operations in Ireland from the turn of the 1980s, by which time union avoidance had become an accepted pattern of US MNC behaviour (Gunnigle 1995). This starkly contrasts with the experience of Pharmaco and Healthco, who established their first plants in late 1960s or mid-1970s—a period when trade union recognition was the dominant pattern (cf. Gunnigle, Collings, and Morley 2005).

Our final Irish case, Logistico, fell midway between these other companies, having recently conceded a limited form of union recognition though still not acknowledging engagement in full collective bargaining. Logistico's decision to locate a new technical support and other call centre activities in Ireland in the mid-1990s was in part influenced by lower levels of employment regulation and the capacity to go non-union. However, as a result of a sustained organizing campaign by one trade union, the company conceded a limited type of union recognition. It was also instructive that Logistico did not engage in any trenchant opposition to union organization. During the union's organizing campaign, the company allowed the union to address the workers, and company executives met union officials privately. The company now provides the union with certain facilities, such as a 'union room' and check-off at source (of union subscriptions), and it pays workplace representatives while these are involved in union activities and training.

Pragmatism on IR issues was even more pronounced in the UK (Ferner *et al.* 2005). Significantly, union recognition and collective bargaining was largely accepted in manufacturing operations like Engco1, Engco2, and CPGco. As in Ireland, this can be explained in large part by the age of the subsidiaries and the circumstances surrounding initial investment in them. Engco1 was established in the UK soon after the Second World War, and the company fell in with prevailing norms: 'you have to remember, it was almost like the union was part of the industry at one time [. . .] if you wanted to do business, you did business with the union and its shop stewards' (union officer, Engco1). Engco2 arrived later, during the 1960s, and general norms were reinforced by local circumstances in this case. Following its preference for establishing 'company towns', Engco2 selected sites for its subsidiaries in medium-sized conurbations suffering the employment consequences of economic restructuring. The terms of subsequent land deals often required engagement with national and local government, and union influence within both ensured that union recognition was secured at an early stage: 'before the very first employee commenced with the company, a recognition agreement was signed with the AEU' (union officer, Engco2). CPGco struggled against these conventions for some time but eventually did likewise and recognized unions for collective bargaining. During our research, shop-floor employees were strongly unionized in all three companies, with near 100 per cent membership in some plants, and unions played prominent roles in dispute resolution.

Three subsidiaries (ITco, EngServs, and Household) maintained non-union environments and one (PharmaChem) had a mix of union and non-union sites. The reasons for this were complex, though, and a simple causal connection to American ownership was difficult to establish. Anti-unionism was certainly apparent in ITco, as discussed later, though it was not clear whether this was attributable to American, British, or sectoral characteristics. Labour market factors certainly dampened demand for union organization in EngServs, where skilled engineers relied predominantly on a highly developed and often overheated occupational labour market. As one put it, 'it is common knowledge that if you want more money you have got to leave and come back or be prepared to leave and hope they will pay you more money'. But asked specifically about direction from America on union recognition, the UK HR director said, 'it's not a policy objective and it doesn't get discussed a lot, I have to say'.

In summary, therefore, attempts to minimize the direct influence of collective bargaining were most apparent in German subsidiaries, where the risks of sharing decision-making were the greatest. In Spain, Ireland, and the UK, by contrast, the predominantly enterprise-based model of IR did not significantly constrain management action or conflict with attempts to establish company-specific rules. Non-union approaches were evident here too, but were not explained so straightforwardly by country-of-origin influences. The age of the subsidiary and sectoral norms, combined with other pressures evident in the host-country context, appeared as important influences here. Provided unionism was circumscribed and allowed subsidiaries to perform to expectations, it was tolerated and accommodated by managers.

Collective Representation

Strong contrasts were apparent too on the issue of collective representation at workplace level. Institutional support for works councils in Germany and Spain was met with pressure to minimize organized collective influence. In advance of new regulations derived from the Information and Consultation Directive, requirements in the UK and Ireland were less onerous and delivered mainly through workplace bargaining with unions.

As discussed earlier, the idea of 'non-union' employment relations does not make much sense in the German and Spanish contexts. Formally, it is the works council which acts at company level but these often comprise union nominees and support for their actions amongst the workforce is not determined by union membership. Consequently, subject to resources, unions are able to influence works council proceedings directly and indirectly. German and Spanish management often played on this ambiguity; marginal levels of union membership amongst workforces were taken to indicate non-unionism. But this could coexist with union influence on the works councils. In the Spanish subsidiary of ITco, for example, one of the most systematically non-union companies in our sample, works council members were CCOO affiliates—the union confederation with the strongest record of mobilizing workers at this level.

Despite the prevalence of works councils overall, a number of strategies were developed to reduce their influence. Spanish subsidiaries of Drugco and Household were keen to maintain a preponderance of non-union committee members. CCOO had unsuccessfully challenged electoral procedures at Household, and the company had prevented workers approaching the union during a restructuring exercise by threatening to withdraw enhanced redundancy packages and to offer only the statutory minima. Works councils sometimes did not meet or were convened only in response to specific events, such as business restructuring. Superior conditions were offered explicitly to hold off demand for union representation: 'we take care of people so the need [for a union] doesn't arise, and therefore we have to be very sophisticated in HR policies' (HR manager, Drugco Spain). In these circumstances, works councils were preoccupied merely with hygiene factors:

The most serious problem we might have is that in summer one of the buses doesn't have air conditioning, or that the afternoon shift had sandwiches made with bread that was a bit stale. When they come, the doors are open. In the factory there are 300 people in three shifts and there have never been any problems. (HR manager, Drugco, Spain)

Where union-backed works council activity was established, as in some ITco subsidiaries in Spain, managers reported tactical responses and a will on occasion to press ahead with decisions that had not been agreed by the *comité*:

Even where there is no agreement with the *comité*, management can always choose whether to implement the change or not. If we do it, the *comité de empresa* might take us to the labour court, it might not. If it mounts a legal challenge, it is the judge who decides if in the end the change can be implemented or not. This is the dynamic in which you find yourself whenever you try to be on the one hand global, and at the same time adapt to local legislation. (HR manager, ITco Spain)

In Germany, *Business Services* created separate companies for support staff and consulting staff. The effect of this was to confine works council representation to the former, which comprised merely one-fifth of the workforce. A number of sophisticated HR policies developed at corporate level were replicated in the company's German subsidiary with a view to keeping works councils at bay:

We have 'best place to work' initiatives. We strive to be an employer who is so attractive that consultants want to join us and stay with us. And that is more than any works council could offer. When the company, all the HR people, and all the senior managers are daily putting a lot of effort into finding ways to make this an attractive place to work, then they are doing exactly the same as what a works council should do. (German HR manager, Business Services)

There was some evidence that the management of works council input was traceable to American influence. In Logistico, works councils were strongly shaped by headquarters' suspicions of IR institutions in other countries. According to subsidiary management, when the first works councils were set up in the late 1980s, there was irritation on the part of company headquarters in the USA. Questions were asked about what a works council was and why it needed to be informed of matters like new pay systems and working time. Such irritation was perceived by subsidiary management as a very clear signal of the strategies expected of them: 'If a works council had been set up, then management had failed in the eyes of the Americans . . . "failed" meaning that was the end of your career.' (German works councillor)

These perceptions strongly shaped managerial responses to the setting up of works councils. For example, when representatives called the first works meeting (*Betriebsversammlung*), which according to the Works Constitution Act can take place during working time without loss of pay, a letter was issued by a law firm initiated by Logistico's German labour relations department threatening a 500,000 DM fine or imprisonment if the works meeting took place. The meeting did eventually occur, with busloads of employees from throughout Germany coming to attend. According to a German works councillor, the main point of conflict was the setting up of works councils:

It was very difficult to set up a works council and it's the same today—I am convinced that [*Logistico*] would do everything to prevent a works council from being set up—both through lawful and unlawful means.

There was a widely held view among German subsidiary management that they were subject to strong pressure to comply with the thrust of headquarters initiatives and that they were expected to deliver particular outcomes and practices regardless of possible works council restrictions, for example:

Management is under strong pressure because there is an expectation that code-termination should not cause any delays. 'This is your task, these are the targets and at the end of the year you have to be at this point.' (German HR manager, CPGco)

This does not mean that it is accepted that we go our special national way just because of codetermination and have an easy life. [Headquarters] still expect that we implement our agenda even under these exacerbated general conditions. In other words: codetermination is no excuse for not achieving our goals. (German HR manager, ITco)

Subsidiary management at Logistico has responded to such pressures by trying to shape the nature of the group works council in such a way as to minimize potential opposition to their plans:

The attitude of management was that 'if a groups works council is to be set up, then we want to shape it'.... They try, unofficially of course, to influence the election propaganda and election strategy in such a way that people who support their views are elected. The group works council is controlled by [Logistico]. Some of its members have been trained in America. They have been very well trained and receive a lot of support. (Works councillor)

In the UK and Ireland, where rights are notably more dilute than in Germany, consultation over organizational restructuring and redundancies was dealt with straightforwardly by union representatives, where unions were recognized. With some minor exceptions, this rarely resulted in sustained attempts to change management decisions. Proposals to close a manufacturing plant in Engco2 generated a public campaign by unions culminating in an invitation to them to discuss the issue at corporate headquarters. Notably, however, the plant was closed following the conventional concession that redundancies would be on a voluntary basis only. Similarly, in Ireland, Healthco was able to outsource work to Eastern Europe and to transfer staff doing 'lower grade' work to a newly created company with only limited opposition from unions on points of detail.

Potentially of greater interest was the impact of newly reinforced rights to consultation in non-union settings. Even before the Information and Consultation Directive, strengthened legal provision required more explicit consultation with 'employee representatives' during the planning of redundancies and transfer of undertakings. In ITco, these requirements were met on an ad hoc basis; that is, consultation was conducted with affected employees as necessary. Some employees, anticipating transposition of the Information and Consultation Directive, pushed for more permanent arrangements but met stern resistance. Those gauging support from colleagues for such a move received prompt responses from the company.

All hell broke loose. I was threatened with sacking for [. . .] incorrect use of [*ITco*] resources. I was threatened with having my task ID taken away, which I thought was a particularly petulant little sideswipe. And this was all because I'd actually taken the initiative to go out to the workforce.

EngServs' British subsidiary, however, opted to introduce a permanent structure for consultation. Since the company operates in a project environment, where staff numbers fluctuate in direct relation to the contracts won in competition, keeping the option of redundancies under review was a constant requirement: 'it doesn't take much to throw it, you are expecting something to come in, if that doesn't come in you are in trouble.' This provided the initial rationale for a permanent structure but, once established, the forum developed very quickly. Managers wished to provide a more 'optimistic' momentum behind meetings and opened the terms of reference to include substantive terms and conditions. At the same time, formal training provided by the Advisory Conciliation and Arbitration Service (ACAS) equipped employee representatives for a wider range of roles. Quasi-bargaining processes were developed in which the forum deliberated over the issues ranging from arrangements for watching international football matches during the World Cup, to parental leave provision and eventually the introduction of an entirely new contract of employment.

Once again, American influence reportedly was not significant in either prompting this innovation or resisting it. Significantly, however, corporate interest did stir the moment that consultation arrangements seemed set to broaden access for unions to strategic decision-making at European level. Corporate managers in EngServs intervened to ensure that subsidiaries did not volunteer to establish a European works council. Were employees to demand one, American managers determined that it would be placed in the UK:

We were never keen, push never came to shove, and if we did we would have put it in the UK because of the lack of unions or strength of unions in the UK. That's where the centre for the European Works Council would have been for [*Eng Servs*]. We wouldn't have put it in Finland because it's strong, neither in Poland or Italy, it would have gone in the UK. (US manager, Eng Servs)

ITco did establish a European works council but emphasis was placed primarily on the dissemination of information. Proactive consultation on strategic matters at European level was kept to a minimum, the preference being for issues to be addressed locally:

What tends to happen at the moment is the emphasis is on management getting it right within country and then thinking, 'oh, should we actually inform the EWC'. Whereas in fact it should be the other way round. They should be informing the EWC and using that as a mechanism to inform the works council in-country.

Once again, the pattern appears to be one of tolerating employee representation within specific boundaries, that is, where it provided consultation arrangements supportive of management decision-making and helped with the implementation of strategies once confirmed. This was evident in most of the UK and Irish cases, but where institutional contexts provided potentially stronger roles for workforces and their representatives, more concerted lines of resistance were apparent and could be traced back to American influence. It is this that explains the relatively robust approach taken towards German and Spanish works councils and in UK subsidiaries covered potentially by European works councils.

CONCLUSIONS

Industrial relations systems in the USA have been moulded substantially by employer opposition to autonomous employee representation, and regulatory systems permit a range of practice determined largely by management preferences at enterprise level. Expectations that these kinds of approaches will be extended to overseas subsidiaries of MNCs are confirmed by survey research and spectacular single cases of companies like McDonalds.

Despite their positioning within an increasingly integrated European economy, our four countries offer distinctive IR contexts. Variation in the range and character of state regulation permit their broad allocation to the *Anglo-Irish* (Ireland and the UK) or the *Roman–Germanic* (Germany, Spain), respectively. While some of these features, such as the form and structure of collective bargaining, has been subject to change, others, such as the constitutional expression of the rights to associate and to strike, are enduring.

It follows that these systems present different levels of challenge to incoming management systems. A greater range of variation might be permitted by the UK system, for example, whilst the German one appears to require compliance to national norms, through the extension of basic statutory rights and those contained in sector-level collective agreements.

The extent to which this conditions different IR *outcomes* is covered in other chapters (e.g. in relation to pay composition). The *procedural* aspects of IR have provided the central focus of this chapter, and the cases exhibit variable and quite complex patterns of influence. In broad terms, the findings appear counter-intuitive; the most determined attempts to minimize union influence were found in Germany and Spain. The UK and Irish subsidiaries, enjoying the greatest leeway to insist on non-union relations, appeared relatively pragmatic and willing overall to accept collective channels.

One simple explanation is available. Opposition to national regulatory norms turns substantially on the challenge it poses to enterprise-based regulation systems of the kind preferred by American companies. Where these are opened potentially to broader influences, as in Germany and Spain, companies attempt to obviate the regulations. Thus, companies took steps to avoid sector-level agreements—or to enter those that permitted them the greatest influence—and to mould the terms of engagement with formally established works councils. In Ireland and the UK, the consequences of conceding unionized relations were not as far-reaching. Whilst non-unionism was sometimes apparent in these settings, it was far from universal.

The most interesting issues arise, however, when the scope of direct American influence is investigated. This can be detected in specific circumstances. Where decisions by national subsidiaries might affect strategic direction in the economic region, through the establishment or operation of European works councils for example, American direction could be quite forceful. Overall, however, the stereotype of centrally driven IR strategies finds only partial support in these findings. Minimal union presence was often attributable to factors other than corporate direction, including particular production or labour market characteristics. Subsidiaries often enjoyed significant autonomy, subject to broad performance targets. The extent of that autonomy varied according to the age of the subsidiary, the greater number of older sites explaining relative stability in the UK for example.

Note

1. In this report we have not provided the full references to any documentation which would reveal the name of the company.

7

Pay and Performance

Phil Almond, Michael Muller-Camen, David G. Collings, and Javier Quintanilla

INTRODUCTION

This chapter examines the management of pay and performance within the European subsidiaries of US MNCs. This subject is of particular interest for a number of reasons. In particular, the centralized and formalized nature of the personnel function in large US firms (see Chapters 10 and 12), alongside the domination of 'individualistic' values and a relative lack of regulation beyond firm level in the USA (see Chapter 3), have long meant that many American firms have been seen as innovative in their management of pay and performance. Historically, many forms of reward management first publicized in the USA have become commonplace in other industrialized countries. For example, Ford's 'efficiency wage' policies, and the tying of wage increases to improvements in productivity, became a central element of the regulation of labour in developed economies for much of the last century (cf. Boyer 1988). Policies, such as gain-sharing and profit-sharing, partially tying the notion of a 'fair day's pay' directly to the economic performance of the firm, also received widespread publicity (Blinder 1990). However, other distinctive features of the American wage–effort bargain, such as the use of highly structured ILMs for manual workers (cf. Osterman 1984a), have been under considerable pressure in the USA itself in recent years, as American employers have become increasingly intolerant of the perceived rigidities of their domestic employment system. Hence, the much-reported decline of the New Deal employment contract (see Chapter 6) has given rise to 'new' forms of payment structures, such as 'broadbanding', and the extension of forms of collective and individual performance pay further down the organizational hierarchy.

More recently, the diffusion of systems of performance-related pay in European countries (EIRO 2001b) is often portrayed as a form of Americanization, as attempts to 'reward contribution' within the bureaucracy of the large organization have been an important factor in managerial attempts to move away from 'Fordist' systems of collective bargaining. Thus, in some respects, the gap in practice between the European subsidiaries of US MNCs and other European employers (cf. Muller 1998) may well have diminished in recent years. To some, systems of formalized merit pay, at least for managers and professionals, have been so widely diffused across indigenous firms across Europe, as well as non-American MNCs, that performance-related pay can no longer be viewed as an 'American' practice (cf. Faulkner, Pitkethly, and Child 2004). Indeed, in this and many other areas of HRM, the cross-pollination of managerial practice, but also of managerial ideology and vocabulary, makes the branding of a given practice as 'American' (or 'Japanese' or 'German') an increasingly difficult exercise. However, as previous research in other areas of labour management has repeatedly shown (e.g. Lorenz 2000; Smith and Elger 2000), the existence of a common label may well mask considerable diversity in the nature of such practices, which in turn may be traced back to societal or business system effects.

Accordingly, this chapter examines the variety of meanings that formulations such as 'performance pay' and 'broadbanding' take in the concrete empirical reality of US firms engaging with the UK, Irish, German, and Spanish employment systems, and how this relates to the wider discussion on home and host-country effects within MNCs. We concentrate on the pay–performance nexus, while acknowledging that this relationship cannot be treated in isolation from the broader pay determination systems within US MNCs and their subsidiaries. Particularly, it is imperative to examine performance and reward management practices for the entire direct workforces of the subsidiaries rather than concentrating only on elites such as international or senior subsidiary managers. In this respect, we depart from much of the international HRM literature, which systematically ignores the issue of pay for non-managers.

After an introduction to national contexts in this area, the chapter presents its empirical findings in three sections: the degree of centralization of pay determination policies and the extent to which this can be described as distinctively American; a brief analysis of how jobs and individuals are classified within wage determination systems; and finally, the management of performance itself.

COUNTRY CONTEXTS

USA

While the relatively underinstitutionalized nature of the American employment system renders the characterization of an overriding US pay determination 'system' a difficult enterprise, it is nevertheless possible to talk of a number of general characteristics within the long-term effort–reward bargain in large US firms (for a more detailed review, see Almond 2004).

First, the heritage of a comparatively close attachment to formal management ideas based on scientific management historically led to wage structures based predominantly on the tasks covered by the work post rather than the characteristics of the individual or his/her level of training (cf. Marsden 1999; Shibata 2002). As in other countries with this sort of system (notably France), employer desire for stability and union pressure for equity gave rise to strong ILMs (cf. Cappelli 1995 Jacoby 1984; Osterman 1984*b*), with jobs defined narrowly within complex job classification systems (Brown and Reich n.d.). Manual workers, in particular, would have strictly defined specialized tasks and, over the course of their career, moved up a seniority-based ladder of job titles differentiated by relatively small increments of pay, and more desirable job characteristics (Brown and Reich n.d.: 3, Cappelli 1995; Mills 1985). Although this system applied most strictly in unionized firms, there is considerable evidence of overspill to non-union 'welfare capitalist' enterprises (Kalleberg et al. 1996; Mills 1985; Osterman 1999).

From the late 1970s onwards, normative arguments about HRM and 'high performance work systems', initially inspired by the Japanese practice, have promoted moves towards more flexible systems of job assignment and continuous skill development, leading to a focus on motivational rewards for company performance, team performance, or skill acquisition. Brown and Reich (n.d.) suggest that the concrete form this move has taken (what they term the 'American high performance model') has been a reduction in the number of job classifications— 'broadbanding'. This has two significant advantages for employers. First, it permits more flexible job assignment by facilitating job rotation. Second, it helps cut costs, as the scope for incremental progression within ILMs is reduced by the amalgamation of intermediate levels in pay hierarchies (Cappelli 1995, 1999*a*; Katz and Krueger 1991; Osterman 1996).

There has also been a change in the nature of systems linking pay to individual performance assessment. First, individual merit pay—at least beyond predominantly output–orientated systems, such as Payment By Results (PBR)—and hence, formal performance appraisals were not widely used for blue-collar employees until relatively recently (Shibata 2002). Equally, although management education in the USA has long argued that pay should be related to performance (Greller and Parsons 1995), there was until recently a strong tendency to compress rankings and/or to evaluate employees generously (Cappelli 1995: 566; Foulkes 1980; Shibata 2002: 642). There has been a notable recent trend, however, towards 'pushing managers to strictly evaluate white-collar employees based on their work results or performance' (Cappelli 1995: 567). The notion of 'performance' has also been expanded to encompass more qualitative assessments of individual competency, teamwork, or accordance with corporate cultural goals such as 'diversity' (see Chapter 8).

One means of ensuring that performance pay discriminates more strongly between better and poorer performers is the use of 'forced distributions', in which line managers are instructed to rank their subordinates in relation to each other, rather than in terms of attaining absolute, preset criteria. Hence, there is typically a requirement to identify a given percentage of 'high' and 'low' performers. Although this practice is not entirely new (cf. Klores 1966), its inherent problem (that line managers may have to place subordinates with objectively adequate performance in the lowest performing group) is significantly magnified if, as is sometimes the case, the results of such evaluation affect the employment security of the appraisee. The eventual 'culling' of poor performers within forced distributions, as initiated by General Electric (Lawler 2002), is linked to the assumption of 'employment at will' underpinning the US employment system, that:

Men [sic] must be left, without interferences, to buy and sell where they please, and to discharge and retain employees at will for good cause or for no cause, or even for bad cause without thereby being guilty of an unlawful act *per se* (*Payne vs. Western & Atlantic Railroad*, Tenn., 1884)

Despite some legal modifications in recent years (cf. Edwards 1995), 'employment at will' remains a strong institutional and ideological norm in the USA (cf. Lichtenstein 2002: 2–3) that does not find parallels in other capitalist democracies. As explored later, attempts by some US MNCs to export 'culling' models to European subsidiaries have encountered a number of problems.

UK

At first glance, one might expect host-country effects in this area to be relatively weak in the UK, given the virtual absence of institutions of wage determination above the firm level. Significant differences between the USA and UK do exist, however. First, the predominant historical form of job allocation/grading is different; in the UK, occupational territories have determined wage structures (cf. Marsden 1999), with jobs being defined by skills on the labour market (historically through the apprenticeship system), and with occupational labour markets predominating over ILMs. Nevertheless, the changes of the last two decades, such as the decline of apprenticeship-based initial training and of collective bargaining, have reduced the institutional effects of this system (Rubery 1994).

Equally, although both the UK and USA are generally grouped together in comparative analysis as 'LMEs' or 'compartmentalized business systems' (Hall and Soskice 2001b; Whitley 1999), and it remains the case that employment protection in the UK is much weaker than in continental European countries, the two countries remain far from identical in this regard. First, institutional employment protection is somewhat stronger in the UK. Workers with twelve months' service cannot be dismissed without good reasons, and although possible reasons for dismissal can be interpreted broadly, the employer must be able to defend the procedures that led to the dismissal. Equally, redundancy should be defendable in terms of the job no longer being required rather than of the performance or capability of the individual. Overall, the underlying ideological construction of the employment relationship does not quite operate under the ultra free-market 'employment at will' assumptions of the USA.

Germany

The central institutions of the German IR system—sectoral bargaining and codetermination (see Chapter 6)—impose a number of effects on the management of pay and performance. First, despite recent challenges to the German system (Bispinck 1997; Hassel 1999; Lane 2000), collective bargaining coverage remains relatively high, at 67 per cent in 2000 (EIRO 2002), and continues to be mainly sectoral in nature, with only a small minority of employees covered by company-level agreements. Sectoral agreements, which classify employees primarily by their level of formal vocational education (Marsden 1999), continue strongly to influence job classification systems even in non-signatory firms (Bahnmuller 2003).

While sectoral agreements, which can be extended to cover non-signatory companies, often constrain the extent of merit pay, the effects of codetermination can also limit employer choice in this area (Muller 1997). The Works Constitution Act grants works councils codetermination rights regarding the fixing of job and bonus rates and comparable performance-related remuneration. Thus, even where companies do not comply with multi-employer bargaining, management is required to gain the approval of works councils before implementing merit pay systems. This process is not always a formality (Kurdelbusch 2002), meaning that variable pay in general has tended to be less widespread in Germany than elsewhere (Lawrence 1991; Muller 1997; Wever 1995), even if the recent partial erosion of the German IR system has led to more firms adopting such practices. Equally, it is extremely difficult to dismiss employees on the grounds of poor performance rankings.

Ireland

Since 1987, Ireland has had a series of neo-corporatist centralized collective agreements setting wage increases (see Chapter 6). This system is grounded in voluntary principles, relying on the moral commitment of the participants to implement agreements achieved through the bargaining process; there is no legal requirement on employers to adhere to the terms agreed. It is hence possible, particularly where local unions are weak or non-existent, to operate outside of national agreements, with pay determined at an 'individual' level based on some performance or grade criteria. In sophisticated non-union MNCs increases would generally be in excess of the national agreement, with the latter representing an external benchmark. Unionized MNCs, which both in the 1970s and in the short period of decentralized bargaining between 1982 and 1987, preferred to engage in enterprise bargaining and to exceed national pay norms, have more recently tended to adhere relatively closely, but not always rigidly, to the central agreements (Geary and Roche 2001). Hence, centralized bargaining, while restraining wage growth in general in return for union influence on wider social and economic policy, does not strongly constrain individual firms in terms of wage growth or grading structures. However, a recent legal judgment, made after our research was completed, stipulates broadly speaking that firms using merit pay systems must give employees overall wage increases no lower than those agreed in the multi-annual national social partnership negotiations. In firms which use merit pay systems to determine base wage increases, the judgment is likely to have some impact on the capacity to award low or zero increases to poor performers on a repeat basis (cf. Higgins 2005).

Models of 'culling' poor performers within a forced distribution are, in theory at least, not an option given legislative constraints. Specifically, all employees with over one year's service are protected by the Unfair Dismissals Act 1977–2001 which, in a manner similar to British legislation, outlines justifiable reasons for dismissal and outlines the procedure which must be followed in dismissing employees (cf. Wallace, Gummigle, and McMahon 2004: Chapter 2). This would require management to follow due process and to allow the employees to improve their performance before they were dismissed. In practice, this would mean that employees should be given realistic performance goals and given a suitable time frame for improvement before the disciplinary process is put in train.

Spain

The Spanish system of bargaining is, in principle, based on sectoral agreements, which may be reached at national or regional level. *Erga omnes* provisions mean that the results of sectoral negotiations legally apply to all enterprises in the sector, regardless of whether they are members of employers' associations. Generally, firm or establishment-level bargaining can only improve on the provisions of sectoral bargaining. In practice, however, the extent to which this system places a constraint on the pay determination systems of foreign MNCs is limited, for two main reasons. First, despite relatively high coverage, the wage levels set in sectoral agreements tend to be relatively low; most 'high road' MNCs (and large Spanish firms) would tend to pay in excess of sectoral minima, either through firm-level collective bargaining or by unilateral management discretion. Second, many sectoral agreements do not cover managerial workers who are classified as 'exempt' employees and have 'individualized' contracts. This particularly applies to many of the Spanish subsidiaries in this study, which have relatively few manual workers. On the other hand, employment protection, at least for those on indefinite contracts, remains very strong, which would seem to present a sizeable obstacle to some of the more aggressive forms of performance management.

DEGREE OF CENTRALIZATION OF PAY POLICIES

We now discuss our findings, starting with the degree of centralization of pay policies. Even allowing for the broad pattern of relatively high centralization within US MNCs (see Chapter 10), there remains perhaps no other element of personnel policy on which the pressures for at least broad commonality of policy are as consistently strong across nearly all the case-study companies in all four countries. The few exceptions to this rule (see Table 7.1), such as EngServs UK and Bankco Germany, are cases where there is very little central coordination over HR policy in the relevant subsidiaries.

Perhaps unsurprisingly, US HQs generally take a strong interest in establishing relatively common reward structures worldwide where possible. In particular, systems of performance management and bonus payment, as well as internal grading structures (at the very least for managers) tend to be highly homogenized. The following quotations are typical:

I think we have worldwide tools now, for example, that look at our compensation practices and test for market reality, equity, consistency, so that we don't have, on the fringe here, different bonus programmes or different payment practices. It's globally evaluated at least twice a year, almost like an audit. We have a performance management system, that's very robust world-wide . . . , that absolutely demands you meet certain criteria and guidelines around performance management. (VP HR, Compuco Ireland)

You won't make a compensation and benefits related decision without [Corporate VP HR's] approval. Compensation and benefits goes all the way back to our corporate office. (HR manager, *Pharmaco* Ireland)

This strong centralizing tendency exists even where HQ allows subsidiaries substantial autonomy in other areas of HR:

We have complete autonomy in relation to training and development, employee relations initiatives, those types of things. On pay, no. Or on any change in benefits. (HR director, HealthCo Ireland)

Centralization often affects apparently trivial issues. For example, one German manager in Household reported that the US HQ was not only closely involved in setting up a pension plan for the German subsidiaries but also had the final say on whether a newly recruited employee was eligible for a bonus or not.

The centralizing tendency is not total, however, and the 'business case' for deviation is sometimes accepted. This does not only apply to institutions which would be regarded by the firms as 'constraints'. For example, in Logistico's Irish call centre, the workforce comprised mainly young and transient foreign national staff. These employees tended to go to Ireland to improve their English language skills and generally did not stay beyond a year or two. Thus they had little interest in pension schemes or other globally standardized benefits available throughout the corporation.

Table 7.1. US influence on pay and performance management in selected case-study companies

Business Services	Performance management system and forced distribution for consultant workforce centrally mandated, with expectation that consultants progress or leave the company. Recent introduction of global variable pay system. All-employee share schemes. Considerable national variation in salary structures, particularly for non-consulting workforces.
Chemco	Company attempts to operate job evaluation system with the same basic principles worldwide for jobs from supervisory level upwards.
	German pay practice chosen for Europe-wide diffusion and is now used in most operations outside the USA, but not in the USA itself. US system not seen as appropriate in Europe due to its higher levels of wage dispersion.
	Global policy of using variable pay for managers. Guidelines for performance management are global, practices determined at European level.
	Global profit-sharing and stock option plans.
Computerco	Broadbanding system, profit-share and stock option plans, and performance management system with managed distribution and risk of dismissal for poor performers—all centrally driven and closely monitored in the USA.
CPGco	Global performance management system, but some latitude for subsidiaries and regions to refine performance criteria, or not to apply individual performance appraisal if this causes resistance among non-managerial workforce, as in the UK and Germany.
	Manual grading structure not uniform.
	Move away from strict forced distribution in performance management. Poor performance increases risk of redundancy in downsizing exercises.
	The USA has no interest in increasing the level of uniformity of wider salary determination, but some attempts to move towards more centralization by the European HQ.
Engco1	Strong central emphasis on uniformity of job descriptions, but some local latitude in practice. Close monitoring of individual promotions.
	Global programmes on individual merit pay and bonuses, although the latter are optional if a 'business case' can be provided.
	Merit pay in practice applies to all non-manual workers, following the US system. Company experimented with forced distribution, but has recently moved away from this.
Engco2	Bonuses and performance pay centrally ordained, with forced distributions and 'culling'-type model recently introduced, against UK resistance, although no dismissals for poor performance have occurred in Germany.
	Intermediate degree of centralization on job grades.
EngServs	Very little HQ impact on the UK policies. Some attempts to impose global performance management system in continental Europe. In Spain, this applied only to senior managers.
Groomco	Tight control of gradings and promotions at higher salary levels. Evaluations of managers must be sent to corporate, also communication with the European HQ to ensure that evaluation accords with the salary structure (German subsidiary has operational control of salary scales within Europe).
	Global performance management system, no forcing or apparent impact on employment security.
	Guidelines set on grading of shop-floor employees, but considerable local flexibility within this.

Table 7.1. (*cont'd*)

Healthco	Global performance management system, high proportions of top ratings must be justified.
	Any change in compensation and benefit policy in subsidiaries must be sanctioned at corporate level.
Household	Performance management system global, no forcing of distribution but eventual risk of dismissal for poor performers.
	Attempts to internationalize the UK broadbanding scheme.
	Generally close control of details of policies.
ITco	Global system, tightly controlled, covering job evaluation and classification, merit pay and performance appraisal system, with forced distribution used to identify candidates for redundancy.
	Some indication of European input into policymaking.
Logistico	Significant involvement of the European HQ in rate of pay increases.
	Corporation see stock options, especially for managers, as important and monitors this policy closely, but control of performance pay is relatively limited.
Pharmaco	Centre approves annual budget for wage increases, and is involved in the planning stage of wage negotiations, but has exerted no pressure to standardize performance appraisal, being content to leave the distribution of wage increases to the subsidiary.
Refresco	Individualized wage determination and performance management system, covering all employees about to be centralized at European level at the time of research.
	Global programme of incentives, stock options, etc.
	Global performance management system, with merit pay covering all employees. At the time of research the link between job description/responsibilities and job grade is similar across Europe, with plans to unify this broadbanding system worldwide. All-employee share schemes.
Softco	Unified global system of competence-based, broadbanded job evaluation.
	Unified global system of stock options (increasingly limited to high status employees) and variable pay for core employees.
	Competence-based performance evaluation programme, originated in Germany but has since been 'reverse-diffused' on a global scale.

In order to address this unusual situation, the Irish operation introduced a flexible benefits programme whereby these employees could take the value of these benefits in the form of record or book tokens (which at the time were not liable to taxation under Irish legislation) or even as cash (which was subject to taxation). Equally, specific labour market circumstances can sometimes be used as a case for deviation from corporate policies on wage increases, as was the case during the Irish 'Celtic Tiger' period, when economic and wage growth in Ireland was much higher than in the rest of the EU.

The general pattern of strong centralization applies particularly strongly to performance pay. In every case, with the exceptions of EngServs in the

UK, and Bankco in Germany, HQ attempted to impose a common system of individual performance pay for those employees covered by it, even if host-country resistance, either from labour or, in some cases, management, meant that this did not always lead to uniformity. Equally, where there was a bonus system for manual workers, this too tended to be centrally ordained. Although in some cases, such as ITco, national subsidiary or European-level managers may have had some say in the formulation of global policy, the resulting formula tended to become an edict which had, in principle, to be universally applied. There was, therefore, a fairly general perception that the means by which pay and performance were linked was of strategic importance, and ought to follow a corporation wide logic. The following quotation is fairly typical of this:

Engco2 has a culture of 'it wasn't invented here so therefore I'm not going to use it and I'm going to tweak it to fit my culture'. And we have encouraged some of that behaviour... but on some things we don't want people to do that, like on our performance management system. (US HQ HR director, Engco2)

In other cases, certain elements of the pay and performance package were, at least in principle, offered to the subsidiary as options, rather than as mandated policy. In other words, there was a centrally coordinated policy, which the subsidiary could choose whether or not to utilize. However, the scope for autonomy could in reality be limited due to the existence of compulsory policies for high-level subsidiary employees. This tended to mean that the pragmatic decision for subsidiary managers was simply to follow the 'optional' policy, as the constraints under which subsidiary choice operated, even for optional practices, were reinforced by the frequent need for subsidiary managers to explain and justify deviations:

[I]f [the country HR manager] wanted to say 'I don't want this central bonus scheme, I want [a different] bonus scheme', then he'd have to agree that with his vice-president, and his vice-president would say 'What's wrong with the *Engco1* scheme?', and that would be quite difficult to do. So its not 100 per cent mandated, but it's not far off! (Senior subsidiary manager, Engco1)

On job grading systems, the picture was more nuanced. For non-managerial workers at least, the local reality tended to be structured quite strongly by national occupational structures and IR systems. However, nearly all of the firms attempted to use a common system of defining jobs internationally. Thus, while difference in the detail of how individuals were allocated to grades might be permissible in order to accommodate to local pressures, a trend towards the establishment of common job descriptions across the corporation was widespread:

The pay practices are probably the most closely controlled out of the corporation on a salary grade structure. That is probably the one thing that even in the loudest days of the business units, there was enforced consistency on. So that it was a meaningful job-to-job description across the company. (Senior expatriate manager in the UK, Engco1)

Indeed, in this case, corporate HQ required specific authorization for individual promotions from supervisory level upwards. Furthermore, individuals at a relatively low hierarchical level were fully aware of this:

And grade . . . if my manager wanted me to be another grade higher, he would have to get it sanctioned by the US, without a doubt, it's not something he could just OK through the UK. (Supervisory employee, Engco1)

Although in reality subsidiary managers were able to maintain some room for manoeuvre by framing job specifications in such a way that HQ would award individuals the grade level that the subsidiary manager desired, the corporate attempt at detailed control remains notable, particularly in the context of a firm that is not otherwise among those of our sample firms most prone to centralization at the level of detail of policy.

Commonality of policy, both in terms of job classification and pay for performance, was often justified in terms of the economies of scale that flowed from a common system, by avoiding duplication of effort. This fairly obvious rationale could be used to defeat the arguments of subsidiary managers for pursuing independent strategies:

They thought (the global performance management system) was better than what I was offering, because it was company-wide and the software was there, and I can't argue with that. (Senior UK manager, Engco1)

With regard to job classification, the argument that uniformity aids cost control acted in a more fundamental way. Complex, multidivisional MNCs, operating in an era of tight cost control under the ideology of shareholder value (see Chapter 3) required a fairly precise idea of how many individuals, performing which jobs, worked in each business unit, and geography, in order to determine whether operations were sufficiently 'lean'. Of particular controversy in the era of downsizing was the identification of the number of managers and 'non-productive', non-customer-facing individuals working within departments. One aid to identifying the roles of employees would be to have uniformity of job and grade descriptions across countries and business units. This could be one justification for establishing a corporate grading system across subsidiaries, even when host-country employment systems required the parallel use of an institutionalized job classification system. At least one firm, ITco, insisted on the establishment of a European-level database, which attempted to go beyond host-country job descriptors in order to get such information as the proportion of managers to employees in different countries. The true picture could be concealed as a result of different national notions of what constituted a 'manager'. As such data could be put to uses which affected managerial job security, even the apparently simple process of counting which individuals were in which roles could be highly political, with host-country units suspected by European-level managers of disguising their true numbers of managerial workers.

Another reason for grade standardization in some of the firms relates to the internationalization of work processes. As there were increasing contacts between employees from different countries, salary and grading differences were becoming more obvious, potentially leading to problems of internal equity. This argument was specifically used by managers of the German subsidiary of Household. Additionally, the establishment of similar grading systems across the managerial hierarchy internationally could help the MNC to identify the best potential talent from its global pool of senior managers.

JOB CLASSIFICATION AND NATIONAL SYSTEMS

In contrast to the 'high performance', single status model, the majority of the subsidiaries in all four countries continued to use pay determination systems which differed significantly between workforce groups. In particular, systems often differed between manual and managerial workforces, or more precisely between those elements of the workforce who were unionized or covered by collective bargaining, and those who were non-unionized (in the British and Irish cases), or exempt from the provisions of collective bargaining (in the Spanish and German cases). Thus in the UK, the central elements of pay determination generally differed between workforce groups. The exceptions to this were EngServs, which followed a model, typical of British firms in its sector, characterized by a strong occupational labour market; and two non-union companies—ITco and Household—which historically followed a variant of what Osterman (1988) would term the American 'salaried model'.

In the three UK subsidiaries studied in which there was both a substantial manufacturing workforce and collective bargaining (CPGco, Engco1, and Engco2), there remained separate systems of job classification for manual workers and managers, with merit pay operating only for the latter (although in Engco1, where non-managerial white-collar staff were not covered by collective bargaining, this group also followed the same performance regime as managers). Thus, the employment system within the subsidiaries constructed definite barriers between different sections of the workforce. As mentioned, US authorization was sometimes needed for promotion between these groups.

In our Irish cases, there were also divides between managerial and non-managerial labour, but these were complicated by 'double-breasting' in two of the firms (Pharmaco and Healthco; see Chapter 6), whereby older plants were unionized and newer ones union-free. This led to a division based on location as well as employee status, with a segmented system in the unionized plants, but a 'performance-based' system for all in the non-union plants. As in the UK, single systems pertained in the entirely non-union firms.

The Spanish cases showed a high degree of variety. There were cases where job classification clearly followed sectoral or firm-level agreements for manual workers, with separate systems for managers (Chemco and EngServs), and a number of cases where this was less apparent. However, the majority continued to fall short of 'single status' type arrangements, with performance management and benefits/bonus regimes differing considerably between groups. Only ITco reported no differences in its wage determination system between different hierarchical groups.

Finally, in Germany, the direct and indirect effects of the sectoral bargaining system meant that systems were generally quite distinct between 'exempt' and 'non-exempt' workers. It is not a coincidence that the only two German subsidiaries with unified systems (ITco and Silico) were among those US MNCs that had long rejected the German sectoral bargaining system.

Broadbanding

As indicated earlier, many large US firms have moved towards 'broadbanding' in their home country, as a means of reducing the costs of the ILM and achieving some degree of qualitative flexibility of labour. These changes are reflected in a number of our cases across different countries, notably in Pharmaco Ireland, Silico Germany, and ITco globally. Given the relative freedom of US MNCs in the UK to restructure grading systems, however, the UK cases are of specific interest and are worth devoting some space to.

For each of the unionized manufacturing subsidiaries (CPGco, Engco1, and Engco2), significant changes to manual grading structures occurred at around the same time as the formal introduction of teamworking. It is therefore probable that the new systems were introduced as part of an attempt to achieve some degree of polyvalence among manual workers, through the reduction of demarcations between different groups.

In each of these three firms, the form taken by the new system was remarkably similar. There was a marked compression of grades, with the number of manual grades reduced to an absolute minimum (only three or four grades were used in practice). Given the continuing distinction, in all three firms, between 'craft' and 'assembly/production' workers, this meant that the possibility of promotion between grades, or any sort of incremental progression, for the majority of the manual workforce was very low, except where former manual workers left direct production jobs to take on supervisory roles. Equally, there was little possibility for intra-grade promotion; within each grade, there was merely a 'training' rate and an 'established' rate.

I think that's a disappointment, I think that's an area where we've missed. What we have at the moment, there's only two, it's basically there's only two, and I think this is an opportunity that we need to work on. There's two rates for the job. If you are an emulsion operator, you'd be S4, you'd either be established rate, or starting rate, training rate. And what it is, training rate, there is a matrix of tasks and activities that you have to learn how to do, there's certain behaviours there with an objective, sort of matrix. Once you're above that certain level, you then become established rate. So there's only two bands, now I think that's an opportunity for us because one of the things I think we now realize is, . . . if you're in that established rate, what is there in there to encourage you to do more than just you need to? (UK manufacturing manager, CPGco)

Each of these firms, then, lacked any forms of competence-related job ladders, or any form of 'strategic pay' aimed at encouraging continuing skills acquisition among the manual workforce. This is despite the fact that such practices are used in one form or other by a significant minority of large firms in the UK (Almond, 1999). The very simple, non-progressive systems adopted in these three firms can probably be related to issues of work organization, in particular the form of teamworking adopted. Teamworking in its more radical sense (i.e. representing a strong break with Taylorism by moving towards a multiskilled workforce) would tend to imply either a move away from a work-post–based system to a competence-based system, or a broadening in capabilities-based classifications within the work-post system. In these firms, however, the form teamworking took was somewhat more limited, consisting mainly of an attempt to reduce demarcation problems rather than to move towards the regular use of workers' multi-functionality. In other words, the form of teamworking adopted in all three of these firms was relatively 'neo-Tayloristic' (Pruijt 2003) with implications for the form of job grading pursued (for a discussion of teamworking in some of the UK cases, see Colling and Clark 2003). Indeed, in CPGco, the move towards teamworking was basically a cultural artefact rather than a reorganization of work or hierarchy—team leaders, for instance, were difficult to distinguish from traditional supervisors, as they did not generally engage in production work, were at a higher hierarchical level and were stationed in offices.

In these firms, then, innovation in the relationship between wage classifications and work organization was limited to a compression in the number of grades, and even this was not necessarily strongly driven by the home country HQ. In CPGco, for example, broadbanding itself was specifically rejected for American operations, where it was felt necessary to retain a grading system with strong echoes of New Deal-type arrangements in order to combat the threat of unionization.

The non-union UK subsidiaries used various forms of 'salaried' models. In two cases, these closely followed established sectoral models. Hence, in all the countries covered, Business Services practised a model widely used among consultancy firms, with salary points within fairly broad categories being determined by appraisal ratings and labour market conditions. EngServs UK used a fairly informal model with very wide grade descriptors and a loosely constructed system of wage progression. Respondents claimed that the latter model was very similar to that used in the wider engineering contracting industry in the UK.

Finally, the most sophisticated and complex system, which in principle covered Spain, Ireland, and Germany, as well as the UK, was that of ITco. This was essentially a globally uniform system, and could be described as a single-status 'salaried model' as all work posts were, in principle, evaluated according to the same criteria. Once again, there was a process of broadbanding. The company moved in the mid-1990s from a complex system in which a very large number of official job titles were allocated to over twenty salary grades, to a system with ten broad bands covering the entire managerial and non-managerial workforces. The positioning of jobs into and within bands was determined according to three factors: skills, leadership requirement, and job scope. Although in principle what was thus being classified remained the required abilities to perform a certain level of job, not the individual, the flexible system of grading was intended to allow new types of work, which emerge relatively frequently in the IT sector, to be allocated easily to grades by line managers. The company also sought actively to reward individual development through the high proportion of pay related to the results of performance appraisal, for which once again there was a common system for all employees.

Thus in the UK, where there are few extra-firm constraints on employer choices, the degree of innovation was not, with the exception of ITco, particularly high. While some managers regretted this, there was, outside ITco, little interest in putting in place 'complex' systems. This is possibly because the—American—aim generally was simplicity and particularly to avoid the complexities of the New Deal system. There were also host-country effects, at least for the firms that were unionized in the UK; union negotiators' distrust of any form of individual appraisal tended to outweigh any interest in employee career progression. Nevertheless, the weakness of any formal ILM mechanisms for non-managerial workers did reflect a relative lack of corporate-level interest in continual upgrading of the skills of the non-managerial workforce.

Pay Determination in The German Subsidiaries

US MNCs policies on basic wage determination were generally more innovative (or challenging) in the more actively regulated German system, where the constraints on wage flexibility posed by the sectoral bargaining system presented a significant issue in a number of cases. As explored in more detail in Chapter 6, only three of the German subsidiaries studied were members of an employers' association and hence, directly covered by sectoral bargaining. Further, none of these simply conformed to the German wage bargaining system. Logistico had joined its employers' association relatively recently (1991) in an attempt to influence the policies of the association. Since 1998, Bankco had been in serious conflict with unions, which involved strike actions and consumer boycott campaigns. The background to this conflict was the centralization of regional call centres into a non-union site, as well as the use of franchisees not covered by collective agreement in branches. Behind this move was management's aim to pay lower and more flexible wages than possible under the collective agreement.

CPGco had moved its operations from the metal industry agreement to a sub-agreement of the chemical industry. The main advantage for CPGco was that the minimum wage for particular positions set by the latter agreement was much lower, thus increasing pay flexibility and leaving more room for performance-related pay. Furthermore, as any employee whose salary was significantly higher than the highest wage defined by the sectoral agreement was an 'exempt' worker, and as this level was much lower in the new agreement, the percentage of non-tariff employees or exempts increased substantially from 70 to 80 per cent of the workforce. Hence, for the majority of the workforce, annual salary increases were no longer guaranteed. An additional advantage of this move from the company's perspective was that CPGco was the largest employer in its new employers' association and thus had a more substantial impact on bargaining outcomes.

Unlike the firms discussed so far, Household was not a member of an employer's association, but was required to comply with the conditions of sectoral bargaining as it belonged to an industry, where all employers are required by law to follow the industrywide agreement. HR managers in Household, and also in Logistico claimed that, because they paid well above tariff, the requirements of the collective bargaining agreements had little impact.

Of the remaining four firms, Business Services, Engco2 and Silico were not covered by sectoral bargaining. Engco2 (with only a small number of employees, all sales and distribution, in Germany) concluded an agreement with its works council to link pay levels to the industry collective agreements and guarantee its employees at least 80 per cent of the annual salary increase of the metalworking tariff, with the remaining 20 per cent determined by assessment of individual performance, while Silico left the engineering sector employers' association in 1974.

ITco used the reorganization of its German operations into several legally independent firms in 1993 to leave the metal employers' association for most of its units. Only its shrinking production sites were still covered by the engineering sector agreement. Although the main reason behind this move was the introduction of the 35-hour working week in the industry, pay inflexibility was also another factor. According to the managing director of the German operations at the time, 90 per cent of annual increases were determined by the industrywide agreement, with only 10 per cent left for individual incentives. The company agreement concluded at the time left much more room for performance-related pay, as is discussed later.

Thus only three of the nine US subsidiaries in Germany complied more or less fully with the requirements of sectoral collective bargaining. In contrast, in six firms we observed that multi-employer bargaining was avoided, or its impact reduced. Overall, it seems that the German labour market institution of multi-employer bargaining does not prove an insuperable institutional constraint for US firms. The German system is primarily constraining on the issue of base pay; once firms pay above the industry tariff, sometimes by careful selection of which regional sectoral agreement they are covered by, there is in fact considerable leeway. Additionally, as explored in Chapter 6, the possibility of establishing company-level understandings, where works councils are compliant, can also offer considerable flexibility in practice. Alongside the general anti-union animus of some of the firms, a desire to avoid pay constraints—particularly to allow more scope for merit pay—was a significant reason why many US MNCs in Germany expended considerable energy to avoid following the standard sectoral system. This was much more of an issue in Germany than in the UK, where a greater degree of flexibility was possible within pluralist IR arrangements.

PERFORMANCE MANAGEMENT

Performance and Pay

A number of different techniques were used to reward either collective or individual performance. First, in all four countries many of the companies usually offered a bonus depending on business results. These varied in nature from the very simple system of CPGco UK, based on corporate performance, moderated by seniority, to cases such as Engco1 and Engco2 UK, where the systems were complex and strategically orientated, aiming to support cultural goals such as teamworking and empowerment. However, their success in achieving such goals was limited by the relatively small financial amounts involved; indeed, in Engco1 UK, a complex system requiring that employees 'demonstrated on a daily basis that they were working within the cultural values' was consolidated into basic pay in order to prevent industrial action over the annual wage settlement. The majority of firms also had share ownership, generally for all employees. In a minority of firms, qualification for bonus schemes or share ownership was dependent on individual performance appraisal (Logistico, Softco, and ITco)

Second, and perhaps unsurprisingly, all of our case-study organizations had performance-related pay for at minimum professional, non-unionized employees, or 'exempt' employees, while in a minority, including the non-union subsidiaries in the UK and Ireland, salaries were adjusted on an individual basis throughout the hierarchy (Business Services and ITco in all the countries studied, plus Compuco Ireland, EngServs UK, Household UK and Refresco Spain).

Performance-related pay systems were generally formal in nature and, as suggested earlier, tended to be standardized within companies across different subsidiaries. Policies were generally developed in the USA before being exported to foreign subsidiaries, although there was a degree of European input in the design of the performance management system in the case of ITco. Hence, within individual firms, the overall nature of performance pay systems did not differ greatly from one European subsidiary to another.

There was no particular commonality between the different MNCs, however, in the proportion of pay determined by the results of performance appraisal, with the financial impact of appraisal results varying from the fairly tokenistic (between 0.5 and 1 percentage point on the wage increase at Pharmaco Ireland) to the significant, as in ITco, where, depending on business performance, the annual pay increase for the best and worst performers on the same hierarchical level could vary by up to 15 per cent, before taking into consideration non-consolidated bonuses, which were also dependent on performance appraisal.

In general, the nature of performance measurement and its consequences do appear to have changed, from a system which offered most employees a form of annual bonus payment, to one which fitted more comfortably with 'strategic' visions of HRM. Equally, the nature of performance criteria had altered: objective criteria based on performance within the job were supplemented by measures of more 'cultural', harder-to-quantify goals such as cooperation within the team, valuing diversity, and so on.

Notably, CPGco, Engco2, and ITco had begun to base performance appraisal, and hence merit pay, not narrowly on business results, but also on performance against competencies, corporate values, or personal qualities and characteristics (for instance, leadership, valuing diversity). In this way, firms attempted to use remuneration to reinforce, and sometimes to change, corporate values, and hence it could be argued that individual performance pay was increasingly being used to support corporate strategy. This could be another reason why such firms were anxious to ensure cross-national uniformity in the area of performance management.

If such measures could be interpreted as belonging to the 'soft', more developmental, side of strategic HRM, then other trends owed distinctly more to 'hard' HRM. In an increasing number of the subsidiaries, not just in the less regulated British and Irish contexts but also in three of the German operations (Business Services, ITco, and Silico), annual pay increases were directly linked to 'merit' via appraisal results, and low performers might not receive any increase at all. At the time of the research, performance-related pay in addition to basic pay was also being negotiated between managers and the trade union for branch employees in Bankco in Germany. Perhaps unsurprisingly, however, strong forms of performance-related pay remained controversial in Germany. For example, one of our German respondents in Business Services reported that global proposals for a strong link between appraisal and merit increases, connected with a high variance in merit pay, created considerable resistance among staff in Germany:

It aimed to produce large differences in pay for performance, i.e. that top perform-ers would receive much higher pay than good or average performers ... which was something we had not had in such an extreme form before. There was a lot of resistance in Germany, and in Austria and Switzerland, because it goes against our culture.... The attitude in Germany is that if someone performs very well, they should be paid very well. But someone who performs well should also be paid well. We didn't want to have such large differences; we found them just too blatant. (HR manager, Business Services Germany)

As a result, the policy was introduced in a weaker form and was further adapted to fit better with German expectations a year later. Similar resist-ance to large differentials in performance-related pay awards was also found in Business Services' Spanish operations. In both countries the policies were, on the face of it, made easier by the fact that the firms operated outside the confines of sectoral collective bargaining systems, as the relevant employees were 'exempts', yet considerable resistance to them remained. In contrast, the pay proposals apparently met with little resistance from the company's British workforce as they were more in line with national sectoral practices. This reflects the fact that barriers to transfer are not always purely institutional, and also reflect societal norms and concepts of fairness.

Institutional factors were still of some importance, however. We have already pointed out that none of the workforce groups covered by collect-ive bargaining in either Britain or Ireland were subjected to individual mechanisms of merit pay. Equally, among non-union groups, care was taken to avoid performance management systems causing workplace unrest or moves towards unionization. For example, in Logistico Ireland, a union official claimed that while pay increases were supposed to be determined through internal performance appraisals for these employees, the company are clever... they never give less than (the increase in the national) centralized agreements so they know we can't really lodge a pay claim or grievance.

Forced Distributions

There was evidence of forced distributions in some, but by no means all, companies. Under such systems, a certain percentage of employees has to be allocated to each performance rating, in order to avoid appraisal 'errors' such as a central tendency or leniency. The chief examples of forced distributions were found in ITco (all countries), Chemco (Britain and Spain), Silico (Germany), Business Services (UK), and Engco2. The logic behind this form of system is explained by a white-collar employee in Engco1:

How much we can afford is a big factor in the performance appraisal because we've only got a certain pot of money that we have.... The way we used to do perform-ance appraisals were that you grade people, you say 1 is excellent, 3 is not so good. And there were also some 4s and 5s, but 4 would be okay you really need to do something, 5 would be you might just pack up your desk and go. Some managers didn't use anything below 3 so they would give 3 to everybody and they would reward people by giving them a 2 or 1. The problem there was that you can have any number of, you can have like a grading of 3, you can have a 3 which was genuinely 3, or you could have a 3 which was, well, it probably should have been 4 or 5 but the managers weren't going to do that. So what corporate did was they brought in a normal distribution that says you have to give 10–15 per cent of your workforce 4 and 5. You can only give 10 per cent of your workforce 1 or 2, therefore the bulk of it is going to be 3. But you have to force people into the 4s and 5s, and you have to reward the 1s and 2s. (White-collar employee, Engco1 UK)

However, in several of our firms we were told that those responsible for assessment resisted placing subordinates in the lowest performance cat-egory and tried to 'play the system', which tended to undermine its logic:

The problem that happened is that with a normal distribution, although corpor-ately you had to get to the normal distribution, each of the departments depending on who shouted the loudest, may well have said there's no way, I can't find anybody in my group to give a 4 or 5. Then it would be up to somebody else in another department to give somebody a 4 or 5, who perhaps if you compared the two people [the result might be different]. (White-collar employee, Engco1)

Because of these problems, *Engco1* moved away from a 'forced' to a 'man-aged' distribution, as also practised by CPGco, Compuco Ireland, and Chemco Spain:

because it's a hierarchical system of evaluation, what I would tend to do for instance on an annual basis is to collect that data and look at the distribution and inevitably it comes out skewed towards better than average. Now, I won't force back, I won't change the numbers, but what I will do is to force back the criteria. I will point out to a manager who has perhaps done ten and it's heavily skewed to above average, I'll say look, those are the measurement criteria, I want you to reevaluate your expectations, were they high enough, given the circumstances? I would force them to re-look at those numbers. If they give me a strong enough argument and came back and said, look, this is a skewed distribution, I genuinely have a better than average group of people, and this is benchmark data I am using this is why, I'll accept it. (European HR manager, CPGco)

IMPLICATIONS FOR EMPLOYMENT SECURITY

The issue of forced distributions is particularly sensitive when the data gathered are not only used to determine pay increases but also affect the job security of the individual. The dismissal of those individuals with poor performance may occur in one of two ways.

The more extreme form is the 'culling' model, where those in the bottom 10–20 per cent are at risk of dismissal. There was an explicit attempt to introduce such a system for managerial employees in Engco2, as part of a drive by a new CEO to make the organization more focused on performance. UK managers made sustained attempts to change this policy, including commissioning an HR academic to discuss how this breached the 'psychological contract'. Although these attempts failed, there is substantial evidence that in practice local managers successfully resisted the spirit of the policy, partly by refusing to place individuals in the bottom category where the groups of employees to be assessed were small, and partly by classifying employees who had already left the firm in the lowest performing category. It is also perhaps worth noting that although Engco2 theoretically practised the same policy in Germany, at the time of research no employee had been dismissed as a result of poor performance ratings.

Business Services (at least in the UK and Spain) also had a policy of 'counselling out' the lowest performers in its consulting workforce, but the implications of this for a consulting workforce were different, as the practice formed part of the 'up-or-out' ILM expectations of this occupational group. There was also the implicit threat in Refresco Spain that 'poor performers can be given training if necessary, but those who don't want to improve become surplus to requirements' (Spanish HR Manager), while similar sentiments were expressed by UK managers in Household.

Elsewhere, while there was no explicit policy of 'culling' the lowest performers in a forced distribution, it is clear that those in the bottom groups were, all things being equal, the most likely candidates to be victims of downsizing, as well as being at risk of being 'managed art' of the organisation more generally. This is particularly clearly the case in ITco. This is to some extent legally questionable, even in the UK, and led to legal challenges in some European countries. It also led to some variation in practice between the national subsidiaries of ITco, despite the uniformity of policy. In the Irish operations, where there was no collective employee influence, managers stressed, in the first place, efforts to rectify poor performance:

I suppose if you took it that there's a likelihood that there is this 10 per cent population in the low, very low bracket, we would have an expectation of ourselves that we would turn 7 per cent of them around and have them performing at least the middle of the road by the end of any given year. (Business Partner, ITco Ireland)

However, the implications for those with repeated poor performance were clear:

The ones that don't move [i.e. improve their rating] would be managed out. Now, that would be a very small amount of people across the board. (Business Partner, ITco Ireland)

I think if you got a 4, the next thing would be your P45 [termination of employment form]. I suppose in that situation, your manager would definitely be telling you before the event if you were going to be a 4. (Employee, ITco Ireland)

The UK situation was similar to the Irish case, with the significant contingent factor that while core employment in ITco Ireland had grown significantly, ITco UK had been prone to restructuring and downsizing. It was acknowledged by UK managers that performance ratings were used to identify candidates for redundancy during these periods. In Germany, as in Ireland, efforts to improve the performance of low-ranking individuals were stressed, this time by a senior works councillor:

[T]here is a very small number of employees every year who do not participate in the development of salaries. In these cases there are, and this is agreed upon [i.e. with the works council], measures in order to lead these [employees] back to performance. And if they perform, they will participate in the next increase in salary. There are measures such as further training, coaching, transfer, etc. And within this system you can make up a missed salary increase in a very short time.

Unlike in Ireland, however, due to collective and legal barriers in Germany, we were unable to find any evidence that poor performance had implications for employment security. In Spain, where the legal barriers to the dismissal of permanent employees are also high, the initial measures for dealing with poor performers were similar to those in Germany. However, if after extensive training the lowest performers were not able to change their rankings over a maximum of two years, they were 'invited' to leave the company, but would receive severance pay well over the legal minimum in order to avoid legal challenges or union conflict.

Despite the legal and institutional problems surrounding forced distributions, and particularly their use to determine employment security, there is evidence that US MNCs could finesse these obstacles. For example, in Compuco Ireland, employees who received a very low ranking on more than one occasion were 'encouraged' to leave the company. In commenting on the fate of employees who received more than one 4 or 5 rating, the VP HR of Ireland stated:

Yeah. I'm quoting numbers off my head now, it's ballpark, but I think there is, of the 4/5 population (those rated 4 or 5) there is 87 of 300 gone. So read the writing on the wall.

When asked if their departure was voluntary or initiated by the company he continued:

I would say 80 per cent voluntarily; others have been told that the future is bleaker and bleaker. It generally doesn't come down to you having to dismiss them. A couple of those cases but that's not typical and my experience is that it doesn't play out that way in most cases.

Nonetheless, this feature of the performance management system of some US MNCs remains controversial, both for legal reasons and because it fails to fit with the societal norms surrounding the employment relationship in European countries.

CONCLUSIONS

As this chapter has illustrated, pay and performance management tended to be quite highly centralized among most case-study firms. US MNCs in general seemed to regard this element of HRM practice as central to their employment systems. In particular, performance management systems were generally highly centralized, and a high degree of cross-national uniformity was expected. The chapter links this both to structural factors, such as the internationalization of career management (see also Chapter 9) and country-of-origin dynamics arising from the entrenched concept of a free market for labour, encapsulated in the notion of 'employment at will'. Additionally, dynamics arising from the increased short-termist pressures on US firms may have led to greater pressure to create relatively uniform systems in areas such as job classification.

Nonetheless, the picture was not uniform. There was variation between firms on a number of dimensions. The nature of specific sectoral or occupational labour markets, such as those for engineering specialists or consultants, produced specific patterns. Equally, differences in the extent of collective coverage caused considerable variations, particularly in the UK where pay and performance management systems for non-managerial workers differed very significantly according to whether trade unions were recognized or not.

The chapter suggested that, at least in the manufacturing firms, job grading systems continue to be embedded in Taylorist and Fordist assumptions. Despite the recent popularity of 'broadbanding', as a means of simplifying and limiting the extent of ILMs for non-manual workers, innovation in this area was in some ways limited. Outside those firms which had developed non-union HRM systems over a long period of time, relatively little attention seemed to have been paid to the potential for linking pay mechanisms to the continued acquisition of manual skills.

The challenge that the majority of our case-study firms presented to host-country employment systems was primarily in the area of individual pay for performance. In particular, the ranking of individuals within performance management systems has become more competitive, as represented by the use of forced distributions, at the same time as becoming increasingly subjective, through the strategic use of performance management to encourage certain 'cultural' behaviours. Elements of this, particularly the links between performance and individual employment security, have caused problems in a number of subsidiaries, due to incompatibilities both in employment law and in social notions of the nature of the employment relationship. It is notable, for instance, that ITco did not attempt to impose a link between performance and employment security in Germany, where there are substantial legal and collective barriers to such a practice. Even in Britain, where the constraints are much weaker, managers' socialized perceptions of fairness sometimes led them to oppose both forced distributions themselves, and so-called 'culling' models. Nevertheless, although there is intra-national variation in the precise operation of performance management systems within individual MNCs, it is notable that where standardized systems were attempted, they tended to remain quite uniform across countries in respect of such elements as performance criteria and the nature of the distribution. This suggests a strong determination by US MNCs to overcome host-country effects in this area, for reasons partly to do with efficiency and cost reduction, and partly with the creation of strong cross-national ILMs for strategic groups of managers and key professionals.

8

Workforce Diversity Policies

*Anthony Ferner, Michael Morley, Michael Muller-Camen,
and Lourdes Susaeta*

INTRODUCTION

This chapter[1] explores international workforce 'diversity' policies within American MNCs. Diversity is in some senses a defining issue of HR policy transfer between countries, since it has its roots in distinctive features of the US business environment—demographic, socio-political, and legal—that have given rise to a particular constellation of 'equal employment opportunity' and 'business case' diversity agendas. There is evidence that US companies are now attempting to internationalize 'diversity', partly in response to the challenges of managing diverse international workforces. This chapter investigates how diversity policies in US MNCs travel to host systems with different demographic patterns and legal traditions, which may make the application of an American diversity agenda appear problematic.

The next section shows how diversity as it has emerged in US corporations reflects a specifically American policy agenda, albeit one that is highly contested. It provides comparative data for the host countries to show how the national political, demographic, and legal traditions vary widely among them. The third section presents the findings from the American case studies. It first investigates the prevalence of corporate international diversity policies in different companies, and then looks at how diversity policy is implemented in subsidiaries operating in the four host countries. In particular it draws attention to the *process* whereby international policy is assimilated, accommodated to, or resisted by actors in the subsidiaries. The fourth section probes the factors underlying the pattern of variation, both across companies and across countries, in the propagation and implementation of diversity policies.

WORKFORCE 'DIVERSITY' AND THE US BUSINESS SYSTEM

The diversity agenda in the USA is deeply marked by tensions between 'equal employment opportunities' (EEO) and 'business case' strands, giving rise to what we have called a 'contested institutional terrain' (Ferner et al. 2005). The former strand, EEO, together with the associated political agenda of affirmative action (AA), has been embodied in a legislative programme stretching back to the mid-1960s. It has generated a host of policies and procedures within companies to ensure legal compliance with its provisions. The business case strand is symptomatic of a more voluntarist corporate approach to 'valuing difference'. In this chapter, 'diversity' is used in the broad sense to encompass both strands and 'diversity management' to refer to the proactive and voluntary development of initiatives at company level.

The racial and social heterogeneity that has marked the USA, deriving first from slavery and later from successive waves of mass immigration, has been a primary influence on the emergence of 'diversity' as a political and corporate agenda. First, ethnic minorities are a high and rapidly growing proportion of the population, and hence both an important source of labour and skills, and a considerable consumer base (SHRM 2002). Currently, ethnic minorities (largely black and Hispanic but also Asian) constitute around 30 per cent of the American workforce—an increase from 22 per cent in the mid-1980s. In relation to gender, women also represent a high proportion of available labour—around 47 per cent of the total workforce, and a majority in ethnic minority communities.

Second, from the 1960s, minorities and women were the protagonists of a civil rights movement that, in tandem with severe racial tensions in the cities, transformed the legislative and political landscape. Title VII of the Civil Rights Act 1964 outlawed discrimination on the basis of race, colour, religion, sex, and national origin, and set up the Equal Employment Opportunities Commission (EEOC) to act on job discrimination. Executive orders imposed affirmative action on companies that wished to do business with the US government. Subsequent legislation outlawed pay discrimination on the basis of sex, age, and disability (Dessler 2001: Chapter 2). Although the legislative framework compelled companies to consider issues of compliance, major lapses, even among 'high profile' companies, were not uncommon and could result in expensive legal action.

The US diversity agenda has long been riven with ambiguity and tensions. The extensive legislation, while acknowledged as among the strongest and most sophisticated in the world, is costly and difficult to enforce, with critics complaining of 'litigious gridlock' (Bond and Pile 1998; see also Baker 2002). One reason is the weakness of the underpinning institutional supports that are important in enforcing statutory provisions in European countries through the interlocking of legal and social regulation, as Rubery et al. (1999) and Whitehouse (1992) have emphasized (see also Metcalf, Hansen, and Charlwood 2001). In particular, collective employee mechanisms of pressure, such as coordinated collective bargaining and well-developed systems of union representation, are notably absent in the US EEO/diversity context. Reflecting this lack of social embeddedness, the concept of AA has become a political battleground, and corporate interests have lobbied periodically for a more voluntarist approach (Dickens 1999).

Partly as a consequence of the contested nature of the terrain, and partly in the light of demographic trends, a concern with compliance has, from the 1980s onwards, been increasingly supplemented by attention to the 'business case' for diversity management (e.g. Cox and Blake 1991; Richard 2000; SHRM 2002). This rests on drawing 'competitive advantage' from workforce diversity. The sources of such advantage are threefold: first, the ability to attract skilled workers from a wider range of sub-communities and to retain them within the company; second, the potential for increasing the demand for a company's products and services by targeting diverse consumers; and third, the scope for improving organizational creativity and learning by harnessing a 'diverse' range of perspectives and ideas (e.g. Cox 1994; Dass and Parker 1999; SHRM 2002). It should be noted, however, that evidence of a link between diversity and business performance is inconclusive (Jehn, Northcraft, and Neale 1999; Kochan et al. 2003).

This voluntarist approach to diversity management is more individualistic than the collective approach to managing diverse employee groups implicit in EEO legislation. In practice, corporate diversity management programmes tend to focus on individual needs and abilities, sometimes serving to heighten rather than diminish inequality between groups (e.g. Agócs and Burr 1996). This is reflected in the substantial slippage in the meaning of diversity. The concept is increasingly used to embrace a wide range of personal characteristics, diluting the focus on disadvantaged groups such as ethnic minorities and women. There are, furthermore, unresolved tensions between the fairness and equity principles underlying EEO and managerial concerns with 'business case' and efficiency rationales (e.g. Bond and Pile 1998). The latter may imply a move away from diversity policies should the business case change (e.g. Dickens 1999). Indeed in certain periods, and for certain kinds of company, the 'business case' has underpinned ruthless exploitation of ethnic and gender divisions in the labour market (e.g. Gordon, Edwards, and Reich 1982). The practical outcome of this 'contested terrain' is that, while the earnings gap for female workers has decreased significantly in recent years (Mishel, Bernstein, and Boushey 2003: 171–2), on other measures, such as pay dispersal between high and low earners, the USA continues to have the most unequal labour market in the developed world (p. 408).

Despite these tensions, formal diversity management programmes are well-entrenched in large US corporations. Three quarters of the largest companies had some form of diversity management programme in the late 1990s (Egan and Bendick 2001: 2). Diversity dimensions were incorporated into a wide range of corporate activities, including leadership development, corporate 'values', recruitment and retention, career development, community relations, and supplier relations. Many companies developed structures of involvement, such as 'diversity councils' and 'affinity groups' for specific sub-groups of the workforce such as women, ethnic minorities, and gay and lesbian employees.

The scant evidence available on diversity programmes in US MNCs (Egan and Bendick 2001; Wentling and Palma-Rivas 2000) suggests that in recent years companies have sought to diffuse diversity initiatives to international operations, particularly as they have acquired increasingly 'diverse' global workforces. International diversity initiatives tend to mirror domestic policies, albeit on a less wide-ranging scale. For example, diversity has been incorporated into common global corporate values; companies have established global diversity teams and administrative structures; and global diversity training programmes have been introduced. In general, though, overseas subsidiaries have had considerable scope to adapt policies to local circumstances.

THE DIVERSITY CONTEXT IN THE HOST COUNTRIES

This section outlines the domestic context of diversity in the four host countries. It highlights significant cross-national differences in levels of ethnic heterogeneity and of female participation in the labour force, and how gender, ethnic, and other dimensions of 'diversity' are dealt with in public policy in different countries. All four countries operate within a framework of EU law. The most important piece of legislation affecting diversity issues is the EU's Employment Directive of 2000, which required Member States to introduce new prohibitions on employment discrimination relating to religion, sexual orientation, and age in addition to regulations covering race- and gender-based discrimination.

UK

The UK legal tradition in this area draws substantially on US legislation (Liff and Wajcman 1996), and differs from much of continental Europe in having a less generic and more highly developed legislative framework. The UK legislation outlaws discrimination in pay and employment on the grounds of gender, national origin, ethnicity, and disability. The key pieces of legislation include the Sex Discrimination Acts 1975 and 1986, the Equal Pay Act 1970, the Race Relations Act 1976, and the Disability Discrimination Act 1995. The UK has in addition adapted to the EU framework of law on employment opportunity: regulations transposing into UK law, EU provisions covering religion and sexual orientation came into force in December 2003, while age regulations were in preparation at the time of writing. UK legislation and jurisprudence have generally emphasized equality of opportunity or 'equal treatment' rather than equality of outcomes. In contrast to the USA, positive discrimination has been discouraged. Remedies tend to be open to individuals rather than groups (see Johnson and Johnstone 2000): i.e. each affected individual has to bring a separate claim. Compared with the USA, unions in the UK have played a greater role in the evolution of legislation (Colling and Dickens 2001; Heery 1998).

The demographic drivers of diversity are also substantially different compared with the USA. Race and ethnic affiliation are less significant in relation to labour market policy. Ethnic minorities account for only 9 per cent of the total UK population. Gender has been the primary basis of labour market segmentation; although the UK has one of the highest female employment rates in Europe, at 65 per cent in 2003, it is highly segmented by employment status: for example, 41 per cent of female employees work part-time in Britain, compared with 18 per cent in the USA.

Germany

The German legislative traditions of diversity are significantly different from the Anglo-Saxon pattern and intertwine with different demographic underpinnings. To a much greater extent than the UK, German legislation will be affected by the incorporation into national law of EU regulation, in particular the 2000 Employment Directive. However, this will only be transposed into German law from 2006 (Müller-Camen and Krüger 2004). There is not yet a legal definition of victimization; some case law has dealt sporadically with the term, but not as comprehensively as required by the European directive (Mahlmann 2002: 26). Likewise, the burden of proof in discrimination cases lies generally with the wronged employee, and there is no reversal of the burden of proof as required by the European directive (except in the area of gender discrimination).

The main anti-discrimination provisions are Articles 3.1 and 3.3 of the German Constitution. The law requires all persons to be treated as equals before the law and outlaws discriminatory treatment on the grounds of sex, parentage, race, language, national origin, religion, political opinions, and disability. However, these provisions pertain to the public sphere and only indirectly affect the private sphere, where provision is vague and ambiguous (Mahlmann 2002: 10). In addition, under the Works Constitution Act (BetrVG), it is the duty of a works council to monitor the company's compliance with legal regulations, among which discrimination provisions are explicitly mentioned (§ 75 BetrVG).

Despite the broad scope of regulation, case law has tended to concentrate on gender discrimination. The legislative approach to gender discrimination is also more proactive compared to the relatively passive approach seen in other areas: Article 3.2 of the Constitution asserts that 'men and women are equal' and subsequent legislation has reinforced the notion of equal rights and equality of treatment (Krell 2001). A further area covered by legislative provision is that of the disabled. Companies with more than 20 employees are required to allocate 5 per cent of their jobs to disabled people or pay a penalty. However, this is a relatively low proportion and in 2001 the percentage of disabled employees in German organizations was only 3.8 per cent (Stuber 2003: 52).

The ethnic composition of the German labour force was transformed by a mass influx of migrant 'guest workers' from the mid-1950s. Between 1955 and 1973 around 11 million guest workers entered the country from southern Europe and Turkey, and there have been subsequent waves of immigration, albeit on a smaller scale, since the 1990s. Currently, over 7 million non-Germans work in the country. In comparison with the UK or France, the impact of migrant populations was initially limited by stringent nationality laws which denied German nationality to those whose forebears were not themselves German, and there has been fierce debate over the role of immigrants in German society. Legal reforms, however, have allowed around 2 million people of foreign descent—mainly second generation 'guest workers'—to become German citizens since 1990.

In this context, German companies have been relatively slow to consider a diversity management agenda (Müller-Camen and Krüger 2004; Wächter et al. 2003). Where these practices exist in German companies, they often only cover gender. Nonetheless, women are not well represented at the decision-making level of German firms: between 5 and 8 per cent of managers and a mere 1 per cent of board members are female (Stuber 2003). 'Explicit agendas covering aspects of diversity other than gender, such as race or ethnicity...' are underdeveloped in most German companies compared with their American counterparts. In this respect it is interesting that Deutsche Bank, one of the few companies to engage strongly with diversity management, merged in 1999 with the US-based Bankers Trust, which in turn had one of the most developed diversity management approaches in the USA. At the same time, however, the institutional embeddedness of diversity is in some respects greater than in the USA, particularly through the involvement of bodies of workforce representation such as works councils in the implementation of policies.

The principal question to be addressed, therefore, is how far US case-study subsidiaries were able, as HR pioneers and innovators, to implement a diversity agenda in the significantly different German environment.

Ireland

Under Article 40.1 of the Irish Constitution, all citizens are held equal before the law. Beyond this constitutional provision, the legislative context for diversity in Ireland was historically dealt with under two key Acts: the Anti-discrimination Pay Act 1974, which prohibited pay discrimination on the grounds of sex or marital status; and the Employment Equality Act 1977, which concerned itself with employment discrimination on grounds relating to gender, marital status, race, religious and political beliefs, and trade union membership or activity. In more recent years the provisions of these two earlier pieces of legislation have been subsumed under two new Acts, which together represent a significant development in Irish equality law. Discrimination at work is dealt with under the provisions of the Employment Equality Act, 1998–2004, discrimination outside the workplace under the Equal Status Act, 2000–2004. Under both Acts, discrimination is prohibited on nine specific grounds: gender; marital status; family status; sexual orientation; religious beliefs; age; disability; race, colour, nationality, ethnic or national origins; and membership of the Traveller community.

The demographics of the Irish labour force are very distinct from the US pattern in relation both to ethnic diversity and female participation. Ireland has been characterized until very recently by a marked gender segmentation, with female employment rates[2] as low as 37 per cent in 1992 (Eurostat 2004). However, in recent years the female employment rate has expanded very rapidly, reaching 56 per cent in 2002. In terms of ethnicity, the Irish population has traditionally been marked by a high degree of national and ethnic homogeneity, with the exception of the Traveller community, numbered in some tens of thousands, which has tended to remain on the margins of the formal labour market. Commentators characterize the 'internationalization' of the Irish labour market in recent years as swift and dramatic, unprecedented in the context of the Irish economy. The growth in the labour market from approximately 1 million in the early 1990s to approximately 1.8 million today has been matched by a growing multiculturalism. In the five-year period to 2003, the number of work permits issued to immigrants rose sevenfold or eightfold to around 48,000 a year. With the expansion of the EU and other geopolitical factors, this growth in 'multiculturalism' can be expected to continue in the future.

Spain

There is broad protection against discrimination under Article 14 of the Spanish Constitution of 1978. All citizens are equal before the law, and discrimination on the grounds of race, gender, religion, opinions, or other social or personal circumstances is outlawed. In the field of employment equality, the Workers' Statute 1980 prohibits agreements or managerial actions that directly or indirectly discriminate for reasons of age or disability. Discrimination is prohibited on pay and working hours on the grounds of sex, racial and ethnic origin, social condition, religion, ideology, sexual orientation, and union affiliation or family relationships with other employees. The Workers' Statute was modified in 2002 to incorporate the principle of equal pay. Other legislation grants rights to breastfeeding mothers.

Since the mid-1990s, collective agreements have increasingly incorporated provisions on non-discrimination, and peak confederal agreements have encouraged the adoption of such provisions by lower-level bargaining. Non-discrimination provisions affected more than a third of employees by 2001. While they are often declarations of intent with few substantive results, there have been limited advances towards more equal opportunities on issues, such as working time, job classifications, promotion, and pay. Generally, collective bargaining has shown more dynamism in building on late-1990s legislation aimed at reconciling work and family life, leading, for example, to negotiated improvements in parental leave and flexible working arrangements.

Spain is similar to Ireland in terms of the gender and ethnic composition of its workforce. As in the case of Ireland, female employment has been low, reflecting the relatively recent transition away from a predominantly rural economy. At the beginning of the 1990s, the female participation rate was by some way the lowest of the EU15, and was still only 32 per cent in 1992 compared with figures of 56 per cent for Germany and 61 per cent for the UK. Although the figure has risen rapidly in recent years, to 46 per cent in 2003, it is still significantly lower than that of the other three countries, and one of the lowest in the EU25 (Eurostat 2004).

Spain was historically characterized, too, by a high degree of racial homogeneity. In recent years, as in Ireland, there has been a large influx of immigrant workers. The foreign component (including EU nationals) of the total Spanish population is currently 7 per cent, having quadrupled since 1998. An estimated 42 per cent of foreigners have an irregular or illegal status. Nearly two-fifths come from Latin America and a further fifth from Africa. Foreigners constitute 4.7 per cent of the Spanish workforce, with concentrations in agriculture, construction, and domestic service, and in the regions of Madrid, Catalonia, and Valencia (data from the Instituto Nacional de Estadística). Immigrant workers are often treated as second-class citizens, working in the black economy in harsh conditions and with little employment stability. However, a growing number have acquired Spanish citizenship and the government has taken steps to regularize the employment status of immigrants.

FINDINGS

This section explores how the diversity policies of the US case-study companies were implemented in these varied national-institutional environments. It first looks at the global diversity management policies disseminated by these firms, then at the subsidiary response.

International Diversity Policies in the Case-Study Companies

In the USA, most of the case-study companies had active diversity policies, often justified by reference to a business case: the need to secure access to 'the pool of talented people'; to reflect the customer base; and to enhance creativity by 'leveraging difference'. There was, however, a certain ambivalence. Some respondents expressed concern about the potential of diversity policy to alienate core white male employees. Others regarded their sector or firm as one that was unlikely to attract female or ethnic minority employees, so made little effort to develop policies for tapping diversity. Moreover, some companies had an uneasy relationship with the domestic EEO agenda, which was seen as burdensome and as creating complications, as with the need to be alert to indirect discrimination ('disparate impact') during redundancy and downsizing exercises.

Thus, the extent to which companies adopted international diversity policies varied considerably (see Table 8.1 for a summary). At one extreme some, like EngServs, made minimal attempts to develop such policies. However, the situation was a dynamic, evolving one. In Computerco in Ireland, diversity had traditionally received little attention. The subsidiary passively followed any central policies and took no active role in developing its own local applications, for instance, in relation to gender; it had no manager with responsibility for diversity. Recently, however, there had been a major European initiative on diversity, led by a corporate VP, with a particular focus on increasing female representation in leadership roles.

Most companies paid at least lip service to diversity, incorporating it into formal corporate values, but then leaving it to subsidiaries to develop policy with little central intervention. This was the case in companies like Engco1 and Chemco, and in Healthco in Ireland. As a result, many subsidiaries adopted a fairly passive approach, neglecting diversity issues in practice. However, other firms, like ITco, Business Services, Engco2, and CPGco established quite complex global structures and policies. Global diversity 'leadership' teams drove diversity policy and set the tone by propagating the corporate message that diversity was a key issue: this was the case in ITco where, exceptionally, the diversity agenda was strongly diffused to and assimilated by national subsidiaries in all four host countries. Tiers of 'diversity councils' at global, regional, and national or site level concerned themselves with the application of diversity policy in their jurisdiction. Corporate websites propounded a firm's philosophy of diversity, detailed policies and structures, and publicized external diversity awards and internal prizes, from the 'Gay Alliance Corporate Leadership Award' to '50 Best Companies for Latinas . . . To Work for'. These companies and others also implemented substantial global training programmes in diversity, and in some instances (e.g. in EngCo2) these were mandatory worldwide. Diversity policies touched on many of the major areas of HRM,

Table 8.1. Summary of diversity policy in selected case-study companies

Company	Diversity as a global corporate value	Global structures of diversity	Global target-setting and monitoring	International diversity training
Business Services	Yes—firm promotes inclusive culture, and harnessing talents of diverse people	Global diversity officer to ensure diversity policy applies worldwide; managers with diversity responsibilities designated at country level Global programmes focusing on women's career development and advancement (e.g. flexible work and work–life balance) Geographies encouraged to 'customize' diversity initiatives to fit locality—e.g. introduction of 'career pauses' in the UK	Yes—ethnic and gender balance used as criterion in monitoring graduate intakes, promotion outcomes No specific quotas in national geographies, but pressures to increase female participation Global reporting on ethnicity and gender balance of senior promotion candidates	Diversity training devolved to geographies; compulsory diversity training in the UK
Computerco	No	Recent European initiative to introduce coordinated diversity approach, leading to appointment of a European vice-president for diversity European-wide mentoring programme for female managers online, anonymous diversity survey to explore views of female employees on firm's working climate, and to establish reasons for female turnover Establishment of networks for women employees, review of recruitment and job posting procedures, campaign to improve the image of IT as a career among diversity groups	No information	European training programmes in confidence building and assertiveness for women, and general awareness training for employees
CPGco	Yes—diversity linked to respect for	Strong internationalization of domestic diversity concerns	Yes—compulsory emphasis on women in global diversity policies:	Diversity/harassment training compulsory but mainly devolved

	individual; aim to become a global leader in integrating diversity into the business	Chief diversity officer responsible for global policy; Global employee diversity networks; Questions on 'valuing diversity' in periodic global staff opinion survey; Global diversity awards; Work-life balance initiative	since 1995 a global target of 50 per cent women in leadership roles; flexibility for local subsidiaries to designate other diversity groups; Regular monitoring of diversity metrics (gender, ethnicity) directly by HQ HR; Senior managers are set diversity targets as part of corporate framework of accountability; proportion of remuneration linked to diversity metrics	to subsidiaries
Engco1	Yes—'diversity' includes 'skills, abilities, experiences and cultural backgrounds'	No	No, although general concerns with increasing representation of non-Americans in leadership teams	No
Engco2	Yes—corporate values include embracing diversity, defined as employees' 'diverse perspectives'	Strong internationalization of diversity policies; International diversity implemented through: corporate diversity council; diversity champions in each business unit; site-level 'diversity councils' responsible for local diversity initiatives; international diversity awards for pioneering sites; global anti-harassment policy	Yes—diversity policy, action plan and progress reporting mandatory globally for business units; universal gender component to plans, but other components left to locality; global monitoring of diversity metrics (women and ethnic minorities), quarterly monitoring of subsidiary diversity action plans; Targets for diverse groups in leadership positions; Senior managers' performance appraisal linked to diversity objectives and metrics	Compulsory standardized diversity training worldwide, monitored by HQ
EngServs	No	No—virtually no internationalization of domestic diversity policy	No	
ITco	Yes—diversity and inclusion as integral to corporate culture	Strong internationalization of diversity policy led by senior vice-president; Emphasis on customer diversity driving workforce diversity initiatives		

(contd.)

Table 8.1. (contd.)

Company	Diversity as a global corporate value	Global structures of diversity	Global target-setting and monitoring	International diversity training
		Multiplicity of diversity networks and affinity groups including a women's 'leadership council' in Europe and women's leadership teams in most countries Tracking of women in high potential and leadership groups Work flexibility policies (e.g. working from home)	Yes—no formal targets/quotas in Europe but unpublicized target 'ranges' for women, e.g. for new hires Discreet tracking of key diversity groups at local/regional level—e.g. metrics on new hires, women in management/executive positions, time between promotions, returners after maternity leave, etc. Emphasis put on diversity management in performance appraisal	Global courses available for use, but no compulsory programmes at global level
Logistico	Corporate culture of 'embracing diversity'	Diversity steering council co-chaired by CEO/Chair and by VP HR, recommending ways of fostering diversity throughout the firm Significant emphasis on ethnic diversity, reflected, e.g. in Irish and German subsidiaries Corporate code of professional conduct and anti-harassment policy and hotline direct to HQ	No targets set though increasing informal pressure on diversity and HQ raises issues, e.g. of diversity in national subsidiaries; attempts to increase the national diversity of the European leadership team	
Pharmaco	Diversity broadly defined to include, e.g. experience outside own country, cross-functional, outside the industry, etc.	No	Corporate policy that board should reflect the customer populations served; Specific US-based metrics to be met on gender and ethnicity, but outside US no specific targets; national/regional monitoring of, e.g. gender composition of talent pipeline; norm of promoting diversity if candidates otherwise equal	No evidence

from recruitment and selection through employee development and promotion to reward and performance management.

Some companies were acknowledged pioneers of the diversity agenda in their host countries. In Germany, ITco was seen as a role model for gender equality. The German subsidiary started its first development scheme for women in the 1960s. In 2001, 25 per cent of its German workforce was female; women occupied 11 per cent of middle management positions and 6–7 per cent of top positions—a much higher proportion than the norm in German industry. Likewise in Spain, where women accounted for a third of the workforce, ITco's subsidiary had achieved a proportion of women in management posts of 18 per cent, a figure that had increased sharply over recent years.

Even in companies with well-developed international diversity objectives, policy tended to focus on gender diversity. This was the case particularly in Spain, Ireland, and Germany, although it was predominantly true of the UK subsidiaries as well. Global 'affinity groups' and mentoring systems for women employees were set up, and some firms set targets for women in high potential groups, promotion pools, or management posts. Supporting measures, such as 'work–life balance' policies, flexible working, working from home, parental leave, and so on, tended in practice to underpin gender diversity more than other aspects of diversity.

Policies on ethnicity (which were a key focus of diversity policies in the USA), disability, or sexual orientation were much less prominent in most companies, and where they existed, subsidiaries generally had considerable discretion in applying them. Ethnic diversity was formally on the agenda, especially in the UK where public policy attention was high, but it tended to be neglected in practice, even in diversity-conscious companies like CPGco and Engco2. Other companies, notably Engco1, also acknowledged that their workforce did not reflect the ethnic diversity of their local labour market, but few if any had measures to address this. In Spain, Ireland, and Germany even less attention appeared to be paid to ethnicity.

There were exceptions to this pattern, however. One was Logistico, whose US operations employed a high proportion of ethnic minority workers and monitored their presence in managerial positions. In Ireland, Logistico placed as strong an emphasis on ethnic and national diversity as on gender. Logistico's German subsidiary was the only German case-study company to address immigration as a diversity issue, monitoring the nationality of its employees. As elsewhere in the company, employees had access to a multilingual anti-harassment hotline direct to corporate headquarters. However, even in this case, the subsidiary did not appear to be under pressure to fulfil targets, such as for non-Germans in leadership positions.

The approach to international diversity in most companies was to set an overall framework rather than a highly prescriptive range of policies. While it might be mandatory for subsidiaries to have a diversity policy, it would be up to them to specify the content. In some companies, subsidiaries were required to set targets or were given central targets, for example, for the number of women on leadership teams, and they were expected to supply metrics against which they could be evaluated. Even where no formal targets existed, the centre might well intervene to ask questions about progress on diversity issues: for example, in Chemco Spain, there were no targets for the number of women the subsidiary had to recruit, or for workforce diversity more generally, but 'there are questions that always come down to us from HQ—"why are there more women in this department than in that one?"' Similarly, in Business Services in Germany there was indirect pressure to increase the number of women in 'consultant' roles: when female consultants left the company, HR had to provide information about the reasons and whether something could be done about it.

Monitoring of gender and other dimensions of diversity could be direct and insistent:

[The international HR director] looks for me to report to him, routinely, on the mix of our population here, our employee base in terms of gender and race and how that's changing and what we're doing about it, day to day. And he asks everybody around the world to do that and that's very high on the agenda. So I have an hour's call with him once a month and that will take up quite a lot of it.
(UK HR manager, CPGco)

In a handful of companies (notably CPGco, Softco, and Engco2) senior managers were appraised against individual diversity targets. Managers could be set targets, for example, for improving employee satisfaction ratings on diversity measures in workforce attitude surveys, or for increasing the number of women in managerial posts.

Diversity in Operation in European Subsidiaries: Resistance, Avoidance, and Compliance

Despite the fairly generic nature of global corporate diversity policies, they evoked ambiguous reactions in subsidiaries. First, there was a strong perception that diversity was a peculiarly American 'obsession'. While British managers did tend to accept that diversity was an issue, especially in relation to the advancement of women within the company, in Spain and Germany, respondents (women as well as men) were much more hostile to the notion itself, denying that there was a problem to be resolved:

For my part, I do not see the 'diversity' theme in Spain as a problem or as an 'issue' or as anything. ([Female] HR manager, Business Services, Spain)

Rubbish. All rubbish. [. . .] They have started with it, with sexual harassment and all these things, all this nonsense. We just smile to ourselves about it and the Americans make themselves ridiculous. No, diversity management, we do not know and we do not want to have to hear about it. Women and men, that is absolutely no issue for us. (HR manager, Bor-Tec, Germany)

It should be stressed that such attitudes were not necessarily representative of employee views. Although we do not have systematic evidence, there are indications that a lack of managerial concern with diversity created problems for female employees. In Computerco Ireland, for example, female respondents expressed frustration at the low percentage of women in managerial positions and spoke of the 'glass ceiling' and 'jobs for the boys'.

Second, subsidiaries were critical of what they saw as the inflexible way in which the diversity agenda was applied, without taking account of local circumstances and needs. Spanish managers in one company, for example, were critical of a centrally set target for women in managerial positions which was, they claimed, rigidly applied even in North African countries whose culture did not easily accommodate women in such posts. The internationalization of the diversity agenda was seen as driven by parochial US concerns. An example was the reference to the Ku Klux Klan in the worldwide anti-harassment policy of one company. In another firm, managers at the European level and in the UK subsidiary argued that the internationalization of diversity was a response to attempts to contain racial tensions (and the ensuing litigation) in the core operating units in the USA. However, European managers queried why attempts to develop a more inclusive corporate culture in the USA should be diffused worldwide. A typical complaint by subsidiary managers, in companies as varied as Engco2, Business Services, and Refreshco, was that the centre wished to collect data from subsidiaries on ethnic diversity using categories designed for the US domestic context, and in circumstances where ethnic monitoring made little sense. The exasperation felt by subsidiaries was well expressed by a Spanish manager:

They were insistent that we should count the number of blacks we recruit. And I told them [HQ], look, in Spain it's difficult to hire blacks. 'Well then, [what about] South Americans, gypsies?' But they they're not graduates. I've got South American people working with me and I've got one or two blacks ... but they're graduates. They're people who fit with me, because also they speak Spanish, you can't just suggest that an army of Ecuadorians should turn up and we should hire them to fill some quotas. [...] We were giving them data from the National ministry of statistics [sic], from the interior ministry on residence permits. So they gave us a lot of work for nothing.... (HR manager, Business Services)

In some instances, where there was a strong European tier of management, it could act as a 'buffer' to ensure that corporate policies were not applied in an inflexible way. In Computerco, for example, the appointment of an American manager as European VP for diversity allowed central policy to be adapted to national circumstances:

We want to take the things that are global and core to our values and share those, but very early on I recognised that I couldn't pick up stuff from America. I had comments to me 'oh great, another damn American programme, you guys are so altruistic and we've got socialistic governments that take care of us and we don't need this stuff'. So very early on I learned I couldn't take anything from America and just drop it in, I had to Europeanize it if you will.

Another complaint from national respondents was that diversity policy could be counterproductive in terms of business goals. For example, targets for women in managerial roles were seen as potentially demotiv- ating for male managers while failing to address the organizational obstacles to the advancement of females, such as the long hours culture typical of US companies. Finally, managers were concerned about the tensions between global diversity policy and national or European law. They pointed, for example, to differences between conceptions of positive discrimination in Europe and the USA. Elsewhere, corporate requests for information on some categories of employee, for example, the disabled, were hampered by privacy protection legislation.

In summary, subsidiary respondents often saw diversity policy as inflex- ible, too insistently applied, driven by American domestic preoccupations, and at odds with European legislative traditions. In the UK subsidiaries, and to a lesser extent in Ireland, most managers were at least receptive in prin- ciple, although they might not see it as particularly relevant. So were man- agers elsewhere in some companies, such as ITco, where the need to address a varied customer base through active diversity policy was widely accepted. But in Spain and Germany, respondents were resistant to the very concept.

Subsidiaries deployed various strategies for minimizing the disruptive impact of international diversity policy, ranging from resistance through adaptation to avoidance or lip service. First, resistance was a commonly observed response, even in companies generally favourable to diversity. Legislative constraints were a significant factor in provoking and legitimizing resistance. For example, CPGco UK resisted targets for women in post partly on the grounds that such targets constituted 'affirmative action' or positive discrimination and were thus at odds with European law. Similarly, in Business Services Spain, an HR respondent resisted ethnic and religious monitoring on the grounds that 'in our Constitution discrimination against people is prohibited, and therefore we don't even ask [...] I *cannot* ask, by law, Article 14 of the Constitution'.

Such resistance, in short, mobilized a rhetoric of legislative compliance to justify itself, although in some instances, since the law was not always clear-cut in its implications, legislative constraints were invoked to resist policies that were opposed on other grounds, normally of business effectiveness in the local context:

We have argued that if we were seen to have targets [for women in management positions] then that would implicitly be positive discrimination. I don't know strictly from a legal point of view whether that would be...but I guess that's what essentially fended off too explicit a target. (HR manager CPGco UK)

The 'business case' was also extensively mobilized, in tandem with compliance arguments, to legitimize resistance; and it was used even when legal constraints were absent. CPGco argued that quotas for women managers, besides creating legal difficulties, would be counterproductive, by alienating male managers and by distracting attention from the organizational obstacles to women's advancement. In Business Services Spain, pressure from the global diversity management structure to increase the intake of female graduates was resisted on business grounds: the proportion of women taking degrees in appropriate disciplines like engineering was low. Under pressure to justify why it did not recruit from graduate disciplines where female graduates were better represented, it argued that male-dominated engineering graduates fitted the target profile and were better suited to the business.

Instances of resistance also occurred where the imposition of a global diversity agenda upset existing relationships between managerial functions and levels. For example, in CPGco's diversity was driven directly by a US-based global HR director. This entailed the imposition of diversity targets on HR managers in subsidiary operations. The UK manager resisted this shift in the focus of his objective-setting from his local business manager to an American-based executive. He argued that global objectives concerned with global diversity policy had little to do with his day-to-day HR activity, which centred on managing employee relations in the plants. This manager saw himself as engaged in a wider struggle with corporate HQ:

over quite what global management of HR means, how workable it is, you know. [...] We are engaged in a very active debate between people like me and the global HR organization about quite how that should work and there are very strong differences of view.

Resistance was usually one of a battery of responses. In most companies it was accompanied by some degree of accommodation or constructive engagement with the policy, particularly by UK managers who were generally more sympathetic to diversity agendas than their counterparts in other countries. Engagement took the form of promoting alternative mechanisms for achieving diversity goals, 'functional equivalents' that would achieve the same end without the perceived disadvantages. While objecting to explicit targets, for instance, CPGco emphasized a policy of building support systems for women by monitoring pools of high potentials, including women candidates on selection short lists, and stressing supporting measures such as work–life balance.

A variant was not so much constructive engagement as 'displacement'. Subsidiaries tried to distract HQ attention from aspects of diversity policy that they were not keen on to those that they felt happy with implementing. A CPGco UK operations manager diverted attention from targets for women in his leadership team by focusing on other mechanisms, such as improving the 'feeder pool', to achieve the same goal in the longer term. The respondent summarized his stance with his worldwide line manager in the following terms: '... don't *count* me, look at the behaviour, look at the things we've put in place, and measure me on how much progress I'm making with those'. He promoted an initiative together with the trade union to examine diversity in the blue-collar workforce and to assess why it was 'not representative, either in terms of gender or ethnicity' of the local community. In doing this, the manager subtly redefined the object of the exercise: the point of monitoring was not so much to increase the diversity of the local workforce, but to 'benchmark' against other local employers and make sure that the subsidiary was consistent with their practice. In this way, lip service was paid to the diversity agenda, while shaping it to local needs and priorities.

In some respects, this was easier to do in a business context, such as that of the UK, where equal opportunities and anti-discrimination legislation forced management attention to a range of diversity issues regardless of the existence of a global corporate agenda on the subject. Ethnic monitoring of recruits, for example, is common practice in UK companies, including in firms like Chemco where diversity policy was not seen as part of the international HR agenda: 'We want to be sure we're getting a broad appeal, and then we know more and more as time goes on about our ethnic mix' (UK HR manager). But this UK context also meant that in companies promulgating international diversity policies, existing activity in the UK subsidiary could be 're-branded' to fit in with the demands of the centre:

What we've learned how to do . . . is to listen to what they say and decide what we're going to do and put it under that same banner. (Operations manager, CPGco UK)

'Displacement' also took the form of accepting a policy in principle, but pointing to practical constraints that impeded progress. When companies were under pressure to monitor and increase participation of ethnic minorities in the workforce, for example, it was possible to argue that this was desirable but impracticable in a context of low turnover, or of recruitment freezes or downsizing. Engco2's efforts to increase the proportion of women in the pool of temporary workers, from which permanent employees were taken on, was hampered by the fact that temps were the first to go when restrictions were placed on workforce size.

A fourth and final strategic response could be labelled 'counter-attack'. This deployed the legitimatory rhetoric of diversity itself, but to ends that embodied the interests of European managers rather than those of corporate headquarters. This response was directed primarily at tackling the dominance within leadership tiers, in Europe and more widely, of American nationals. Several companies, notably Business Services, Logistico, and CPGco, argued strongly for a greater representation of non-Americans in senior positions, by 'fast-tracking' if necessary. Corporate HQ managers were sometimes sympathetic to such a revision of the notion of diversity, and some firms, notably Pharmaco, emphasized the national diversity of their global leadership team.

Thus corporate diversity policies were disseminated to European subsidiaries through a complex process of negotiated adoption and adaptation. While some companies, such as Engco2, adopted the paraphernalia of diversity with little demur, in other cases (particularly Business Services and in CPGco), there was a dynamic of central demand and subsidiary response, counter-demand and counter-response. This may be illustrated by the efforts of CPGco in Europe to deflect central demands for quotas on women in management, and by the resistance of Business Services in Spain to diversity monitoring and targets. The insistent probing quality of central intervention and the dogged determination of the subsidiary to resist measures seen as inappropriate is illustrated by the case of Business Services (as recounted by a manager in the Spanish subsidiary) summarized in Box 8.1.

Box 8.1 DIVERSITY TARGETS AND MONITORING IN *BUSINESS SERVICES* SPAIN

The centre first proposed that the Spanish subsidiary monitor the number of black employees. Once the subsidiary had convinced the HQ that this was not appropriate in the Spanish context, there was discussion of alternative ethnic groups such as Gypsies or South Americans. The Spanish were able to argue that these too would be an inappropriate basis for target-setting because of their illegal status and/or lack of adequate qualifications. The HQ then modified the focus of 'diversity' to include cultural or regional diversity. The Spanish suggested that cultural diversity would encompass regional variety—Basques, Catalans, and so—and argued that they were already diverse in that respect. They anticipated other possible avenues for future HQ thrusts on diversity—such as religious diversity—and made pre-emptive defences against them by invoking the provisions of Spain's Constitution. The HQ then returned to the question of recruiting more women. When Spain replied that their target market, graduate engineers, had a low proportion of women, the HQ probed the possibility of targeting graduates in arts subjects. Spain countered that these graduates did not have the necessary profile.

VARIATIONS BETWEEN COMPANIES AND COUNTRIES: EXPLAINING THE PATTERNS

Overall, therefore, international diversity policy was a prominent feature of many case-study companies. But it was not transposed smoothly to subsidiaries. Even when sympathetic, European subsidiaries frequently contested, adapted and deflected aspects of the diversity agenda which they saw as driven by American preoccupations. Diversity, American-style, was regarded as unsuited in certain respects to European national contexts and counterproductive to subsidiaries' business aims.

Nonetheless, within this broad picture, international diversity policy, and the extent of local implementation, varied considerably between companies and host countries. This section examines explanations for the patterns of dissemination observed.

Variation between Companies

Differences in structural characteristics of companies, in particular the degree of international integration of operations and markets, and the composition and skills profile of their labour force, appear to be a significant source of variation in diversity management. This is in line with Florkowski's strategic contingency model of diversity in MNCs (Florkowski 1996), according to which international policy reflects a combination of product-market and labour-market pressures. Following Florkowski, it could be expected that companies (such as ITco) that aim to serve customers who are diverse in ethnicity and gender would have a more developed diversity agenda. The degree to which that is internationally standardized and propagated would depend partly on the diversity of overseas markets and partly on the degree to which corporate integration mechanisms exist at international level. The more highly integrated are MNCs, in terms of operations and product markets, the more highly integrated one could expect international diversity policy to be. ITco appears to fit this characterization: the strong diversity ethos across its international operations may be seen as reflecting the high degree of global integration of its operations and markets. At the other end of the spectrum, EngServs needed to respond to country- and region-specific pressures (see Colling and Clark 2002) and placed very little emphasis on diversity.

Business Services was structurally similar to ITco, in that it operated in a similar sector and served large, integrated, multinational clients. But as we have seen, the 'internalization' of the diversity ethos was weaker, international diversity policy aroused significantly more resistance, especially in Spain, and diversity arrangements were less uniformly entrenched. This can perhaps be explained by other features of the company, such as a heritage marked by the ethos and structures of the partnership form. This militated against highly directive top-down HR policy and encouraged a more collegiate style of international HR policymaking.

A further structural characteristic is the nature of the target labour force. This would seem to explain in part both the degree of diversity and its specific focus. Firms like ITco and Business Services relied on a highly skilled, professionalized, and expert core labour force to provide their services. Such skills were scarce and the companies could be expected to be swayed by a business case for seeking suitable labour among the widest range of groups within the labour market. This could also explain Business Services' reluctance to accept American definitions of diversity: it simply did not believe it could optimize its access to scarce skills by doing so, given the nature of the

Spanish labour market (notably the marginalization and lack of qualifications of much of Spain's ethnic minority labour force, and the strongly gender-segmented structure of graduate qualifications). In manufacturing companies, the 'perverse' business case—*against* diversity—may be seen as coming into play: it is possible to speculate that firms were concerned to preserve the homogeneity, stability, and cohesion of blue-collar workforces, through such mechanisms as inter-generational and family recruitment, and this militated against ethnic diversity. This appears to have been the case in CPGco and in Engco1, both of which retained ethnically quite homogeneous manufacturing workforces even where there was a significant ethnic minority presence in the local labour market.

In general, employee testimony collected in the UK case studies shows very little awareness of the diversity agenda, and little evidence of a practical impact on the working life of employees other than managerial and professional groups. The one exception, Logistico in Germany (and to some extent, in Ireland), with a high percentage of immigrant employees, may also be seen to support this analysis. Given the unskilled or semi-skilled nature of much of the work of operatives in the logistics industry, it may be predicted that companies will seek to minimize the costs of access to cheap sources of labour. These are likely to be found among immigrant populations which are less well-integrated, lack skills and qualifications, and are less susceptible to collective organization—a point made by Royle (2000) in reference to McDonald's recruitment practices in Germany.

Nonetheless, structural factors do not account for the vigour with which international diversity policy was pursued (at least with respect to gender) in some case-study companies. In particular they cannot explain the marked difference between Engco2 and a relatively similar engineering company, Engco1, which had at best a rudimentary international diversity agenda. This contrast demonstrates the space for strategic choice within structural constraints. The choice, in this case and also in CPGco, seems to stem from the effect of the strong and persistent philosophy of the founding family on the managerial ethos of the company. A statement on diversity by Engco2's founder, dating from the early 1980s, was frequently quoted as the under-pinning of contemporary diversity strategies. Moreover, the diversity agenda was of a piece with the distinctive variant of welfare capitalism pursued by the company, based on a strong ILM and high workforce commitment. In this context, the company's deployment of corporate 'culture', including diversity, could be seen as a tool of international competitive advantage by defining the company both for internal stakeholders, and for an external audience, notably customers and potential recruits.

Variation between Countries

The case studies reveal considerable differences between countries in the extent to which international diversity policies were applied, in the meanings given to 'diversity', and in subsidiary responses. Managers in Germany, Ireland, and Spain tended to be more negative and disengaged towards diversity than those in the UK. The 'internalization' (Kostova 1999) of the diversity agenda was most evident in the UK, though even here there was frequent conflict with HQ over the modalities of dissemination and implementation within the British environment. A key issue, therefore, is how global diversity policies are accommodated within host business systems with distinct legislative frameworks, socio-political traditions, and demographic characteristics.

One line of explanation for the differences focuses on the openness of different host business systems to the diffusion of US HR practices. It could be argued that the greater prominence of diversity in UK subsidiaries reflects the British business system's openness to US influences. However, this is problematic for a number of reasons. The Irish business system, with similarly marked Anglo-Saxon traits, could be seen as even more open to American HR innovation, given the dominance of US FDI in the country. Yet commitment to diversity was restrained in most of the Irish subsidiaries. Moreover, Spain, with its high proportion of foreign capital in major sectors of the economy, and its adoption of an Anglo-Saxon business education model, may be seen as having considerable scope to assimilate dominant American business repertoires. But Spanish subsidiaries were at best lukewarm and at worst contemptuous towards HQ diversity initiatives.

Another possible explanation for variation lies in demographic differences. Two demographic factors stand out. First, Britain has by some way the highest female employment rate, with Spain by some way the lowest, and Germany and Ireland in intermediate positions (see earlier section). The divergence has been considerably reduced by rapid growth in female employment in Spain and Ireland, but even as recently as the mid-1990s, the Spanish rate was little more than half the British. Second, Britain's ethnic minority population is far larger and longer-established than in Ireland or Spain; while Germany as we have seen is a special case because of the traditional transience of immigrant workers, and the unavailability of naturalization for those of non-German descent until recent years.

But these structural features provide at best a partial explanation of differences. They do not explain, for example, why Britain and Germany, with similar percentages of ethnic minority members of the labour force, have conceptualized the issue of ethnic minorities and citizenship (and employment) in such different terms. And a simplistic demographic approach to the salience of the diversity agenda begs the question of *why* there are such varied female participation rates in the four countries. The answer clearly has something to do with the dynamics of social and industrial structure—for example, the impact on female work roles of a comparatively late transition to modern, industrial economies in Ireland and Spain. But it also seems to lie in the interaction between demographic factors and the way in which these are incorporated into and processed through social movements and through political debate and action. These processes result in concrete legal frameworks covering discrimination and equal opportunities, in the shaping of female labour market participation through the structure of welfare states, and ultimately in cognitive frameworks and assumptions that guide behaviour in firms. In the UK, both gender and ethnicity have been the focus of political debate and social action, and outcomes have been embodied in legislation since the mid-1970s and have subsequently forced their way onto corporate agendas. The legislative agenda has been more muted in the other countries and has been driven primarily by EU regulation rather than by the mobilization of interest groups at national level. With the exception of the UK, ethnicity has been largely absent from debate until very recently. Action has failed to coalesce around the issue of gender and the 'glass ceiling', as witnessed by the extremely low levels of women in managerial positions in Germany. Nonetheless, mechanisms of social 'embeddedness' of diversity may be stronger in some respects in Germany because of the role played by collective representation institutions in enforcement of equal opportunities.

Finally, national demographic characteristics clearly interact with company labour market strategies. For example, given Logistico's need to recruit large amounts of relatively low-skilled and low-cost labour, it made sense to target immigrant labour in Germany and hence to stress nationality as a key dimension of its diversity strategy. Unfortunately, it was not possible to gain access to Logistico in Spain, but one may speculate that policy would have been to target immigrant (and often ethnic-minority) labour, because—in strong contrast to Business Services—it was not seeking highly qualified labour. Similarly, the development in Ireland of competitive advantage in the provision of international call centre services may increasingly lead subsidiaries in companies such as Computerco, ITco, and Logistico (where the primary focus of the Irish operations was a multilingual call centre), to target ethnic, or at least linguistic and national diversity in certain sectors, despite the continuing relatively high degree of ethnic homogeneity of the workforce overall.

CONCLUSIONS

The workforce diversity agenda is an interesting instance of policy diffusion since it can be traced in a relatively direct way to features of the American business system; international diversity policy is largely an expansion of domestic policies driven by specific US concerns. This has resulted in a lack of fit between diversity elements and host-country contexts, and has provoked considerable resistance from subsidiaries. Nonetheless, there is considerable variation among companies and countries in responses to diversity. This has been explained by a combination of structural factors and more contingent strategic and political choices by actors at national and organizational level.

In short, diversity has to be seen as a *constructed* agenda. It is driven by certain external conditions, such as a high proportion of ethnic minorities in the labour force, the emergence of civil rights movements and ensuing legislative frameworks, and so on. But it is then purposively articulated and defined as a terrain for corporate action. This process of articulation is well-established—though still highly contested—in the USA. It has occurred in a more muted fashion in the UK with its relatively well-developed EO agenda, relatively high proportion of ethnic minorities, and its mimetic relationship to US business hegemony. But it is more alien to traditions of political and corporate action in the other three countries; although even here, the situation is a dynamic one as countries, and companies, respond to changing demographic patterns, political agendas, and legislative frameworks.

Notes

1. We are particularly grateful to Trevor Colling for some incisive comments on earlier drafts of this chapter.
2. Defined as the number of women aged 15–64 in employment as a percentage of the total female population of the same age group.

9

The Management of Managerial Careers

Peter Butler, David Collings, René Peters, and Javier Quintanilla

INTRODUCTION

This chapter is concerned with managerial resourcing and development in the subsidiaries of US MNCs. Large US firms have long sought to school managers, both technically and culturally, through the erection of strong internal labour markets (ILMs), that is, closed systems restricted to very limited ports of entry (Doeringer and Piore 1971: 47). This has particularly been the case with firms of the 'welfare capitalist' variety. In recent years, however, the systemic bureaucracy inherent in ILMs has come under increasing pressure, amid drives for flexibility and leanness, often manifest in programmes of downsizing and delayering. The growing influence of the market as a mode of economic and social organization (Grimshaw et al. 2001: 26) has prompted some commentators to proclaim the demise of the traditional internal managerial career, based on guaranteed employment (McGovern, Hope-Hailey, and Stiles 1998: 463) and steady career progression (see, in particular, Cappelli, 1995, 1999b; Cappelli et al. 1997). These influences are depicted as being especially pervasive in the USA, given the pressures to increase shareholder value as a result of the growing influence of institutional investors (Cappelli 1999b: 151). In view of such claims, this chapter seeks to shed light on the dynamics of managerial resourcing in the study companies; evaluate the pressures for change; and, consistent with the theoretical focus of this volume, explore how these tensions are being played out within the particularistic context of the host environments in which the subsidiaries operate.

The following section gives an outline of the somewhat variegated US approach to managerial resourcing. The discussion then moves on to critically consider the current challenges facing those organizations traditionally reliant on the internal development of managerial talent. As will be discussed, there is an emergent friction between external influences and the formerly dominant internal logic that prompted the creation of entrenched ILMs. Given that our central preoccupation lies with the overseas subsidiaries of MNCs, some background comparative data are subsequently provided on the traditions of managerial resourcing in each of the four host countries. This acts as a backdrop to the presentation of the research findings. Here we consider the ongoing commitment to the ILM, explore the pressures for change, and probe the extent to which the outcomes are significantly coloured by host country norms. In the concluding section, we evaluate the contribution of the findings to two important streams of literature: comparative institutionalism and international career management.

THE US MANAGERIAL 'MARKETPLACE'

In stereotypical portrayals of the US 'market-orientated' (Dore 1989) business system, firms are characterized by high labour turnover, both for managers and non-managerial staff, and by multiple ports of entry (e.g. Dore 1989; Evans, Lank, and Farquhar 1989). Career patterns show much greater mobility between firms than 'organization-orientated' (Dore 1989) business systems such as Germany. Accordingly, American managers are characteristically depicted as having a predominantly external framework for career management, seeing high mobility as natural (Thompson et al. 2001: 50) with training and development, like general education, regarded as an individual's responsibility (p. 54). According to Handy et al. (1988: 51), this stems from the prevailing sense of the market, whereby society is perceived as a marketplace for talent, as well as for goods and services.

There is, nevertheless, a long tradition, particularly in larger US firms, of insulating employees from market pressures by the creation of ILMs—a phenomenon that has proved relatively stable over time across large sections of US industry (Cappelli et al. 1997: 16). A defining feature of US managerial development is thus the marked degree of heterogeneity. While there are unresolved issues pertaining to the origins of ILMs (cf. Osterman 1984b), broadly, their genesis may be tracked back to the early part of the last century, as an organizational solution to a specific constellation of factors: threats of unionization; labour scarcity; and government regulation—with the emergent professionalization of the personnel function acting as a strong catalyst (Jacoby 1997: 280–1). Within certain organizations, what was essentially a pragmatic internal solution sublimated into a more philosophical welfare capitalist variant (Jacoby 1997). This approach counted many of the major names of American business among its adherents, including Eastman Kodak, Polaroid, Sears Roebuck, Thompson Products (subsequently TRW) DuPont, Eli Lilly, IBM, Procter & Gamble, and Standard Oil (Jacoby 1997).

While this model served to protect employees generally from the vicissitudes of market conditions, managers were early on accorded privileged status. As Cappelli et al. (1997: 18) argue, one legacy of the influence of scientific management, and the separation of task and conception, was that 'employment policies treated managers as the essence of the organization, [and] therefore worthy of substantially greater protection than was offered to other employees'. One corollary was that 'for practical purposes, managers had a job for life, subject to minimally acceptable performance'.

Within this format, and indeed in US organizations more generally, a further traditional element has been the emphasis placed on general, rather than specialist, managerial training. This is reflected in the proliferation of business 'majors' and MBA qualifications amongst corporate entrants, which provide a general grounding in the language and methods of business (Handy et al. 1988: 53–9; Locke 1996). As Hansen and Wilcox (1997: 193) note, technical expertise is respected, but often thought to be out of touch with the overall culture of management and business. One outcome is that American technical experts are rarely promoted into executive management. As will be discussed, this is in marked contrast to the functional chimneys that are characteristic features of corporate managerial education in several of our host countries.

PRESSURES FOR CHANGE

Over the last decade or so, it has become a commonplace for commentators to proclaim the demise of ILMs and of 'corpocratic' (Kanter 1989) careers within a single organization. The essence of such accounts is that the need for organizational restructuring, through downsizing and delayering, and ongoing preoccupations with numerical flexibility, has eroded the ILM as a site for the development of loyalties and productive skills. Organizations are increasingly coming under strain to restructure the way they operate, giving rise to a more market-mediated form of employment relationship. Such pressures have prompted Cappelli (1995: 573) to argue that 'there has been a trend or shift towards employment practices associated with markets outside the firm, and away from arrangements based on other criteria that typically reflect the internal interests of the firm.' The challenges to the ILM are generally regarded as being especially significant in their implications for middle hierarchical positions (Grimshaw et al. 2002: 96).

This dynamic has been articulated conceptually as both a repositioning of the psychological contract, and a switch to a new 'moral covenant' (Heckscher 1995: 39). One group of commentators has depicted this as involving a transition from guaranteed *employment* to one of guaranteed *employability*, with employment security reserved for an elite cadre of high performers (McGovern, Hope-Hailey, and Stiles 1998: 463–4). Others envision an emergent 'spot market', akin to neo-liberal models of labour market analysis, with career planning increasingly 'outsourced' to managers themselves (Cappelli 2000). A common theme however, is a suggestion of the demise of previously durable ties between employers and employees.

The implication of Cappelli's position is that ILMs originally constructed to meet the internal logic of the organization on the grounds of efficiency, have been swept away by pressures *external* to the organization, owing to the growing dominance of markets as a form of economic and social organization. This simple counterposing of external influence over a formerly dominant internal logic, however, has met with criticism. As Grimshaw et al. (2001: 26) argue, any transformation of ILMs is ultimately driven by conditions both external *and* internal to the firm (see also Osterman 1987: 59). This suggests that a more nuanced set of outcomes is likely to arise. While the dismantling of the traditional 'pillars' (Grimshaw et al. 2001: 25) of the ILM may have some influence on short-run financial performance, the impact of, for example, violations of the psychological contract on motivation and commitment may have more enduring consequences. Indeed, in this, as in other areas of HR policy, we might expect to see some oscillation in policy as the inherent tensions are played out.

The interplay of external and internally derived influence takes on a greater degree of complexity still within the subsidiaries of MNCs, because of the interaction with host-country effects. As Calori, Steele, and Yoneyama note (1995: 58), there is a mix of 'culture specific imperatives and contingencies', which can act to counterbalance the unimpeded transfer of policy in this area. Simply put, there are very different cultural assumptions about what makes a manager (Sparrow and Hiltrop 1994: 376). Attempts to transfer work and career development approaches from one country to another have often failed to consider the cultural differences that influence foreign acceptance (Hansen and Wilcox 1997: 195). Hence, we might expect corporate policy vis-à-vis managerial resourcing to be coloured by host-country norms to a greater or lesser extent. That is, such policy may be subject to local constraints and contestation when it comes into contact with differing management systems. To further develop this theme, in the section that follows, we provide sketches of the distinguishing features of managerial development in the four host countries. While to various degrees there is a tradition of internal managerial development, there is significant nuance in the precise operationalization.

MANAGERIAL DEVELOPMENT IN THE HOST COUNTRIES

Britain

Sparrow and Hiltrop (1994) suggest that in the context of management training and development, the only thing that Britain shares with the USA is not being continental European. Certainly in contrast to the USA, the managerial role has not traditionally been seen as a high status occupation (Handy et al. 1988: 163). Only after the Second World War did large corporations start to think in terms of formal managerial careers; recruit people as potential managers from the universities; and initiate formal education and training programmes. Even by the 1980s, after taking population size into account, the US output of MBA, postgraduate, and undergraduate managerial qualifications continued to dwarf that of Britain (p. 168). Britain's lagging performance in this area was highlighted by series of influential reports in the mid-to-late 1980s (Constable and McCormick 1987; Handy 1987; Managham and Silver 1986), which expressed concern at the poor quality and limited resources devoted to management development (see Storey, Edwards, and Sisson 1997: 39–43 for a review).

Nevertheless, the British model does show some affinities with its US counterpart. There is again a tradition, particularly in large companies (e.g. Shell and ICI), of recruiting people on leaving education and providing them with a mix of training and early experience geared to a long-term career in one organization. Similarly, the British system mirrors the USA in emphasizing the values of independence and autonomy. Nearly two decades ago, long before the purported dawn of the 'boundaryless career'

(Arthur and Rousseau 1996), Handy and his colleagues found that managers regarded careers as their own property and were consequently highly sensitive to the need for portable qualifications (Handy et al. 1988: 176).

There are nevertheless further significant points of difference. In marked contrast to the USA, training is characteristically functionally specific, giving rise to narrow definitions of job responsibilities. Most graduate employees are recruited for pre-determined technical or functional jobs (Evans, Lank, and Farquhar 1989: 128). Only later on are individuals with generalist potential given more broadly based training, after they have mastered 'key career-anchor jobs' (Sparrow and Hiltrop 1994: 381). Indeed, a major criticism made by the *Constable and McCormack Report* (1987) was that few managers gained experience beyond one function. Certainly, as late as 1988 there had been little development of horizontal fast tracks, allowing high potential employees to gain functional experience (Handy et al. 1988: 172). In this sense, there are similarities with the German model (see later) in that organizations prefer their recruits to specialize in one area, with lateral movement only occurring somewhat belatedly for aspiring generalists. This emphasis on 'functional chimneys' has traditionally been reinforced by the dominance of the professions (e.g. law, accountancy, marketing, and HR). The aim of professional accreditation is specialization, and it was never intended to provide a pathway towards general management (p. 174).

Ireland

In common with Britain, the lack of competitiveness of the Irish economy for much of the post-war period has been linked to the poor training of managers (Heraty and Morley 2000: 21–2). However, as Monks (1996: 727) has argued, there is a major difficulty with defining the nature of Irish personnel practice, and management development is no exception. Such conceptual problems are compounded given the recent ascendance of FDI, which has ensured that that any emergent Irish 'model' has been subject to a multitude of potential influences. The volatility of the Irish economy over the last twenty years or so, however, has perhaps been the key factor impacting upon organizational strategy in this area, rather than ownership per se.

Broadly, such data as there are suggest an increasing reliance on the building of integrated ILMs (Hearaty and Morley 2003). According to the Cranet E-survey (formerly the Price Waterhouse/Cranfield Project), the 1990s saw an increase in a range of indices characteristic of structured ILMs including succession planning, high-flyer schemes, and formal career plans (Heraty and Morley 2000: 30). This trend was particularly pronounced amongst organizations with 200 or more employees. This would appear to be related to the specific dynamics of the Irish labour market. Throughout much of the 1980s, Irish economic growth was sluggish and unemployment escalated, giving rise to an over-supply of labour in most sectors. Consequently, 'dipping' into the ELM was a ready option for employers (Gunnigle 1992: 8). However, the post-1994 period saw the emergence of the 'Celtic Tiger' economy with economic growth figures three to four times the EU average, feeding into skill shortages (Heraty and Morley 2000: 22). As Heraty and Morley (2003: 77) argue, in such a context, organizations are increasingly under pressure in the war for managerial talent. This, combined with employee developmental expectations, would appear to be driving the emphasis towards ILMs. Nevertheless, while the *trend* may well be in this direction, the majority of Irish companies continue to eschew managerial developmental strategies such as succession plans and formal job rotation (Heraty and Morley 2000: 30). This would suggest that the sourcing of Irish managers mirrors the US and British situations in being somewhat hybridized.

Germany

German managerial development is quite distinct from the US variant. Germany is a society that emphasizes the importance of *technik*, the fashioning of useful artefacts, and subject matter (Handy et al. 1988: 126). A defining feature is thus the functional or technical orientation of big business (Evans, Lank, and Farquhar 1989: 125), giving rise to a specialist, rather than generalist managerial approach (Hansen and Wilcox 1997: 199). As Sparrow and Hiltrop (1994: 377) note, German managers do not 'manage' in the round but are instead seen to 'manage something'. Managerial entrants, increasingly graduates from polytechnics and universities, do undergo an initial period of job rotation. This allows the company to find the job most suited to the individual (Evans, Lank, and Farquhar 1989: 125). However, ongoing multi-functional mobility is limited to a few 'elitist recruits' or non-existent (p. 127), and even these high-potential employees must first and foremost be technical experts in a given field (Hansen and Willcox 1997: 197). One consequence of this approach is that skills are predominantly skewed towards technical competence, rather than general management. A corollary is fairly rapid promotion, given that German employees do not have to prove their competence in different positions of the same level.

This much having been said, in common with the USA there is a long history of large German companies operating ILMs (Windolf and Wood 1988: 148). This is predominantly a manifestation of the German emphasis on stability in organizational life, reflected more widely in the stability of supplier–client relationships and shareholder groupings (Calori et al. 1995).[1] German managers have traditionally expressed strong attachments to their profession, sector, and firm, characteristically spending their whole career within a single organization (Calori, Steele, and Yoneyaman 1995), with criteria for promotion skewed towards expertise, seniority, and longevity (Hansen and Wilcox 1997: 200). Set within such a model, job changing and the introduction of outside hires is often regarded as disruptive (p. 199). Interestingly, German managers have also been recorded as having an input into such career issues as the suitability of transfers (see, e.g. Deller and Flunkert 1996: 8), suggesting the existence of proprietorial rights over career, somewhat akin to their American and British peers.

Spain

While the first business school was established in Bilbao as far back as 1916 (Sparrow and Hiltrop 1994: 385), the data available on Spanish HR practices are somewhat scant (Bayo-Moriones and Merino-Díaz de Cerio 2001: 189); those pertaining specifically to managerial development even more so. What emerges, however, is a model that shows some marked similarities to the Germanic system. Traditionally, managerial careers have been developed in one organization and in a specific functional area (Flórez-Saborido, Rendón, and Castro 1992: 53). Mobility between organizations has not been very frequent. This reflects both the traditionally low level of competition for managerial staff between Spanish companies and the limited incentives for employees to move given the practice of awarding promotion predominantly on the basis of seniority (Aguilera 2004; Flórez-Saborido, Rendón, and Castro 1992). Intra-organizational geographic mobility has likewise been limited. This stands in marked contrast to the wider Latin European system, exemplified by France, where it is common for young graduates to be sent on international assignments, serving as attachés to senior managers (Lawrence 1993). In 1983, the average length of service in Spanish companies with over 200 workers was 15 years, even higher than Japan.

Overall, the traditional reliance on ILMs appears to be holding up, notwithstanding the increased competition for managerial staff, evidenced in the growing use of head-hunting organizations (Flórez-Saborido, Rendón, and Castro 1992: 52). Bayo-Moriones and Merino-Díaz de Cerio's survey (2001: 189) of Spanish manufacturing plants indicates a heavy reliance on internal promotion as a means of filling senior managerial posts. Such a focus on internal resourcing has been related to facets of business culture, notably the traditional resistance to geographical mobility, both within the country and internationally; the strong preference for employment stability; and the existence of a business culture that historically has reinforced internal promotion (Camelo et al. 2004: 955).

There is nevertheless evidence of erosion of traditional practice as the Spanish system of corporate governance evolves towards a hybrid model that adopts practices from different systems, especially the Anglo-Saxon one (Aguilera 2004: 9). Spanish accession to the European Community in 1986 was the catalyst, giving rise to a fivefold increase in foreign investment (López-Claros 1989: 9)—a trend that has been sustained following the 'regulation by deregulation' (Aguilera 2004: 26) of financial and labour markets. Such investment, particularly targeted at mergers and buy-outs of Spanish companies, has had a significant impact on managerial practice (Flórez-Saborido, Rendón, and Castro 1992: 41), especially promotion criteria. The importance formerly placed on seniority in promotion decisions appears to be diminishing, with an increasing reliance on appointment on merit (Flórez-Saborido, Rendón, and Castro 1992: 52). Hence, Martín et al.'s study (2001) of leading Spanish industrial firms indicated that preference is now accorded to career management based on performance and skills, rather than seniority.

EMPIRICAL FINDINGS

When considering the robustness of ILMs, the characteristic approach is to invoke Doeringer and Piore's account (1971) of the 'classic pillars' of ILMs—limited external recruitment, rigid and unresponsive pay structures, and steady internal career progression—and to map change along these vectors (see, e.g. Grimshaw et al. 2001; McGovern, Hope-Hailey, and Stiles 1998). The foregoing analysis likewise draws upon this model, and initially, we focus on the theme of career progression as a means of organizing the data; this in effect calls for a focus on process-orientated issues. Under such a formulation, the traditional managerial career within ILMs may, at its simplest, be conceptualized as a manpower flow comprising a range of activities, including graduate recruitment, selection and development of 'high potential' employees (hipos), formal succession planning, and the use of inter- and intra-functional developmental activities (see Table 9.1 for a summary of findings). An evaluation of the ongoing robustness of these practices sets the context for an examination of the emergent challenges to ILMs in which issues pertaining to the recruitment of experienced hires and to pay are afforded closer scrutiny.

Graduate Recruitment

Most of the companies had well-established graduate training schemes operating at subsidiary level. Indeed, in interviews graduate entry was often depicted as the 'life blood', and as dictating the very 'life cycle' of these firms. Particularly in internet recruitment, great emphasis was placed on marketing the organization as 'employer of choice' to prospective graduates. There was a marked homogeneity in the way companies sold themselves to candidates, offering very formalized graduate development and training programmes. However, some organizations were clearly preoccupied with attracting 'very qualified, upwardly mobile people', rather than graduates per se. Such 'brand' differentiation was clearly evident at ITco, Business Services, Engco2, and Healthcare. These companies were explicit in their desire to 'identify and hire the best talent on campus'. In return, they offered new recruits the promise of high-calibre peer groups and steep learning curves.

The importance attached to graduate recruitment was reflected in the rigour of the selection procedure. This was generally centrally coordinated at global or European level. Thus at Business Services (where 100 per cent of consultancy staff came via this route), there was a highly standardized global selection process, using the same interviewer training, identical interview forms, and a standard framework of competencies worldwide. Up until very recently the firm's entire annual worldwide cohort of several thousand recruits had attended an induction programme in the USA 'for a period of weeks to get indoctrinated into the *Business Services* way' (HQ global HR manager). Latterly, however, on cost grounds there had been a shift to a 'virtual' computer-based initiation process. The standardization of practice was viewed as essential given the marketing of the organization as a global brand, with multinational clients expecting consistency in worldwide service delivery. Similarly, ITco utilized a Europe-wide testing centre model that had been developed in recent years. This template, initially piloted in the UK, comprised business

Table 9.1. Developing managers in selected US MNCs

Company	Graduate recruitment	Functional rotation	International mobility	High potentials and succession planning
Business Services	Elite graduate recruitment, highly standardized globally	Frequent cross-project and function movement	High and project linked	'Up-or-out' market-oriented hipo development approach (typical of sector)
CPGco	Specific targeting of science and engineering graduates,—two-year induction through various assignments	Inter-functional mobility but limited movement between businesses	International moves for hipos coordinated at regional level	Highly formalized and coordinated management development process for hipos with several years experience in the company, linking in with global succession plans
Engco1	Graduate recruitment but also promotion from shop floor	Frequent horizontal mobility encouraged by move away from functional 'silos'	International movement generally done on ad hoc basis through contact networks, but increasingly prerequisite for career advancement at global senior levels	Formalized succession planning for top 150 posts worldwide, with more informal system of hipo development at lower levels
Engco2	Elite graduate recruitment however, still some promotion of senior personnel from shop floor	Limited horizontal mobility, functional chimney particularly strong for engineers	Importance of international experience for career prospects	Global hipo process relatively recently developed
ITco	Elite graduate recruitment, Europe-wide testing centre model	Cross-functional experience seen as key to future promotion, esp. in generalist areas	International assignment essential for career development	Early identification of hipos on entry; highly formalized global succession planning based on performance and development reviews tracking top stratum in each subsidiary
Logistico	Limited importance of graduate recruitment, emphasis on promotion through the 'ranks'	Cross-functional experience crucial for future promotion	International experience essential for advanced career development	Succession planning for senior managers under strong regional coordination, with senior position-filling based on European pool of managers

games, interviews, and tests, in an array of areas including financial logic, numeracy, and communications. However, even within the confines of a centrally imposed format, there was some room for local creativity. Thus in Germany, both ITco and Silico had been active in setting up a new route of entry via vocational training for high school graduates, in preference to post-university entrance. Irish subsidiaries were especially proactive. ITco employed a college liaison manager, as a means of developing strong working relations with universities and technological colleges. A recent initiative was the establishment of an 'academic council', charged with identifying and developing areas of mutual interest between university departments and ITco units. Likewise, at Pharmaco, professors at both local and national universities forwarded to the subsidiary lists of their brightest graduates on an annual basis. These tight academic linkages are arguably reflective of the small size of the Irish economy, increasingly acute skill shortages and the fact that year-on-year only a limited number of companies recruit from a finite labour pool, allowing close relationships to be built.

One or two companies, however, were exceptional in affording limited importance to graduate recruitment. This was the case at both Compuco and Logistico. In the former, there had never been any specific graduate recruitment in the Irish subsidiary. At Logistico, the low status of graduate recruitment is explicable in terms of the strong ethos of encouraging employees to work their way up from the 'shop floor'. The ILM was perpetuated by the systematic appraisal and development of non-managerial staff, rather than by graduate recruitment. As our German informants pointed out, there was a long tradition of hierarchical mobility, especially for drivers. Within the UK subsidiary, a key element of this approach was the creation of a specialized assessment centre to identify future managerial talent, again a local initiative. This instance of 'reverse diffusion' was in the process of becoming part of a wider corporate approach to management development. The two engineering firms, Engco1 and Engco2, also relied to some extent on managers who had worked their way up from the shop floor.

Functional Rotation and International Mobility

Across most companies there was a relatively high degree of horizontal (or job) mobility. However, this was particularly pronounced within the British subsidiaries. For example, a significant proportion of HR managers had been brought in from other functional specialisms. Such movement was often formalized through cross-functional development pathways. The process had been afforded added stimulus in certain instances, for example Engco1, because of the move away from functional silos to business units. In some companies (e.g. Drugco) this was at odds with the wider sectoral pattern. Senior managers placed great emphasis on such functional mobility as a means of 'keeping employees tested', and nurturing future managerial talent. Indeed, a common perception was that 'if you weren't moving, you weren't being successful' (manager, Drugco UK).

At EngServs, UK lateral movement, which predominantly took the form of movement between projects, was viewed as a natural response to the cyclical nature of the industry: during periods of downturn there was a need to find jobs for valued employees who might otherwise be 'poached'. More broadly, rotation between functions and projects gave employees a more rounded set of competencies, especially important for future generalists. The tendency to move managers across functions was reinforced by the trend away from functional organizational structures to ones based on international business divisions. However, in some instances (most notably, Engco1 and CPGco), there were concerns that that business 'silos' were replacing functional ones, making it difficult for managers to move between businesses. This was particularly noticeable at CPGco, where senior business managers, having invested in employees, were loath to release up-and-coming talent.

While mobility within and between functions was a feature of management development across the UK subsidiaries, the frequency of change in assignments was particularly rapid in some instances. At Engco1 and Drugco, the average length of tenure in some functional areas was two years or less. However, most significant in this respect was Business Services, where staff were continually 're-created'. The project-based environment of consulting dictated that there was de facto rotation at eighteen-, twelve-, or even six-monthly intervals as staff moved between assignments. Potential executives were rarely in the same role for more than twelve or fifteen months.

The emphasis upon horizontal mobility also came through in the Irish and German data. This was exemplified in two of our core case studies, ITco and Logistico. At ITco, cross-functional experience was viewed as a prerequisite for future promotion opportunities, again particularly important for aspiring generalists. These findings were echoed at Logistico, where functional rotation was a precondition for personal development. Thus, it was essential that experience, in say accountancy, be complemented by tenure in an operational position. The results are particularly notable within the German context, suggesting some erosion of hitherto dominant functional career ladders.

The widespread use of lateral rotation was giving rise to evident tensions. This was particularly the case in certain Spanish subsidiaries, where respondents were often seen to be resistant to the 'zigzag' style of management unleashed by very rapid job rotation. At Refresco, for example, there were concerns that the tendency to rotate people 'American-style' every two to three years, didn't give employees 'time to learn anything', perhaps reflecting the traditional Spanish preference for functional specialization. Indeed, at Drugco this was a cause of friction between HR and various functional areas. Tensions arose because of the desire of HR to promote flexibility at the expense of the specific skills required in particular departments. One upshot of this 'push back' was a tendency for Spanish employees in this organization to remain in specific roles for longer than their British counterparts, notwithstanding the global tracking of the process by the US board.

Functional rotation was generally complemented by the use of geographical movement as a developmental tool. Indeed, this was generally viewed as the *sine qua non* for hipo status (see later) and *ergo*, appointment to senior managerial level. This was the case at Chemco, Logistico, ITco, Softco, Engco2, and Household. The following comments were fairly standard:

There's very much, I think, that perception, certainly from the European side, that this is one of the requirements [for senior management]. You have to be willing to move, you are blocking your career if you say you will not move. There is definitely a glass ceiling. (Managers CSC, Logistico, Ireland)

In many instances (e.g. Logistico, Chemco, Bankco, CPGco, and ITco), the process was formally coordinated at regional level and systematically programmed into career planning. However, in others, the process was both more ad hoc and less dogmatically prescriptive. Thus, for example, at Engco1 potential overseas assignees were asked on an annual basis whether or not they would *consider* an international assignment. Of the four host countries, Spain was again an outlier in that there was relatively little movement by managers to other subsidiaries. This resistance to mobility was causing problems due to bottlenecks. One Spanish subsidiary, Groomco, had sought to circumvent such recalcitrance through a process of filtration, asking candidates at the point of pre-selection if they were mobile.

Interestingly, the rationale underpinning international rotation was not exclusively developmental. What came through strongly was the desire to preserve the integrity of the ILM. It was the only way in which internal resources could provide sufficient flexibility to fulfil the requirements of different parts of the organization, without recourse to outside hires and the associated problem of cultural contamination. This was particularly so at Drugco where there was an ageing senior managerial cohort; at Business Services, where there were intermittent shortages of critical skills in certain regions; and in the smaller companies such as Household, where consumer products had only a few thousand employees across the world. Another factor driving the requirement for international experience was the growing importance of cross-national organizational structures, particularly global business units. This meant that the career horizon for aspiring managers was increasingly within business 'silos', but at the same time international.

The Management of High Potentials and Succession Planning

An increasing trend in managerial development over the last twenty years or so has been the granting of privileged status to high-potential managerial entrants or 'high flyers', both as a means of developing future executives for mid- and upper-career level jobs, and to enhance retention of high calibre candidates (cf. Thompson et al. 2001: 22–3). Indeed, given the closed nature of ILMs, the pressing need to decrease the cycle time required to identify leadership needs, assess current talent, and develop high performers is particularly acute (see Burke 1997: 19). Hence, the identification of a high-potential managerial cadre, groomed to advance rapidly through the corporate hierarchy is of crucial importance.

The case-study firms generally had formal management tools for the development of high-potential managerial talent. In some instances hipos were selected from amongst the annual graduate intake. In others, assessment centres or career development workshops for employees with some experience were popular. Characteristically, the hipo process was globally coordinated and managed, although in some cases this was done at European level (e.g. Chemco), and this was quite recent in some companies (e.g. Engco2). Typical development activities included ongoing training needs assessments, leadership programmes, and planned rotational assignments for experiential learning. Typically, the cohort would be tracked against a competency framework on an annual basis. Echoing Derr, Jones, and Toomey's findings (1988) regarding hipo management in large US enterprises, a further commonality was the emphasis placed on total flexibility for this group. Interestingly, this came through in all host countries, including Spain, suggesting some erosion of the traditional resistance to overseas movement—at least amongst this elite grouping.

Beyond these broad similarities, however, there were some clear distinctions, particularly in the timing of hipo selection. Such nuance was very much driven by corporate policy, rather than being coloured by host country influence. Evans, Lank, and Farquhar (1989: 128–9) have remarked that the age at which potential should be identified is a problematic area, pointing to trade-offs between potential identification at entry level, or after some years of proven technical experience. As Burke (1997: 22) argues, a problem with the former strategy is the 'crown prince syndrome', whereby hipos 'perceive they have been anointed as the chosen few'.

Such dilemmas were evident in the case-study firms. For example, under the highly formalized management development process at CPGco, graduates were only identified after they had been in the company for four or five years. The process was explicit and transparent, with the cadre of hipos informed of their status. Similarly, Chemco used a European assessment centre for experienced hires, with candidates made fully aware of the significance of the exercise. By contrast, ITco utilized a model of early selection in which the managerial cohort was assessed on entry for executive or 'high-flying' potential. Hipos were typically not given an indication of their status before the age of 30. This heterogeneity in approach accords with Evans, Lank, and Farquhar's comment (1989: 124) that there is a diversity in American patterns, not least in the timing of the 'tournament', compared with the broad uniformity evident in other models of managerial development; for example, the elite cohort, late selection approach used in Japan (see also Handy et al. 1989; Storey, Edwards, and Sisson 1997). Distinctive (although typical of its sector) was Business Services, which pursued an 'up-or-out' strategy. After several years as professionals, members of its graduate intake who would not make the grade were 'counselled out' at the point of transition to managerial positions.

Closely allied with hipo identification is the administering of succession planning—the process whereby existing managers are identified to succeed outgoing or retiring managers, often within a specific timescale. Succession planning was widely used across the case-study companies. Indeed, in several instances this process was prioritized as the pre-eminent HR issue, and subsidiaries were left in little doubt of the need to toe the line. However, there were significant differences in the formality of the process, the time horizons, the degree of coordination, and the relative importance of 'technical' as opposed 'political' criteria (Friedman 1986).

In most organizations, the formalization of processes was very much a function of hierarchical level, and there was again an absence of a detectable host-country effect. Thus, at Engco1 formalized executive succession planning took place for the top 150 corporate positions. Below this, and for most managers at subsidiary level, a less-regulated approach predominated. This was depicted in the UK subsidiary as a 'networking-type, buddy-buddy system' (HR manager), often driven by informal anecdote about people's reputation. Eventual success was seen to depend on the patronage of business champions and the operation of informal networks. Similarly at *Pharmaco*, while the planning covered the top three levels of the organizational hierarchy, at subsidiary level, corporate HQ did not question the credentials of the people involved. The requirement was simply to have 'names in boxes'. At Groomco, our Spanish respondents noted that such a list was not even a mandatory requirement for subsidiaries, although it existed in the majority of countries. In several firms a more penetrative, centrally scrutinized model was applied, with globalized talent inventories drilling further down the corporate and subsidiary chain. These organizations had sought to move away from a reliance on informal perceptions and networking at subsidiary level. That is, there was a shift from political to more objective technical criteria.

Corporate monitoring was well established at CPGco, whose centrally coordinated formal development process extended out to subsidiaries, acting as a conveyor belt for filling 'critical positions' through a central clearing system. The process was particularly sophisticated at ITco where there was a standardized approach, involving performance/development reviews based on a number of definitions set down at corporate level. The reviews formed the basis for succession planning, and were used to track the top fifty people at subsidiary level.

Distinctive amongst our companies were the two computer manufacturers. Silico applied a rather idiosyncratic approach, advertising top managerial posts internally every three years. Compuco was the least-developed organization in terms of its succession planning. While one manager at the Irish subsidiary did claim that there was a corporate succession plan, even she acknowledged that it was poorly maintained, noting that it was out of date even before it was on paper, perhaps reflective of the company's relative youth as an MNC.

COUNTERVAILING PRESSURES: TOWARDS A HYBRID APPROACH TO THE MANAGEMENT OF MANAGERIAL CAREERS

Changes to 'Supply' and 'Assignment Flow'

Taken as a whole, the earlier data point towards a strong ongoing commitment towards the internal development of managers. Nevertheless, it was also clear that companies were reviewing the efficacy of their policies in the light of the business uncertainties and pressures for change reviewed earlier in the chapter. This was in turn resulting in some erosion of the strategy of relying predominantly on home-grown managerial talent. This accords with Sonnenfield, Peiperl, and Kotter's modelling (1988) of career policy as a coherent and internally consistent set of variables, configured by the strategic behaviour of organizations (see also Kanter 1984). Within this formulation, career policy reflects a range of environing influences, such as the stability of markets, barriers to entry, market dominance, monopoly power, and the need for innovation and dynamism. Changes to such exogenous factors are predicted to be reflected in movements along two dimensions: supply flow, which captures the extent to which an organization relies on the external or internal labour market, and assignment flow, the degree to which individual mobility (e.g. assignments and promotion decisions) are based on individual performance or group contributions. While still controversial (see Baruch and Peiperl 2003, for a critique), Sonnenfield's model is useful heuristically as a means of conceptualizing the dynamics of corporate career systems, given that it captures both inter- and intra-organizational movement.

The efficiency of an emphasis on internal supply flow rests partly on employers' needs for firm-specific skills (Mylett and Zanko 2002; Kanter 1984). It was evident that there was significant movement along this dimension towards a greater reliance on 'outside hires' as firms responded to external pressures. CPGco was a case in point. This organization formerly operated in a stable product market with predictable skill requirements. However, there had been much erosion of the ILM as the company had sought to institute a career system more attuned to contemporary product markets and technology where skill needs were difficult to anticipate. Over the previous decade the company had been exposed to increased international competition. One response had been to diversify into new high-margin areas, particularly products based on rapidly evolving digital technology. CPGco had in turn bought in the required skills it needed by hiring experienced employees:

My perception is yes, it is far more accepted to bring in people at mid-level than it has been in the past. In the past it would have been promotion from within first, second and third choice. And a poor fourth would have been external. Now it's generally acceptable to bring in an external person if the right competencies are there. (Senior UK manager, CPGco)

The erosion of CPGco's once insular culture was symbolized by the recent appointment of the first CEO from outside.

A similar scenario was played out at several other companies. ITco, formerly regarded as a bastion of the ILM with an ingrained 'job-for-life' ethos, saw its solid market position in manufacturing eroded from the 1980s. Its recovery was based on a shift in the balance of operations away from manufacturing into the higher-margin area of IT service provision. This triggered an erosion of the ILM as the company was required to look externally for the necessary competencies. The influx of external managerial talent, while now commonplace across the British, German, and Spanish subsidiaries, had been particularly pronounced in Ireland. This was due to the rapid recent growth in the Irish operation, where it was accepted that the experience of local managers was low. Interestingly, the resultant integration of fresh ideas was seen as a very positive spin off, suggesting some downgrading of the erstwhile belief in the necessity for strong cultural ties. Similar findings were reflected elsewhere. Pharmaco Ireland was aware of the problems of 'cloning' generated by a complete reliance on the ILM. One HR adviser pointed to the inherent danger of new ideas being retarded if new blood were not recruited into the organization on a regular basis.

Amongst our case-study companies, Logistico was exemplary in its determination to fill managerial posts internally; even CEOs to date had been assigned from within the corporation. The maintenance of the status quo is explicable first, in terms of Logistico's presence in a traditionally low-tech sector with predictable skill demands, and; second, the entrenched position of the company in a sector where there are nevertheless significant barriers to entry, not least the requirement for a well-coordinated logistical infrastructure. However, there was an awareness of tensions resulting from the ILM, due to recent rapid overseas expansion. In terms of the requirement for international mobility, this was perhaps the most autocratic of our sample, adhering rigidly to a regiocentric (Heenan and Perlmutter 1979) model of staffing, whereby key positions are filled by the best person in the region, in this case Europe. The highly prescriptive nature of policy in this area was a cause of some unease amongst some junior managers, not yet on the international 'wagon train', fearful that the company's 'blinkered' stance could represent a barrier to subsequent repatriation.

A further problem was that the creation of the German subsidiary predated most other European subsidiaries by some fifteen years. One consequence, given the entrenched ILM, was that Germans predominated among senior managers at regional level. This was clearly a source of embarrassment to a firm committed to the principles of diversity (see Chapter 8). Nevertheless, Logistico continued resolutely to avoid importing managerial talent, preferring instead to fine-tune the ILM by extending and modifying the fast-track management programme, for example, by rolling out the British assessment centre initiative. The company thus stands as a useful illustration of the degree to which there is still managerial 'strategic choice' within the constraints imposed by changing market pressures.

The enhanced inflow of personnel in most companies, giving rise to increasingly hybridized approaches, was similarly accompanied by changes in 'assignment flow'. Overall, the data suggest that the ILM was moving away from the classic economists' ILM model of seniority-based promotion, towards a more meritocratic model, less sheltered from the vicissitudes of market pressures. This was manifest in strategies of performance management (see Chapter 7) and an emerging 'core–periphery' approach to managing managers. Exit via retirement was no longer taken for granted, and in some organizations consistently underperforming managers were just as likely to be 'managed' or 'counselled' out. There was a growing desire to retain high-performing managers, rather than managers per se. At ITco, for example, while the notion of a job-for-life had gone, British respondents stressed the danger of losing the more competent people. As a corporate HR manager noted, 'you know, attrition could be at 30 per cent, but if it's people that aren't adding value then you don't care'.

Headquarters, however, did not have a totally free hand to initiate policy in this area. In some host settings, the more brutal facets of corporate strategy were perforce diluted to comply with local norms. Ultimately, there would appear to be limits as to how far market rigours can be introduced unimpeded into certain national settings. As discussed in Chapter 7, the GE model of culling the bottom tranche of performers was not an option for Irish subsidiaries, although there was evidence of it being utilized in the UK. It was similarly evident that in Germany the shift to a more contingent system of reward was problematic for institutional reasons. Thus at Business Services, global proposals for a more variable pay structure had met with resistance amongst consulting staff. This gave rise to the introduction of the policy in a weaker form. Similarly at CPGco, at the time of the research the proposed linking of performance appraisal to merit increases was proving controversial.

The Impact of Restructuring

The trajectory of managerial careers was also in a state of flux as a result of organizational restructuring, enacted through episodes of delayering, downsizing, and mergers. A common practice was the stripping out of management layers at the regional headquarters. This had significant implications for management near the top of the subsidiary hierarchy. Consider, for example, CPGco. Here the leaner organizational structure was undermining vertical mobility by eliminating jobs at the European regional level. The 'strategic' posts were increasingly based at corporate and business division headquarters in the USA. As a result, career advancement for senior managers entailed moving to America—a step that was not necessarily seen as attractive. The company was acutely aware that frustrations with regard to career progression could result in an exodus of talent and sought to stem the tide through the increased provision of lateral career opportunities and the 'handcuffing' of employees through stock options and retention bonuses.

The transition towards flatter, leaner organizational structures at subsidiary level was likewise resulting in leakages of talented employees due to frustrated career expectations. This was particularly the case in the UK, plausibly because of the greater culture of career mobility. HR managers regarded the increasing emphasis on lateral movement as, at best, a partial solution:

Certainly in sales and marketing when I was there, people would join as marketers and they would get bored within three to four years. Being a flat lean organization they'd find that there wasn't the next job, a direct ladder. We'd say well you can move to the side, move into sales, and they'd say well it's the same grade, I'm not doing that. (UK HR manager, Household)

One outcome was a new sense of realism, with several of these formerly paternalistic organizations becoming 'less hysterical' about employees wanting to join other companies. Indeed, in the current climate, talented departees who subsequently wished to return were more likely to be welcomed than debarred for reasons of disloyalty.

CONCLUSIONS

The data presented in this chapter feed into two important streams of literature. First they inform the debate on the trajectory and dynamics of managerial labour markets. *Pace* an increasingly influential body of literature, our findings do not indicate the demise of internal managerial careers, or a shift to 'a new open-ended relationship driven by market forces' (Cappelli 2000: 23). Rather, the findings support Grimshaw et al.'s prognosis (2001) that changing market conditions have given rise to new sets of tensions within the operation of ILMs, rather than neutralizing their role as a site for the reproduction of managerial skills and corporate culture. Thus graduate entry, the development of employees regarded as high potential, and medium-term succession planning all remain firmly in place. Following Piore (2002: 274), this may be partly explicable in terms of the increasing reliance on project and teamworking. To be sure, the managerial skills required could be drawn from the competitive labour market. However, ultimately managerial competence relies on knowledge and experience of the *specific* domain in which such skills are applied. As Pfeffer (1998: xviii) has argued, what 'provides long-term advantage are those things that are core to the firm and not readily duplicated by competitors—and purchases on the open market cannot be sources of unique or distinct capabilities'.

There are clear affinities with the literatures on the resource-based view of the firm; and, more specifically, the learning organization (see, e.g. Senge 1991), that see knowledge as something which is stimulated and produced through ongoing social interactions or 'cognitive partnerships'. That is, through knowledge creation, individuals shape and transform the social/interactional environments within which they work, enhancing organizational potential and competitiveness (Lee et al. 2004: 8).

It is nevertheless clear that, in line with earlier work by McGovern, Hope-Hailey, and Stiles (1998), the traditional career model has been significantly 'downsized', particularly as a result of changing technologies requiring the rapid importation of new skills. Similarly, the shift to more flexible organizational forms through the process of downsizing and delayering has had an impact, giving rise to increasingly truncated career ladders. Career movement in many settings is thus more likely to be horizontal than vertical, increasing outflows as result of 'pyramid squeeze' (Kanter 1984: 125) and frustrated career expectations.

The findings similarly contribute to debates on corporate control and subsidiary autonomy. For the most part, the management of managers was centrally conceived and coordinated. Management development was regarded as an area of corporate rather than subsidiary responsibility. In this regard the corporate hand had unquestionably been strengthened by the growing importance of the regional tier, with policy on graduate recruitment and international assignments, for example, generally coordinated at this level. Within this area of HR policy there was very little scope for contestation and few opportunities for local HR personnel to act as 'interpreters of the local environment' or to secure a degree of autonomy through charter building. The manifest lack of host country influence lends support to Rosenzweig and Nohria's thesis (1994), that managerial development is more susceptible to central influence than HR generally, as there is less pressure on firms to be 'isomorphic' to local business culture.

Yet headquarters did not have totally free hand. More specifically, the attempted diffusion of a distinctly Anglo-Saxon version of the ILM had met with resistance, notably in some German settings. The emphasis upon the individualization of the relationship between managers and their firms, captured in the emphasis on tighter performance standards through contingent pay, had met with stiff opposition. Such practice was widely regarded as anathema to the more egalitarian German culture. In this respect at least, 'customs, norms and politics' (Osterman 1994: 324) *had* been influential. This accords with Sparrow and Hiltrop's (1994: 47) observation that there is a difference between the USA and UK (as representatives of the Anglo-Saxon approach to HRM) and other European countries, in relation to the desirability of sharing organizational risk with individuals. This suggests that the ability of US MNCs to move their European subsidiaries towards more meritocratic, individualized, and target-driven modes of ILM will remain, in some settings, the source of local contestation and continuing uncertainty.

Note

1. For non-managerial employees legislation has also been important. Under the Works Constitution Act, works councils are entitled to demand that vacancies are filled internally. For executive staff (employers with 'managerial functions') the Works Constitution Act does not apply.

Part IV

The Findings: Structure, Process, and Dynamics

10

Centralization

Anthony Ferner, Paddy Gunnigle, Javier Quintanilla, Hartmut Wächter, and Tony Edwards

INTRODUCTION

This chapter considers one of the most complex issues in the management of employment relations in multinationals: the balance between central control and subsidiary autonomy in policy and practice. American MNCs have a reputation for centralizing control of HR policy and applying it in a standardized way across subsidiaries internationally. But the existing, largely survey-based literature, gives few clues as to the reasons why this should be so. Moreover, it provides little insight into the internal organizational mechanisms that create and maintain a particular pattern of centralization and autonomy, as the approach is generally static, and does not explore the dynamics of centre—subsidiary relations over time. This chapter uses the methodological advantages of the case-study approach, particularly its ability to investigate processual aspects of organizational behaviour, to explore patterns of centralization—autonomy in US MNCs.

After briefly revisiting the wider literature on centralization and autonomy, it provides a broad-brush picture of the degree of centralization and standardization of HR policy in the case-study companies. It then attempts two main tasks. First, it examines the factors that drive change in the balance between central control and subsidiary autonomy over time. In doing this, it picks up a theme of earlier chapters, the ability of actors at different levels of the corporation to influence policy choices. Second, it explores the patterns of similarity and difference underlying the centralization—autonomy balance in different host countries.

CENTRALIZATION VERSUS LOCAL AUTONOMY IN THE MANAGEMENT OF EMPLOYMENT RELATIONS

The well-worn cliché of the international management literature concerning the need for both global integration and local responsiveness (e.g. Bartlett and Ghoshal 1998) finds perhaps its most vivid expression in the dilemmas of the HR function itself. On the one hand, research shows that across a range of management issues, central control in MNCs is least forcefully exerted over HR/IR matters (e.g. Young, Hood, and Hamill 1985). On the other, considerations of efficiency, consistency, and equity encourage companies to adopt transnational structures of centralized control and coordination and to implement standardized policies as far as possible. Rosenzweig and Singh (1991) conceptualize this as the tension between two rival 'isomorphic' pulls: between the framework imposed by the corporate centre and the institutional constraints of the host environments in which the multinational operates. HRM itself comprises a range of heterogeneous issues which embody this tension to different degrees. Rosenzweig and Nohria (1994), in their study of HR in foreign multinationals in the USA, found that 'rank-and-file' IR issues, such as wage determination, hours of work, job contracts, and redundancy procedures, were more susceptible to the local isomorphic pull of the host environment; while other areas, such as management development or employee communication, were more prone to the institutional pull of the wider corporation.

Schmitt and Sadowski (2003) have conceptualized the balance between competing pressures for central control and local autonomy using the analogy of 'fiscal federalism'. They argue that the optimal degree of centralization occurs when the sum of costs of centralization and those of decentralization is minimized. The costs of decentralizing include the foregone scale economies in the design and application of personnel systems, and the loss of internal consistency. This argument may be reinforced by invoking Taylor, Beechler, and Napier's analysis (1996) of strategic international HRM: central managers in MNCs are more likely to diffuse central HR policies and competences where these are seen as contributing to the international competitiveness of the company. In Schmitt and Sadowski's terms, decentralization costs would include foregoing the competitive advantage deriving from the international propagation of effective HR practices developed by the centre. Conversely, the costs of centralization include the cost of accessing relevant know-how which is often held locally; increasing control costs as the number of subsidiary units rises; costs of violating the regulations and norms of the local systems in which subsidiaries operate; and the costs of frustrating the preferences of subsidiary actors, which are likely to vary cross-nationally. The higher the costs (and the lower the benefits) of decentralization compared with centralization, the more likely are personnel practices in the subsidiary to be influenced by central policy.

In recent years, greater attention has been paid to the dispersal of strategic functions from a monolithic corporate headquarters across a range of international operations. In what have been called 'federal' or 'heterarchic' structures (e.g. Hedlund 1986), subsidiaries assume worldwide or regional responsibility for a particular business, product, or management function such as R&D. Watson and Roth (2003) refer to this phenomenon as 'lateral centralization'. Thus while activities are coordinated and globally centralized, the 'critical point or focus of decision-making is at the subsidiary level, not at headquarters (p. 137). This does not change the essence of the Schmitt and Sadowski approach, merely the locus of centralization.

Schmitt and Sadowski's analysis provides a flexible framework for analysing the degree of centralization. It can accommodate, for example, national-institutional considerations. Institutional constraints in areas such as employee representation—for example, codetermination legislation in Germany—can be seen as raising the costs of centralization, since to evade the constraints requires the development of costly avoidance strategies and may antagonize local actors both within the MNC and outside it. The framework can also incorporate differences due to sectoral factors. For example, in sectors where activities are highly integrated cross-nationally, the costs of decentralization and the benefits of centralization, including the scope for economies of scale, may be higher than in more 'multidomestic' industries.

The Schmitt and Sadowski approach suffers from a number of problems, primarily its excessively rationalistic assumptions: the degree of HR centralization depends on the application by top corporate management of a positivistic cost–benefit calculus. This is to downplay the incalculability of many of the costs and benefits of HR centralization or autonomy, resulting from the uncertainty of outcomes, the difficulty of quantifying outcomes even where they are known, and the 'causal ambiguity' (Szulanski 1996) of management practice whereby it is unclear what particular effect causes what outcome. At first sight, the framework is also incapable of accommodating another notable aspect of centre–subsidiary relations that has been touched on in earlier chapters: the pervasive organizational micropolitics accompanying the creation, transfer, and implementation of HR policy within the multinational. In theory, micropolitics can be incorporated as an element in the cost–benefit calculus. For example, if a subsidiary resists implementation of a global HR policy, the centralization costs include the costs of the resources required to overcome subsidiary resistance. As is argued later, where the perspective of this book departs from the Schmitt and Sadowski approach is in seeing structured differences of interest, and their continual interplay, as an inherent property of MNCs.

THE NATIONALITY EFFECT IN CENTRALIZATION–DECENTRALIZATION

A considerable body of research examines the degree of centralization of HR/IR issues in MNCs (for a detailed review, see Ferner et al. 2004). Over many years, comparative studies have uncovered distinctive patterns of centralization in MNCs of different national origin. Policies tend to be devised by the corporate centre and are more likely to be standardized internationally in US MNCs (e.g. Child, Faulkner, and Pitkethly 2000; Harzing 1999; Negandhi 1983). HR/ER tends everywhere to be less centrally controlled than other management functions. Nonetheless, HR tends to be more centralized in US companies than in, for example, German or Japanese MNCs; US HQ plays a significant role across a range of issues from employee representation, through collective bargaining to payment systems and training issues (e.g. Gunnigle 1995; Negandhi 1983; Young, Hood, and Hamill 1985). For example, Björkman and Furu's data (2000: 709) 'showed support for MNC home-country effect on the top management pay mix structure: US MNCs seemed more likely to utilize a high proportion of variable pay'.

Case studies (e.g. Martin and Beaumont 1999) have confirmed this picture, showing that US MNCs tend to have standardized international policies in such areas as pay systems and performance management. US companies also exert strong, albeit generally less formalized, central control in such areas as employee representation. Thus, several case studies have reported global policies on union avoidance in American MNCs; in extreme instances such policies have been moderated only minimally by host-country regulations supporting collective representation (see, e.g. Royle 2000).

Studies have likewise found that US companies tend to formalize their international HRM policies to a greater extent than other MNCs, in the sense that policies are codified in the form of written statements, codes of conduct, and so on. Formalization has been associated in turn with a relatively high degree of standardization, that is to say a tendency for policies to be applied in similar or identical ways across a range of operations (see, e.g. Harzing 1999; Kopp 1994).

FINDINGS

The Prevalence of Centralized Global HR Policy

The findings across the four countries confirm in very broad terms the picture of the centralized management of international HRM. There is a pattern of global standardized and formalized policies in a number of areas. Centralized policy was most notable in the management of performance, particularly for managers and in the use of performance-related pay and bonus systems; in other aspects of pay, such as share ownership and market positioning of pay levels relative to competitors (see Chapter 7); in management development and succession planning (Chapter 9); and in employee communications, especially through the use of global staff attitude surveys and the dissemination of global cultural values (see Table 10.1 for an overview of findings for the case-study companies). Other areas where global policies were frequent include the management of workforce 'diversity' (see Chapter 8), and guidelines for relations with unions (see Chapter 6). Finally, policies for the management of managers, especially of senior managers and those with high potential, tended to be more centrally controlled than those for other employees (cf. Scullion and Starkey 2000).

The HR manager of CPGco's Spanish subsidiary usefully distinguished between highly prescriptive and standardized 'policies' and broad 'guidelines' (*directrices*):

In the three areas [of management development, performance related pay and performance appraisal] there is uniformity and the policies are followed in every country in the world. They are 'policies' because they go beyond 'guidelines'. They are written down and are obligatory. For example, a guideline would be if the parent company tells you that you have to appraise employees once a year. In CPGco they tell you 'you have to appraise employees once a year following this particular model and filling in this particular form'.

In some areas of HR practice, the high degree of prescribed standardization was a notable feature. Policies on performance management tended to be

Table 10.1. Patterns of centralization in case-study companies

Firm (country studies)	General	Systems of central control	Role Europe/region and international business divisions	Areas of centralized HR policy
Bankco (D/GB)	Absence of central HR policies in many areas, esp. in corporate and investment banking side, reflecting anti-bureaucratic ethos of dominant merger partner, but with some global HR programmes.	Information on headcount and labour costs is collected and compared regularly. Norm on pay levels of median positioning in labour markets.	Strong impact of business division on the nature of HR policy—more standardized policy within retail banking; minimal central HR policy in other areas. Considerable regional autonomy in determination of HR policy, with centralization of some functions, e.g. recruitment, at European level.	Strongly standardized global policies in executive compensation. Global stock ownership programme being introduced. Increasing attempts to inventorize and manage talent globally, e.g. through development of global leadership competences. Corporate 'philosophies' rather than policies in areas such as diversity.
Business Services (D/E/GB)	Standardized global policy developed through virtual international networks and project teams.			Standardized English language employee satisfaction surveys conducted throughout the company. Graduate orientation programme for all new graduate recruits to consultancy business worldwide. Global system to identify and manage high potentials, including assessment system to facilitate international transfers.
Chemco (E/GB)	Some subsidiary autonomy within general guidelines set by European HQ.		Increasing centralization of HR from corporate HQ following change of CEO, reducing region's role.	Highly standardized global employee performance and development system. Global profit-sharing scheme for supervisors and above.

Compuco (IRL)	Formerly considerable autonomy for HR function in Irish subsidiary, with central influence exerted through tight control of costs. More recent assertion of greater central control of HR policy linked to growing public profile, and in response to labour market problems. Still emphasis on overall control through results rather than processes, with IRL management free to develop own policy solutions.	Rising use of HR metrics on attrition, absenteeism. Corporate monitoring of outcomes of performance appraisal and management development processes. Direct central intervention on specific HR issues, e.g. in move from temporary to permanent contracts in Irish subsidiary.		Introduction of global employee opinion survey. Common toolset for managing compensation, albeit customized slightly for various regions, emphasizing the evaluation and reward of operational performance. Global management training programme, with some local adaptation. New diversity initiative instigated by HQ although with location-specific adaptation. Standard global Compuco 'code of conduct' disseminated to all employees. Stereotypical US non-union management philosophy evident in Irish subsidiary.
CPGco (E/D/GB)	Increasing HR autonomy for international business divisions, sometimes conflicting with centralization within regions.	Strong control of headcount through regular monthly reporting. Ceiling for subsidiary pay rises set by European HQ. Quarterly reports to region on fulfilment of training targets.	Increasing centralization within region, e.g. approval of senior appointments. Some Europe-level functions (e.g. remuneration) contracted to country operations. Use of virtual European structures.	Standardized performance evaluation system, ESOPs. Prescriptive central guidelines on pay (e.g. at risk per cent in bonus scheme). Global policy of pay being at mid-point of market Global system of identifying high potentials, coordinated from HQ. 40 hours training per employee, centrally monitored. Central global opinion survey, linked to senior subsidiary managers' performance measurement. Cultural values driven from centre, formalized relatively recently. Worldwide diversity policy with metrics and link to appraisal; detail left to affiliates, but must include gender issues

(contd.)

Table 10.1. (*contd.*)

Firm (country studies)	General	Systems of central control	Role Europe/region and international business divisions	Areas of centralized HR policy
EngServs (E/GB)	Relative weakness of central financial and HR systems but pressures for globalization leading to review of functions including HR.		European HQ with strong policy role in HR and other matters, but not covering division that UK is part of.	
Engco1 (GB)	Network-based 'pooled' control rather than 'command and control' policy. Much central policy notionally optional, but non-compliance needs to be justified.		Weak coordination in Europe above country level. Move to strong international business divisions from 1990s.	
Engco2 (D/GB)	Direct influence of owner and family on company 'ethos'. Strong central influence; cost-driven standardization, subsidiaries have to make 'business reasons' case for departing from global policies.	Monthly monitoring, coordinated by finance function, of HR issues such as staffing levels, employee performance and pay rises. HQ routinely compares performance of comparable production sites. Large, well-resourced central HQ function. Global HQ directive to cut costs by 10%.	International business division increasingly important but regions less so; HR director of one division is UK-based.	Increasingly standardized global HR policy in areas of diversity, performance management and teamworking. Global policy of using forced distributions of appraised performance to weed out underperforming employees. Global policy to be at median pay levels. Formal worldwide corporate mission introduced, following consultation with subsidiaries.
Drugco (E/GB)	Subsidiaries have leeway to develop their own policy within			Standardized global performance management system for all employees

	flexibly applied central guidelines. Cohesion underpinned by dominant corporate culture, strong ILM, and widespread informal networks.	combining measurement against objectives and 'leadership behaviours', with mandatory performance management training for new employees. Global corporate programme of executive stock options. Standardized employee survey worldwide every 2 to 3 years. Identical corporate values worldwide.	
Healthco (IRL)	Unusual degree of subsidiary discretion in most HR issues, although most local initiatives seen as congruent with HQ policy. Some move to greater corporate control of policy as costs rise.	Worldwide programme to monitor performance evaluations in subsidiaries since 2001, although large parts of new system based on Irish existing practice. Introduction of requirement on subsidiaries to have succession plans in place but little prescription of detail.	
Household (D/E/GB)	Impact of owning family still strong - UK plant closure plan vetoed by owner. Global restructuring and rationalization initiatives In HR, tendency to centralization/globalization though with local flexibility. Recent move to business divisions; businesses dominate business/region matrix.		Growing importance of European regional level, leading to reduction in country autonomy. National HR managers have European responsibilities. Shared HR (and other) services for Europe located in London.
Healthcare (E/GB)	Considerable devolution of HR to European region		Europe able to challenge central HR policy guidelines. European role in headcount control, training, executive compensation. European project teams to handle plant closures.

(contd.)

Table 10.1. (contd.)

Firm (country studies)	General	Systems of central control	Role Europe/region and international business divisions	Areas of centralized HR policy
ITco (D/E/GB/IRL)	Fluctuations from highly centralized, to countries, to regions/global businesses. Currently tight corporate control of HR with little scope for subsidiary adaptation, even in tightly regulated employment relations systems, e.g. Germany. Progressive global standardization of HR policy.	Strong central control of budget processes. Regular reviews and visits from HQ to ensure subsidiary conformity. Importance of intranet in dissemination of HR policy. Global data 'warehouse' storing HR information from all locations in central database; provides each business with information on appraisal, recruitment, etc. at local, European, and global levels.	1990s move away from 'country-centred' HR to increasing role of businesses. Coupled with centralization within Europe of HR delivery: Europe-wide management of graduate recruitment, international assignments, and routine HR inquiries through HR call centre. Europeanization of communications, reducing 'country flavour'.	Standard global performance management system with little scope for local adaptation plus worldwide bonus system based on business results and appraisal rating; performance-related pay a fundamental tenet. Standardized centrally driven leadership competences model used to manage executive resources. Standard corporate 'cascading communication' system, 'open door' approach to management–employee communication, and global staff survey. Diversity policy centrally driven but with regional traits. Strong corporate commitment to avoid union presence in subsidiaries where possible.
Logistico (D/GB/IRL)	Centralized approach, but some limited scope to customize centrally determined policies. Some differences between organic growth subsidiaries (e.g. Germany) and acquired (e.g. UK), with former more standardized on central practice.	Use of standard written policy manual for managers covering area of HR as well as customers, shareholders, and the community; supplemented by global 'code of conduct' giving detailed guidance to managers on running the business. Focus on standard work practices and time measurements	Role of European region still limited, reflecting relatively small weight of non-US operations in global company. European region functions as transmission belt between HQ and subsidiaries, mainly concerned with adapting and translating HQ global policy for the region, esp. given growth through acquisition. Role in allocating pay budgets to individual countries.	Centralized performance management system. Control through European HQ of management development and succession planning in subsidiaries. Standardized global employee opinion survey, associated with employee focus group discussions. Centrally driven corporate communications programmes, including globally standardized pre-work communication meetings. Some local management adaptation of the benefits plan to optimize tax.

Pharmaco (IRL/GB)	Growing central control of HR in Irish subsidiary reflecting increasingly strategic status of its manufacturing operation.	Strict HQ control of headcount through budget process. Regular collection of HR metrics; global best practice teams; corporate audits of subsidiary practices. Global cost-cutting directives. Central monitoring and approval of IRL pay bargaining.	European HQ collates subsidiary HR metrics on headcount, turnover, absenteeism, employee survey data, and performance review scores.	Strong explicit corporate values propagated from centre, but IRL able to customize for local context. Increasing central influence on management training.	advantages for IRL employees: corporate 'recommendation' to minimize potential of expansion of unions. Recent HQ attention to global diversity policy.
Refresco (E/GB)	Recent change from highly centralized to decentralized structures, including HR, reflecting refocus on making 'global brands local'; retention of strong central control over issues of quality and innovation.	Global guidelines of being at market median on pay	Decentralization from HQ to four broad regional units and lower level European group comprising individuals located in national subsidiaries.	Performance management system centralized at European level. Centrally designed programmes for senior management development, with regional/local adaptation.	
Softco (E)	Highly centralized, with subsidiaries seen as agents of HQ; however, there is some scope for local HR initiatives at the margins.	Management processes and tools highly centralized and directed by HQ. Biannual reporting through budget process of HR metrics, including headcount, hirings, HR climate.	Mix of territorial and international business structures, with European region as intermediate level overseeing subsidiary implementation. HR policy imposed by the centre.	Highly centralized HR policies, including in areas of performance management, employee survey, diversity objectives.	

much the same everywhere, and subsidiaries were expected to conform in detail to central policy, for example, in the use of standardized appraisal forms and processes. Elsewhere, as in the area of workforce diversity, central intervention more often took the form of 'guidelines' requiring subsidiaries to have a policy but without specifying it in detail. There were also more ad hoc interventions, for instance, directives requiring across-the-board cuts in headcount, as in Engco2, or restraining pay increases worldwide within fixed limits, as occurred in PharmaChem. The centre also exerted control through direct oversight of aspects of HR in subsidiaries. In Pharmaco Ireland, for example, collective bargaining was closely scrutinized:

... every strategic decision must be approved by them—what we can go to, the communications approach, the mechanisms of setting up a negotiations team. We can delay and argue for anything that's grey, but they're always on the end of the phone. (HR adviser, Pharmaco IRL)

Centrally driven policy went hand-in-hand with large central HR departments, which devised policy for the whole MNC (see Chapter 12), and with a framework of HR control and reporting. Subsidiaries were monitored through routine reporting of data on headcount, employee costs, the results of employee surveys, data on employee appraisals and training, and other HR metrics. Compliance with global policies was carefully monitored. In some cases, regular corporate 'audits' of HR/ER were conducted.

More informal, less systematic mechanisms for the control and monitoring of HR included the use of expatriate American managers. Some companies, such as Engco1 and Engco2, made considerable use of expatriates from company HQ either to regional offices or to particular sites. In some cases their role was to oversee operations and ensure that company policies and procedures were functioning well; in others, it was to transfer technical expertise. More generally, they were 'carriers' of corporate cultural values. As a respondent in ITco Ireland noted, '... They are bringing people over from the older sites to continue to spread the ITco philosophy.' However, their use was by no means widespread in all companies. In the Irish case studies, their presence tended to be much reduced after the initial phase of subsidiary operation, and operational control passed almost entirely into the hands of Irish managers. American managers rarely operated in the HR function at country level, though there were exceptions; in Engco1, for example, US managers drove the development of the UK HR 'shared services' function (see Chapter 12), while in Pharmaco

Ireland, which had little history of expatriates, a recently appointed US HR executive had been used to restructure the HR role in Ireland.

The increasing adoption of electronic global HR information systems enhanced central control by increasing HQ's ability to collect and analyse comprehensive information; at the same time it significantly reduced the costs of central control. A notable development was the creation of a global HR data repository or 'warehouse' in ITco. National subsidiaries supplied data to the repository and would be called to account for inconsistencies. The information could also be used to compare countries against benchmarks, for example, for the ratio of managers to non-managerial employees, and hence to assist the centre in driving through cost-cutting programmes.

This broad picture holds in general terms across host countries, despite significant variations between companies. In one or two, notably EngServs in the UK and, until recently, Compuco in Ireland and Drugco in Spain, HR was managed in a relatively decentralized fashion. In all cases, decentralization reflected factors peculiar to individual companies or sectors, rather than host-country influences. EngServs UK, for example, constituted a large proportion of the MNC's operations (and a still larger proportion of its profits), reflecting its privileged position in expanding former colonial markets, and the sector required detailed knowledge and interpretation of local market conditions. Drugco Spain's considerable autonomy, already declining at the time of the research, derived from the subsidiary's origins as a joint venture with a well-established and successful Spanish partner. The partner's credibility in the wider company allowed it to follow its own path until the subsidiary became a wholly owned operation in the 1990s. Compuco Ireland's parent company was not concerned with the detail of HR practice in its subsidiaries, focusing on global cost reduction through innovation in the value chain. As long as business targets were met, subsidiaries were autonomous in HR matters. While business performance remained paramount, however, in recent years a central HR role at corporate level had developed as a result of perceived problems in labour market positioning and in corporate image, and the company was introducing more centralized policies in such areas as performance management and pay, training and development, and diversity.

In Germany, where the degree of employment relations regulation is strongest, central influence was still strongly felt in companies such as ITco, as has been seen in earlier chapters. For example, ITco Germany followed the highly prescriptive global corporate pay and grading system. As a German ITco manager commented, the existence of codetermination law:

... doesn't mean it's accepted that we go our special national way just because of that fact. We are not expecting to have it easier. [HQ] still expect us to implement our agenda even under these more difficult conditions. In other words, codetermination is no excuse for not achieving our goals. [...] Maybe this might take a little longer.

In an earlier article (Ferner et al. 2004), we attribute the strength of central HR policy to the influence on US MNCs of a number of features of the American business system. First is the 'dominance effect' (cf. Smith and Meiksins 1995) that derives from the preeminence of the American system in the world economy. American superiority encourages the presumption that policies developed within the context of the US business system provide competitive advantage when transferred overseas. Second, US companies have developed an appropriate management 'technology' to manage overseas operations in a centralized fashion. This can be seen as the path-dependent effect of the early drive to serve continental mass markets, leading to the development of a unique set of what Chandler (1990) terms 'organizational capabilities': the organizational structures, management control systems, and professionalized management functions—including HR—capable of coordinating geographically dispersed operations (see Chapter 3). Such capabilities may be adapted to the needs of managing international operations. That is, they make practicable the cross-national transfer of US practices. Moreover, particularly in companies, such as ITco, CPGco, and Engco2, from the 'welfare capitalist' tradition, with their emphasis on securing the long-term commitment of the workforce to the goals of the company, there was a strong incentive for cohesive, consistent management of the workforce as a whole.

The American business system has been adept at (partially) circumventing the problem of the 'context-generalizability' of policies (that is, their ability to function effectively outside their original national-institutional context), not least by codifying and standardizing elements of practice and by providing efficient mechanisms for cross-national dissemination and monitoring of implementation.

Within this overall picture of centralized HR, however, there was some significant variation among companies and across host countries. There was also evolution in the nature, location, and degree of centralization over time. The following paragraphs explore the dynamic relationship between central control and subsidiary autonomy. The discussion then

goes on to probe the way in which the balance of centralization—
autonomy is *negotiated* by actors at different organizational levels,
focusing on the varying scope for negotiation afforded by different
national-institutional settings.

The Dynamics of Centralization—Autonomy

While centralization was the keynote, its precise nature varied significantly, and there was considerable oscillation at the margins between
central control and subsidiary autonomy in relation to HR/ER matters.
Such change partly reflected the longer-term evolution of product markets. A notable example is provided by ITco. In the 1970s, central controls
over HR were sharply tightened, as part of a more general centralization
process. In the 1980s, however, there were moves to allow greater autonomy to national subsidiaries, to give them flexibility to respond to local
markets. During this period, national subsidiaries that were seen to have
earned their own autonomy through strong financial performance had
considerable scope to go their own way on HR. Corporate crisis led to a
readjustment in the early 1990s. At the same time, the downside of
decentralization had become evident in the costly 'duplication of effort'
across subsidiaries, and in policy proliferation that obstructed efforts to
service international clients. These factors led to renewed HR centralization and a significant loss of control by subsidiaries. However, the new
bout of centralization was primarily effected at regional level and within
international business divisions, rather than at the level of the global
corporation.

In some cases, such transformations affected the MNC as a whole. This
was the case in ITco, but also in Engco2, whose move to greater standardization of global HR policy paralleled the increasing importance of non-US
operations. In other cases, changes in the degree of centralization affected
the relationship between HQ and specific subsidiaries. Prime examples are
Pharmaco and Healthco in Ireland, both traditionally autonomous subsidiaries under almost exclusively Irish management. In both, a combination of increased cost pressures at home and competitive pressures in
their target markets meant that manufacture of some standard products
was becoming less viable, attracting greater HQ attention. In response,
these subsidiaries lobbied successfully at the centre to produce new,
higher-margin products. In Pharmaco's case, the size and importance of
the Irish manufacturing facility was increased and consequently so was
the potential for global disruption of product flows. This in turn led to a

tightening of corporate controls and reporting relationships, greater HQ intervention in HR/IR, and the dispatch of a US HR manager to the subsidiary. This can be seen as a specifically Irish effect, since a feature of the institutional context was the transition from a low-wage to a higher-wage, higher-skill economy through the 1980s and 1990s, changing the logic of production there away from standard, cost-sensitive, and price-competitive products towards greater value-added products.

While some of this 'oscillation' between poles of centralization and decentralization can be attributed to responses to long-term changes in product markets, it sometimes reflected more contingent and short-term factors. Indeed, there seems to be a strong element of 'mimetic isomorphism' as companies respond to the example of successful pioneers. In some companies there was a constant evaluation of the balance between central HR control and subsidiary autonomy, and of the locus of centralization. This reflected companies' attempts to balance the conflicting demands of, on the one hand, global integration to achieve economies of scale and consistency of approach, and, on the other, of local differentiation to adapt to local markets and to host national-institutional contexts (cf. Brooke 1984). The relationship was a volatile one, with constant subtle adjustments, and the occasional sudden restructuring of the balance, prompted by, for example, the arrival of a new CEO, as in Engco2, and also in Chemco as discussed later. Another important trigger for adjustment was takeover or merger. Bankco had been formed from the merger of a financial services company with highly standardized global HR systems and policies, and a more 'entrepreneurial' dominant partner that subsequently 'threw out the HR rule book', leaving much HR policy to the subsidiaries:

[The pre-merge company had] very structured, almost rigid processes around evaluation, promotions, you name it. When I came into the [post-merger] business I was horrified that that kind of stuff just didn't exist. I was horrified on the one hand, but extremely... erm, it was almost uplifting that, hell, you know we can do a lot of things which I could never have done before, because you're unconstrained by the policy manuals. [...] And of course there's two sides to the coin, you know, it does mean we're probably re-inventing the wheel, it probably means we're doing things twice, it probably means we aren't learning from each other, so there's a lot of downsides.... (European HR director)

This pattern of oscillation may be linked to features of the US business system, particularly the tradition of constant corporate experimentation with organizational forms. This reflects the relative 'under-institutionalization' of the US system and the weakness of ties to other actors in the American 'LME'; this in turn permits and indeed encourages companies to respond rapidly to short-term changes in their environment as the cost–benefit calculus of different modes of organization changes (Ferner et al. 2004). However, it is clearly not confined to such MNCs: Scullion and Starkey (2000), for example, report considerable swings from centralized to decentralized HR management and back again in their study of thirty UK MNCs.

Centralization to the Region and the International Business Division

An important aspect of the evolution in the centralization–decentralization balance was the continuous revision of the relative roles played by corporate HQ, the region, international business divisions, and the national subsidiary. The salience of the European regional level within the structure of MNCs, reflecting primarily the increasing political and economic integration of the EU and the consequent creation of a European 'regulatory space', has been noted by observers (e.g. Marginson 2000; Marginson and Sisson 1994). Regional structures also offer cost advantages to MNCs, avoiding unnecessary duplication of corporate functions such as HR at the level of each national subsidiary. Finally, they provide a way for HQ to have a single regional 'interlocutor', aggregating inputs from disparate national subsidiaries.

ITco's recentralization in the 1990s was notable for the way in which authority (across a range of functions, not just HR) was drawn up from the subsidiaries to the regional level, with the creation of regional functions for recruitment and selection, compensation, HR planning, and the management of expatriates. A regional HR call centre was also established. There were similar developments in other companies such as CPGco. As a result, the role of the national HR function was reduced (see Chapter 12) and the subsidiaries' autonomy seriously eroded. However, as Pulignano (2006) has shown in her study of European sites of a US electrical engineering and chemical company, not all regional aggregation is necessarily bad news for national subsidiary autonomy. Particularly where the regional organization is staffed by Europeans with an understanding of national-institutional differences, the regional tier may have the effect of providing a buffer between corporate HQ and the subsidiary, increasing the latter's freedom of manoeuvre. We observed this phenomenon in a number of companies. In Logistico Ireland, for example, local management felt that they were 'pushing at an open door' in talking to the region about national differences:

...most of the top positions in Europe (HQ) are filled by Europeans now, with experience in different European countries, who understand the way the business works in Europe and it is easier to... communicate and deal with them. (HR manager)

The buffer effect of the region was further enhanced where the regional HR function was staffed by national HR managers wearing a second, regional hat. This was the case in several companies, including CPGco and PharmaChem. In the latter, for example, national managers came together in a regional HR council and had responsibility for HR in different business divisions within Europe.

However, the buffer effect of the region was not always sustained. In Chemco, the region had previously been structured around specialist HR competences located within different national subsidiaries; the 'centre of excellence' for compensation, for example, was in France, and it liaised with corporate HQ on behalf of the European region. Policies reached the European subsidiaries through the mediation of the European level. But at the beginning of the decade, a major restructuring, prompted by the arrival of a new CEO, led to a loss of regional authority and a strong reassertion of corporate influence through the propagation of global, standardized policies in areas such as performance management:

The joke is that we once had... twenty countries in Europe where there was a Chemco company and we had 25 appraisal systems and five of them were in Italy! Now we only have one. (UK HR manager)

Likewise, a system of pan-European leadership competences, that had been taken up as a model for the global company, was summarily replaced following the restructuring by one imposed from the corporate HQ.

Less ambiguous than the changing role of the region was that of international business divisions, in other words structures for managing all the operations of specific groupings of products or services within the overall MNC. In many companies, business divisions were assuming greater 'bottom-line' responsibilities. This led to the devolution of some international HR functions from the corporate centre to the businesses, while at the same time the international businesses absorbed control over HR from national subsidiaries. This pattern was marked in ITco, Engco2, and CPGco. In these companies the businesses had a strong international HR structure (see Chapter 12), often crossed with a regional organization in a business–geography matrix. The logic of devolution of HR to international businesses was that different businesses had varying policy needs. In banking, for example, different subsectors such as retail and corporate banking, had very different HR requirements:

[they are] almost completely separate businesses... different employee profile, different compensation, everything is different, different talent development process. Therefore you can understand to a large extent why there's not... greater corporate cohesion in terms of HR policies because you've got very different businesses, and that's why... there are some like share options and shares where that can be global, not a lot else. (European HR director, Bankco)

The relations between the regional and business component could be tense, particularly since they represented two conflicting organizing principles: cost minimization through the provision of standard HR 'services' at regional level; and tailoring of HR to specific needs of different international businesses. Such tensions in turn fuelled the constant shifts in the centralization–autonomy balance.

Power, Interests, and National-Institutional Resources: The 'Negotiation' of the Centralization–Autonomy Balance

As argued earlier, rationalistic approaches to the degree of centralization have tended to depict it as the outcome of a careful cost–benefit calculation by senior corporate executives. Our findings in contrast highlight the way in which centralization–autonomy is *negotiated* by actors at HQ and in the subsidiaries: the way the balance is defined and how it operates in practice are the outcome of organizational politics fuelled by a variety of power resources in the hands of actors at different levels. As noted, Schmitt and Sadowski's fiscal federalism model (2003) could in principle accommodate micropolitics by including costs of resistance in the cost–benefit calculus. This, however, still retains a top-down, static flavour and does not capture the constant jostling at the margins as the balance of centralization–autonomy is continually contested: different groups try to increase their freedom of manoeuvre, or to engage in bargaining over the terms of central control, deploying a variety of power resources linked in many cases to specific features of local institutional settings.

The limits to the negotiation process should also be stressed. First, autonomy in HR policymaking also had costs for subsidiaries. They would have to devote considerable resources to developing systems that could otherwise be available 'off-the-shelf' from HQ: why 'reinvent the wheel' was the attitude in subsidiaries such as Engco1 UK. Subsidiaries' motivation to resist centralization was not, therefore, unqualified. In any case, resistance was only one possible strategy. Compliance could also be part of a negotiating strategy, in order to gain flexibility in other areas of activity. Pharmaco Ireland, for example, used a strategy of compliance as part of its pursuit of new mandates for higher value-added investment, seeing leverage to be gained from going with the grain of corporate policy rather than resisting central control.

Second, micropolitical relations in US MNCs were set within a broader context of 'dominance effects' deriving from the US's hegemonic economic position. Much of what the corporate centre attempted to do would be accepted by subsidiaries because of the acknowledged preeminence of the USA. This mindset was explicitly expressed by one respondent, in Drugco Spain. The subsidiary, he claimed, would never give a blanket rejection to HQ proposals:

You have to listen. First, because no one calls into question the position of the US. US management is recognised worldwide, many [business] gurus are American, etc. And also, of course, they're the boss.

The sense of cultural deference contained in this extract could perhaps be understood as reflecting the fact that Spain's economic development and modernization are relatively recent, and that its evolving modern business model is largely based on the absorption of foreign, predominantly Anglo-Saxon, exemplars (Ferner, Quintanilla, and Varul 2001). In Ireland and the UK, the attitude was more one of cultural 'empathy' than deference. Subsidiaries understood what the Americans were trying to do and shared a similar managerial mindset. A perception of US superiority was more muted in Germany, with its strong indigenous management traditions, although it was not entirely absent: successful, innovative American companies, such as Silico and ITco, were considered to be in the vanguard of modern HRM to which many German companies aspired.

Within this context, the micropolitics of centralization was observed in relation to both policy creation and implementation. As detailed in other chapters (especially Chapters 11 and 12), subsidiary managers in Engco2 attempted to gain a greater say in the development of global HR policy, with mixed success. There were instances in other companies where subsidiary HR functions helped shape global policies, either by providing a model as the basis of an international policy, or by participating in a policy development process through various international HR forums (see also Tregaskis, Ferner, and Glover 2005).

More commonly, micropolitics was manifested in subsidiary resistance to central HR policies seen as inappropriate for local circumstances, or in attempts to modify their mode of application. One example of resistance was in Engco2 UK. Local HR management responded to a global directive to achieve a 10 per cent cut in headcount on a given timescale by arguing that this would transgress established consultation and negotiation procedures in the plant. Eventually, the timescale was relaxed to allow for union consultation and employee 'buy-in'. UK managers in Engco2 also resisted corporate attempts to impose a rigid forced-distribution system of performance appraisals. Concerned about the impact of forced distribution on the 'psychological contract' with 'solid performers', local management softened the impact of the system by exploiting uncertainty over the definition of the size of the relevant reference groups (see Chapter 7).

Another area of contestation of central directives was pay policy. In Engco2 UK, managers successfully resisted a global pay freeze on the grounds that a pay rise for the following year had already been agreed with the unions; to breach this agreement, it was argued, could lead to industrial conflict and a breakdown in trust (see Edwards, Colling, and Ferner 2004). A similar incident took place in PharmaChem. UK management strongly opposed a mandatory global pay limit on the grounds that it would force the subsidiary to treat workers at its non-union site less favourably than workers at a unionized site, since the latter would have the industrial muscle to breach the limit. In other words, local management played on the MNC's preference for preserving non-union relations where possible.

The micropolitical game was particularly evident in Germany subsidiaries since local management required considerable ingenuity to apply global HR policies within the constraints of codetermination and of the German business system more generally. Some subsidiaries used this institutional context to deflect central HR policies. As a respondent in Household Germany put it,

What do we do [if we have to introduce something we do not like]? We build a sort of shadow organization around it, and do our normal business at the local level. These are the political games in organizations through which one tries to stay alive and be profitable.

In Bor-Tec Germany, several changes of ownership in the US parent had encouraged German management to develop a strong sense of protectiveness towards the local operations. The subsidiary's management culture strongly emphasized technical know-how, helping to maintain subsidiary competitiveness despite high labour costs. A strong feeling of cooperation and mutual trust developed, helping to ward off interventions from the USA. Anecdotally, there was evidence that German management successfully resisted US attempts to transfer a model of 'self-directed work teams' that did not sit well with the established engineering culture in the

German firm, and which would be regarded with scepticism by the firm's well-trained and highly experienced *Facharbeiter* (skilled workers).

In ITco Germany, as seen in Chapter 7, the relationship with the works council provided local management with room for manoeuvre in applying the highly standardized global pay and grading system. In particular, the collective bargaining agreement had a role in specifying the factors for grouping jobs into pay grades, and promotion was dependent on qualifications rather than appraised performance.

Sources of Subsidiary Influence

These examples throw light on the subsidiaries' sources of influence and the resources that they were able to deploy to push back the frontline of HQ's centralizing tendencies. Such resources may be divided into two broad, and sometimes interacting categories: company or sectoral factors; and factors generated by the host institutional setting.

First, subsidiaries acquired bargaining resources from aspects of their structural position within the wider MNC. A more systematic exploration of the impact of structural factors on the degree of centralization requires a more large-scale, quantitative approach. However, our case studies point to certain typical processes whereby structural factors are exploited by subsidiaries to enhance their freedom of manoeuvre.

Where subsidiaries were brownfield acquisitions with specialist expertise (e.g. parts of Engco1 in the UK), where they had originated in joint ventures (e.g. Drugco Spain), or where there were frequent changes of US parent (e.g. Bor-Tec), they could be expected to have greater scope for autonomous action. The subsidiary's position in the corporate value chain, and its success, relative size, and profitability were also important sources of bargaining power, although their implications were more ambiguous. Pharmaco Ireland acquired a strategic role in the supply of key products, giving it more bargaining power but at the same time attracting greater scrutiny from HQ. A more low-key role could keep a subsidiary 'off the corporate radar': this was the case with Healthco Ireland, although its avoidance of scrutiny was compromised by the weakening viability of the model of producing low-cost standardized products.

Subsidiaries also exerted influence through their ability to exploit tensions between different corporate HR policies or principles. Such tensions provided them with a legitimatory rhetoric for resistance. This was seen in the PharmaChem example when opposition to globally imposed pay restraint was couched in terms of support for the principle of encouraging non-union operations. In Drugco UK, the same mechanism was visible in HR's opposition to plans for headcount reductions, on the grounds that such an approach would compromise the company's people-driven ethos.

Second, subsidiaries derived significant resources from their embeddedness within the host institutional environment. They could leverage their role as privileged interpreters of the local environment. This provided them with justifications for opposing standardized central policy, or for securing modifications. Since institutional constraints were rarely clearcut in their implications, even in highly regulated countries such as Germany (Wächter et al. 2003), they could become a 'contested terrain' between subsidiary and HQ. Perhaps because of the relative absence of institutional constraints (especially on HR) in the US business system, HQ management could be unresponsive to subsidiary arguments based on local institutional constraints. HQ could also take steps to reduce the 'interpretative gap' (cf. Ferner et al. 2004) by, for example, dispatching expatriate managers to scrutinize local operations.

However, subsidiaries could also draw in other ways on the local institutional environment. In particular they could form alliances with other local actors, including workforce representatives (cf. Kristensen and Zeitlin 2005). This was notable in both Germany and the UK, and there were also instances in Ireland. In Healthco Ireland, a shop steward recounted how the local collective agreement contained a clause on compassionate leave that conflicted with US policy. When the agreement was reported to HQ, the relevant page was held back. In Engco2 UK, a de facto and informal 'unholy alliance' was formed by local HR management with the unions over the handling of the corporate redundancy programme: the unions played their part by confirming that there would be negative consequences for employee morale and industrial relations if the original US plan were implemented.

Alliances between local management and the works council were observed both in Bor-Tec and Silico in Germany. In these cases, however, the causality was reversed: management challenged aspects of central policy as a way of gaining credibility and cementing alliances with the works council, crucial for a working relationship that could deliver company policy in other respects. Bor-Tec management, by modifying a corporate redundancy scheme to include costly measures, such as an outplacement service, was able to increase its prestige in the eyes of the works council. In Silico, management signed a works agreement, about splitting the company into two parts, that was not in line with American specifications (see Chapter 12).

However, there were signs that such alliances, particularly in Germany, were being disrupted by the Europeanization of HR. On an increasing number of issues, decision-making on HR/IR now transcended national borders. In the words of one CPGco works councillor,

The influence of Geneva is increasing all the time. I'm not happy about it . . . we're becoming a virtual company where employees no longer have direct contact with their managers. . . . As a works councillor, I don't like it at all because the direct contact with decision-makers is no longer there . . . often we can no longer get to them.

Similar sentiments were expressed by an ITco councillor:

. . . we used to be able to negotiate directly with German management, now everything has to be checked with Paris to make sure that both standardized European processes and national regulations are observed.

Finally, there was a deep ambivalence in the stance of subsidiary management, especially in the German case. Though in some cases local managers resisted or deflected central HR policy, in other instances they chose to use their detailed understanding of the local environment to further the interests of HQ. For example, they helped the centre to find ways round institutional constraints in order to implement standardized global policies in the German operations. In CPGco Germany, management secured greater pay flexibility by reclassifying certain employees as 'exempt' (*aussertariflich*) so that they were subject to individual contracts of employment and not covered by rates stipulated in collective agreements. As seen earlier, local management were aware that HQ expected them to achieve objectives regardless of codetermination and other constraints. In companies that maintained a strong ILM (see Chapter 9) and provided a wide range of career opportunities at the region or even at global level, local managers had an active interest in finding ways for standardized policies to be implemented. In short, managerial career paths influenced whether subsidiary managers used their local managers to thwart or to promote central intentions.

CONCLUSIONS

This chapter has tried to dig beneath the often-observed centralization and standardization of HR policy in US MNCs by focusing on processual aspects of the relationship between subsidiaries and HQ.

While endorsing the findings of previous research, it qualifies them in several respects. First, it suggests that there are variations between companies that can be ascribed to a range of structural factors, such as entry mode (acquisition vs. greenfield), sector, role of the subsidiary within the MNC, and so on. The contribution here has been to examine the process through which they influence the degree of centralization.

Second, a key aspect of the centralization–autonomy balance is its dynamism and volatility as it shifts in reaction both to long-term transformations in product and labour markets, and to more short-term and contingent pressures. A central element is the constantly evolving relationship between four distinct levels in MNCs: corporate HQ, international business divisions, global regions, and national subsidiaries.

Third, the balance is—to some degree—negotiated by corporate actors at different organizational levels pursuing differential interests through the deployment of a range of resources, some of which importantly derive from actors' embeddedness in local institutional contexts.

Fourth, there are some differences across host countries in the degree of application of standardized policies. This reflects a complex array of factors. Most obviously, national constraints in highly regulated systems impose limits on the applicability of internationally standardized policies. However, such constraints are not necessarily obstacles to policy centralization as the generally compliant stance of Spanish subsidiaries makes clear. Despite the existence of quite extensive regulations governing both individual and collective aspects of the employment relationship, Spain's evolution as an NBS made it more susceptible to the influence of US 'dominance effects' than say Germany (or even the UK).

Nonetheless, national-institutional contexts in the host countries provide a source of power and influence for local managers as interpreters of local constraints to HQ. This was seen in all countries, including Spain where, as discussed in Chapter 8, local managers used rhetorics relating to institutional constraints in order to shield the subsidiary from the full impact of central employee diversity policy. The national-institutional setting also gave local management differential scope to forge alliances with other local stakeholders. The desire and need to maintain such relationships provided a motive to challenge rigid central policy in the first place, as well as a power resource with which to resist central pressures. This was most clearly seen in Germany, where the 'collaborative market economy' predisposed managers to forge strong and lasting links with other stakeholders including organized labour. But it also occurred to some extent in the UK and Ireland.

In short, therefore, the chapter reinforces the argument of the volume as a whole that, while MNC behaviour ultimately reflects a range of structural factors to do with market, technology, and sector, MNCs' responses to these factors are mediated by organizational politics. Actors at different levels are embedded within distinctive national-institutional domains, which shape their perceptions of structural constraints and strategic opportunities and which also give them access to a range of institutionally specific power resources that they may deploy in pursuit of their interests. The ensuing micropolitics shapes the balance between central control and subsidiary autonomy.

11

Innovation and the Transfer of Organizational Learning

Tony Edwards, David G. Collings, Javier Quintanilla, and Anne Tempel

INTRODUCTION

It is commonly argued that a key factor shaping the competitive position of MNCs is their capability to identify innovations made within the firm and subsequently transfer these across their operations. For example, Hymer's pioneering work (1976) on MNCs argued that as firms internationalize they transfer 'a whole package of resources' across their operations in different countries. Bartlett and Ghoshal (1998) identify the ability to utilize practices that enhance competitiveness across the firm—which they refer to as the pressure to achieve 'worldwide innovation'—as one of the most important competences of MNCs. In a similar vein, Gammelgaard, Holm, and Pedersen (2004: 195) argue that 'to an increasing extent, the success of MNCs is considered to be contingent upon the ease and speed with which valuable knowledge is disseminated throughout the organization'.

This chapter examines the process of innovation and organizational learning in US multinationals. This is potentially a very broad area, so we limit ourselves to one aspect of organizational learning, namely the ways in which an innovative employment practice is identified in one part of a firm's operations and then transferred to sites in different countries. This is an important phenomenon not only because it has the potential to affect the competitive position of the multinational itself but also because it can cause change within the business systems in which MNCs operate by introducing novel practices that are subsequently adopted in other firms. Some observers see this as occurring through a process of beneficial 'upgrading' in which efficiency-enhancing innovations are introduced to an economy; for others, however, it is more to do with practices that clash with local institutions being introduced through coercion.

The chapter has the following specific aims. First, we review various perspectives on the transfer of employment practices in MNCs and how this can contribute to the competitive advantage of firms, contrasting 'information-processing', 'contingency', 'NBS' and 'micropolitical' approaches. The second aim is to briefly review the evidence concerning the transfer of practices from the domestic operations of American MNCs to their foreign subsidiaries, drawing on the findings of earlier chapters. Third, and most significantly, the extent to which the case-study firms transfer practices that originate in their overseas operations is considered.

ORGANIZATIONAL LEARNING, TRANSFER, AND THE COMPETITIVE ADVANTAGE OF MNCS

The issue of how and why MNCs derive competitive advantage from transferring practices across borders has been approached from a number of different perspectives. In this section, we review the basic premises of four of these. The first can be termed the information-processing approach and is exemplified in the work of Gupta and Govindarajan (1991, 2000). This view sees transfer as mainly about the spread of information from a 'donor' unit to a 'receptacle' or recipient for this information (Gourlay 2005). The considerable attention devoted to this perspective can be seen as a consequence of the increasing focus on 'knowledge-based' firms (Edwards and Ferner 2004).

There are two main variants of this information-processing approach. One of these is that used by economists in attempting to explain why firms grow internationally. For example, Buckley and Casson (1976) used as their starting point the question of how foreign firms can compete effectively with indigenous firms given that they lack the expertise and contacts in that host country. Their answer was that a multinational must possess a source of competitive advantage that local firms do not have, enabling them to overcome the disadvantage of being foreign. Where this is the case, a second question arises: why would a foreign firm look to use this competitive advantage itself rather than license or franchise it to a local firm? Their answer to this was that it may be difficult to reach a licensing or franchising arrangement, particularly for an 'intangible' asset, such as knowledge, as there is a degree of uncertainty as to how much knowledge is really worth and how other firms may utilize it. Thus, where a foreign firm possesses a source of competitive advantage which it cannot easily license to a local firm then it must set up foreign subsidiaries in that country if it is to reap full returns on its unique competencies. This has become known as 'internalization'; a firm looks to transfer its sources of competitive advantage internally rather than externalize them to other firms. The implication of this line of analysis is that MNCs will transfer practices from the home country to host countries, something that we term 'forward transfer'. In this sense, the transfer of practices is about the extension of knowledge and practices residing in the home country to new operations in other countries.

The other variant of the information-processing approach, the resource-based view of the firm, allows for the transfer of knowledge in a number of directions across sites within MNCs. This approach figures strongly in the model of IHRM developed by Taylor, Beechler, and Napier (1996) who argue that a multinational's competitive position is shaped by the nature of the 'organizational competencies' that it possesses and how the firm transfers these across its organization. As they put it: 'in order to provide value to the business, the (strategic international) HRM system of global firms should be constructed around specific organizational competences that are critical for securing competitive advantage in a global environment' (1996: 960). They argue that transferred practices can be developed anywhere within the organization and go in any direction (Taylor, Beechler, and Napier 1996: 967).

Both variants of the information-processing perspectives have limitations, however. One very significant weakness of a 'donor' and 'recipient' model of knowledge transfer is that what is transferred may alter during this process. That is, a practice may undergo a process of 'hybridization' as it is interpreted differently in a new context. Acknowledging this opens up the need to examine the role of distinct NBSs in shaping the transfer process and also raises the issue of the role of actors within MNCs as active agents in shaping the transfer process. Before doing this, we address a further weakness in the information-processing perspective, namely that it fails to fully acknowledge variations between MNCs in the extent and nature of transfer.

This issue is a central part of the 'contingency' approach. As Edwards Ferner, and Sisson (1993: 7) note, 'much effort has been devoted to devising typologies to distinguish different kinds of MNC. Usually some notion of "strategic contingencies" relating to market and environment is used as the basis of differentiation.' The essence of this perspective is that there are systematic variations between firms in the extent to which they engage in cross-national transfer and that these can be explained with reference to key aspects of the way that MNCs are organized.

225

One example relates to corporate structure; the key lines of organization that link units within a multinational together shape the likelihood that transfer will occur. For instance, Marginson et al. (1995) argue that MNCs that organize their units into international product-based divisions have greater potential to pursue common policies across their sites than do those in which units are grouped into a series of national subsidiary companies. Indeed, the authors show that the HQ of the former type of multinational are more likely than the latter to deploy international policies on the management of labour.

In focusing principally on the characteristics of firms that shape the transfer of innovations, the contingency perspective can be complemented with one that considers the 'embeddedness' of firms in distinctive national-institutional contexts. Thus the third perspective is the 'institutional' approach, which examines the way in which institutions facilitate and constrain the learning process. One aspect of this is the evidence concerning the 'country-of-origin effect', which suggests that institutional effects lead to transfer flowing from the country in which the firm originates, with the implication that 'learning' is mainly in one direction. This has, of course, been a theme of the book; for example, as we have seen, the transfer of practices in the field of performance management in US MNCs, such as 'forced distributions' in the appraisal of staff, tend to be strongly shaped by practices that are established in the firms' domestic operations.

Some recent literature on MNCs based on an institutional approach examines the way in which innovative practices can originate in the foreign subsidiaries of MNCs and subsequently be transferred across sites—a phenomenon known as 'reverse transfer'. This literature has shed light on the ways in which NBSs shape such transfer through their influence on the 'receptiveness' of sites in the home country to innovations from other countries and the 'diffusibility' of practices, which refers to the ease with which a practice can operate in a different context from that in which it originated (Edwards and Ferner 2004).

Building on this notion of diffusibility, the institutional approach has also been used to show how practices, whether initiated at home or abroad, are adapted to fit the new context and therefore change character once transferred. One example is that German MNCs in the UK maintain the emphasis on training that is characteristic of the home country—a 'culture of training' as Dickmann (2003) calls it—without attempting to re-create the precise training practices that operate in Germany. The process in which a practice alters in form as it operates in a new context is known as 'hybridization'.

While the institutional approach has much to commend it, a focus solely on extra-firm institutions pays insufficient attention to the internal workings of the multinational. Thus a fourth approach centres on the preferences and agendas of various groups of organizational actors and how they exert influence within the firm. This political approach stresses the way in which sources of power are held by a range of groups of actors and, consequently, the transfer process is contested. This approach is evident in a range of studies of MNCs. One theme has been the way that the HQs of MNCs 'instil order' across operations in divergent institutional contexts (Morgan et al. 2003) through, for example, the use of 'reward and punish' tactics in investment decisions (Mueller and Purcell 1992). Another theme has been a focus on the way that actors at unit level use the resources they control to block the transfer of those practices they see as challenging their interests (Broad 1994). A further theme that is evident in the political literature is one that shows how those in the foreign operating units struggle to exert influence across the firm through earning themselves 'mandates' or 'charters' from the HQ (Birkinshaw 2000).

This political approach shows how learning is 'politicized' in that it is a process that various groups look to influence through the use of whatever resources they control. Therefore, it can complement the institutional approach in explaining how practices are 'hybridized'; practices alter in form not just because they are adapted to fit the new institutional context but also because of the deliberate actions of actors who are seeking to protect or advance their own interests.

We have seen that the information-processing approach needs to be complemented with other perspectives to generate a full understanding of the process of transfer. In particular, an integrated perspective should incorporate the role of structural features of organizations in giving rise to inter-firm variation—the role of national institutions in shaping and constraining the substance of transfer and the micropolitics of life in MNCs as a key aspect of the process of transfer. It is such an integrated approach that we look to utilize in the rest of the chapter.

FORWARD TRANSFER AND PERCEPTIONS OF COMPETITIVE ADVANTAGE

A major theme of the book has been the way in which the 'Americanness' of US MNCs comes through in their tendency to transfer practices from the USA to their operations in the four countries we have examined. This section builds on the findings relating to the transfer of American-style practices in general and to the centralized decision-making on HR issues in particular to argue that many American MNCs consider the domestic business system to provide sources of competitive advantage that can beneficially be spread to other sites.

As we saw in the previous chapter, policy-making on international HR issues tended to be highly centralized, formalized, and standardized across our case studies. While some exceptions to this were apparent, such as the findings in EngServs in the UK, in the main a clear attempt to transfer home-country practices to their foreign subsidiaries was in evidence. The transfer of practices to European operations was clear in such areas as performance management, diversity, work organization, and collective relations (see Chapters 6–8). This suggests that organizational learning was relatively restricted in that American MNCs relied primarily on knowledge and expertise that they already possessed before internationalizing rather than scouring their international operations for new knowledge and expertise.

One of the clearest indicators of the home country's role in providing sources of competitive advantage was the development of formal statements of values and mission at the international level that were modelled on the American versions. The UK data threw up a number of examples of this in firms such as Household, Refresco, and CPGco. It was also a major theme of the data in the other three countries. Companies, such as ITco and Pharmaco, had gone to some lengths to communicate formal statements of values to their Irish operations. In Spain and Germany, the trouble that had been taken to translate value statements demonstrated the emphasis that senior management placed on instilling these values. The use of formal statements of value and guidelines was particularly striking in Logistico, where a detailed policy book, designed at corporate level, outlined the policies which the company believed in and offered guidance on the way to take management decisions. Every managerial employee worldwide possessed a copy, and its principles were also communicated to all new employees through induction training. The policy book consisted of four 'pillars': employees, customers, shareholders, and community, with the employee pillar containing the company's key HRM policies and serving as a guide to the general approach to HR worldwide.

The assumption that home-country ways are inherently superior was showing no signs of disappearing. One possible hypothesis might be that the longer the firms operate internationally, the less focused on the home country they become. However, this is not what our data suggest. One illustration is Pharmaco in Ireland where the training of people in detailed procedures was increasing:

They (corporate) are getting more involved in ensuring, that even in matters that I believe, are below where they are responsible for, we'll say, communicating data to New York, they are now making sure that these people are adequately trained in whatever the requirements are. They are taking a greater interest in that'. (Irish HR manager)

As we saw in Chapter 10, one line of argument by way of explaining this is that the foreign operations of US MNCs are relatively small in terms of the overall size of the companies. Accordingly, many of the subsidiary managers argued that there was a parochial and inward-looking approach to international HR policy-making: policies were designed with an American workforce in mind and then rolled out to the international operations, being adapted almost as an afterthought. For example, the policy book in Logistico was designed on the basis of the US operations. There had been moves to design a policy book specifically for the company's international operations that would not be dominated by American concerns, but this idea did not come to fruition, apparently because only a small proportion of the firm's operations (accounting for only 11 per cent of total employment) were located outside the USA.

An exception was Business Services, however, where an evolution in policy-making was noticeable. In the past, policies had been designed in America and then rolled out throughout the company. However, senior managers had sought to change this:

because a lot of time was wasted in developing stuff that was actually applicable for the US market, and was a very good idea for the US market, but actually then when you tried to roll it out globally, it didn't make sense at all'. (UK-based global HR manager, product market unit)

This changed as more leadership positions began to be awarded to non-Americans and more use was made of international project teams to develop policies and concepts:

There are now no project teams which are made up solely of Americans and in which people from Europe and Asia are not involved. (German HR manager, financial services market unit)

Notwithstanding this exceptional case, in various ways the data point to the limitations of the information-processing approach. The transfer of practices such as those in the area of diversity and collective relations appeared to have little to do with a rational assessment of the costs and benefits of applying global policies (see, e.g. Chapter 8), nor was the process merely a question of transmitting information from one willing 'recipient' to another. Rather, the transfer of practices in these areas seemed to have more to do with the firms' embeddedness in the American business system and the way this institutional context created a lasting influence that informed development of international HR policies.

The evidence concerning forward transfer also demonstrated the importance of the micropolitics of transfer. There was evidence indicating that staff in the corporate HQ saw the transfer of home-country practices as an important way of justifying their own position and maximizing their claim on resources. One theme of the data is of subsidiary actors going along with corporate policies, either because they saw the transfer as usefully supplying them with practices that fitted situations they encountered or because they did not see it as in their interests to challenge corporate HQ. This was particularly the case for those practices that were going with the grain of local institutions. In the UK for example, there was relatively little resistance in firms such as ITco to practices designed to enhance the number of women in management positions since this has become an issue that many British organizations are facing up to anyway. However, another theme of the data from subsidiaries was that transfer was sometimes opposed by managers and employees, as we have seen. Actors in the subsidiaries of MNCs control resources that give them some degree of influence and they are able to use this at times to block transfer or alter the way that transferred practices actually operate. One way in which they could achieve this was to use the space that they had from corporate monitoring to deviate from corporate policies. For example, in the Irish operations of Healthco, managers indicated some such deviation; 'what the HQ don't know won't hurt them', as one respondent put it. But resistance could also be more explicit and overt. Some evidence was found in the German subsidiaries particularly in the area of pay and performance management. For example, in CPGco, the German HR manager successfully fought for the variable pay system in Germany to exclude a forced distribution. In such cases, resistance is often partially successful in that the practice is transferred but is adapted and operates differently—the process of 'hybridization' that we referred to earlier.

Therefore, the evidence concerning forward transfer points to the need to go beyond an information-processing perspective. In particular, it suggests that there is a high degree of variation between firms and that it is a process that is conditioned by institutional factors and micropolitical processes. These are points that we develop in the next section, which examines the scope for site level actors to exert influence across the multinational.

REVERSE TRANSFER

In this section we seek to establish the extent of 'reverse transfer' in our case-study firms and consider the way in which this phenomenon can be a key facet of organizational learning in MNCs. However, we also identify a number of barriers to reverse diffusion. In analysing this phenomenon, we make use of a distinction developed in earlier work between 'evolutionary' and 'transformative' transfer. The former refers to diffusion that is directed towards an optimal mix of practices within an existing modus operandi, leading to only modest changes to employment relations in the firm's domestic plants; the latter type of reverse transfer shifts the firm to a new modus operandi, thereby bringing about more radical change (Edwards and Ferner 2004).

The Evidence of Reverse Transfer

One theme of the data was of apparent openness to reverse transfer. Many respondents argued that their firm was open to learning from across its sites and that where actors in the subsidiaries could demonstrate the efficiency of a new practice, then this could be adopted across the organization. For example, there was evidence from the Irish subsidiary that Logistico attempted to take advantage of what was going on in the subsidiaries by regular audits of the way they worked. Another example was at Softco where the firm held 'Best Practice Fairs' that had the goal of facilitating the transfer of expertise across its sites.

There were some clear examples of reverse transfer. One was at ITco where one channel through which it could occur was known as 'Best of Breed'—a programme designed to allow subsidiaries to identify practices that could beneficially be deployed elsewhere, enabling subsidiaries to spearhead the transfer process. The initial steps towards reverse transfer had also apparently come in the form of the job grading system. This was originally a UK initiative that was 'sent up the lines' and became policy in the European operations, though apparently not across the whole company. There was evidence that the British operations had also introduced the practice of establishing individual business targets as part of the appraisal system, and this was something that was transferred back to the USA. This was going with the grain of the company's policies on appraisal, constituting a relatively minor adaptation to them, and hence it was evolutionary in its impact.

In Drugco there was evidence that the Spanish subsidiary had introduced the information system SAP. It appeared that the Spanish part of the firm was keen to be seen as a good corporate citizen and was eager to display its innovative potential. Thus one respondent described the process:

The whole organization today works with SAP, but we were the pioneers in 1997. We realized that the company wanted to introduce SAP and we were the first to be interested. They thought it would be ideal for us to be the pioneers, given that our 'best practices' were already recognised in other respects. We successfully implemented SAP in finance, HR and manufacturing while, for example, France only implemented it in HR and finance.

To the extent to which the Spanish subsidiary was seen as innovative, it was clearly going with the grain of the approach of the wider firm; as the quote indicates, the introduction of SAP was clearly favoured by the parent firm.

There was also evidence of reverse transfer from Silico in Germany. A process unique to the German subsidiary that came under scrutiny was a working time system which subsidiary management had developed together with employee representatives in the 1980s to increase the flexibility of the German operations. Under this system, employees worked 40 hours a week and were paid for 38, with the surplus credited to 'working time accounts'. The credit could be used, for example, for extending parental leave or for further part-time study. For managers, the agreement allowed the plant to be closed temporarily in response to changes in demand, thereby saving the costs of laying off staff. During the late 1990s, a corporate mandate was issued that all employees would have to work the equivalent of six days extra per year in order to help the company out of its economic crisis. Subsidiary management in Germany used this opportunity to present its working time system to HQ management. In the words of the German HR director:

I went to them and said this is the way we do it in Germany, I presented it in their terminology... I pulled out all the stops, saying 'all German employees are included in this and we don't have to ask them or to consult the employee representatives in order to increase working time as you [corporate HQ] have stipulated because the system allows such flexibility'.

The corporate model for dealing with fluctuations in demand drew on the German practice in important ways. Most significantly, it became corporate policy for employees to have 'working time accounts' that allowed for flexibility in working time. While these were not implemented in other locations through a detailed collective agreement as they had been in Germany, the transfer of the practice to American operations was evidence of reverse transfer.

In *Engco2* there was also an instance of reverse transfer. The firm's move into new geographical markets and the associated rhetoric of making the firm more 'global' was used by managers in the UK and other foreign operations as an argument to persuade HQ that the policymaking process should incorporate the inputs of those based outside the USA (see also Chapter 12). The US HQ dominance provoked a 'mini-rebellion' at a global HR conference, and during the course of our research, a team was established to redesign the performance management system. The team was led by one of the British conference 'rebels' on a three-year assignment at HQ, coordinating a multinational team of eight people from six countries. It was envisaged that the team would allow actors from across the company to influence the policy formation process and, while it did not operate in as participative a way as some had hoped, the review did incorporate practices from outside the USA into the new system. The prime example of this was the inclusion of a competency-based appraisal system that was pioneered in the UK. This is clear evidence of reverse transfer. It was of an evolutionary rather than transformative kind because the competency-based appraisal system was a refinement of a principle already set by the working party's brief of tying performance management more closely to training needs.

In Engco1 there were three examples of reverse transfer. The division that we examined was organized around an international network of sites that had complementary roles and were expected to cooperate with each other. One illustration of this collaboration involved the transfer of the 'shared services' concept within the HR function across business divisions. The British HR function had pioneered 'shared services' for pensions, and this generated interest in America. The British innovation had some influence on the company's shift towards the adoption of shared services in HR globally, but was described as the 'tip of the iceberg' since senior HR staff at corporate HQ were already moving in this direction.

A share purchase plan was a second illustration of reverse transfer at Engco1. The firm has a worldwide plan under which an employee could buy shares to the value of between 1 and 6 per cent of salary. The company supplemented this with shares of the same value. One manager described the way that this practice originated in Britain:

[The UK site] was the first facility in the world that put stock ownership, subsidized stock ownership, on the factory floor. Now it's done in a lot of places.

This innovation went with the grain of the firm's emphasis on 'variable' pay, supplementing a pre-existing profit-related bonus and, even more importantly, the concept of stock ownership itself was not new, just the extension of it to shop-floor workers.

A final illustration of an innovation at Engco1's UK sites concerned teamwork. The innovation comprised a novel layout for the production line involving a reorganization of teams. These teams elected 'coordinators', held meetings every morning to discuss performance, and were required to maintain a 'continuous improvement processes' book. The largest American plant drew on the British innovation in implementing an almost identical plant layout. The operations manager of this plant indicated that they had drawn on the developments in the UK site which had been 'very successful in doing that' and went on to describe a 'lot of meetings with (the UK plant) on how they did it and things they would have done differently'. This case of reverse transfer certainly had a significant impact on the organization of production and work group relations. However, the concept of teamwork already existed and, hence, the changes were relatively minor adaptations to existing practices rather than radical shifts to new ones. Therefore, all three of the UK initiatives were going with the grain of the company's established direction and, hence, were evolutionary rather than transformative.

The company with the highest incidence of reverse transfer appears to be Business Services. This firm had gone to considerable lengths to capture, codify, and subsequently transfer organizational knowledge across borders. The firm was one where formalized structures encouraged reverse transfer, and it seemed to be effective in transferring codified forms of knowledge; the 'mining' of databases was a key part of this. Central to these attempts was a set of computer-based learning tools and a number of mechanisms capable of storing knowledge in a way that made it readily available for global use within the company, thereby creating 'knowledge capital'. As one respondent described it:

So all of the best practices, all of the learnings from key projects around the world—we have what's called the 'Knowledge Exchange' which is a place where all of that is stored and housed, content architecture, search engines, how to find the information, how to harvest it, how to categorize it in a way that's easily accessible by our people. (HQ HR manager)

There were examples of reverse transfer from each of the three subsidiaries investigated. For example, the UK operations were among the first in the company to manage a large outsourcing project. The way this was handled, involving staff being incorporated into Business Services, became the model for how outsourcing should be handled across the firm; it became known as the 'blueprint' for this:

The [supermarket] project became essentially a case study for what to do and what not to do in managing the workforce or employees of an outsourcing arrangement and those dos and don'ts and methods and practices have been well documented and are now part of the foundation of how we look at managing employees in other outsourcing units. (HQ HR manager)

Some of the staff active in the outsourcing deal in Britain subsequently advised on the introduction of similar arrangements in other countries. In developing a significantly innovative practice, this appears to be a transformative reverse transfer.

In Germany, a leadership training programme was developed to support new partners with little leadership experience. It was drawn up against the background of the rapid growth of the German subsidiary where young partners were quickly promoted into positions where they were responsible for managing a team of consultants and acquiring new business from clients. It proved to be a success in Germany and was then developed into a global leadership development programme.

An idea was developed in Spain to set up centres where repeatable work which did not have to be done on-site with clients was done in packages. This too was subsequently adopted globally. The part of the workforce performing these tasks was managed separately from other groups. The logic of this arrangement was that it offered the management skills of Business Services to firms on a 'repeatable' rather than a tailor-made basis, something that distinguished such work from consulting. One respondent described it thus:

The model was something that started in Spain which was getting a group of skilled people that was a separate workforce that supported the consulting practice in terms of providing repeatable solutions on a day-by-day basis, so...actually they set up two or three centres in Spain to support the consulting practice and that model is what's become our [repeatable activity] workforce. And again some of our key leaders out of Spain are the ones that are helping us again take that model and set up centres both outside the US in places like China and India and Manila, but also setting up the [repeatable activity] workforce centres within countries, so within the US or France, etc. So again, that was a concept that was done totally in Spain that we leveraged, frankly, everywhere. (HQ HR manager)

The impact of this practice, involving as it did a major change in the way that the workforce was managed, was unquestionably transformative.

Such transfer was widely seen as legitimate and expected in Business Services, both in the national subsidiary and at business-unit and corporate HQ. It was premised on the professional ethos that permeated the global company, which assumed that talent and expertise could reside in any location. Transfer was also assisted by strong, formalized, functional and business unit networks which explicitly focused on identifying and propagating best practice. This was complementary to an extensive and rigorous effort to codify, formalize, and catalogue the basis of professional knowledge across the company; in other words, there were structures in place to ensure that tacit knowledge was made as far as possible explicit, and hence more easily transferable. This relatively high propensity to reverse transfer probably reflects factors to do with the sector. The activity of professional service firms such as Business Services was based on a highly skilled and qualified global workforce composed of professional experts.

How significant an impact did the process of reverse transfer have on employment practice in the American operations? The answer is a mixed picture. In Business Services, there were a number of important, apparently transformative, instances of reverse transfer that were key to the way that firm generated innovations. In addition, there were a number of instances of evolutionary reverse transfer, notably in Engco1 but also in ITco, Drugco, Silico, and Engco2. However, these instances of evolutionary transfer were, by definition, minor amendments to existing practices and in many of the case studies there was only one instance that could be identified. In addition, reverse transfer was absent in many of the other case-study firms. Thus it was not possible to identify any specific practices that had been the subject of reverse transfer in firms, such as Bor-Tec, Softco, CPGco, EngServs, Pharmaco, and Logistico, despite the talk of openness to innovations coming from across the company. It is conceivable that some instances of reverse transfer went undetected, though it is likely that most instances would have been uncovered by multiple interviews with respondents at a number of levels and across countries. The overall picture, therefore, seems to reveal that reverse transfer occurs only to a restricted extent—certainly, it is much rarer than forward transfer— and where it does occur its impact seems to be evolutionary in the main. In other words, the extent to which the case-study firms engaged in learning from their foreign subsidiaries was quite minor, with the exception of Business Services. The next section seeks to identify explanations for this limited impact and the variations between the firms.

Barriers to Reverse Transfer

One type of explanation for why the impact of reverse transfer may be limited focuses on the institutional constraints arising from the NBS of the home country. (For more detail on the following arguments, see Edwards et al. 2005.) One instance of this in US MNCs was the way in which the dominant institutions in the USA have given rise to patterns of employment practice that managers are reluctant to disturb with innovations from other countries. An initial expectation might be that the deregulated nature of the American labour market will give managers in the US operations a free hand to engage in reverse transfer. However, pre-existing personnel policies and practices in the American sites can present a barrier to reverse transfer.

In welfare capitalist firms, HR policies are carefully and systematically constructed as part of an attempt by managers to keep out unions, and managers may be unwilling to disturb this balance with innovations from other countries. One illustration of this was CPGco. The British operations of CPGco introduced a form of 'broadbanding' of pay grades (see Chapter 7). A senior manager from the UK site looked to push this innovation to the USA. However, the American sites did not introduce the practice, apparently because of the union avoidance policies that were a key part of the firm's welfare capitalist heritage. The main US site closely monitored its pay levels and structure in relation to unionized firms. In this context, the British innovation of simplifying the pay system into a small number of bands was unattractive to American managers. The pay structure in the American plant emphasized seniority provisions, while the British system involved a closer relation between pay and skills. Furthermore, the American plant retained multiple job grades, apparently representing an attempt to emulate the structures, and improve on the levels, of pay in nearby unionized firms. If the British practice had been implemented in the USA, some US workers would inevitably have perceived themselves to have lost out from the changes, relatively or absolutely, and this might therefore have provided fertile ground for unions to make membership gains. In this way, the commitment to retaining non-union status in welfare capitalist firms constrains the scope for innovation by managers.

It is not just the welfare capitalist firms in which such barriers exist. In those firms still bearing the legacy of New Deal IR, the detailed procedures and elaborate pay scales, together with the need to negotiate major changes with employee representatives, would make a significant reorganization of pay grades, for example, problematic. For these reasons, therefore, the patterns of employment practice to which the institutional framework in the USA gives rise do not give US MNCs a free hand to engage in reverse transfer as might have been anticipated, particularly in relation to issues such as pay systems.

A second characteristic of the US business system that might impede reverse transfer is the fluctuating nature of basic strategy and structure in large American firms. We noted in Chapter 3 that an LME as in the USA would tend to make firms open to 'radical' innovations, including practices that are reverse transferred and that may represent a significant departure from established practice. However, the frequency with which large American firms make changes to their core strategies and associated structures in general, and the swift and dramatic responses to changes in market conditions in particular, creates a context in which reverse transfer is inhibited. While the ease with which resources can be moved from one use to another in the USA may allow companies to reinvent themselves with dramatic shifts into new areas, as Hall and Soskice (2001b) argue, this fluidity appears to impede the international coordination that is necessary for reverse transfer to occur. Building close links between site-level actors in different countries takes time, often involving a lengthy process of coalition-building and cross-national learning (Birkinshaw 2000). Arguably, in 'CMEs' like Germany or Japan, company structures and strategies change more gradually and respond to changes in markets in a slower, more measured manner; this type of corporate heritage in the parent company may provide a more stable, and therefore more conducive, context in which reverse transfer can take place.

One example of how fluctuations in corporate strategy impeded reverse transfer was EngServs. During the 1990s the firm had begun to move away from its highly decentralized organizational form, strengthening global corporate functions and reversing previous understandings about operational sovereignty at subsidiary level. This came partly as a response to major problems in some operations that had led to legal challenges to the company. The introduction of global corporate functions appeared to increase the potential for reverse transfer, since the absence of strong mechanisms linking the US sites to those elsewhere had previously been a key barrier to such transfer. The highly profitable UK operations were well placed to serve as donor units for new practices in view of these developments. However, the appointment of a new CEO led to a dramatic reversal of the strategy of building global functions, seriously curtailing the scope for reverse transfer. Compounding this was a tendency for the US operations to respond to downturns with deep job cuts, particularly among the expensive process engineers. Arguably, this limited the scope for the US part of the division to upgrade itself—through introducing practices developed in the foreign subsidiaries, for example—when conditions changed. In short, the move to global corporate functions including HR was too short-lived to allow the British operations a sufficient opportunity to carve a role for themselves as pioneers of new practices for the rest of the firm.

A different approach, but one which also draws on national-institutional frameworks to explain barriers to reverse transfer, is to focus on the nature of host business systems. One theme of the data is that many instances of reverse transfer originated in the UK (see Table 12.1). One factor that may explain this is the extent to which there are compatibilities between key institutions in the host systems and the American business system. Thus, in the same way as many corporate policies could be adopted with relative ease in the UK because they went with the grain of local institutions, so too was there more scope for UK practices to be adopted in domestic operations or to become part of corporate-wide policies. In contrast, it may be hypothesized that reverse transfer is less likely to flow from German subsidiaries because of the greater institutional distance between host- and home-country institutions, limiting the scope for German practices to be adopted in the USA or to be absorbed into corporate-wide policies.

Linked to this, actors in the UK are better placed than their German counterparts to influence global policy formation because it is easier for them to 'speak the language of the Americans' as one of our respondents put it. This may allow them to bargain effectively for their position to be adopted. This is related not only to the advantages that UK (and Irish) managers have in terms of language but also in terms of perceived similarity of culture. There are a number of cases, notably CPGco, ITco, and Bor-Tec, where German interviewees stressed the special relationship that UK managers had been able to build up with corporate managers. There was evidence of this even in Business Services where, despite the extensive channels open to subsidiary management outlined earlier, a German HR manager still complained that 'it takes a lot before someone from Continental Europe or Asia is promoted into a leadership position'.

Table 11.1. The incidence of reverse transfer in selected case studies

Firm	Sources of influence from subsidiaries	Existence of mechanisms capable of facilitating transfer	Evidence of reverse transfer
CPGco	Sizeable operations in the UK and Spain, with large production facilities; substantial employment in Germany though production sites closed in 1990s	Strong mechanisms for coordinating policies across borders, such as international working groups; much use of international assignments	**No clear evidence** UK site introduced 'broadbanding' involving a form of teamwork and a fall in the number of pay grades—pushed to the USA but not taken up; Moves by UK operations to share anti-harassment training not taken up by HQ; No evidence of reverse transfer from Germany, Spain
EngServs	UK by far the most profitable part of the company; UK controlled the division of which it was a part	Traditionally very weak mechanisms, confined to very limited transfer of staff at senior levels and infrequent international committees	**No clear evidence** UK operations developed new 'individualized' payment system; similar system introduced into other European sites, possibly influenced by UK, but not incorporated into global policy
Logistico	European operations minimal significance in terms of overall operation; Business largely concentrated in the US	Quite regiocentric organization; Opportunities for personnel and information sharing within regions (in this case Europe), but only limited possibilities of transfer to US; Little expatriate flow in either direction outside regions	**No clear evidence**
Pharmaco	Irish operations relatively significant in context of corporation; number of key products entirely manufactured and tableted in Irish operations	Numerous formal mechanisms to bring about transfer; examples include common IT systems and reporting, transition training for employees moving into senior managerial roles, use of standard codes for financial reporting	**Evidence of reverse transfer from IRL**— Working time system presented to corporate management as possible solution to flexibility problems—evolutionary reverse transfer because it influenced the way in which working time was managed in domestic operations
Silico	German subsidiary largest operations outside of US	Mechanisms to compare processes and practices, supported by common IT framework	**Evidence of reverse transfer from Germany** Working time system presented to corporate management as possible solution to flexibility problems—evolutionary reverse transfer because it influenced how working time was managed in domestic operations

		Clear evidence of reverse transfer
Engco2	Sizeable UK operations serving European market; use of 'global' firm rhetoric to legitimize subsidiary involvement in global HR policy process	Postings of subsidiary staff in key positions in HQ, e.g. to review firm's performance management system; Regular international meetings of HR function	**Clear evidence of reverse transfer** New performance management system led by Briton on three-year posting at corporate HQ; Evolutionary reverse diffusion with inclusion of competency-based appraisal; Senior UK HR manager involved in development of 'templates' to facilitate greater subsidiary involvement in policy formation, but later fell by the wayside
ITco	Changing structure led to more scope for subsidiaries to play part in policy development; growth of UK operations in 'outsourcing' market increased its influence	Existence of strong mechanisms for developing common HR policies—national-level structures reduced to minimal role; Much use of international assignments	**Clear evidence of reverse transfer from UK** Appraisal system, involving setting and assessing goals for each individual on annual basis—partly developed in UK so clear evidence of evolutionary reverse transfer; UK people influential in European HR function; HR 'call centre' for Europe located in Britain, though closely modelled on similar centre in the US
Engco1	Significant operations in UK—basis for serving European markets difficult to serve otherwise	'Inpatriation' of key figure from largest UK site to largest American site; Informal international network among managerial staff	**Clear evidence of reverse transfer** UK site developed new system of teamwork on shop floor subsequently implemented in US plants—clear evidence of evolutionary reverse diffusion; British operations pioneered development of stock ownership for factory workers—clear evidence of evolutionary reverse transfer, now part of worldwide policy; UK HR function involved in development of 'shared services', took on lead role across the division—clear evidence of evolutionary reverse transfer
Business Services	Sizeable and well-established operations in UK, Spain, and Germany, each subsidiary had specialist expertise in certain market segments; Partnership ethos: 'partner mentality is everyone equal and everybody's idea is as good as the next man's'	Strong formalized networking, regular, formal functional meetings often using virtual methods; Standardized methodology for codifying knowledge	**Clear evidence of transformative reverse transfer** Spanish subsidiary pioneered new workforce structure for consultancy support operations, with major ramifications for international firm; rare example of 'transformative' reverse transfer; UK innovation in electronic filing of performance assessment forms, taken up globally; UK outsourcing example; Leadership development programme, piloted in Germany—clear evidence of evolutionary reverse transfer, provided basis for corporate programme; System for assessing software skills and needs developed by consortium of European subsidiaries; Used across Europe and may be globalized in future; Development of 360°feedback in French operations, subsequently made global

A related factor is that variations in the extent to which subsidiaries across countries are the source of reverse transfer are also shaped by how senior managers in American MNCs perceive the host business systems in terms of economic performance. Arguably, this may lead US MNCs to the UK and Ireland since they are widely perceived to be performing more strongly than the German or Spanish economies. In this respect, a common message emanating from our German data was the negative perception on the part of American senior management of the German business system. This perception was clearly communicated to subsidiary management and centred on the issues of inflexibility, high-labour costs, and long decision-making time as shaped by the institutions of collective bargaining and codetermination. It was felt particularly strongly in manufacturing companies such as ITco, Silico, and CPGco, and led to significant restructuring of the German sites away from production to service activities, entailing associated workforce reductions in the 1990s. Against the background of such perceptions, it is perhaps not surprising that there was not more evidence of reverse transfer from our German data. However, while the British, and possibly Irish, operations may be better placed than their German and Spanish counterparts to influence the nature of international HR policies, it may be that the basic compatibilities in the business systems means that reverse transfer is mainly evolutionary when it originates in these two countries. In contrast, while the German and Spanish subsidiaries are less commonly the source of reverse transfer, it is possible that when it does occur it is more likely to constitute a major change to the MNC's modus operandi and, therefore, be transformative in nature.

A focus on national institutions is revealing in some ways but does not explain variations between case-study firms. To achieve such an explanation, we consider how structural features of the organizations themselves promote or retard reverse transfer, and give rise to some variation in the extent of reverse transfer across firms. One characteristic of organizations that affects the incidence of reverse transfer is the extent and tradition of central influence on employment policy (see Chapter 10). In highly centralized companies, such as ITco, Engco2, and CPGco, this influence did not close off all scope for innovations at foreign subsidiary level. Indeed, our evidence indicates that the UK sites often looked to expand their role within the wider firm through supplying expertise and knowledge to other sites. However, the centralist tradition does appear to have created a significant organizational group that may resist reverse transfer, namely, a well-staffed and influential HR function at corporate HQ. This group may feel threatened by the increasing influence of subsidiaries in the policy-making process, fearing that the logic of this development will be a reduction in headcount at the centre and a fall in the status of HQ staff within the organization. Consistent with this reasoning, Ferner and Varul (2000) found that middle-ranking managers in the corporate HQs of German MNCs resisted the reverse transfer of 'Anglo-Saxon' practices and were most able to do so where the domestic operations formed the bulk of the company. Therefore, the failure of many US MNCs to engage in reverse transfer may be a result of political activity by those in HQ, who see their prominent role in policymaking threatened by subsidiary involvement. Arguably, this contrasts with the way that many MNCs of other nationalities are structured. For example, in a case study of a Swedish MNC Hayden and Edwards (2001) argued that the 'Swedishness' of the firm gave rise to an openness to learning from other countries.

Evidence indicative of this is found in Engco2. In this firm, the partial break with the HQ-driven model of developing global HR policies (see earlier) clearly posed a threat to many in the central HR function, and the new model based on engaging HR staff from across the world only came about after insistent demands from foreign managers. The gradual reversion to the HQ-driven model and the downplaying of participative policy formation represented the removal of this threat. The privileged claim on resources of the corporate HR function was raised directly by one of our British respondents in CPGco who expressed amazement at the number of people in the corporate HR function. Where this is the case, it might be argued that there is likely to be resistance to reverse transfer; the importing of practices from elsewhere would imply that some of the central policymaking staff were redundant, and those adversely affected might mobilize whatever resources they controlled to oppose the process.

While a highly centralized approach is not conducive to reverse transfer, neither is a highly decentralized approach. Thus in EngServs, the most decentralized of our case-study firms, the absence of integrative mechanisms across sites restricted the scope for innovations generated in foreign subsidiaries to be transferred back to the USA. It was in those firms with a 'network' structure, involving interlinkages between subsidiary companies but without a controlling HQ, that there was rather more scope for reverse transfer. Thus in Business Services foreign operations were afforded a more significant role in the policy formation process. As we saw earlier, HQ was favourably disposed towards modelling corporate-wide policies on innovations made in Spain, Britain, and Germany. The structure of the division of Engco1 that we examined was also conducive to the reverse transfer of the teamwork practice. While production was not as highly networked as was the case in Business Services, it was structured in such a way as to allow foreign subsidiaries to have responsibilities beyond their own country and to generate cooperative rather than strongly competitive relations between sites.

A further structural factor is the nature of regional structures within US MNCs. There is evidence that MNCs emphasized the European, as opposed to national or global, elements within their structures. Within our case studies, the European dimension to the structure was particularly important in ITco and CPGco, and to a lesser extent in EngServs (see Chapter 10). Such structures can provide a focal point for European subsidiaries to influence the development of global policies. Indeed, in CPGco the European entity appeared to have some influence on the development of global policies on such issues as variable pay. However, another impact of the increasing emphasis on the regional dimension was to generate close links between European sites, but simultaneously to curtail direct contact between the European and American sites. Indeed, in one of the case-study companies, Bor-Tec, European HR managers convened a meeting to develop a strategy of resistance against what they saw as a very ethnocentric, centralized approach by HQ. British subsidiary management sought to prevent this from happening and refused to have any part in it as they feared that this would damage their relationship with HQ.

Regional integration can promote a degree of networking and subsequent transfer of practices across sites within regions, but its impact on reverse transfer is ambiguous. Of course, where firms are organized around a business–geography matrix, the business dimension of the structure can still promote reverse transfer and the strengthening of regional structures within US MNCs may actively promote transfer from Canada or Mexico, though this is likely to be constrained by the relative size of the Canadian economy and the low 'value-added' role that Mexican subsidiaries of US MNCs sometimes play.

ITco is a case where the regional dimension of a 'matrix' structure (based on regional and divisional elements) was particularly strong. In this firm many aspects of HR, such as recruitment, the management of international assignments, and routine administrative enquiries, were centralized at European level. The UK operations had pioneered several initiatives within the European HR function, such as the operation of the administration centre, but appeared to have a much more limited role in developing policies in North America. The story in EngServs is similar. The UK operations enjoyed something of a 'regional mandate' within Europe and the Middle East, leading the creation of new subsidiaries in this area and managing them for a time. This privileged role coupled with the highly profitable nature of the British operations, positioned it well to serve as a donor of new practices to the USA. However, the regional mandate meant that it had no formal role in doing so, and it had much less influence on the other side of the Atlantic.

The micropolitical approach can be used to supplement the institutional and contingency approaches. The data provide numerous instances in which the role of groups of actors within the firms was crucial in shaping the extent and nature of reverse transfer. One aspect of this is the reaction to senior American managers' perceptions of subsidiary operations and the host business system in which they were embedded.

This was an important feature of the German subsidiaries. Subsidiary management at ITco and CPGco reacted relatively passively to HQ's negative views of the German system, being prepared to conform to HQ policies even if this meant challenging local institutions (Tempel et al. 2004). In contrast, subsidiary management at Silico adopted a strategy of attempting to redefine these negative perceptions and actively shape the restructuring process in the German operations:

> It is of fundamental importance to get involved in the process. With the level of labour costs we have here, we have to look to those activities where we can add value. There's no point in us competing for printer production. We'd have no chance. That's why we have to compete for activities where we can use our competitive advantages, our high skills levels. That is something that we have done intensively in the last few years.

Management's ability to do so was reinforced by the fact that the German subsidiary was Silico's largest operations outside the USA. This strategy is mirrored in the reverse transfer of the subsidiary's working time system, with subsidiary management seeking ways to make corporate management aware of the innovations they developed in order to increase flexibility and to present the system as a possible way forward for the company's US sites.

In contrast to CPGco, ITco, and Silico, the German operations of Business Services did not suffer from HQ's negative perception and this may have increased the likelihood that they would be seen as a source of innovation. The nature of the workforce, with a high proportion of young, professional workers, enabled subsidiary management to circumvent collective bargaining and codetermination. Workflow planning and working time—two key factors influencing the competitiveness of consulting firms—could therefore, be shaped unilaterally by management without the restrictions of the Works Constitution Act and could be managed in line with global specifications.

The ability of local management to exert influence within the wider firm is also strongly shaped by the profitability of the operations they control. Highly profitable sites or groups of sites are clearly more likely to be viewed as key players within the firm by corporate management, and they can use this as a resource either to argue that they should be allowed some autonomy in implementing global policies or that innovations they have made should be adopted across the company. One illustration was Business Services' adoption of the Spanish model of concentrating particular types of 'repeatable' work in a separate organization; this innovation was credited by corporate managers with contributing to the highly profitable state of the Spanish operations.

CONCLUSIONS

The main conclusion of this chapter is that the transfer of practices in US MNCs tends to be principally in one direction, namely from the centre to the foreign operations. In this sense, the findings fit with the claims in the academic literature and the main findings of the book of a strongly ethnocentric approach in US MNCs. Thus, corporate HQs often overlooked practices developed in Europe that subsidiary managers argued were potentially useful to the rest of the group. In those instances where practices were subject to reverse transfer, it was generally 'evolutionary' in that its impact on US domestic operations represented a fine-tuning of a set of practices within a given overall approach and was rarely 'transformative' in the sense of moving the firm to a new modus operandi.

What, then, does the evidence tell us about the four approaches to organizational learning in MNCs outlined at the beginning? The 'information-processing' approach clearly has limitations. In particular, it tells us little about how systematic differences in NBSs shape the nature of transfer. Instead, we have developed an institutional approach to transfer in US MNCs. This has pointed to the existence of institutional barriers to reverse transfer from the home country, such as the tradition of welfare capitalism and the frequent changes in corporate structure and strategy that the American business system presents. It has also pointed to the way that actors in the foreign subsidiaries of US MNCs are differentially placed to bring about reverse transfer according to the nature of the institutional framework in which they are embedded. Despite the significant insights that the institutional approach brings, however, it does not explain variations between firms of the same nationality and for this we have incorporated a 'structural' dimension into our explanation. This focuses on such factors as the legacy of centralized influence, patterns of corporate ownership, and the nature of regional structures. The institutional approach also needs to be complemented with an awareness of the contested nature of transfer, focusing on the way that actors' interests are either enhanced or challenged by reverse transfer. Therefore, we have adopted a pluralistic perspective drawing on multiple approaches in the search for a full understanding of the transfer process.

In sum, the analysis in this chapter suggests that the 'transnational' structure advocated by Bartlett and Ghoshal (1998) as the solution to the challenges of managing across borders is not much in evidence in our case-study firms. A key aspect of a transnational firm is the ability to transfer expertise across its organization, yet US-based MNCs appear to be adept at doing this only in one direction. With the exception of Business Services, a firm that was unusual in that it had only recently ceased to be a partnership, the case-study firms engaged in substantial transfer from the USA to their foreign operations but relatively little transfer in the opposite direction. The embeddedness of US MNCs in the American business system has of course been a central part of our explanation for their approach to managing their international workforces throughout the book; in this chapter, we have extended this line of analysis to explain their domestic orientation to the generation of innovations.

12

The Role of the International Personnel Function

Hartmut Wächter, René Peters, Anthony Ferner, Paddy Gunnigle, and Javier Quintanilla

INTRODUCTION

The design of the personnel department is the result of a continuous organizational process, embedded in the overall structural development of the company. There is a substantial body of international comparative literature on HRM as a normative model. Within this literature, however, the nature of the HR function itself is generally neglected. This chapter tries to deepen the understanding of the role of the personnel function in US MNCs by exploring its international operation and the evolving challenges it faces in the context of the historical development of the function in the USA.

A central analytical question is how diverse institutional influences are reconciled (or not) in the operation and role of the function within and across national borders. While the business literature has attempted to consider the evolution of the HR function in terms of generic cross-national tendencies—for example, the devolution of HR responsibilities to line managers, the function's attempts to seek a role as 'business partner' and 'change agent', and the changing balance between routine administrative work and more 'strategic' functions (Ulrich, 1999: 34)—much of this predominantly prescriptive literature has tended to generalize US preoccupations and models, to the neglect of cross-national variety in the organization, role, and boundaries of the personnel function.

Host business systems affect the design of the HR function in MNCs in many ways. In Germany, for example, the tradition of vocational education has led to an apprenticeship system that affects career paths and the number of layers in organizations (cf. Wächter and Stengelhofen 1995: 92). As a result, the HR function in MNC subsidiaries in Germany has to find ways of responding to the institutional conditions of the national context. Nationally specific arrangements within the function then have to be integrated with a cross-national structure for the management of personnel within the global corporation. The chapter therefore explores the role and structure of US MNCs' HR within different national subsidiaries, how these fit with a broader conception of the function's role at international level, and how resulting tensions are managed as the function evolves over time.

The empirical section analyses the case-study companies' personnel departments in different countries and on a supranational level. In particular, two themes are explored: the changing relative significance of personnel structures at national, regional, and international business levels and the influence on personnel's structure and role of efficiency-seeking agendas in the case-study firms.

A number of internal organizational dimensions may be examined in order to understand the evolving role and structure of the personnel function. First, the HR department can, broadly speaking, be organized by function. De Cenzo and Robbins (1996) characterize the typical (non-union) US HRM department as divided into four different functions: employment management, including hiring and firing; compensation and benefits; training and development; and employee relations. The chapter considers how the influence of the US institutional environment is reflected in such functional specialization within personnel departments.

A second dimension of the personnel function is size. Quantitative data on the size of personnel departments in Europe (Van Ommeren and Brewster 1999: 35) indicate that the country of origin exerts an influence on the size of personnel departments. In subsidiaries of American companies, departments are reported to be 9–10 per cent larger than subsidiaries of European organizations. Unfortunately, we lack systematic data across companies and countries on the size of the function. But quantitative comparisons are in any case problematic. They raise significant problems of comparing like with like, where, for example, large administrative functions, such as payroll administration have been outsourced, or where large numbers of employees provide cross-unit services, sometimes at an international level (e.g. in HR call centres). We return to the implications of such structural developments later.

A third dimension for capturing the role of the personnel function is its relative hierarchical position. This can be analysed at the subsidiary as well as the multinational level. The 'Cranet' surveys have measured the status of HRM in different European countries according to whether the head of the HR function has a place on the main board (for details on the four countries see Brewster, Mayrhofer, and Morley 2004). The results suggest that the function occupies a similar hierarchical position in UK and Irish companies, has shown a strong increase in Germany, and in Spain exhibits the highest hierarchical level of all countries.

However, such surveys are problematic. First, results may be biased by the inclusion of MNC subsidiaries. Both the extent of foreign ownership and its composition by county of ownership is likely to impact on the findings in a given country. This may result in an 'import' of a high value for the hierarchical position of the personnel function in a country such as Ireland with a high level of US FDI. Second, data need careful interpretation in the light of national-institutional arrangements. For example, at the beginning of the 1990s the personnel function in Germany was apparently characterized by a low-hierarchical position (see Brewster, Larsen, and Mayrhofer 1997: 10). This is surprising since the representation of the HR function on the board is stipulated by law. The *Arbeitsdirektor* (labour director), elected by the majority vote of the supervisory board (except in coal and steel), deals with personnel issues in companies with more than 2,000 employees (for details see Blessing and Otto 2004). Companies with fewer than 2,000 employees usually have very few people on the board, and the assignment of responsibilities is not as specialized as in other countries.

In short, survey data are of limited value, and the hierarchical position and influence of the function needs to be explored through the detailed analysis of the micropolitics of its relationship with the corporation as a whole, at different organizational levels; this is the focus of our own empirical investigation.

A fourth dimension of the personnel function is its development over time. Its dynamic reflects, first, the pressures of operating in different institutional environments that are themselves changing; and, second, the need to adapt to changing market contexts, competitive pressures, and technological developments as these affect the MNC's strategic choices and objectives. As a result of such dynamic external pressures, the structural relationships between different parts of the function, notably between the HR function at HQ and in different national subsidiaries, is in a state of flux, subject to periodically intense pressures for change.

In summary, the chapter uses case-study data to investigate the role, structure, hierarchical position, and evolution of the personnel function in US MNCs. To explain distinct patterns, it draws on historical approaches to the development of the HR function, in detail for the USA and more briefly for the European countries.

THE DEVELOPMENT OF THE PERSONNEL FUNCTION IN PARENT AND HOST BUSINESS SYSTEMS

The features of the American business system and of the European host countries have been described in Chapters 3 and 4. We now focus in more detail on the evolution of the HR function in the parent business system and in the four host countries.

Historical Development of the Personnel Function in the USA

The personnel function in large US firms has developed its own distinctive features. First, in contrast to more highly regulated systems such as Germany, where a fairly prescriptive institutional framework shaped the role of the function, in the US it has been characterized by its 'proactivity' (Lawrence 1996: Chapter 9). The reasons lie in interrelated historical strands in the evolution of the American business system outlined in Chapter 3. American companies, averse to union interference in management prerogative, actively sought ways of deterring a union presence and encouraging the commitment of workers to their firms. In this task, the personnel function played a key role, devising innovative policies for pay and benefits and for employee communication and involvement, and establishing strong ILMs. Well before the First World War, major companies were implementing career-based, stable employment structures, and their strategies gave rise to new employment departments to administer them (Jacoby 1985, 1997).

A further factor encouraging proactivity was the state's unusually weak role in provision of welfare functions. This prompted companies to fill the vacuum themselves by providing for the welfare needs of employees, at a time when other countries were decisively moving away from the corporate welfarism model (Jacoby 1997).

This tendency towards proactivity has been consolidated by the fact that, even in its unionized sectors, the US business system lacks the coordinating and framework-setting role of institutional levels beyond the firm that continue to play a significant role in European systems of IR. Hence the decisions of corporate personnel functions in US firms are shaped to a far lesser degree by the constraints of higher-level regulation. This greater latitude allows and indeed encourages a greater range of personnel policies and approaches.

A second broad feature of personnel in the USA is its relatively early definition as a professional function. This partly reflected the early emergence of large firms and the increasing complexity of their organizational structures and management systems. The separation of personnel issues from the daily job of managers on the shop floor resulted in specialist personnel departments, performing various tasks for the organization. Moreover, the adoption of scientific management and the resulting rationalization of work roles invoked a number of specialized functional requirements such as time and motion study, the codification of job requirements, and job descriptions (Baron et al. 1986: 358). Tendencies to formalization and growth in the function were strengthened by government intervention in the two World Wars (Baron et al. 1986; Jacoby 1985: Chapter 5). Later, government intervention in the form of complex legislation on civil rights and EEOs encouraged the further growth of sub-specialisms within personnel function, for example, to monitor legislative compliance and then to develop the 'business case' for workforce diversity (see Chapter 8).

A final element in the characteristic formalization of the US personnel function was the rapid development of company-based collective bargaining as a result of the New Deal model. The construction of a 'web of rules' regulating lay-offs, rehiring, and promotion, as well as grievance handling (Jacoby 1985) developed the formal structure of the function. Collective bargaining was also a major force behind the consolidation and codification of the fragmented wage structures that had resulted from decentralized, uncoordinated wage setting by plant managers and foremen. In non-union firms, similar codification of pay structures was important for defensive reasons, to ward off unionization.

The third broad characteristic of personnel management in the USA, already discussed in Chapter 3, is the sharp distinction between unionized and non-union firms. In non-union companies, particularly those adopting the 'welfare capitalism' brand of non-unionism, the personnel function came to develop a strategic role (Foulkes 1980: Chapter 5; Jacoby 1997). Top personnel executives were sometimes part of the core group of corporate policymarkers, helping to propound and interpret the corporate founding philosophy and empowered by their ability to brandish the union threat. They also developed a role as a 'third force', mediating between workers and line managers and acting as the 'guarantor' of employee rights (Jacoby 1997).

The proactive personnel policies of such firms—strong ILM for core personnel with sophisticated recruitment and selection techniques, individualized pay related to performance, and a strong emphasis on a culture of corporate 'community' aimed at winning employee commitment and deflecting unionization—can be seen as the precursors of the prescriptive model of personnel that from the 1980s increasingly came to be labelled 'HRM' (see Guest 1989; Storey 1995 for discussion of the evolution of 'HRM' as an ideological concept).

In the unionized sector, a division of labour emerged within the personnel function, between personnel specialists and those responsible for managing IR and jointly administering the 'web of rules' in what Kochan, Katz, and McKersie (1994: 36) call a 'symbiotic relationship' with unions. IR specialists developed organizational interests bound up with collective bargaining and their relationships with union officials. Later, as the unionized sector dwindled, and as unionized firms increasingly relocated to non-union locations, the influence of the personnel specialists increased at the expense of IR professionals.

Finally, the strength of the function in the USA—the relative absence of constraints from institutional frameworks of legislation or other supraorganizational arrangements—has also been its weakness. The emergence of a specialist function separate from line management, together with the problems of calculating the costs and benefits to the company of a staff function, such as personnel, prompted criticism from efficiency-oriented management from early on. As a result, the personnel department has always been under pressure to justify its existence and to prove its contribution to profitability and business success. This pressure has intensified over the last twenty-five years with the growth of international market competition, and the increasing orientation to shareholder concerns. Changes of recent decades have also called into question HR's role in the organizational hierarchy, underlining the predominance of other functions such as finance. Nonetheless, recent research suggests that HR professionals have maintained a significant niche role in US companies, partly by espousing the ideology of shareholder value and by concentrating heavily on executive issues rather than administrative or operational ones (Jacoby, Nason, and Saguchi 2005).

In short, therefore, American personnel management has followed a distinctive trajectory: proactive, focused on firm-level strategies, bureaucratized, and formalized in structure and policies from an early period, institutionally and philosophically bifurcated between labour relations and personnel roles (especially during the middle decades of the twentieth century), and intensely preoccupied with policies for attracting commitment of employees to the industrial community of the firm rather than to the collective values of trade unionism. However, it has struggled to play a strategic role in the wider corporation—a struggle intensified by the erosion of welfare capitalism in the face of international competition and shareholder value pressures in recent years.

The Host Country Traditions of the Personnel Function

While the evolution of the personnel function partly reflects 'internal' factors, such as organizational size and complexity and management style and culture, it is also significantly shaped by external forces such as labour or product market pressures, the IR system, and state legislative intervention (Beer 1984). In addition, tendencies towards professionalization of personnel have a marked influence. Such 'normative pressures' emanate partly from the activity of professional HR associations whose members try 'to define the conditions and methods of their work' (DiMaggio and Powell 1983: 152).

In the following section we concentrate on these external influences and briefly describe the different traditions in Spain, Germany, the UK, and Ireland, showing that systematic cross-national differences in contextual factors have led to different patterns of evolution of the personnel function in different countries.

SPAIN

The current HR territory in Spain was mainly shaped by the democratic reforms at the end of 1970s in the aftermath of the Franco era. Unions had been suppressed and declared illegal during the fascist dictatorship, so employee rights played a minor role. Employment relations were governed by a rigid and comprehensive set of labour regulations imposed by the state. Major labour law reform, starting with the *Estatuto de los Trabajadores* (Workers' Statute) in 1980 and continuing through subsequent legislation, changed the situation dramatically (Campos e Cunha, Obeso, and Pina e Cunha 2004: 170). The representational rights and organizational structures of unions were defined in detail, and a statutory system of workplace representation based on the *comité de empresa* (works council) was introduced. This significantly shapes the terrain on which employment relations are conducted in Spanish firms, and hence the role of the personnel function. Labour market regulation is still extensive despite liberalizing reforms in the 1990s. The nature of work contracts and labour market flexibility are highly influenced by these regulations, and labour courts play an important role (cf. Quintanilla, Susaeta, and López 2004: 135).

Furthermore, the evolution of personnel as a management function in Spain has been conditioned by the 'dualist' structure of the Spanish economy. The predominance of family-owned small- and medium-sized companies has hindered the development of professionalized management and is reflected in the traditionally weak management education system. For a long time Spanish HR managers were not highly educated, and the HR function lagged behind other corporate functions in adopting new management techniques and standards (cf. Valle, Martin, Romero 2001: 247). However, the MNCs that entered Spain in large numbers from the 1970s contributed to the rapid professionalization of management functions, including HR. This has been further encouraged by the modernization of social structures under democracy, including the reform of education systems and of labour market regulation. There has been a rapid growth of Anglo-Saxon–style business education programmes closely patterned on the MBA model of American business schools (Quintanilla, Susaeta, and López 2004: 136).

In response to the rapid changes in the Spanish business system over the last thirty years, the personnel function has shown a high degree of adaptability (Ferner, Quintanilla, and Varul 2001; Muller-Camen et al. 2001). This malleability makes Spanish subsidiaries a strategic test bed for the implementation of innovative HR practices despite an environment that in some respects remains highly regulated.

GERMANY

The role of the personnel function in Germany is viewed by outsiders as 'overwhelmingly legalistic, reactive, short-term, and operational' (Ferner 1997: 30; Lawrence 1993). There can be no doubt that German personnel departments are organized in reaction to labour market regulation and codetermination exigencies (e.g. Spie and Bahlmann 1978), particularly the Works Constitution Act. Wächter and Stengelhofen (1995) stress the 'juridification' of the function in response to the need to interpret and manage the implications of the complex statutory environment. Moreover, personnel professionals at company level have tended to lack a major role in collective bargaining, which is conducted primarily at regional-sectoral level; their task has generally been one of application of agreements reached elsewhere. Thus the scope for autonomous, proactive initiatives by the personnel function is somewhat restricted in German companies.

Partly as a result of this context, the function has tended to lack the professional identity and profile of its counterparts in countries such as Britain. However, in response to the debate over the *Standort Deutschland*, a considerable change in labour market legislation has been taking place in recent years. American MNCs have been prominent in challenging the rigidities of German regulation (cf. Wächter et al. 2003: 106), and this is likely to have consequences for the future role of personnel in German companies.

UK AND IRELAND

In many respects HRM in Ireland and the UK has developed along the same lines. Even after the Irish independence from Britain in 1921, some institutional conditions affected the two systems in an analogous way. The close links between the labour markets and identical institutions (e.g. some trade unions or the major HR professional organization, the CIPD—see later) have left similar marks in the two systems (Atterbury et al. 2004: 44). The 'pluralist tradition' of IR has however been challenged by several factors, including extensive FDI. The attractiveness of both the UK and Ireland for foreign investors results from low labour costs, light regulation of the labour market, and weakened trade unions. The openness and small size of the Irish economy have prepared the ground for MNCs to exert a strong influence. MNCs are seen as the major source of innovations in personnel practices as well as of greater specialization of the HR function (Gunnigle 1998). As a result of the pluralist stamp of the Irish business system, personnel was traditionally concerned with the management of IR. However, the function's low involvement in companies' strategic decision-making has changed in the last two decades. Despite different development paths in respect to IR, survey data suggest that HR departments in both countries have gained far more acceptance and influence on corporate strategy (Atterbury et al. 2004).

PROFESSIONAL ORGANIZATION OF THE PERSONNEL FUNCTION

Professional associations of personnel managers exist in all of the researched countries. However, history, organizational objectives, and the degree of embeddedness in the respective national-educational contexts differ significantly. The Spanish Association for Personnel Managers, the AEDIPE, founded in 1964, has assumed the role of disseminating foreign best practices in HR between Spanish companies (Campos e Cunha, Obeso, and Pinae Cunha 2004: 170). The driving force behind this development is the pragmatic desire to catch up with global HR standards. The rhetoric of HRM abounds also in the UK's Chartered Institute of Personnel & Development (CIPD) as well as in the German association, the DGFP. Whether this reflects the diffusion of HRM into practice is, of course, open to debate.

The creation of the German HR association, the *Deutsche Gesellschaft für Personalführung* (German Society for Personnel Management, DGFP), was a response to the welter of post-war labour legislation in such areas as collective bargaining structures and employee representation. The association was founded (under a different name) in 1952 in order to exchange experiences and reduce uncertainty. Affiliation is based on corporate rather than individual membership, and even today the association is designed to support practitioners by offering seminars or initiating practitioner networks (for a detailed analysis see Lee and Limberg 1995), rather than as a 'qualifying association' through which members gain professional qualifications on the UK CIPD model. Education in large German companies is mainly provided by the state, hence the DGFP exerts only an indirect influence on qualifications of personnel managers.

The DGFP differs in many respects from the CIPD, which was founded as early as 1913. Initially established by owners and managers concerned with workers' welfare, the CIPD's range of tasks has broadened significantly. One of the CIPD's key roles is as a 'qualifying association'. Through the introduction of education schemes and examination in accredited colleges, the association has restricted entry and eventually moulded a profession for personnel specialists. In the light of the individual membership it is not surprising that the CIPD today is one of the largest organizations of personnel specialists in the world (Lee and Limberg 1995), proportionately more significant with its membership of 120,000 than the Society for Human Resource Management (SHRM) in the USA (with a membership of 190,000). The American body has a less dominant role in professional accreditation than the CIPD, although the trend is towards greater certification, particularly in the light of the increasing specialization of the function as a result of legislation, corporate internationalization, and so on.[1]

In summary, therefore, the evolution of the profession in the different host countries has responded to different institutional contexts and has been shaped by the different functions and agendas of professional bodies.

THE INTERNATIONAL STRUCTURE AND ROLE OF THE PERSONNEL FUNCTION: EMPIRICAL EVIDENCE

The Organization of the Personnel Function

A number of broad features characterized the organization of the personnel function in the case-study companies, although there were differences reflecting factors such as the extent of diversification and/or the development stage of the organizational structure (cf. Hill 2003: 432–51). At HQ level there was generally a global HR function responsible for integrating HR issues worldwide and involved in the overall strategic decisions of the MNC. The function at this level tended to be horizontally organized, spanning different business units.

At host-country level, the HR function generally reported to the head of the national subsidiary but was also functionally linked, through a 'dotted line' relationship, to HR at a higher organizational level. In a few companies this was global HQ, but more frequently it was an intermediate tier—normally the region, but in some cases a global business unit. Contact between the national HR function and global HQ tended to be minimal, although in some companies annual conferences brought HR professionals from different national subsidiaries together with HQ and regional HR officials. The role of the region was generally to disseminate global policy to the national operations. To varying degrees, it developed or adapted policy to ensure its applicability to the specific requirements of the location. But in the more centralized companies the region functioned as hardly more than a transmission belt, or 'errand boy' as one respondent termed it, on behalf of corporate.

In some regions, particularly where there were disparities in subsidiary size, smaller subsidiaries came under the authority of the HR function in a larger subsidiary. In complex regions with large numbers of subsidiaries, there could be subregional clusters of countries. This is the case, for example, in Logistico: the UK HR director also had functional responsibility for HR in the 'Nordic' region, whose HR directors reported to him. In most firms with such clusters, these usually formed around language or cultural heritage, such as German-speaking, Nordic, or Romance-language countries.

The regional organizational layer could also take the form of a virtual organization, in that to varying degrees its functions were provided by HR managers from different national subsidiaries wearing a second, European 'hat'. This was the case in PharmaChem, and in Business Services where functional groups at European regional level were drawn from managers in the national operations. In CPGco, some of the specialist functional expertise was provided in this way: a Paris-based manager was responsible for European training and development and a Germany-based expert for compensation and benefits.

This form of regional HR organization could disrupt local relationships within subsidiaries. ITco, for example, assigned responsibility for regional policy areas such as pay, working time, and internal promotion rules to individual national HR managers. This solution caused considerable confusion and frustration on the part of works councils in Germany, who were used to negotiate on these policy issues with local management: codetermination on personnel and social programmes is one of the most important areas of works council influence in Germany. Companies of this size generally have several joint committees of HR management and works council on such issues, and the works council may be considered a co-author of most HR policies in an enterprise. This was the case in ITco, where the works council traditionally played a strong role. With the new regional set-up, however, the HR department was unable to answer questions raised by the works council, whose initiatives ended in a vacuum.

The importance of global business units in most of the firms gave rise, especially in large MNCs, to complex matrix structures in HR. In ITco, the main business units within national subsidiaries had HR 'partners' who represented business unit needs to the HR function. At regional level, the HR director coordinated HR functions both in national operations and in international business units operating in the region. Cross-cutting this was a third matrix dimension, that of HR 'processes', comprising different specialisms such as recruitment and selection, remuneration, and training and development. In some cases, there were tensions between regional and business roles. In CPGco, the desire to build strong global businesses was seen by key HR players to be impeded by a powerful regional tier, and hence power increasingly flowed from the regions to the global businesses.

A wide variety of communication and coordination mechanisms were used to link different units and levels of the HR function. These included periodic meetings of HR professionals from different countries and task forces or working groups to develop or adapt policy in different functional areas of HR. In some companies—Business Services was a notable instance—regular functional meetings took place virtually, through telephone conference calls and videoconferencing. Electronic communication, including email and the intranet, was also important where members of an HR team were located in different countries. In some companies (e.g. CPGco), virtual international teams were constituted to drive policy innovation in such areas as '360° feedback', or leadership training programmes. Such international coordination mechanisms were also a means of capturing 'best practice' in HR and disseminating it to operations in other parts of the MNC (see also Chapter 11).

In some instances, the exchange of experience in regional or other international meetings evolved into an institutionalized 'best of breed forum' (Pharmaco). The best practice system was supposed to compare policies in each subsidiary in order to find and disseminate the most efficient as fast as possible through the whole organization.

Headquarter Influence on the Local Personnel Function

As has been argued in earlier chapters, strong HQ influence over personnel strategies and policies was pervasive in most of the companies in all countries. HQ HR departments had a major role in propagating standardized personnel policies internationally. This was partly driven by the fact that companies generated a growing proportion of their income outside the USA, and therefore perceived the need to structure the HR function on a global basis.

Moreover, the HR function was a key player in the dissemination of a global corporate culture as a 'glue' to integrate the different parts of the MNC. This was the case in Household, a relatively small, family-owned company, which relied less on programmes and procedures to integrate its policies worldwide than on instilling corporate values through, for instance, the 'targeted' selection of employees who fitted with the culture.

As described in Chapter 10, the centre commonly mandated standardized policies in such areas as performance appraisal; pay systems—especially for managers—including variable pay, share ownership, and stock options; management development and the handling of 'talent' or 'high potentials' and of international assignees; and employee communication. Even in countries such as Germany, with relatively strong institutional constraints of their own to act as a countervailing force to centrally driven MNC policy, it was not uncommon to find that local personnel managers had almost no flexibility on policy.

Central control was manifested not only through global policies and cultural 'glue', but also through 'hard' management controls in areas such as headcount. Corporate HQ, and beneath it the region, generally had a role in determining headcount in subsidiaries, limiting the scope for local operations to recruit employees. This was a crucial element in central HR control: 'it would be impossible to drive performance . . . , profitability and growth if each country was free of this control' (manager, ITco, Ireland). Such control was becoming increasingly sophisticated as a result of developments in IT. Many companies were implementing global HR information systems (HRIS) using such specialist software programmes. In ITco, a global 'data warehouse' permitted tight control over the number of managers, sales staff, and other groups through the firm's HRIS, allowing corporate HQ to identify opportunities for delayering.

Logistico had one of the most centralized HR functions. It had developed working methods and standardized equipment, which were seen as the source of competitive advantage over indigenous firms. National HR departments strictly enforced company rules and regulations, laid down in detailed policy books. Standardized practices were disseminated globally, in such areas as working methods, training and safety, employees' appearance, the use of 'pre-work communication meetings', annual surveys of employee attitudes, and employee stock ownership plans.

This relatively centralized pattern restricted the role of the local personnel function. At the same time, however, there were areas of flexibility. First, as discussed in Chapter 10, although some companies were moving sharply towards increasing centralization of HR, the balance between central control and subsidiary autonomy was constantly shifting, both in response to structural changes in markets and technology, and as a result of the micropolitical struggles of organizational actors at different levels.

Second, mandatory central policy often only applied to restricted groups of employees, for example, top managers: in CPGco, a company with about 75,000 employees, the standard performance appraisal system covered approximately 800 people worldwide.

Third, as discussed in more detail in Chapter 11, national managers in some companies, including CPGco and Engco2, were drawn into global HR policymaking processes through participation in working parties and similar mechanisms, and were hence able to influence the policies that would affect them. (However, the evidence for this in our case studies is rather limited, and even in Engco2 where the process went furthest, it appeared to have stalled by the end of our research—see later.)

Finally, the comparative prominence and status of HR in US parents and the function's integration into the corporate business strategy process could also be expected to impact on the role of HR at subsidiary level, in the sense of encouraging the function to play a role as 'business partner' in the local operation. This was particularly true for the German case where

HR managers would not normally play a business strategy role. This was expressed by an HR manager, in Household, Germany as follows:

[In our company] an HR manager participates in business meetings, in which a German HR manager would typically never take part and the HR manager is also asked about products. So, I too give my input if business decisions are about to be made.

The Personnel Function and the Search for Efficiency

One of the principal factors underlying the dynamics of the personnel function, and the evolving relationship between different levels, was the search for efficiency, uniformity, and cost control. This was driven in turn by the intensification of international competition and by the reaction of corporate policymakers to the pressures of financial markets over share performance. It was facilitated by technological innovations within the personnel function itself, notably the use of international HRIS allowing more sophisticated and rapid analysis of data about different staff groups and activities.

Personnel functions in many of the case-study companies were under intense cost pressures. In Engco1, a senior HR executive at corporate HQ maintained that:

you know, some things that HR people do ..., they seem warm and fuzzy and the right thing to do, [but] we're looking for a return on investment in everything that we do ... there is what we call the value proposition.

Formal rates of return were stipulated for HR initiatives such as the shared services centres, and the process was closely monitored:

... when we commit to saving, let's say with the shared services model, that we're going to save X number of dollars, we have to report back to the executive office every year that says here's where we are on this three- or five-year plan. . . . (Senior HR manager at corporate HQ)

In a number of companies, the cost dynamic was reflected in falling HR staff numbers. Over a period of a few years, Engco2's UK HR department, several dozen strong, was cut by the 20 per cent mandated by HQ. This was partly as a result of the introduction of shared services in personnel (see later). In ITco Spain, there were twenty-six employees in the HR department at the time of our fieldwork (in 2001); a decade earlier there had been twice as many. Moreover, it was planned to reduce HR staff numbers by one employee a year, and departmental costs were being cut by 10 per cent annually. HR management acknowledged that 'we don't contribute income or margins, we spend', and increasingly it saw its role as one of reducing the cost burden it imposed on the profit-generating part of the business by improving the efficiency of its operations. In the words of a senior Spanish HR manager:

What I tell them is the following: your salary is paid by the business units, they are our clients and if it's done badly, what will have to happen is that everyone will be made redundant and the service will be contracted out to an outside company.

This cost dynamic had ambiguous effects on the evolution of the personnel function. For instance, it could work against the prevailing trend of building separate personnel capacity within global businesses, since an efficiency case could be made for achieving economies of scale by providing HR services across businesses. The efficiency logic thus generated a notable phenomenon, the use of 'shared services', both across businesses within a country and also across countries. In Engco1, shared services were explicitly depicted as a reaction to extensive devolution of HR responsibilities over previous years to the main global businesses; they were part of the company's search for 'synergies' and the avoidance of duplication in HR provision.

The rationale for shared services was partly a Taylorist one of separating out low value-added, routine administrative work from higher value-added activity. Moreover, by concentrating this routine activity in shared service centres, subsidiary HR functions could become more closely linked to local line management needs and less functionally differentiated from them. HR functions could aspire not only to cut costs but also focus on more strategic business roles such as 'winning the war for talent' or, in the words of one respondent, 'allowing the line HR leader to become a consultant, a business partner, a value-added resource as opposed to an administrative picnic planner' (HQ HR manager, Engco2). The concept was seen as applicable to a wide range of HR activity: recruitment; compensation and benefits; family-oriented services; travel; company car policy; payroll administration; the management of international assignments; training; and pensions. At the time of our research, global HQ in Engco1 was planning to implement the concept of service centres for routine HR administration, combined with global centres of HR expertise having 'design control' (the term borrowed from the language of product design in the company) in areas such as compensation and benefits or succession management, on a worldwide basis within the company.

An important development in the search for efficiency through shared services within the personnel function was the introduction of international HR call centres, in ITco, Engco1, Drugco, and other firms. Engco2 had plans for a global call centre for routine enquiries from staff, though plans were put on hold as a result of cost cutting. The company nevertheless used the shared services concept to achieve economies of scale across business divisions within national operations, both in the USA and in the UK. For the first three years of the UK system, sites were not allowed to go outside the firm but had to buy services from the service centre; thereafter, the centre was to compete with external providers, increasing the efficiency pressures on the function. The ITco HR support centre for European operations, originally based in the UK and later transferred to eastern Europe on cost grounds, responded to routine personnel queries on such issues as pay, maternity rights, and holiday entitlement. The centre employed individuals with specialized language skills and country-specific HR knowledge. More complex problems were referred back to country HR departments to deal with.

Companies also reduced the burden of routine personnel work by increasing use of the intranet, allowing employees to access their individual employment information on pay, pension value, leave, and so on. In ITco, the website was backed up by a hotline inquiry number. This, together with the international HR call centre, allowed direct contact with employees to be reduced: 'HR managers, HR partners and HR specialists in Ireland do not work directly with employees, with the exception of the staffing team who interview and issue contracts of employment' (HR manager, ITco Ireland). A similar 'self-service' model was implemented in Silico, where a Web portal offered personal information on items, such as pensions and payroll to individual employees, who thereby assumed administrative tasks of which the HR department was relieved.

The increased transparency to which such developments gave rise could cause problems. In Engco2, when a telecommuting policy, designed for the USA, was put on the intranet, a regional office contacted the international HR director about implementing the policy in its region. However, the centre was concerned that the country in question did not have a tradition of working from home free from direct supervision, and that few employees would have the domestic arrangements to make the practice feasible. The centre therefore resisted the request for the policy to be implemented outside the USA.

The HR outsourcing was relatively unimportant as a source of efficiency savings. In Engco2, there was some outsourcing of personnel functions. In the larger American MNCs, however, outsourcing appeared to be of lesser importance, because size permitted economies of scale and HR tools were unique to the company. Engco1 explicitly downplayed the value of outsourcing on the grounds that greater, ongoing savings could be made by improving inefficient in-house processes.

Finally, these developments, including the introduction of sophisticated data management systems, tended to increase the HR role of line managers and reduce the direct administrative role of personnel professionals. As an HR manager in ITco Ireland explained,

Our HR system requires managers to be responsible for the integrity of the data for their direct reports. Changes in status, grades, promotions, etc. need to be initiated by the manager and approved by next level manager and HR. The onus is on employees to view their personal details to ensure that their basic details such as address, contact numbers, bank details, etc. are accurate. Many mandatory compliance-training requirements such as [on the] code of conduct are computer-based training activities. The onus is on employees and managers to ensure completion.

The Politics of Personnel: Local Reactions to HQ Dominance

In Chapter 10, the micropolitics of the relationship between HQ and subsidiaries was discussed in detail. Here it is worth reiterating that the respective roles of personnel offices at different organizational levels were not set in stone, nor purely dictated from on high by the corporate centre. As other chapters have made clear, there were constant tussles at the margin to define and redefine the ambit of activity. This involved negotiation and give-and-take, as in the example of Engco2's bargaining with the centre over the implementation of a redundancy programme, discussed in Chapter 10.

The role of corporate HR in the USA was not always favourably regarded in the subsidiaries. Central HR was sometimes seen as over-resourced and underemployed, enjoying the luxury of having staff with specialist expertise, whereas overworked HR personnel in the subsidiaries had to be generalists. In the words of one UK HR director, 'I'm thinking are these all staff people? Where do they have the luxury of having all these people working on, you know, one guy spending all his time about diversity. . . . ?' Serious conflicts could emerge between HQ and local HR managers particularly where corporate HQ was active in establishing global HR policy. This was seen in Engco2, where policies on diversity, teamworking, performance management, and corporate culture were all being rolled out in the drive to develop standard global HR policy. In such circumstances, complaints arose in subsidiaries about what was seen as unreasonable central intervention.

In extreme cases, subsidiary HR managers saw the centre as undermining their area of discretion, and strongly resisted. In one of Engco2's UK sites, when HQ demanded the sacking of a long-service employee for saying something that contravened the code of conduct, the site HR manager opposed the sacking:

Myself and the plant manager had to sort of stick our heels in fairly loudly to say look, if you want to come and run this business, fine, fire me and him, but if we're going to run this business, then you've got to let us run this business.

Eventually, subsidiary management got its way, but only after considerable argument with the centre.

While the resistance from UK HR managers to corporate directives seems to have been mostly based on the desire to protect their scope for autonomous initiative, in Germany, local resistance was determined by the constraints of codetermination. As seen in earlier chapters, HQ did not generally accept codetermination as a reason for non-compliance. German HR managers had to fight hard to explain local institutional constraints to the US HR function. They found it particularly difficult to communicate the impact of codetermination on manpower planning: in bargaining between works council and management, the latter wished to retain some negotiating room by avoiding total transparency on headcount. HQ's demands made this difficult. As one HR manager in CPGco put it,

(Headcount) is of utmost importance. It is beyond description the time we spend on it . . . . Are costs important or heads? Actually, we should look at how I can reach my goals with a certain budget, but apparently heads are easier to count . . . . The topic headcount could take up the whole evening. I could write a book about it.

CPGco, a non-union company in the USA, was initially very concerned about the introduction of codetermination on the company board in Germany. After fears proved exaggerated, HQ left codetermination to the local company. However, central HR retained an annual global employee survey, directed to individual, rather than collective, concerns such as satisfaction, promotion possibilities, and work–life balance. This reflected central HR's conception of its role at least partly as 'employee advocate', stemming from its welfare-capitalist heritage. From such a perspective, German-style codetermination would be deemed unnecessary. The uneasy compromise that emerged in companies such as CPGco and Silico was that the global HR function reluctantly and not altogether comprehendingly accepted the constraints of the German statutory framework, and in return local management appreciated that the constraints were not an acceptable excuse for failing to achieve corporate objectives.

What is key in this dynamic is the way in which local HR functions were inserted into a set of structured relationships with other 'stakeholders'. Their mode of functioning, and to some extent their *raison d'être*, were bound up with these relationships, especially in a highly regulated environment such as Germany. This may be illustrated by an incident at Silico's German production site. The local HR manager faced the dilemma of whether to follow HQ specifications or to avoid antagonizing the local works council and abide by the stipulations of the Works Constitution Act. Silico raised its reputation with the works council when it signed a work agreement prior to HQ approval.

We have signed work agreements which were not in line with [American specifications]. You have to be prepared to take some flak, but once it is signed there is nothing they can do about it. For example, we adopted a different approach to the splitting of the company here. We had to negotiate an *Interessenausgleich* [reconciliation of interests in the event of workforce reduction] with the works council and we had to explain to the employees why the split into two separate companies made sense .... If you can't explain that and you lose the confidence of people at that point it gets difficult. In Germany if works councils object to a *Betriebsübergang* [transfer of an establishment, the legal precondition for *Interessenausgleich*], the legal consequence is that you have to retain the old structure. That is why you have to go it alone at that point. (HR manager, Silico Germany)

In the two cases of EngCo2 in the UK and Silico in Germany, the resistance of local HR managers to executing HQ regulations strengthened the standing of subsidiary HR. In both, the need to act consistently at the local level and to retain the trust of employees and their representatives, was the driving force behind these conflicts. In the UK case, the web of local relationships reflected the fact that the subsidiary was heavily unionized and had been so since its establishment (see Chapter 6). Such 'embeddedness' was far less evident in the Spanish case studies. In few of the companies were unions strongly present so that the kind of long-term bargaining relationships described by Ortiz (2002) were generally absent. Moreover, in many of the firms, works councils were inactive or absent, and where present were generally regarded as constraints to be tolerated (and manipulated) rather than as partners. Being part of an international company could thus be seen by the Spanish HR function as a way of loosening local constraints on it, rather than as an imposition to be resisted through local alliances.

On some occasions, subsidiary HR managers established cross-national alliances to negotiate their case with the centre. For example, in Bor-Tec, the most important European location was the UK. Its sites, particularly in the Scottish oilfields, were coordinated by the largest business unit, in London. Because of size, tradition, and its direct link to US HQ, London also had an impact on the smaller subsidiaries in Europe. During our research, a first regional meeting of HR managers from various European countries took place in Germany. The agenda was set by European HR managers, carefully avoiding any hint of 'rebellion' against US HQ and British dominance. However, representatives from HQ HR in the USA did not participate, because of flight insecurity following 11 September 2001. So the conference served only half its purpose. It strengthened the sense of togetherness and sharing of experience among HR managers in Europe. But the latent conflict with American HQ was unresolved.

A second example, referred to in Chapter 11, was the so-called 'mini-rebellion' against central control in Engco2. This grew out of subsidiaries' dissatisfaction with the degree of HQ influence as the latter sought to develop a standardized global approach to HR. At the company's annual global HR conference in 1999, there were repeated criticisms of central HR's dominance. Criticism was fuelled by resentment at HQ's veto of a UK employee share scheme and its subsequent imposition of a scheme with minimal consultation. Many from outside the central HR function spoke up to argue that centralized policies were not being formulated in a globally inclusive way. The business case put that the existing centralized process was ineffective: 'what has happened here is that they are designed in [corporate HQ] by corporate, they get it issued, they then a lot of pushback because it doesn't work in one region' (European HR manager). These concerted protests were successful in altering the agenda of the conference, and were the catalyst for a new, more inclusive, procedure for generating international HR policies, involving personnel functions from outside the USA.

However, this incident also illustrates the limitations of resistance by local HR to the centre's agenda. When the HR policy design 'template' was applied to the development of a new global performance management system, the multinational team was led by a UK manager, seconded full-time to the project at US HQ. But as detailed policy work began, it became increasingly difficult to involve the international team members—not least because their resources were stretched by budgetary cutbacks and travel restrictions—so that in effect the project was driven by the HQ personnel function together with the seconded UK manager, in relative isolation from international inputs. In short, the process was not nearly as participative as had been intended.

By the end of our research, Engco2's much trumpeted 'global templates' were no longer in evidence, and one senior HR manager argued that in reality the process was disproportionately driven by US concerns. This respondent cited the ongoing review of leadership development as an example, describing how people outside the USA had been 'marginalized'. In the words of one senior HR director in the USA, '[influence on policy] from outside into the USA? There might be some, but I'm not aware [of it]. No . . . It is harder, maybe because of the mentality that we are the parent.'

CONCLUSION

Specific features of American HRM are clearly reflected in the structure of personnel departments in American MNCs and in the extent to which the HR policy agenda remains driven from the corporate centre. National traditions seem to be of less importance for the organization and professionalization of personnel departments in the subsidiaries, although the broader institutional context, particularly in Germany, continues to have an impact, notably by embedding local personnel functions in networks of relationships with other actors such as works councils.

HR departments at all levels are under mounting pressure to reduce costs and to produce results in terms of business profits. This has led to an increasing exploitation of modern information technology, including HR call centres, intranet, teleconferences, and advanced HRIS. In turn, this has led to a division of labour between 'routine' or 'transactional' HRM and more strategic and higher value-added work, and has encouraged the transfer of HR operational responsibilities to line managers. Such developments have also had the result of increasing the transparency and consistency of policy cross-nationally, particularly useful for smaller and less well-resourced subsidiaries, although this generates sometimes unwelcome pressures for uniform application. They also encourage personnel to seek a more strategic role as 'business partner', although the extent to which this is possible is still an open question.

Finally, the constant shifting of responsibilities and roles between the personnel function at different levels partly reflects the attempt to come to terms with the evolving external environment of international markets and competition, and with the intensifying pressures for 'shareholder value'. But it also reflects—as we have stressed throughout this volume— the dynamic process of interest negotiation between actors at different organizational levels and within different institutional domains. In this, they draw on the institutional supports of their local environment, as well as on their ability to construct (sometimes transient) alliances with their counterparts in other national subsidiaries. However, our fieldwork suggests that the ability of subsidiary personnel functions to form an effective counterweight to the centre's agenda is rather limited.

Note

1. We are grateful to Professor Sully Taylor for her personal communication on the professionalization of the function in the USA.

13

Conclusions

Phil Almond, Trevor Colling, Tony Edwards, and Anthony Ferner

INTRODUCTION

The research project on which this volume is based investigated the cross-national transfer of IR and HRM policies and practices within US MNCs. In particular, it sought, through qualitative, in-depth case-study research, to investigate the extent and nature of 'country-of-origin effects' (Ferner 1997), resulting from the embeddedness of US MNCs in the American business system, on the management of HR in such firms within Europe. In other words it sought to analyse the extent to which US MNCs carry out their activities abroad on the basis of competencies, cognitive frameworks, and modes of operating which were developed in the US business system. It also set out to examine how such effects interact with the various other 'organizational fields' (see Chapter 2) within which these firms operate. In particular, it investigated the relationship between country-of-origin effects and the effects of the embeddedness of subsidiaries within distinct NBSs in Europe. To this end, subsidiaries in two 'compartmentalized' business systems with 'Anglo-Saxon' systems of labour law (Ireland and the UK) were investigated alongside those in one archetypal 'coordinated' business system (Germany), and one country—Spain—with relatively extensive legal codification of the employment relationship. The selection of firms also aimed to allow some investigation of the potential effects of other, non-national, organizational fields, including those emanating from the level of the sector.

Broadly speaking, our case studies have confirmed that a number of important country-of-origin effects exist. The previous chapters have analysed how many of the HR-related operations of US MNCs can be traced back to their embeddedness within the US business system. This has been seen to affect not only the nature of substantive policies in areas such as collective IR, pay, performance and career management, and the management of diversity, but also the structure of the HR function itself, levels and processes of managerial decision-making, and the nature of cross-national organizational learning. In each case the relevant chapters have sought to trace the observed behaviours, structures, and policies back to the firms' embeddedness within the US business system, which in turn is related to the specific nature of the development of US capitalism. Historical features, such as the typically US development of sophisticated management 'technologies' to manage large, complex firms across wide geographical distances; the legacy of mass production and Taylorism; the decades-long contrast between unionized and sophisticated non-union sectors of business in developing alternative models of labour management; the flexible and open nature of labour and product markets; and the legal, political, and economic consequences of a culturally and ethnically diverse labour force, continue to have effects on the way large American firms manage their human resources, both at home and abroad. In short, the evidence of this project demonstrates that, for American MNCs at least, embeddedness in the country of origin continues to matter.

Yet, as our cases also illustrate, the effects of US MNCs' embeddedness in their domestic business system are far from consistent, either in their nature or their operation. Neither are they deterministic, or even always easy to distinguish from other elements of the structures within which the various actors within MNCs make decisions. This concluding chapter therefore tries to shed light on the interplay between different elements of the structures within which HR policy is formulated within US MNCs. It will also point towards some implications for future research.

US MNCs: STRATEGY AND STRUCTURE

As Chapters 2 and 3 of this volume reflect, any attempt to trace the effects of various elements of 'structure', or, in new institutionalist terminology, 'organizational fields', is a complex affair. This section revisits some of the arguments of Chapters 2–4 of this volume, in relation to home and host business systems, as well as the sectoral and micro-organizational levels, in the light of the empirical evidence collected during the course of the research programme.

The Country of Origin Effect

A number of fairly general patterns emerged in the course of the research, which may be said to distinguish 'Americanness' from other national models of the organization of human resources. First, at one level, our findings confirm those of other studies: US MNCs continue to have a tendency to operate in a relatively centralized manner, managing through standardized formal systems, processes, and policies (see Chapter 10). The majority of our case-study organizations, therefore, were markedly 'ethno-centric' in the way they were organized, as is evidenced not only by the widespread forward transfer of HR policy but also by the relative lack of 'reverse diffusion' of policies from subsidiaries into US operations (see Chapter 11), at least in the sphere of HRM. In some cases, international *policy* (although, importantly, not necessarily international *practice*) was little more than domestic policy, formulated for the US context, writ large. This was perhaps most clearly the case with regards to workforce 'diversity' policies in a substantial proportion of the case-study firms (see Chapter 8).

The general pattern of centralization can partly be explained by reference to the historically overwhelming predominance of the American domestic market for most US MNCs. But several of our companies were highly internationalized—many had more than 50 per cent of their work-force overseas (see Chapter 5). The formalized, bureaucratic control systems of managerial capitalism, on which US MNCs founded their organizational capabilities domestically, therefore seem to survive even in highly internationalized firms. These centralizing tendencies have, if anything, been reinforced by recent pressures towards short-term financial accountability of business units.

These findings are significant given the arguments of one important strand of the international management literature, which, reflecting a general trend within the social sciences towards a narrative of decentralized 'networks' (Castells 1996), proclaims a tendency towards 'transnational' corporations. Such organizations, it is argued, are no longer best viewed as hierarchies, with the home-country headquarters at the apex and foreign operations as subordinate, but as 'heterarchies', with managerial decision-making dispersed among the network rather than concentrated at the top of a hierarchy (Nohria and Ghoshal 1997).

While several of the case-study organizations were organized primarily by product divisions, as predicted by the heterarchical model, our examination of the cross-national coordination and control of HR in mainly large and relatively integrated MNCs gives little support to ideas that HR itself is becoming increasingly managed on a 'transnational' or heterarchical basis (see Chapter 10). This is not to say that those in managerial positions within foreign subsidiaries have no influence. As Chapters 10 and 12 reflect, policy and practice are often affected by international networks of managers, and subsidiary managers in particular are sometimes keen to use such networks. However, such networks, whether they are deliberately put in place by headquarters to shape policy or emerge more informally as a result of interaction between managers from different national operations, at most complement, rather than replace, existing hierarchical control systems.

In general, then, our cases showed very little sign of a widespread shift in formal control away from corporate headquarters. The argument that US MNCs remain relatively centralized in policymaking is supported by evidence on the structure of the personnel function, reported in Chapter 12. Traditional features of the US personnel function, which are in turn embedded in the twentieth-century development of the American business system, continued to be strongly reflected in the international structure of HR management. In the majority of firms, HR structures were quite bureaucratized and formalized. Although there was some variation, where host-country IR systems made it unavoidable, generally the structure of the personnel function remained quite similar across different national subsidiaries. This in itself has aided US MNCs to follow relatively uniform strategies across different national operations. Particularly in those firms with a tradition of 'welfare capitalism', the ethos of personnel functions internationally reflected concerns with employee commitment and corporate culture.

In recent years, cost-cutting pressures, and the decline of organized labour, have posed challenges to the personnel function both in the USA and elsewhere. Chapter 12 reports on how many of the case-study firms reacted to these challenges by splitting 'strategic' and 'administrative' components of the HR function. Moreover, companies were making use of international shared service centres, usually located in countries with relatively 'flexible' and low-cost labour markets. Alongside this, regional structures of personnel management were taking on new roles in attempting to ensure uniformity both of the structure of the personnel function, and of policy itself, across different European countries. In general, regional functions were charged with implementing global policy overwhelmingly shaped in the USA, and where necessary making limited adjustments, rather than having significant autonomy to shape HR strategy at the European level.

In examining the extent and nature of cross-national organizational learning within the HR sphere, Chapter 11, as indicated earlier, largely confirms the pattern of centralization. There was very extensive evidence of 'forward diffusion', in other words the transfer of American HR policies overseas (see later), but generally little evidence that overseas subsidiaries were being used as a source for learning that could be applied in the USA. This seemed to be partly an effect of the relative size of American operations in the majority of the MNCs concerned, and partly a reflection—albeit a somewhat counter-intuitive one—of the very 'openness' of the American business system.

This apparent contradiction can be explained in several ways. First, as has been argued elsewhere, particularly by American writers with an interest in developing 'progressive' systems of HRM, a deregulated NBS may reduce the 'constraints' on management decision-making but is not necessarily conducive to widespread innovation in areas such as work organization or employee involvement (Turner 1991; Kochan and Osterman 1994; Levine 1995). Thus, while it has often been argued that highly productive arrangements emerge as a management reaction to institutional constraints in countries such as Germany and Japan, the very lack of such constraints enables lower-road forms of competition in the USA. Clearly, this argument can be extended to the internal processes of HR policy transfer within MNCs: US MNCs would encounter difficulties in importing policies which were heavily context-dependent, such as arrangements for increasing qualitative flexibility that originate as employer reactions to the German vocational training and codetermination systems. Equally, the centralized, formalized structures of management on which US MNCs have based their international competitive advantage may not lend themselves to processes of learning from foreign operations. And, as Chapter 11 also reminds us, it would be wrong to view the US employment system as somehow being 'constraint-free'; examples are given of cases where potentially beneficial innovations, such as simplifications of payment systems, were not adopted because these might impact on the architecture of employment systems originally designed by the managers of welfare capitalist firms in order to avoid unionization.

SPECIFIC EFFECTS ON HR POLICY AND PRACTICE

Chapters 2 and 3 make the point that the 'compartmentalized' nature of the American business system means that the institutional arrangements governing economic behaviour afford firms a considerable margin of manoeuvre to deploy a range of strategies. In other words, while more regulated, or coordinated, NBSs will tend to impose a high degree of national uniformity, HR policy and practice will have a much higher degree of heterogeneity in the USA. This is not to argue that managerial practice in countries such as Germany or Japan, shows no substantial intra-national variety. Rather, variation within such systems is more likely to revolve around a standard model, while the less formally structured American business system—and particularly its employment system—is more likely to allow notably different models of organization and behaviour to coexist. In other words, several 'clusters' of outcomes may be apparent, with more differentiation between them that might be the case elsewhere.

Most obviously, employers in the USA do not have to contend with strong statutory systems of worker representation, nor, outside a few relatively isolated pockets, with well-organized and resourced trade unions. This has given rise historically to a heterogeneous range of American sub-models for the management of collective relations—the unionized and proceduralized IR model stemming from the New Deal, the 'welfare capitalist' model (Jacoby 1997), where paternalist HR strategies have successfully been deployed to avoid union influence, and finally the 'low road' model of non-unionism (see Chapters 3 and 6). In this relatively 'unconstrained' context, in which the power of unions to achieve collective representation against a determined employer has never been strong, contingent factors, such as the personal philosophy of owners or founding families, have come to assume a particular importance in explaining the trajectory taken and choices made by the firm in the IR sphere.

The different IR models are not static in their nature, however. The last three decades have seen sustained challenges, not only, as has been widely reported, to New Deal-type unionized IR (cf., Kochan, Katz, and McKersie 1994), but also to the welfare capitalist model. This is in some ways ironic given that the human relations-style innovations of welfare capitalist firms were frequently promoted in the 1980s as an alternative to the New Deal system and to IR pluralism in general, both in the USA and abroad. The challenges came partly from much greater international competition, initially from Japanese firms and subsequently from elsewhere in Asia. The capacity of welfare capitalist firms in particular to sustain paternalist policies, such as employment security and above-market wage levels, has historically been underpinned by very secure and often monopolistic product market positions. A second challenge came from the changes in the corporate governance system that put much greater pressure on American firms to deliver higher and quicker returns to shareholders. Both these developments eroded the 'internal settlements' central to New Deal unionism and welfare capitalism. Equally, changes in the balance of power between capital and labour should not be neglected. The decline in trade union power in the USA, reflected in indicators such as membership density and collective bargaining coverage, and in the declining union effect on wages, has created a situation in which traditionally 'high road' firms perceive less need to pursue strongly paternalistic HR policies in order to achieve their goal of avoiding unionization. These developments are linked to trends in the case studies: the boundaries between the New Deal pluralistic, welfare-capitalist, and lower-road styles of IR and HRM were becoming blurred; while true welfare capitalism was withering away as formerly paternalist firms moved decisively away from policies of employment security and embraced a 'market-driven' approach to internal management, through mechanisms such as competitive performance ranking.

One might reasonably ask, therefore, to what extent the distinction between the three broad styles of employment relations management remains useful and appropriate in the analysis of the international operations of US MNCs. Where the American parent had a distinctively welfare capitalist heritage, we examined whether traces of this were still visible in employment relations in its European subsidiaries. With regards to approaches to trade unions and employee representation, the picture is mixed. There were cases of welfare capitalist firms with a long history of exporting their broader HRM system in order to avoid unions where possible, or at least to minimize collective influence in the more densely regulated European systems (see Chapter 6). In these cases, union avoidance remained a key tenet of global HR policy in spite of sometimes decisive moves away from standard features of the welfare capitalist approach such as employment security. However, Chapter 6 also shows that firms with welfare capitalist traditions in the USA did not always export the anti-union ethos globally or consistently, and in some cases adopted a pragmatic approach to foreign operations.

On the other hand, the existence of even strong unions at home was, perhaps unsurprisingly, no guarantee of a pluralist approach abroad. This is because IR style is not always simply a matter of strategic choice; many firms deal with unions because they have to, rather than because they want to. Firms whose senior managers had experience of dealing with unions and New Deal-style contractualism in their home base could be particularly keen to use union avoidance techniques where possible, both at home and abroad, and to communicate a preference for non-union operations throughout the global company, as Chapter 6 recounts.

Chapter 7 reports on a high degree of centralization in the area of pay and performance management. The chapter notes that US control of internal job grading and classification systems was often tight, and that the more internationally coordinated firms frequently attempted to control the numbers of workers and managers at the various hierarchical levels within subsidiary operations, rather than relying solely on budgetary controls. Equally, particularly notable was the determination of the headquarters' HR functions to ensure not only that subsidiaries implemented individual merit pay—at least for workers not covered by collective bargaining—but to ensure that, as far as possible, uniform systems of performance pay and management were used across the corporation. The chapter argues that this degree of centralization can be explained both by structural factors, such as the existence of an international ILM for senior managers, and also by the desire to impose a certain degree of cultural uniformity in the aims which workers, and particularly managers, pursue. This desire to bridge potential differences in interest between managers (and sometimes other employees) at different organizational levels through the formal incorporation of 'cultural' goals into performance management systems can be seen as a reflection of the concept of hegemony referred to in Chapter 2. While this may not be unique to US MNCs, the fact that the performance measurement systems were generally exported from the USA, with little influence from the managers of foreign operations, ensured that such 'cultural' measurements were within the norms of the US business system. In other words, the formal nature of the wage–effort bargain was constructed following American norms and values.

Chapter 7 also reflects on the increasingly summative and competitive nature of performance evaluation, through competitive ranking and the risk that low rankings would lead to zero pay increases, and/or the eventual threat of dismissal or redundancy. We argue that this reflected the juridical assumption of 'employment at will' that underpins the US employment system but which is not replicated elsewhere in capitalist democracies, even those such as the UK or Ireland that are generally classified as LMEs. Hence, forced distributions, particularly where they had some impact on employment security, not only posed problems for managers in countries with relatively dense collective and legal regulation of the employment relationship such as Germany. They also provoked managerial resistance in the UK from managers unwilling to use them, where the lowest performers were at some risk of dismissal, reflecting the fact that managerial understandings of the nature of the employment relationship continue to differ between the UK and the USA. The use of a similar practice in one US company—not part of this study—recently led to a successful legal challenge in Ireland.

Chapter 8, which explores the issue of diversity policy, also showed strong country-of-origin effects, although in this case, corporate policies reflected more recent demographic, social, political, and legal developments than was the case in many other areas of policy. Specifically, while there was variation among the case studies in the extent of diversity policies, both in the USA and internationally, it is possible to trace the general shape of such policies to anti-discrimination legislation and affirmative action measures resulting from civil rights and gender equality movements of the 1960s and 1970s, and to corporate reactions to such developments. The notion of diversity has to some extent moved from being simply a regulatory constraint to a concept reinterpreted as a normative value communicated in management education, which has been reinterpreted in a more managerially acceptable light in the process. As with performance-related pay, which has changed over the last two decades in many large firms, diversity management too has altered in a way that reflects social, political, and economic changes in the USA.

In particular, the emphasis of corporate equality policy has moved away from an earlier focus on legal compliance to what is often seen as a more proactive stance. This is based on acceptance of the normative message that a more encompassing diversity management programme can aid corporate performance, through 'recruiting the best' and satisfying the expectations of customers. In a political context in which much of the equal opportunity policy programme is hotly contested, the voluntaristic development of 'diversity' programmes at corporate level can also be seen as a means of reinterpreting the equality agenda in a way that is more acceptable to corporate decision-makers. There remained, however, substantial variation between case-study firms in the scope of diversity policy within the USA. Chapter 8 explains this variation both in terms of structural factors and more contingent strategic choices made by actors at the organizational level.

To the extent that it is internalized by managers, the 'business case' argument is likely to lead corporations to seek to export the concept of diversity management overseas. This was reflected in our case studies, at least among those firms with relatively well-developed diversity programmes in the USA. Although policies were not generally simply transposed into foreign environments, the content of such policies often seemed to reflect concerns more typical of the USA than of the host countries.

Chapter 9, on the management of managerial careers, examines one of the central apparent contradictions in the US employment system. On the one hand, the US employment system is based on 'market' assumptions to a much greater degree than those of its international competitors. On the other hand, the ILM has long been central to employment regulation in large firms in the USA, both for manual workers and, as the chapter explores, for managers. The chapter investigates whether such ILM systems for managers form part of the international employment system of US MNCs, and the extent to which established patterns of career progression have survived the increased pressures towards the marketization of the employment relationship arising from increased international competition and the influence of institutional investors.

Some of the findings here are unsurprising. The traditional career model of gradual progression up a predictable career ladder has been made unviable by the pattern of corporate downsizing and the flattening of hierarchies. However, this did not mean that the logic of the ILM was no longer present in our sample of firms; the ILM still represented a site for the reproduction of managerial skills and corporate culture, albeit one with more internal tensions than previously, and above all one which was much more competitive and less sheltered. Despite the pressures on older models of career progression, the corporations generally still preferred to recruit from within where feasible, and many of the managers to whom we spoke, both at subsidiary and at headquarters levels, had very long periods of service in their firms.

The notion that US MNCs continue to take internal career development—for managers—seriously is given support by the fact that in most cases, management development was clearly regarded as an area of corporate rather than subsidiary responsibility. In the more globalizing firms, the corporate perception was that the firm was attempting to develop a worldwide ILM for talent, hence this area, along with performance management, tended to be controlled quite tightly by the corporate centre. Whether global internal markets for managerial talent were actually achieved was another matter, however. Many continental European managers, in particular, remained far from convinced that they had equality of access to senior corporate management roles. Nevertheless, the ILM was being adapted, often with difficulty, to new economic conditions and to foreign operations, rather than simply withering away.

Sector Effects

If the American employment system allows a greater range of outcomes than occurs in other systems, then it is logical to expect more internal differentiation within the system between firms pursuing different organizational goals and different types of business strategy, and to anticipate a greater impact of 'organizational fields' such as *sector*. Some of the differences in HR strategies, policies, and structures between our different cases can be partly explained by sectoral differences; in particular, in many ways processes within EngServs were distinct from those in most of our other cases. This could be traced back to this firm's position within the engineering contracting industry—a high level of dependence on former colonial markets of the UK, and more generally the specific nature of risk in large-scale project contracting (Colling and Clark 2002). Such findings are potentially replicable across firms operating within similar sectoral and product market dynamics.

This raises the question of how 'sectoral effects' should be integrated with NBS or societal effects. There has been a notable recent trend in cross-national comparisons to answer this question by positing that sectoral, or product-market, effects counteract national effects in such a way as to make the latter of decreasing importance. This has in turn given rise to the notion of 'converging divergences' (Katz and Darbishire 2000)—the argument that international convergence, and intra-national divergence, increasingly exist alongside each other.

Empirical confirmation of this notion is beyond the scope of this volume. However, a wider point on the relationship between sectoral and national effects remains: just as those according primacy to differences in NBSs have to attempt to *explain* cross-national differences, rather than just point them out on an empirical basis, so it is necessary to explore the explanatory force of 'sectoral effects' in slightly more detail.

The notion of sector when used in the analysis of international firms encompasses differences across a range of dimensions: the nature of firms' product markets; the degree of international integration of operations (including not only production/service provision, but also research and development, distribution and marketing, and so on); the nature of occupational labour markets, the skills profile of the workforce, and predominant patterns in the organization of production and the labour process; and the characteristics of sectoral 'governance', in other words the systems governing issues such as the definition of skills, training, the acquisition of professional qualifications, and technical standards within sectors. Unsurprisingly, therefore, the notion of sector is rather slippery, since sectors may be highly visible and tightly specified—like automobiles or civil aviation—or much more diffuse—like IT. It may not be easy to determine which sector a firm actually operates in, particularly where it straddles several sectors, and/or where it is involved—as was the case of several of our companies—in both manufacturing and the provision of services.

Equally, sectoral effects themselves are hardly independent of national effects: for example, the sectoral governance system of the chemical industry is very different in Germany compared with the USA (see, e.g. Hollingsworth, Schmitter, and Streeck 1994). One obvious example here is how a 'sector' is delimited for IR purposes. In multidivisional firms, there is often a potential mismatch between IR sector and product-market sector. Yet both are likely to have an impact on IR and HRM. For example, Engco1 desired to move away from the New Deal pattern of IR partly in order to escape automobile sector pattern bargaining: while US producers remained relatively protected on their home market, Engco1 operated in the more competitive and globalized capital products market. Similarly, a number of firms moved between different sectoral IR arrangements in Germany. This partially represented the changing realities of the business, such as a move from production to service provision, but was also done for political reasons, to neutralize union influence on decision-making.

Further dangers of conflation arise where sectors are dominated by firms of a given nationality, as is the case, for example, in the field of IT. In such cases, it becomes increasingly difficult, and perhaps futile, to distinguish whether predominant HR patterns result from sectoral effects, or from the embeddedness of nearly all major players in the American business system.

Nonetheless, variations on some of the dimensions listed earlier may give rise to distinctive sectoral patterns of behaviour and interests that to some extent cut across nationality effects. There are, internationally, commonalities driven by the nature of sectoral labour processes, markets, and governance regimes. But broad sectoral patterns have long been noticeable in the organization of work and the labour process; for instance, automobile factories in different countries appear to be more similar to each other than to retail banks operating in their respective home countries. It is unclear why new technologies of production and management should be more likely than older innovations, such as the moving assembly line or scientific management, to lead to a pattern of cross-national convergence within sectors. Such a proposition would be difficult to confirm without access to comparable multilevel, in-depth qualitative research over a number of decades.

None of this is to deny that sectoral factors have a role to play in the explanation of our findings. Sector-related factors, such as the degree of international integration of operations, appear to be strongly linked with the existence of highly standardized international policies in such areas as pay and performance and management development. International integration is also associated with the existence of mechanisms of knowledge transfer such as international HR committees and working groups. This is presumably because different units in internationally integrated companies are interdependent and hence more reliant on the cross-border diffusion of knowledge and best practices. Nevertheless, there is considerable evidence of an interaction, or even opposition, between such sectoral factors and American country-of-origin effects, in that the centralized and ethnocentric US management approach poses considerable barriers to the transfer of knowledge from operations outside the USA, even in highly integrated companies, for reasons explored in Chapter 11.

Host-Country Effects, Transfer, and Politics

Among our sample, which generally consisted of relatively integrated US MNCs, attempts to impose relatively uniform international structures and policies across different national subsidiaries were commonplace. However, as all the empirical chapters reflect, it was frequently not possible for firms to transfer policies and structures wholesale, without adaptation to the host-country context. Equally, in many areas, even where policies were mandatory in subsidiaries, their application in reality was less than uniform across different national operations. In other words, there was a degree of adaptation, or hybridization of policies, as their nature and meaning was shaped and interpreted by host country managers, and, sometimes, trade unions.

At a most basic level, such adaptation and hybridization reflect the fact that policies shaped by the American business system sometimes have to be adjusted to fit with host-country legal frameworks. That is, certain policies are either obligatory or prohibited in some societies, thus reducing the legitimate scope for strategic choice. While such constraints applied across a full range of policy areas in the case-study companies, national systems of collective employee representation and bargaining, as well as employment protection regimes, were particularly obvious in their effects. However, this pattern may partly reflect the scope of our research: it is likely, for example, that national training and working-time regimes would also have significant effects, but these did not form as central a part of our fieldwork.

Taking account of host-country effects, however, is by no means a simple matter of understanding what is legally permitted in a given national system, or even what is the predominant practice in the relevant national-sectoral organizational field. This is to put too much emphasis on extra-firm institutions, and too little on organizational politics at different levels within the firm. As this volume has explored in detail, different actors at all levels of the organization will always retain some scope to pursue aims and goals of their own. Even where actors at corporate level issue explicit guidelines or edicts, these may be circumvented or interpreted liberally. Such 'negotiations of order' are clearly rendered more complex in multilayered international firms. In the case of outcomes within the foreign subsidiaries of MNCs, they cannot simply be read off from a broad understanding of host-country business systems, but are the result of various actors, with different power resources, negotiating what the nature of such host-country effects actually are.

Because of this, the real force of many host-country 'constraints' is highly variable, and can be said to be partially dependent on the HR strategies of the corporation as a whole, and/or those of subsidiary managers. In other words, as was argued in Chapter 2, an analysis of the transfer of HR policies within MNCs has to take account of the role of power and actors' interests in *shaping*, as well as responding to, institutional constraints.

In one sense, the effect of host-country effects may be *less* than an examination of formal legal constraints would lead one to believe. One way of avoiding constraints, of course, is simply to disobey regulations, to find ways of neutralizing the national 'organizational field', as McDonald has been shown to do in the field of collective IR (Royle 2000). It should be noted that such challenges to host-country systems are not confined to obviously lower-road firms. For example, ITco managers in Spain were willing to overrule the views of their workforce representatives and, in principle, risk legal challenge, which, however, rarely materialized. Similarly, in a number of case-study firms, approaches to employee dismissal failed to accord with the letter of the legal host-country 'constraint' (see Chapter 7). Firms, in other words, may 'shape' the host-country institutional 'field' by ignoring, or finding ways around, some of its apparent exigencies. In so far as such practices are not successfully challenged, and are economically viable, they in turn begin to shape the very nature of the host-country institutional 'field', in that they invite imitation from indigenous enterprises. In short, host-country regulatory effects are often malleable in their effects on practice, and foreign MNCs in general are perhaps in a stronger position than most firms to explore the extent of such malleability.

In other ways, however, the effects of the host-country 'field' go far beyond mere 'constraints'. What is transferred, and the ultimate shape of policies in practice, is not just determined by the direct regulatory effects of institutions, but also by the expectations of workers and managers in the country. The frames of reference affecting subsidiary level actors, which have their origins in these actors' 'embeddedness' in the host country business and societal systems are therefore important in shaping HR outcomes. Most obviously, among our cases, German, and indeed British, subsidiaries, often applied corporate policy on trade unions and collective representation in a more pragmatic and accommodating way than the parent company did. In particular, German managers would attempt to sell to sceptical American managers the benefits of workplace codetermination. In some British subsidiaries, local managers saw little reason to challenge the position of manual workers' unions, in spite of indications from American management that unionized IR were to be avoided where possible.

In some cases, such societal effects on the cognitive and normative frames of reference of host-country managers and workers caused more overt host-country resistance to rule-setting higher in the MNC. An example is the open resistance by managers in EngCo2 UK to the use of forced distributions for performance ranking for 'culling' underperformers. Only after failing in an open challenge to global policy did UK managers resort to undermining the functioning of the policy by stealthier means.

On the whole, the HR policies of US MNCs perhaps unsurprisingly posed the greatest challenge to the most densely institutionalized host-country system featured here. Many of the firms challenged the German system of employment relations on a number of counts, and simple conformance with the German system was rare. In particular, companies challenged the institution of sectoral bargaining, as detailed in Chapter 6, and were innovators in the area of performance-related pay. Even in Business Services, where the workforce consisted largely of business consultants, the extent of gaps in pay between better and worse performers that were required by the global organization exposed tensions with the host business system. There were also clear attempts among American MNCs to challenge the perceived lack of working-time flexibility in Germany. This was, in some cases, one reason behind the firms' challenges to sectoral bargaining systems.

This is not to say, however, that US MNCs have posed no significant challenge to the more compartmentalized business systems of the UK or Ireland. While the changes in UK IR of the last twenty-five years mean that large non-union firms, of varying national ownership, are no longer as rare as they once were, clearly the original role of firms such as ITco in challenging IR pluralism helped create the vision of non-union HRM. More recently US MNCs in Ireland have played an important role in moving the employment relations system away from pluralist assumptions at firm level, not least through the practice of 'double breasting' (see Chapter 6).

In short, therefore, the interaction of home- and host-country effects at subsidiary level reflects the reshaping of norms, expectations and rules, which affect both the nature—or operationalization—of policies at the local level, and the nature of the host-country system itself. A complex hybridization of policies and practices is, in short, part of the process of international transfer.

One reason why these processes of transfer are complex, and require in-depth research across different units of the MNC, is that MNCs cannot be reduced to rationalistic, economic calculating machines, with firm-level technocrats making decisions about the costs and benefits of transferring given practices to given national environments, as is sometimes assumed in the international management literature (see the critical comments in Chapter 10). On the contrary, as we have stressed throughout this volume, MNCs must be analysed as structures of power and influence, with coalitions of interests—themselves of varying degrees of permanence and stability—constantly seeking ways to accommodate different perspectives and objectives. MNCs pursue their goals and activities through groups and actors at different organizational levels and in different roles and functions. These groups have their own interests and often control power resources, ranging from finance to knowledge and skills, with which they can exert leverage that may run counter to the formal line of control.

Global Dominance Effects

The concept of dominance effects refers to the idea that dominant or hegemonic states are able to exert organizational, political, and technological influences that invite dissemination and adoption across the global capitalist system (Smith and Meiksins 1995). At the level of the firm, dominance effects create an incentive on the part of firms to emulate the practices that they perceive to contribute to the success of firms in dominant countries. Conversely, firms that originate in dominant countries have an incentive to take advantage of what they see as the factors that gave rise to the economic strength of the country of origin by 'exporting' key practices to their foreign subsidiaries.

Such dominance effects are of some significance in our analysis. American economic performance—and, of course, geopolitical dominance—may mean that the policies of US MNCs are seen as more legitimate, at least by managers, and hence invite less resistance than might otherwise be the case. As was mentioned in Chapter 12, Spanish managers, in particular, have long seen American management as the model to which to aspire, while even German managers, who until recently have had a strong indigenous model of management, are showing increased levels of interest in imitating many typically 'American' managerial practices.

All this might be another reason for supposing that country-of-origin effects may be particularly strong in US MNCs. It does, however, pose an analytical problem, in that imitation by non-American MNCs of what have traditionally been seen as American practices may make it difficult to separate out American country-of-origin effects from the wider, international 'system' effects of 'global Americanization'. Clearly, certain elements of American HRM, which can be demonstrated to have roots in the American NBS, have more recently been imitated by non-US firms. The widespread use of formal systems of merit pay is one example of this; there are also some indications that globalizing firms from outside the USA have increased tendencies to use formal diversity policies that appear fairly similar to those of US MNCs.

Before concluding that such trends constitute convergence on an American model, however, it is important to investigate practices in some depth. It is necessary, for example, to be aware that the existence of performance-related pay does not necessarily lead to the forms of performance management analysed in Chapter 7. More comparative research is still required, therefore, on the forms which such apparently hegemonic policies actually take in practice. Given the history of 'convergence' on dominant forms of organization and HRM, from Taylorism, through to Japanization, it is probably sensible to suggest that such imitation of American structures and policies as is undoubtedly taking place outside the USA will continue to be influenced by distinctive business and societal system effects, leading to a pattern of variegated hybridization rather than simple convergence.

Dynamic Embeddedness?

Business systems evolve over time, altering the rationalities of actors embedded in them. We have seen that the erosion of both the American pluralist and welfare capitalist styles of management have been strongly related to the push for 'shareholder value', which in turn is a trend reflecting developments in the American political economy, not least changes to the pension system, as well as a reaction to the perceived poor performance of the managerial capitalist firm in the 1970s. This has, in several of our cases, given rise to a reassertion of strong centralization, albeit of a type somewhat different from previous models.

Moreover, business and societal system changes have clearly altered the 'space' in which managers make decisions across virtually the full range of personnel policies. In some cases, entirely new concerns have created new spheres of action and constraint; the emergence of diversity policy as an important concern of the managers of US MNCs, both at home and abroad, is very clearly related to social change in the USA affecting normative and cognitive understandings about the labour market roles of different groups.

In other spheres of personnel policy, there has been something of a 'reinvention' of what is seen as 'American'. The managerial capitalist pattern of governing the ILM, based on the stability offered to both employer and employee through stable job classification systems with regular promotion dependent primarily on service, clearly was seen as a constraint some time ago. At least as far as managers are concerned, however, the ILM has not been replaced (see Chapter 9); instead it has become increasingly based on the older American norm of the individualistic, competitive labour market.

These and related changes to the American business system are not always adequately reflected in cross-national typologies of business systems. The USA may have always been a 'compartmentalized business system' (Whitley 1999), or an LME (Hall and Soskice 2001b), but to continue to use such classifications does not necessarily capture fairly important changes in coordination patterns within firms, which have had important effects on employment policies. This point is explored further in a later section.

POTENTIAL DIRECTIONS FOR FUTURE RESEARCH

Our research has provided considerable support for the notion that the country of origin has an important structuring effect on MNCs with national origins in the USA. Several directions for further research may be outlined. First, our examinations of the operations of US MNCs within 'LMEs'—the UK and Ireland—have shown that a categorization of NBSs using broad-brush typologies may not always be adequate for the analysis of the internal diversity within each type of business system, particularly as regards IR and HRM. There are very clear differences between the UK, Ireland, and the USA in the micro-regulation of labour, with consequences for the coordination of HR in US MNCs. Further research should, therefore, not only contrast policies in countries with obviously different types of NBS, but also look for the important differences in detail that exist between host NBSs of a broadly similar type.

Second, however, there are also clearly arguments for examining even broader differences in host environment than those examined in this book. Our research has concentrated on national subsidiaries in developed market economies within the EU, limiting the range of variation since all are subject to an overarching tier of supranational regulation. Clearly, there is much potential in conducting similar research which examines operations in developing and transition economies. While the comparative analysis of employment relations has tended, for the sake of simplicity, to focus on countries with relatively similar levels of economic development, comparisons between subsidiaries in less similar countries may give rise to useful findings. Particularly, whether the degree of economic development in host countries affects US MNCs' propensity to attempt to impose uniform policies in such cases is an interesting and open question.

Third, for reasons of access the current research has not investigated the important sub-group of US MNCs that pursue a 'low road' strategy of employment relations and HRM, exemplified by McDonald (Royle 2000) and many imitators. While systematic cross-national research in such enterprises is, for obvious reasons, far from easy to conduct, more research is clearly needed on enterprises which follow the low-road IR strategy in order to provide a clearer, fuller picture of the range of possible models of international HRM thrown up by the US business system.

Fourth, the impact of country of origin is likely to vary from one parent-country business system to another. The behaviour of US MNCs is likely to have been profoundly shaped by the global systemic dominance of the

USA, economically, politically, and militarily. Dominance effects, in short, are likely to have magnified the influence of country-of-origin effects. Further research is needed in the ways in which MNCs from 'non-dominant' countries of origin manage their HR and employee relations internationally (cf., e.g. Ferner and Varul 1999; Hayden and Edwards 2001). It may be hypothesized that such firms are more likely than US MNCs to be 'geocentric' in their willingness to adopt models of international HR from business systems other than their parent.

Finally, systematic research is needed to obtain a fuller picture of how country-of-origin effects—and host-country effects—interact with other structural effects, such as sector, mode of entry, and age of operations in host economies,[1] and how organizational actors exploit the different resources that such variables make available to them. In particular, there are likely to be differences in the power resources of different organizational actors according to whether subsidiaries are—or were originally—brownfield sites, and where the current structure of the MNC is a result of the integration of a number of existing companies and workplaces. In this respect, the pervasive nature of intra-organizational negotiation between units over strategy, as highlighted particularly by Kristensen and Zeitlin (2005), is perhaps more likely to be predominant in the merged enterprise investigated by those authors than in long-established unitary enterprises that have internationalized through a process of organic growth. Such variables are significant, and need to be specified precisely in future qualitative research.

Note

1. ESRC-funded research, conducted by Anthony Ferner with colleagues at Warwick Business School, King's College London, and Leicester Business School, is currently investigating the relations between organizational characteristics and employment relations practices of multinationals in the UK, by means of a large-scale survey (see ESRC award number RES-000-23-0305).

RESEARCH METHODOLOGY

INTRODUCTION

This appendix briefly outlines the design of the research project on which our empirical arguments are based. It discusses the use of multiple case studies covering four countries and the rationale for the selection of countries and cases. It then summarizes research methods, particularly the use of semi-structured in-depth interviews, and other forms of data collection. It touches on issues of validity and reliability and covers some of the major limitations, in principle and in practice, of the approach adopted.

RESEARCH DESIGN

The primary aim of the project was to understand how US MNCs manage their workforces across a range of different foreign host contexts. As explained in Part I, underlying this objective was a conceptual framework that saw MNCs as operating across national-institutional domains that influenced their action. The objectives were, therefore:

- To identify the nature and extent of the 'embeddedness' of US MNCs in their domestic NBS, and in particular how this context influences their approach to the management of HR/ER;
- To explore how such influences are transmitted to US MNCs' subsidiaries abroad;
- To investigate how transferred policies and practices are adopted in the different national-institutional environments of the hosts countries in which US MNCs' subsidiaries operate.

These research aims determined the broad research design. The overall study was undertaken in four host countries with differing business and institutional environments. As detailed in Chapter 4, they range from Germany, with a highly regulated set of labour market and employment relations institutions operating within a 'collaborative market economy' framework; to Ireland and the UK, which are more 'permissive' environments where the scope for managerial choice with respect to the labour market and to the management of employment relations is much wider. Spain occupies an intermediate position, with highly prescribed institutions in some respects, but with an evolving business culture closer in nature to that of the USA and other 'LMEs'. This approach was designed to allow the exploration of whether distinctively 'American' features of US MNCs survive transplantation to different host countries, and whether they manifest themselves in different national 'variants' according to changing environmental constraints, or according to particular sectoral patterns.

Use of Case Studies

The focus on questions of *process* necessitated the use of an in-depth case-study methodology to permit the unravelling of complex causal linkages; the exploration of similarities and differences between corporate policy and actual practice in subsidiaries; and the dynamics of informal bargaining processes between HQ and subsidiary within MNCs. The research design relies on multiple case studies in order to widen the generality of theoretical constructs (see Eisenhardt 1989): for example, to see how far some notion of 'Americanness' is common across different sectors and kinds of company, and to assess how far processes based on cross-national 'negotiation' of policy implement is typical of a range of contextual circumstances.

Cases were chosen on the basis of 'theoretical' rather than 'statistical' sampling (Yin 1994), that is to say for their potential contribution to theory-building, rather than to statistical analysis as in a survey approach. The case studies cover key theoretically important variations: for example, union versus non-union (especially of the 'welfare-capitalist' variety); internationally integrated sectors (such as electronics or chemicals-pharmaceuticals) versus less-globalized sectors, serving primarily national markets; companies dependent on large numbers of highly skilled professional employees (e.g. pharmaceuticals or business consultancy services) versus those relying predominantly on unskilled and semi-skilled labour (e.g. logistics services); and so on.

The project attempted to study a number of firms that were present across several of the host countries so that direct comparisons could be made. This was possible in a number of cases: notably ITco, in all four countries; CPGco and Business Services, in the UK, Germany, and Spain; and Logistico, in Germany, Ireland, and the UK. In other cases, we were able to study a company's operations in at least two countries (e.g. Household in Germany and the UK: Drugco and Bankco in Spain and the UK).

Multi-country cases were not practicable in all cases, for a number of reasons. First, some countries did not have significant operations in more than one of the hosts (Engco1 and Engco2 are examples). Second, to focus on case studies of companies that operate across several of the host countries considerably restricts the range of cases available. Third, even where within-case, cross-national comparisons are possible, they need to be treated with some caution, since in some firms, there is an international division of labour. For example, ITco Ireland was primarily a manufacturing location, while ITco UK focused on the provision of business services; EngServs in the UK and Spain operated in two very different business sectors. Fourth, in some cases where cross-national comparisons would have been desirable, they proved impracticable because of difficulties of access. This was the case in Pharmaco, for example, where good access was secured in Ireland, while planned access in the UK failed owing to merger developments. Finally, and more broadly, strict cross-country case comparisons risk missing the broader picture. As Hall and Soskice (2001*b*) argue, different kinds of company are likely to fit in with the specific 'institutional complementarities' of different host business systems. Thus, there is likely to be some specialization in the sorts of firms attracted to each host. Empirically, the structural composition of US FDI varies significantly from country to country (a focus on IT and pharmaceuticals/healthcare in Ireland, on engineering, business services, and consumer products in the UK, for example).

In all, seven firms were investigated in depth. A further eight companies were the subject of significant case studies (see Chapter 5 for more details on the case-study firms). These case studies involved multiple interviews with respondents across a range of organizational roles and at different organizational levels (see later).

Research Methods: A Multi-Level Approach

A distinctive feature of our approach was the attempt to gain multi-level perspectives on the case-study companies. This contrasts with much conventional international business research that predominantly focuses either on senior strategic management tiers, or on lower levels of the MNC, such as the subsidiary—but rarely both. Most, though not all, of the main case studies incorporate the perspectives of both the headquarters 'view from above' and the subsidiary 'view from below'. This research technique contributed to data triangulation and served to highlight tensions and differences of interpretation between the subsidiary and parent; not least around issues of monitoring and enforcement. In addition, in several instances testimony was obtained from managers either with European regional responsibilities, or with leadership roles within international business divisions. This took account both of the increasing use of matrix organizational structures and of the growing importance of regional and business division tiers as intermediate levels between global HQ and national subsidiaries (see, e.g. Chapters 10 and 12).

Research Methods: The Use of Interviews

The major tool of data collection was the in-depth interview. Fieldwork began in the spring of 1999 and continued until late 2004. In total, 281 in-depth interviews were conducted in the case-study companies. In addition, a further fifteen interviews—six in Germany, six in Spain, and three in the UK—were undertaken in minor case studies of six other firms (see Chapter 5). In total researched was carried out in twenty-one organizations. Details are provided in Table A.1.

While in total around 300 separate interviews were undertaken, the quality of research access varied significantly. In some companies, thirty or more interviews

Table A.1. Case-study firms and interviews by country

Company	Sector	Interviews				
		German	Irish	Spanish	UK	HQ
Core companies						
Business Services	Business consultancy and technical services	4	*	3	2[a]	3[b]
CPGco	Consumer and medical products	3	*	5	16	6
Engco1	Capital engineering equipment	*	*	*	32	4
Engco2	Manufacturing capital engineering equipment	1	*	*	19[ac]	6
EngServs	Process plant construction services	*	*	4	22[ac]	2
ITco	IT equipment and services	3	16	5	18	10
Logistico	Logistics services	4	9	*	2	1
Secondary companies						
Bankco	Banking and other financial services	2	*	*	3[a]	a
Chemco	Industrial, consumer, and health care products	*	*	5	1	*
Compuco	IT equipment	*	11	*	*	5
Drugco	Pharmaceutical products	*	*	7	1	1
Groomco	Consumer products	*	*	5	*	1
HealthCo	Pharmaceuticals	*	14	*	*	*
Household	Consumer household products	1	*	1	4	1
Pharmaco	Pharmaceuticals	*	12	*	1	*
Refresco	Soft drinks	*	*	4	1	*

Number of German interviews	18
Number of Irish interviews	62
Number of Spanish interviews	39
Number of UK interviews	122
Number of European interviews[d]	19
Number of US interviews	21
Total number of interviews	281

Note: Number of interviewees may differ from number of interviews, since some interviewees were interviewed more than once, and conversely some interviews were with multiple respondents.

[a] Includes interview carried out with UK-based respondent with international business unit level responsibilities.

[b] Exceptionally, a single interview is counted as three, since three managers with widely different functional roles were interviewed together in a 3-hour interview.

* Employment numbers are provided of subsidiaries only where research was undertaken. An asterisk does not necessarily indicate an absence of corporate presence within a particular country.

[d] Interviews at European HQ (sometimes including other geographical areas such as Africa) were carried out in the following companies CPGco (4); Compuco (5); Drugco (1); Household (2); ITco (6); and Logistico (1).

[c] Includes group discussion with members of a consultative forum.

were conducted (encompassing actors from both the subsidiary and the US headquarters). At the other extreme, however, were cases that were restricted to a single interview, usually with an HR manager.

In the major case studies, the strategy was to interview a variety of respondents to obtain a multifaceted perspective. This involved, first, interviewing across different organizational levels—predominantly at national subsidiary level, but also at global, regional, and international business division headquarters.

Second, it meant interviewing managers from a range of functions. While most respondents were from the personnel function, in the major case studies managers in the finance and operations functions were also interviewed, in order to place HR in a broader organizational context. Most managers interviewed were senior within their function, but interviews were also conducted down to supervisory level.

Third, in the UK, it was possible to obtain an employee perspective in the main case-study companies. Thus in each of five companies (ITco, CPGco, Engco1, Engco2, and EngServs), between eight and ten employees were interviewed, providing a counterpoint to the managerial account. These interviews were generally carried out following the gathering of the managerial data. Where possible a range of non-managerial respondents were interviewed in concentrated bursts over two days. This enabled the UK team to follow an iterative approach, pursuing incidental themes between interviews, checking and building knowledge of work processes, relationships, and perceptions of distinct American corporate features. In addition, union officials and workplace representatives were interviewed where workforces were collectively organized.

Interviews averaged between one and two hours in length, though a small number lasted up to three hours; employee interviews tended to be shorter, around 40–60 minutes. Both processual and substantive issues were covered. The former included questions of policy design, transfer, implementation, adaptation, monitoring, and control. More generally, processes of negotiation over and resistance to international policy initiatives were studied. Substantive areas comprised the full range of HR issues, ranging from recruitment and selection to training and development, corporate culture, the management of performance, employee communication and involvement, work organization, and collective employee relations. However, the focus was on areas emerging from previous research, or in the course of our own research, as key indicators of US MNC distinctiveness. Such issues include employee representation, especially the recognition of unions, and (an emergent issue) the management of workforce diversity. Questions were also asked about overall organizational structure and about the structure and operation of the HRM function.

The length of the fieldwork phase, extending over more than five years, allowed research teams to make repeated visits over time to the major case companies. This in turn enabled issues to be followed as they developed, and the stability and durability of particular policies, structures, and approaches in HR/ER to be assessed.

A standardized basic interview schedule was developed detailing the issues to be covered across the case studies. This tool was used by each of the country teams and adapted to fit local circumstances. In addition, the schedule was supplemented by other lines of questioning in the light of the specific features of the company or of the respondent. Templates for respondents from different functions and organizational levels were appropriately adapted. Separate templates were used for employee respondents and for interviews with employee representatives.

Documentary Sources of Data

The project made extensive use of both primary and secondary documentation. The former included company policies and pro formas, for example, for appraisal systems, statements of corporate culture, and so on. Publicly available documentary material included sources such as the US Securities and Exchange Commission (SEC) filings (especially Form 10-K) and company websites. These were used to obtain both background data on corporate organization, operations, location, and employment; and a broad 'feel' for organizational context and culture expressed through formal statements of mission, visions, values and credos, and so on. Finally, previous published studies of some of the case-study firms were widely drawn on, particularly for the historical background of companies' evolution. While such sources are cited at various points in the book, care has been taken to do so in such a way as not to betray the anonymity of the case-study companies.

Data Analysis

Across the countries, all but a handful of interviews were tape-recorded and fully transcribed; transcripts were cross-checked against original tapes. Interview transcripts were widely circulated among team members within a country, and in some cases across countries.

A systematic common coding structure was gradually developed over the course of the project. The coding comprised a 'branching tree structure', with a small number of primary 'nodes' covering product markets; corporate structure, culture and control systems; the personnel function; and substantive HR/ER issues. Each main area was subdivided, sometimes repeatedly. For example, HR/ER issues were broken down into pay and performance, training and development, communication and involvement, expatriation, employee representation, and so on. Partly reflecting the need to manage a greater volume of data, the UK material was analysed using QSR N5 qualitative software; other teams employed manual coding.

Validity and Reliability

While there is much debate over the applicability of notions of validity and reliability of data to qualitative research (e.g. Bryman and Bell 2003: 270–6), the plausibility of qualitative analysis depends on ensuring that procedures for data gathering and analysis are as rigorous as possible. A number of steps were taken to enhance rigour.

First, the multi-level design provided repeated triangulation of data from different sources within a case-study company: triangulation between HQ and subsidiary accounts; between accounts of HR managers and those of other functions, and of line managers; and between the testimony of managerial respondents and that of employees. Moreover, interview data as a whole were triangulated through the use of primary and secondary documentation.

Second, the long duration of fieldwork—taking place over more than five years—allowed repeated reinspection of assumptions and interpretations, as well as the collection of validating accounts of a single respondent at different points in time.

Third, internal 'reliability' was ensured in a number of ways. The same interview instrument was available for use across the international 'consortium' of researchers. The same coding structure was used to analyse data. Moreover, there was considerable 'cross-interviewing', in which members of one national team participated in interviews conducted by other national team. This took place at several different points during the lifetime of the project. The circulation of fully transcribed interview notes, together with periodic international project meetings, allowed emerging intellectual themes to be identified and developed.

Finally, 'respondent validation' was secured by means of feedback reports to respondent companies in each of the four host countries. The Irish and Spanish teams, for example, prepared detailed reports for each of their main case-study companies, while the UK team produced a comprehensive 60,000 word overview of findings, which was sent to all managerial respondents. Such feedback provided respondents with the opportunity to correct inaccuracies and to comment on analysis and interpretation. The UK report also formed the basis of a feedback workshop in December 2003 to which participating companies and academic experts were invited.

LIMITATIONS OF THE RESEARCH DESIGN

Broader issues of 'external validity', and in particular how far findings can be carried over to other settings, for example, in terms of country of origin and host context, are taken up in the conclusion. Here, a number of limitations of the research design in principle and practice need to be acknowledged.

In relation to the implementation of the design in practice, a number of limitations have already been alluded to. First and foremost, data are patchy across countries, for reasons to do with research organization and resourcing. As a result the quality and quantity of the data are variable, and we have inevitably had to accept gaps in our coverage of issues and companies. Problems of access have also made for less systematic data that we would have liked in certain areas. For example, some companies granted relatively good access in one host offering only limited access in other, or denying it altogether. It also proved to be impossible to get as wide a range of companies as planned. Most notably, 'low road' non-union companies, reliant on low-skilled, low-paid, unorganized labour, are unsurprisingly absent from our sample of countries, despite efforts to recruit at least one such firm.

In terms of issues of principle, the research is limited by the fact that this is not a strictly comparative study: US MNCs are not compared systematically with equivalent MNCs from other countries in order to isolate distinctively American features in comparison say with French, German, or Japanese traits. Instead, we have relied on detailed 'process tracing' (e.g. Mahoney 2003: 363–5; see also Hall 2003), following through how characteristics of US companies can be traced back to features of the US business system, how behaviour is influenced by the various host environments, and how particular events work themselves out through the interaction of players at different organizational levels.

The reason for this research design is partly practical, partly methodological. At a practical level, in dealing with large companies in predominantly oligopolistic international markets, the number of firms available for study is relatively small. Given the practical problems of gaining access for detailed research, a strictly comparative research design runs the risk of collapse if access cannot be secured to comparable companies from the different countries.

More fundamentally, there are considerable problems of comparing like with like. It is difficult to find matching companies from different countries, simply because different NBSs give rise to major variations in the nature of companies that are hard to hold constant, and indeed which are part of what makes US companies distinct from say German or Japanese firms. For example, NBSs differ very much in the nature of the corporate structures and forms of organization that they throw up (e.g. multidivisional vs. 'holding company' structures); in their sectoral patterns of foreign investment (e.g. Japanese dominance in electronics and engineering compared with US concentration in sectors such as chemicals, distribution, business services, software, and engineering); in their modes of foreign investment (with Japanese companies relying more on 'greenfield' and organic growth and less on growth through acquisition, compared with US firms), and in the historical timing of the internationalization process ('early' US foreign investment compared with 'late' Japanese internationalization).

Although the present research design is not strictly comparable, members of the team have previously carried out research on multinationals of different national origin (notably British and German) (see, e.g. Edwards and Ferner 2004; Ferner and Varul 1999), and there is a considerable literature on the behaviour of Japanese MNCs in the field of HR/IR (e.g. Elger and Smith 2005). Our research findings can therefore be compared to a certain extent with results from studies of MNCs of other nationalities.

A further limitation is in the choice of host countries. While the four hosts in this study differ on a range of interesting and relevant criteria, they are also limited by virtue of being western European. This means that all operate within and are shaped by the supranational institutional framework of the EU. Hence, the range of variability is strictly constrained.

Finally, despite the major strengths of the case-study method in unpicking complex causal mechanisms and tracing management processes in detail, its limitations should be acknowledged. In order to assess behaviour across MNCs of different origin, qualitative case studies need to be complemented by large-scale quantitative survey research in order to conduct a systematic appraisal of variables such as sector, structure, mode of international growth, and so on. This would enable researchers to confirm whether 'pure' country-of-origin effects persist even when such variables are held constant.

References

Adams, R. (1993). 'The North American Model of Employee Representational Participation: "A Hollow Mockery" ', *Comparative Labor Law Journal*, 15(4): 4–14.

Adams, R. J. (2003). 'Why American Workers Are So Disorganized', *Human Resources and Employment Review*, 1(1): 11–36.

Agócs, C. and Burr, C. (1996). 'Employment Equity, Affirmative Action and Managing Diversity: Assessing the Differences', *International Journal of Manpower*, 17(4/5): 30–45.

Aguilera, R. (2004). 'Corporate Governance and Employment Relations: Spain in the Context of Western Europe', in H. Gospel and A. Pendleton (eds), *Corporate Governance and Labour Management*. Oxford: Oxford University Press.

Allen, R. K. (1997). 'Lean and Mean: Workforce 2000 in America', *Journal of Workplace Learning*, 9(1): 34–42.

Almond, P. (1999). The Social Context of Human Resource Management: An Anglo-French Comparison. Unpublished Ph.D. thesis. Manchester: UMIST.

—— (2004). 'The Management of Pay, Wage Classifications and Performance in the UK Subsidiaries of US MNCs'. Paper presented to conference on *Multinationals and the International Diffusion of Organizational Forms and Practices*. IESE, Barcelona, 15–17 July.

Amoore, L. (2000). 'International Political Economy and the "Contested Firm" ', *New Political Economy*, 5(2): 183–204.

Appelbaum, E. and Batt, R. (1994). *The New American Workplace: Transforming Work Systems in the United States*. Ithaca, NY: ILR Press.

Appelbaum, E. and Berg, P. (1996) 'Financial market constraints and business strategy in the US'. In J. Michie and J Grieve-Smith, (eds.) *Creating Industrial Capacity: Towards Full Employment*. Oxford: Oxford University Press, pp. 192–221.

Arrowsmith, J. (2002). 'MNC Databases: Report on Data Gathering'. Unpublished Project Team Report. Coventry: IRRU.

Arthur, M. and Rousseau, D. (1996). *The Boundaryless Career: A New Employment Principle for a New Organisational Era*. New York: Oxford University Press.

Atterbury, S., Brewster, C., Communal, C., Cross, C., Gunnigle, P., and Morley, M. (2004). 'The UK and Ireland: Traditions and Transitions in HRM', in C. Brewster, W. Mayrhofer, and M. Morley (eds), *Human Resource Management in Europe: Evidence of Convergence?*, London: Elsevier/Butterworth-Heinemann, pp. 29–72.

References

Auerbach, J. (1966). *Labor and Liberty: The La Follette Committee and the New Deal.* Irvington.

Babson, S. (1999). '*The Unfinished Struggle: Turning Points In American Labor, 1877–present*'. Lanhan, MD: Ravman and Littlefield.

Bachrach, P. and Baratz, M. (1970). *Power and Poverty: Theory and Practice.* New York: Oxford University Press.

Bacon, N. and Blyton, P. (2000). 'High Road and Low Road Teamworking: Perceptions of Management Rationales and Organizational and Human Resources Outcomes', *Human Relations*, 53(11): 1425–58.

Bahnmuller, R. (2003). 'Des deux côtés de la convention collective: Formation des salaires et politiques salariales dans les firmes couvertes ou non par les conventions collectives', *Chronique Internationale de l'IRES*, 81: 1–15.

Baker, A. (2002). 'Access vs. Process in employment discrimination: Why ADR suits the US but not the UK', *Industrial Law Journal*, 31, 2, 113–34.

Barnard, C., Clark, J., and Lewis, R. (1995). The Exercise of Individual Employment Rights in the Member States of the European Community. *Research Series*, no. 49. London, Department of Employment.

Baron, J. N., Dobbin, F. R., and Jennings, P. D. (1986). 'War and Peace: The evolution of modern personnel administration in US industry, American Journal of Sociology, 92, 2, 350–83.

Barry, F. (2002). 'FDI and the Host Economy: A Case Study of Ireland'. Unpublished Paper presented at National University of Ireland, Galway, 8 November.

Bartlett, C. and Ghoshal, S. (1998). *Managing Across Borders*, 2nd edn. London: Hutchinson.

Baruch, Y. and Peiperl, M. (2003). 'An Empirical Assessment of Sonnenfeld's Career Systems Typology', *International Journal of Human Resource Management*, 14(7): 1267–83.

Bayo-Moriones, J. and Merino-Díaz de Cerio. J. (2001). 'Size and HRM in the Spanish Manufacturing Industry', *Employee Relations*, 23(2): 188–206.

Beaumont, P. and Harris, R. (1992). ' "Double-breasted" recognition agreements in Britain', *International Journal of Human Resource Management*, 3(2): 267–83.

—— and Townley B. (1985*a*). 'Non-Union American Plants in Britain: Their Employment Practices', *Relations Industrielles*, 40(4): 810–25.

—— and Townley, B. (1985*b*). 'Greenfield Sites, New Plants and Work Practices', in V. Hammond (ed.), *Current Research in Management*. London: Frances Pinter, pp. 163–79.

Beer, M., Spector, B., and Lawrence, P. R. (1984). *Managing Human Assets*. New York: Free Press.

Berger, S. and Dore, R. (eds) (1996). *National Diversity and Global Capitalism*. Ithaca, NY: Cornell University Press.

Bernstein, B. (1970). *Politics and Policies of the Truman Administration*. Chicago, IL: Quadrangle Books.

Birkinshaw, J. (2000). *Entrepreneurship in the Global Firm: Enterprise and Renewal.* London: Sage.

—— and Fry, N. (1998). 'Subsidiary Initiatives to Develop New Markets', *Sloan Management Review*, 39(3): 51–62.

Bispinck, R. (1997). 'Deregulierung, Differenzierung und Dezentralisierung des Flächentarifvertrages: Eine Bestandsaufnahme neuerer Entwicklungstendenzen der Tarifpolitik', *WSI-Mitteilungen*, 8: 551–61.

—— (2003). 'Das deutsche Tarifsystem in Zeiten der Krise – Streit um Flächentarif, Differenzierung und Mindeststandards', *WSI-Mitteilungen*, 7: 395–404.

Björkman, I. and Furu, P. (2000). 'Determinants of Variable Pay for Top Managers of Foreign Subsidiaries in Finland', *International Journal of Human Resource Management*, 11(4): 698–713.

Blair, M. and Kochan, T. (2000). *The New Relationship: Human Capital in the American Corporation.* Washington, DC: Brookings Institution.

Blanchflower, D. and Freeman, R. (1992). 'Unionism in the United States and Other Advanced OECD Countries', *Industrial Relations*, 31(1): 56–80.

Blessing, K. and Otto, K.-P. (2004). 'Arbeitsdirektor', in E. Gaugler, W. A. Oechsler, and W. Weber (eds), *Handwörterbuch des Personalwesens*, 3rd edn. Stuttgart: Schäffer-Poeschel, pp. 207–16.

Blinder, A. (1990). *Paying for Productivity: A Look at the Evidence.* Washington, DC: Brookings Institution.

Blyton, P. and Turnbull, P. (1994). *The Dynamics of Employee Relations.* London: Macmillan.

Bond, M. A. and Pile, J. (1998). 'Diversity Dilemmas at Work', *Journal of Management Inquiry*, 7(3): 252–69.

Bowen, D. E., Galang, C., and Pillai, R. (2002). 'The Role of Human Resource Management: An Exploratory Study of Cross-Country Variance', *Human Resource Management*, 41(1): 103–22.

Boyer, R. (ed.) (1988). *The Search for Labour Market Flexibility: The European Economies in Transition.* Oxford: Clarendon Press.

—— Charron, E., Jürgens, U., and Tolliday, S. (1998). *Between Imitation and Innovation. The Transfer and Hybridization of Productive Models in the International Automobile Industry.* Oxford: Oxford University Press.

Bram W., Deatin, S., Nash, D., and Oxenbridge, S. (2000). The employment contract: from collective procedures to individual rights', *British Journal of Industrial Relation*, 38, 4, 611–29.

Bratton, J., Helms Mills, J., Pyrch, T., and Sawchuk, P. (2004). *Workplace Learning.* Ontario: Garamond Press.

Braverman, H. (1974). *Labor and Monopoly Capital.* New York: Monthly Review Press.

Brewster, C., Larsen H. H., and Mayrhofer, W. (1997). 'Integration and Assignment: A Paradox in Human Resource Management', *Journal of International Management*, 3(1): 1–23.

References

—— Mayrhofer, W., and Morley, M. (eds) (2004). *Human resource Management in Europe: Evidence of Convergence?* London: Elsevier/Butterworth-Heinemann.

Broad, G. (1994). 'The Managerial Limits to Japanisation: A Manufacturing Case Study', *Human Resource Management Journal*, 4(3): 52–69.

Bronfenbrenner, K. (2000). *The Uneasy Terrain: The Impact of Captial Mobility on Workers, Wages, and Union Organizing*. Report to the US Trade Deficit Review Commission, New York, School of Industrial and Labor Relations, Cornell University.

Bronfenbrenner, K., Friedman, S., Hurd, R., Oswald, R., and Seeber, R. (1998). *Organizing to Win: New Research on Union Strategies*. Ithaca: ILR Press.

Brooke, M. Z. (1984). *Centralization and Autonomy*. London: Holt, Rinehart & Winston.

Brown, C. and Reich, M. 'Company HR Policies and Compensation Systems: Implications for Income Inequality', *NCW Working Paper No. 14*, Berkeley, CA: University of California.

Bryman, A. and Bell, E. (2003). *Business Research Methods*. Oxford: Oxford University Press.

Buckley, P. and Casson, M. (1976). *The Future of the Multinational Enterprise*. London: Macmillan.

—— and Enderwick, P. (1985). *The Industrial Relations Practices of Foreign-Owned Firms in Britain*. London: Macmillan.

Buesa, M. and y Molero, J. (1996). 'El capital extranjero', in J. L. García Delgado, R. y Myro, and J. A. Martinez (eds), *Lecciones de Economía Española*, 2nd edn. Madrid: Civitas, pp. 539–59.

Bureau of labor Statistics (BLS) (2004) *Union Membership in 2003*. Washington DC, BLS, United States Department of Labor.

Burke, L. (1997). 'Developing High-Potential Employees in the New Business Reality', *Business Horizons*, 40(2): 18–25

Calori, R., Steele, M., and Yoneyama, E. (1995). 'Management in Europe: Learning from Different Perspectives', *European Journal of Management*, 13(1): 58–66.

Camelo, C., Martín, F., Romero, P., and Valle, R. (2004). 'Human Resource Management in Spain: Is it Possible to Speak of a Typical Model?', *International Journal of Human Resource Management*, 15(6): 935–58.

Campos e Cunha, R., Obeso, C., and Pina e Cunha, M. (2004). 'Spain and Portugal: Different Paths to the Same Destiny', in C. Brewster, W. Mayrhofer, and M. Morley (eds), *Human Resource Management in Europe: Evidence of Convergence?*, London: Elsevier/Butterworth-Heinemann, pp. 161–88.

Cappelli, P. (1995). 'Rethinking Employment', *British Journal of Industrial Relations*, 33(4): 563–602.

—— (1999a). *The New Deal at Work: Managing the Market Driven Workforce*. Boston, MA: Harvard Business School Press.

—— (1999b). 'Career Jobs are Dead', *California Management Review*, 42(1): 146–67.

—— (2000). 'Managing Without Commitment', *Organizational Dynamics*, 28(4): 11–24.

—— Bassi, L., Katz, H., Knoke, D., Osterman, P., and Useem, M. (1997). *Change at Work*. New York: Oxford University Press.

Castells, M. (1996). *The Rise of the Network Society*. Oxford: Blackwell.

Cerny, P. (2000). 'Political Globalization and the Competition State', in R. Stubbs and G. R. D. Underhill (eds), *Political Economy and the Changing Global Order*, Don Mills, Ontario: Oxford University Press, pp. 300–9.

Chandler, A. (1962). *Strategy and Structure*. Cambridge, MA: MIT Press.

—— (1977). *The Visible Hand*. Cambridge, MA: Harvard University Press.

—— (1990). *Scale and Scope: The Dynamics of Industrial Capitalism*. Cambridge, MA: Belknap Press.

Child, J. (1997). 'Strategic Choice in the Analysis of Action, Structure, Organizations and Environment', *Organization Studies*, 18(1): 43–76.

—— Faulkner, D., and Pitkethly, R. (2000). 'Foreign Direct Investment in the UK 1985–1994: The Impact on Domestic Management Practice', *Journal of Management Studies*, 37(1): 141–66.

Clark, I. (2000). *Governance, The State, Regulation and Industrial Relations*. London: Routledge.

Clemens, E. and Cook, J. (1999). 'Politics and Institutionalism: Explaining Durability and Change', *Annual Review of Sociology*, 25: 441–66.

Coates, J., Davis, E., Emmanuel, C., Longden, S., and Stacey, R. (1992). 'Multinational Companies' Performance Measurement Systems: International Perspectives', *Management Accounting Research*, 3: 133–50.

Colling, T. (2001). 'In a State of Bliss There Is No Need for a Ministry of Bliss: Some Further Thoughts on Welfare Capitalism'. Leicester Business School Occasional Papers, no. 62. Leicester: De Montfort University.

—— and Clark, I. (2002). 'Looking for "Americanness": Home-Country, Sector and Firm Effects on Employment Systems in an Engineering Services Company', *European Journal of Industrial Relations*, 8(3): 301–24.

—— and Clark, I. (2003). 'The Character and Diffusion of Teamworking Programmes in the British Subsidiaries of Two American Multinational Companies'. Paper presented at *International Human Resource Management Conference*, Limerick, June.

—— and Dickens, L. (2001). 'Gender Equality: A New Basis Mobilisation?', in M. Noon and E. Ogbonna, (eds.), *Equality, Diversity and Disadvantage in Employment*, Basingstoke: Palgrave, pp. 136–56.

Collings, D. (2003). 'HRD and Labour Market Practices in a US Multinational Subsidiary: The Impact of Global and Local Influence', *Journal of European Industrial Training*, 27(2): 188–200.

Constable, J. and McCormick, R. (1987). *The Making of British Managers: A Report for the BIM and CBI*. Corby: British Institute of Management.

References

Costa, M. T. (1996). 'La empresa: características, estrategias y resultados', in J.-L. García Delgado, R. Myro, and J. A. Martínez (eds), *Lecciones de Economía Española*, 2nd edn. Madrid: Civitas, pp. 285–303.

Cox, R. (1987). *Production, Power, and World Order*. New York: Columbia University Press.

Cox, R. W. (2000). 'Political Economy and World Order: Problems of Power and Knowledge at the Turn of the Millennium', in R. Stubbs and G. Underhill (eds), *Political Economy and the Changing World Order*. Don Mills, Ontario: Oxford University Press, pp. 25–37.

Cox, T. (1994). *Cultural Diversity in Organizations*. San Francisco: Berrett-Koehler.

—— and Blake, S. (1991). 'Managing Cultural Diversity: Implications for Organizational Competitiveness', *Academy of Management Review*, 5(3): 45–56.

Crouch, C. (1993). *Industrial Relations and European State Traditions*. Oxford: Oxford University Press.

—— and Streeck, W. (eds) (1997). *Political Economy of Modern Capitalism. Mapping Convergence and Diversity*. London: Sage.

Cully, M., Woodland, S., O'Reilly, A., and Dix, G. (1999). *Britain at Work*. London: Routledge.

D'Art, D. and Turner, T. (2003). 'Union Recognition in Ireland: One Step Forward or Two Steps Back?', *Industrial Relations Journal*, 34(3): 226–40.

Dass, P. and Parker, B. (1999). 'Strategies for Managing Human Resource Diversity: From Resistance to Learning', *Academy of Management Executive*, 13(2): 68–80.

De Cenzo, D. and Robbins, S. (1996). *Human Resource Management*, 5th edn. New York: Wiley.

Deery, S. (1995). 'The Demise of the Trade Union as a Representative Body?', *British Journal of Industrial Relations*, 33(4): 537–43.

Deller, J. F. and Flunkert, U. (1996). 'Recruitment and Development of Up-And-Coming Managers in Germany and Japan: An Exemplary Comparison', *Career Development International*, 1(2): 5–9.

Derr, B., Jones., C., and Toomey, E. (1988). 'Managing High Potential Employees: Current Practice in Thirty Three US Corporations', *Human Resource Management*, 27(3): 272–90.

Dertouzos, M., Lester, R., Solow, R., and the MIT Commission on Industrial Productivity (1989). *Made in America: Regaining the Productive Edge*. Cambridge, MA: MIT Press.

Dessler, G. (2001). *A Framework for Human Resource Management*, 2nd edn. Upper Saddle River NJ: Prentice Hall.

DeVos, T. (1981). *US Multinationals and Worker Participation in Management. The American Experience in the European Community*. London: Aldwych.

Dicken, P. (2002). *Global Shift*, 4th edn. London: Paul Chapman.

Dickens, L. (1999). Beyond the Business Case: A Three-Pronged Approach to Equality action, *Human Resource Management Journal*, 9(1): 9–19.

Dickmann, M. (1999). Balancing Global, Parent and Local Influences: International Human Resource Management of German Multinational Companies. Unpublished Ph.D. thesis. London: Birkbeck College.

—— (2003). 'Implementing German HRM Abroad: Desired, Feasible, Successful?' *International Journal of Human Resource Management*, 14(2): 265–83.

DiMaggio, P. J. (1988). 'Interest and Agency in Institutional Theory', in L. Zucker (ed.), *Institutional Patterns and Organizations: Culture and environment*. Cambridge MA: Ballinger, pp. 3–21.

DiMaggio, P. and Powell, W. (1983). 'The Iron Cage Revisited: Institutional Isomorphism and Collective Rationality in Organizational Fields', *American Sociological Review*, 48: 147–60.

Djelic, M. (1998). *Exporting the American Model: The Post-War Transformation of European Business*. Oxford: Oxford University Press.

Djelic, M.-L. and Quack, S. (eds) (2003a). *Globalization and Institutions—Redefining the Rules of the Economic Game*. London: Edward Elgar.

—— and Quack, S. (2003b). 'Governing Globalization: Bringing Institutions Back In', in M.-L. Djelic and S. Quack (eds), *Globalization and Institutions: Redefining the Rules of the Economic Game*. Cheltenham: Edward Elgar, pp. 1–14.

—— and Quack, S. (2003c). 'Conclusion: Globalization as a Double Process of Institutional Change and Institution Building', in M.-L. Djelic, and S. Quack (eds), *Globalization and Institutions: Redefining the Rules of the Economic Game*. Cheltenham: Edward Elgar, pp. 302–33.

Doeringer, P., Lorenz, E., and Terkla, D. (2003). 'The Adoption and Diffusion of High-Performance Management: Lessons from Japanese Multinationals in the West', *Cambridge Journal of Economics*, 27(2): 265–86.

—— and Piore, M. (1971) *Internal Labour Markets and Manpower Analysis*. Lexington: Heath.

Dore, R. (1989). *Japan at Work: Markets, Management and Flexibility*. Paris: OECD.

Doremus, P., Keller, W., Pauly, L., and Reich, S. (1998). *The Myth of the Global Corporation*. Princeton, NJ: Princeton University Press.

Dörre, K. (1996). 'Globalisierungsstrategien von Unternehmen - ein Desintegrationsphänomen? Zu den Auswirkungen grenzüberschreitender Unternehmensaktivitäten auf die industriellen Beziehungen', *SOFI-Mitteilungen*, 24: 15–28.

Dundon, T. (2002). 'Employer Hostility and Union Avoidance in the UK', *Industrial Relations Journal*, 33(3): 234–45.

Dunning, J. (1998). *American Investment in British Manufacturing* (revised and updated edition). London/New York: Routledge.

Economist, The (1997). 'Green is Good: Advantages of Ireland as a Host for F.D.I.', 17 May, 343, 8017: 21–4.

Edwards, P. (ed.) (2002). *Industrial Relations: Theory and Practice*. Oxford: Blackwell.

—— Ferner, A., and Sisson, K. (1993). 'People and the Process of Management in the Multinational Company: A Review and some Illustrations', Warwick Papers in Industrial Relations, no. 43. Coventry: IRRU.

References

Edwards, R. (1995). 'New Prospects for American Labor: A Proposal', *Organization*, 2(3): 375–91.

Edwards, T. (2004). 'The Transfer of Employment Practices Across Borders in Multinational Companies', in A.-W. Harzing and J. van Ruysseveldt (eds), *International Human Resource Management*. London: Sage, pp. 389–410.

Edwards, T., Rees, C. and Coller, X. (1999). 'Structure, Politics and the Diffusion of Employment Practices in Multinationals', *European Journal of Industrial Relations*, 5, 3, 286–306.

—— and Ferner, A. (2002). 'The Renewed "American Challenge": A Review of Employment Practices in US Multinationals', *Industrial Relations Journal*, 33(2): 94–111.

—— and Ferner, A. (2004). 'Multinationals, Reverse Diffusion and National Business Systems', *Management International Review*, 24(1): 51–81.

—— Colling, T., and Ferner, A. (2004). 'Comparative Institutional Analysis and the Diffusion of Employment Practices in Multinational Companies'. Paper presented to conference on *Multinationals and the International Diffusion of Organizational Forms and Practices*, IESE Barcelona, 15–17 July.

—— Almond, P., Clark, I., Colling, T., and Ferner, A. (2005). 'Reverse Diffusion in US Multinationals: Barriers from the American Business System', *Journal of Management Studies*, 42(6): 1261–86.

Edwards, T., Coller, X., Ortiz, L., Rees, C. and Wortmann, M. (2006). 'How important are national industrial relations systems in shaping restructuring in MNCs?', *European Journal of Industrial Relations*, 12, 1.

—— Coller, X., Ortiz, L., Rees, C., and Wortmann, M. (forthcoming). 'National Industrial Relations Systems and Restructuring in MNCs: Evidence from a Cross-Border Merger in the Pharmaceuticals Sector', *European Journal of Industrial Relations*.

Egan, M. and Bendick, M. (2001). 'Workforce Diversity Initiatives of US Multinational Corporations in Europe'. Unpublished paper, Washington.

EIRO (European Industrial Relations Observatory) (1997). 'Germany: The Use of "Hardship Clauses" in the East German Metalworking Industry', EIRO on-line www.eurofound.ie DE9703205, March.

—— (2001*a*). 'Industrial Relations in the EU, Japan and USA, 2000', EIRO on-line, www.eiro.eurofound.ie/2001/11/feature/tn0111148f.html

—— (2001*b*) 'Variable pay in Europe', EIRO on-line, www.eurofound.ie TN0103201S, April.

—— (2003*a*). 'Germany: Works Council Members Prefer Sectoral Agreements', EIRO on-line, www.eurofound.ie DE0310203, October.

—— (2003*b*). 'Germany: Collective Bargaining System Under Pressure', EIRO on-line, www.eurofound.ie DE0312202, December.

—— (2004). 'Annual Review for Spain', EIRO on-line, www.eiro.eurofound.eu.int/feature/es0401203f.html

—— (2004*a*). 'Germany: Coverage of Collective Agreements and Works Councils Assessed', EIRO on-line, www.eurofound.ie DE0401106, January.

—— (2004b). 'Transnational: Trade Union Membership 1993–2003', EIRO on-line, www.eurofound.ie TN0403105, March.

—— (2004c). 'Germany: Trade Union Membership Losses Increased in 2003', EIRO on-line, www.eurofound.ie DE0405202, May.

Eisenhardt, K. M. (1989). 'Building Theories from Case Study Research', *Academy of Management Review*, 14(4): 532–50.

Elger, T. and Smith, C. (1994). *Global Japanization? The Transnational Transformation of the Labour Process*. London: Thomson.

—— —— (2005). *Assembling Work: Remaking Factory Regimes in Japanese Multinationals in Britain*. Oxford: Oxford University Press.

—— —— (2006). 'Theorizing the Role of the International Subsidiary: Transplants, Hybrids and Branch-Plants Revisited', in A. Ferner, J. Quintanilla, and C. Sánchez-Runde (eds), *Multinationals, Institutions, and the Construction of Transnational Practices: Convergence and Diversity in the Global Economy*. Basingstoke: Palgrave.

Elteto, A. (2000). 'Foreign Direct Investment in Spain and Hungary: Main Patterns and Effects with a Special Regard to Foreign Trade'. Ph.D. thesis, Budapest University of Economic Sciences and Public Administration.

Enderwick, P. (1985). *Multinational Business and Labour*. London/Sydney: Croom Helm.

—— (1986). 'Multinationals and Labour Relations: The Case of Ireland', *Irish Business and Administrative Research*, 8(2): 1–12.

Eurostat (2004). *Employment Rate: Female %*. Data available on http://europa.eu./int/comm/eurostat/

Evans, P., Lank, E., and Farquhar, A. (1989). 'Managing Human Resources in the International Firm: Lessons From Practice', in P. Evans, Y. Doz, and A. Laurent (eds), *Human Resource Management in International Firms: Change, Globalization, Innovation*. Basingstoke: Macmillan, pp. 144–61.

Fairris, D. (1997). *Shopfloor Matters: Labor Relations in Twentieth Century American Manufacturing*. London: Routledge.

Faulkner, D., PitKethley, R., and Child, J. (2004). 'International Mergers and Acquisitions in the UK 1985–1994: A Comparison of National HRM Practices', *International Journal of Human Resource Management*, 13(1): 94–111.

FAZ (2000). 'Consumerbank denkt über Franchise-Betriebe in Deutschland nach, Erfolge in Belgien/Gewerkschaften befürchten Aushebelung des Tarifvertrags', 4 August, 16.

Ferner, A. (1997). 'Country of Origin Effects and HRM in Multinational Companies', *Human Resource Management Journal*, 7(1): 19–37.

—— (2000). *The Embeddedness of US Multinational Companies in the US Business System: Implications For HR/IR*. Leicester Business School Occasional Paper no. 61, Leicester: De Montfort University.

—— (2003). 'Foreign Multinationals and Industrial Relations Innovation in Britain', in P. Edwards (ed.), *Industrial Relations. Theory and Practice*, 2nd edn. Oxford: Blackwell, pp. 81–104.

Ferner, A. and Edwards, P. (1995). 'Power and the Diffusion of Organizational Change Within Multinational Enterprises', *European Journal of Industrial Relations*, 1(2): 229–57.

Ferner, A. and Varul, M. Z. (1999). *The German Way? German Multinationals and the Management of Human Resources in their UK Subsidiaries*. London: Anglo-German Foundation for the Study of Industrial Society.

—— —— (2000). ' "Vanguard" Subsidiaries and the Diffusion of New Practices: A Case Study of German Multinationals' *British Journal of Industrial Relations*, 38(1): 115–40.

—— Quintanilla, J., and Varul, M. Z. (2001). 'Country-of-origin Effects, Host Country Effects and the Management of HR in Multinationals: German Companies in Britain and Spain', *Journal of World Business*, 36(1): 107–28.

—— Almond, P., and Colling, T. (2005*a*). 'Institutional Theory and the Cross-National Transfer of Employment Policy: The Case of "Workforce Diversity" in US Multinationals', *Journal of International Business Studies*, 36(3): 304–21.

—— —— Clark, I., Colling, T., Edwards, T., Holden, L., and Muller-Camen, M. (2004). 'The Dynamics of Central Control and Subsidiary Autonomy in the Management of Human Resources: Case Study Evidence From US MNCs in the UK', *Organization Studies*, 25(3): 363–91.

Ferner, A. and Varul, M. Z. Colling, T., and Edwards, T. (2005*b*). 'Policies on Union Representation in US Multinationals in the UK: Between Micro-Politics and Macro-Institutions', *British Journal of Industrial Relations*, 43(4): 703–28.

Fichter, M. (1982). Besatzungsmacht und Gewerkschaften: zur Entwicklung und Anwendung der US-Gewerkschaftspolitik in Deutschland, 1944–1948, Opladen.

Flanders, A. (1964). *The Fawley Productivity Agreements. A Case Study of Management and Collective Bargaining*. London: Faber & Faber.

Flórez-Saborido, I., Rendón, M., and Castro, M. (1992). 'Human Resource Management in Spain', *Employee Relations*, 14(5): 39–59.

Florkowski, G. (1996). 'Managing Diversity Within Multinational Firms for Competitive Advantage', in E. Kossek and S. Lobel (eds), *Managing Diversity*. Oxford: Blackwell, pp. 337–64.

Foulkes, F. (1980). *Personnel Policies in Large Nonunion Companies*. Englewood Cliffs, NJ: Prentice Hall.

Friedman, S. (1986). 'Succession Systems in Large Corporations: Characteristics and Correlates of Performance', *Human Resource Management Journal*, 25(2): 191–213.

French, M. (1997). *US Economic History Since 1945*. Manchester, Mancherster University Press.

Fukao, M. (1995). *Financial Integration, Corporate Governance and the Performance of Multinational Companies*. Washington: Brookings Institution.

Galbraith, J. (1967). *The New Industrial State*. London: Hamilton.

Gall, G. (2001). 'Management Control Approaches and Union Recognition in Britain'. Paper presented to the *Work Employment and Society Conference*, University of Nottingham, September.

Gammelgaard, J., Holm, U., and Pedersen, T. (2004). 'The Dilemmas of MNC Subsidiary Transfer of Knowledge', in V. Mahnke and T. Pedersen (eds), *Knowledge Flows, Governance and the Multinational Enterprise: Frontiers in International Management Research*, Basingstoke: Macmillan, pp. 195–207.

Geary, J. and Roche, W. K. (2001). 'Multinationals and Human Resource Practices in Ireland: A Rejection of the "New Conformance Thesis" ', *International Journal of Human Resource Management*, 12(1): 109–27.

Gennard, J. and Steuer, M. (1971). 'The Industrial Relations of Foreign Owned Subsidiaries in the United Kingdom', *British Journal of Industrial Relations*, 9(2): 143–59.

Ghoshal, S. and Nohria, N. (1993). 'Horses for Courses: Organizational Forms for Multinational Corporations', *Sloan Management Review*, 34(2): 23–36.

Gordon, D., Edwards, R., and Reich, M. (1982). *Segmented Work, Divided Workers: The Historical Transformation of Labor in the United States*. Cambridge: Cambridge University Press.

Gourlay, S. (2005). 'Knowledge Management and International HRM', in T. Edwards and C. Rees (eds), *International Human Resource Management*. Harlow: Pearson, pp. 151–71.

Gramsci, A. (1971). *Selections from the Prison Notebooks*. New York: International Publishers.

Greller, M. and Parsons, C. (1995). 'Contingent Pay Systems and Job Performance Feedback', *Group and Organization Management*, 20(1): 90–108.

Grimshaw, D., Ward, K., Rubery, J., and Beynon, H. (2001). 'Organisations and the Transformation of Internal Labour Markets', *Work, Employment and Society*, 15(1): 25–54.

—— Beynon, H., Rubery, J., and Ward, K. (2002). 'The Restructuring of Career Paths in Large Service Sector Organisations: "Delayering, Upskilling and Polarisation" ', *The Sociological Review*, 50(1): 89–116.

Guest, D. (1989). 'Personnel and Human Resource Management: Can you Tell the Difference?', *Personnel Management*, 1: 48–51.

—— (1990). 'Human Resource Management and the American Dream', *Journal of Management Studies*, 27(4): 377–97.

—— and Hoque, K. (1994). 'The Good, the Bad and the Ugly: Human Resource Management in New Non-Union Companies', *Human Resource Management Journal*, 5(1): 1–14.

—— —— (1996). 'National Ownership and HR Practices in UK Greenfield Sites', *Human Resource Management Journal*, 6(4): 50–74.

Gunnigle, P. (1992). 'Human Resource Management in Ireland', *Employee Relations* 14(5): 5–22.

—— (1995). 'Collectivism and the Management of Industrial Relations in Greenfield Sites', *Human Resource Management Journal*, 5(3): 24–40.

References

Gunnigle, P. (1998). 'Human Resource Management and the Personnel Function', in W. Roche, K. Monks, and J. Walsh (eds), *Human Resource Management Strategies: Policy and Practice in Ireland*. Dublin: Oak Tree Press, pp. 1–23.

—— Morley, M., and Turner, T. (1997). 'Challenging Collectivist Traditions: Individualism and the Management of Industrial Relations in Greenfield Sites', *Economic and Social Review*, 28(2): 105–34.

—— O'Sullivan, M., and Kinsella, M. (2002). 'Organised Labour in the New Economy: Trade Unions and Public Policy in the Republic of Ireland', in D. D'Art and T. Turner (eds), *Irish Employment Relations in the New Economy*. Dublin: Blackhall Press, pp. 222–58.

—— Turner, T., and D'Art, D. (1998). 'Counterpoising Collectivism: Performance-Related Pay and Industrial Relations in Greenfield Sites', *British Journal of Industrial Relations*, 36(4): 565–79.

—— Collings, D. G. and Morley, M. J. (2004). 'Die Personalpolitik amerikanischer multinationaler Unternehmen in Irland', in H. Wächter, and R. Peters, (eds.), *Personalpolitik amerikanischer Unternehmen in Europa*. München: Mering, pp. 153–78.

Gunnigle, P., Collings, D., and Maley, M., (2006). 'Accampanying Global Capitalism? State policy and industrial relations in American MNCs in Ireland', in A. Femer, J. Quintanilla, and C. Sánchez-Runde (eds), *Multinationals, Institutions, and the Construction of Transnational Practices: Convergence and Diversity in the Global Economy*. London: Palgrave.

—— —— and Morley, M. (2005). 'Exploring the Dynamics of Industrial Relations in US Multinationals: Evidence from the Republic of Ireland', *Industrial Relations Journal*, 36(3): 241–56.

—— —— —— McAvinue, C., O'Callaghan, A., and Shore, D. (2003). 'US Multinationals and Human Resource Management in Ireland: Towards a Qualitative Research Agenda', *Irish Journal of Management*, 24(1): 7–25.

Gupta, A. and Govindarajan, V. (1991). 'Knowledge Flows and the Structure of Control within Multinational Corporations', *Academy of Management Review*, 16(4): 768–92.

—— —— (2000). 'Knowledge Flows within Multinational Corporations', *Strategic Management Journal*, 21: 473–96.

Habukkuk. (1960). *American and British Technology in the Nineteenth Century: The Search for Labour-Saving Inventions*. Cambridge: Cambridge University Press.

Hall, P. (2003). 'Aligning Ontology and Methodology in Comparative Politics', in J. Mahoney, and D. Rueschemeyer (eds), *Comparative Historical Analysis in the Social Sciences*. Cambridge: Cambridge University Press, pp. 373–404.

—— and Gingerich, D. (2004). 'Varieties of Capitalism and Institutional Complementarities in the Macroeconomy: An Empirical Analysis', *MPIfG Discussion Paper*, 04/5. Cologne: MPIfG.

—— and Soskice, D. (eds.) (2001a). *Varieties of Capitalism*. Oxford: Oxford University Press.

—— —— (2001*b*). 'An Introduction to Varieties of Capitalism', in P. Hall, and D. Soskice (eds.), *Varieties of Capitalism. The Institutional Foundations of Comparative Advantage*. Oxford: Oxford University Press, pp. 1–68.

Hall, M. (2005). 'Assessing the information and consultation of employee regulations', *Industrial Law Journal*, 34 (2).

Hamann, K. and Martínez Lucio, M. (2003). 'Strategies of Union Revitalisation in Spain: Negotiating Change and Fragmentation,' *European Journal of Industrial Relations*, 9(1): 61–78.

Handy, C. (1987). *The Making of Managers: A Report on Management Education. Training and Development in the USA, West Germany, France, Japan and the UK*. London: National Economic Development Office.

—— Gordon, G., Gow, I., and Raddlesome, C. (1988). *Making Managers*. London: Pitman.

Hansen, C. and Willcox, M. (1997). 'Cultural Assumptions in Career Management: Practical Implications from Germany', *Career Development International*, 2(4): 195–202.

Harrison, B. (1997). *Lean and Mean: Why Large Companies will Continue to Dominate the Global Economy*. New York: Guilford.

Harzing, A.-W. (1999). *Managing the Multinationals: An International Study of Control Mechanisms*. Cheltenham: Edward Elgar.

Harzing, A. W. and Sorge, A. (2003). 'The Relative Impact of Country of Origin and Universal Contingencies on Internationalization Strategies and Corporate Control in Multinational Enterprises: Worldwide and European Perspectives', *Organization Studies*, 24(2): 187–214.

Hassel, A. (1999). 'The Erosion of the German System of Industrial Relations', *British Journal of Industrial Relations*, 37(3): 483–505.

—— (2002). 'The Erosion Continues: Reply', *British Journal of Industrial Relations*, 40(2): 309–17.

Hayden, A. and Edwards, T. (2001). 'The Erosion of the Country of Origin Effect: A Case Study of a Swedish Multinational Company', *Relations Industrielles/Industrial Relations*, 56(1): 116–40.

Heckscher, C. (1995). *White Collar Blues: Management Loyalties in an Age of Corporate Re-Structuring*. New York: Basic Books.

Hedlund, G. (1986). 'The Hypermodern MNE: A Heterarchy?', *Human Resource Management*, 25(1): 9–36.

Heery, E. (1998). 'Campaigning for Part-Time Workers', *Work Employment and Society*, 12(2): 351–66.

Heidrick and Struggles (1991). *Der Vorstand/ Geschäftsführer Personal: Kompetenzen und Verantwortung für Unternehmens- und Personalpolitik in den 90er Jahren*. München: Heidrick & Struggles.

Heraty, N. and Morley, M. (2000). 'Human Resource Development in Ireland: Organizational Level Evidence', *Journal of European Industrial Training*, 24(1): 21–33.

—— —— (2003). 'Management Development in Ireland: The New Organizational Wealth', *Journal of Management Development*, 22(1): 60–82.

Herbst, L. (1989). *Option für den Westen, vom Marshallplan bis zum deutsch-französischen Vertrag.* München: Deutscher Taschenbuch Verlag.

Higgins, C. (2005). 'Analog Told to deal with Pay for Non-Union Group', *Industrial Relations News*, 14, 7 April.

Hill, C.W.L. (2003). *International Business*, 4th edn. New York: McGraw-Hill/Irwin.

Hofstede, G. (1984). *Culture's Consequences: International Differences in Work Related Values.* Beverly Hills: Sage.

Hogan, M. (1987). *The Marshall-Plan: America, Britain, and the Reconstruction of Western Europe, 1947–1952.* Cambridge: Cambridge University Press.

Hollingsworth, J. (1997a). 'The Institutional Embeddedness of American Capitalism', in C. Crouch, and W. Streeck (eds), *Political Economy of Modern Capitalism.* London: Sage, pp. 133–47.

—— (1997b). 'Continuities and Changes in Social Systems of Production: The Cases of Japan, Germany and the United States', in J. Hollingsworth and R. Boyer (eds), *Contemporary Capitalism: The Embeddedness of Institutions.* Cambridge: Cambridge University Press, pp. 265–308.

Hollingsworth, J. R. and Boyer, R. (eds) (1997a). *Contemporary Capitalism: The Embeddedness of Institutions.* Cambridge: Cambridge University Press.

—— —— (1997b). 'Coordination of Economic Actors and Social Systems of Production', in J. R. Hollingsworth and R. Boyer (eds), *Contemporary Capitalism. The Embeddedness of Institutions.* Cambridge: Cambridge University Press, pp. 1–47.

—— Schmitter, P., and Streeck, W. (1994). *Governing Capitalist Economies. Performance and Control of Economic Sectors.* New York/Oxford: Oxford University Press.

Hollingsworth, J. R. and Schulten, T. (1998). 'Globalisation and the Future of Collective Bargaining: The Example of the German Metalworking Industry', *Economy and Society*, 27(4): 486–522.

Hyman, R. (2001). *Understanding European Trade Unionism.* London, Sage.

Hymer, S. (1976). *The International Operations of National Firms: A Study of Direct Foreign Investment.* Cambridge, MA: MIT Press.

Ichniowski, C., Kochan, T., Levine, D., Olson, G., and Strauss, G. (1996). 'What Works at Work?' *Industrial Relations*, 35(3): 299–333.

Innes, E. and Morris, J. (1995). 'Multinational Corporations and Employee Relations: Continuity and Change in a Mature Industrial Region', *Employee Relations*, 17(6): 25–42.

International Federation of Exchanges (2005). *Annual Report.* International Federation of Exchanges: www.fibv.com

Invest in Spain (2004). www.investinspain.org

Jackall, R. (1988). *Moral Mazes.* Oxford: Oxford University Press.

Jacobi, O., Keller, B., and Muller-Jentsch, W. (1998). 'Germany: Facing New Challenges', in A. Ferner and R. Hyman (eds), *Changing Industrial Relations in Europe.* Oxford: Blackwell, pp. 190–238.

Jacoby, S. (1984). 'The Development of Internal Labour Markets in US Firms', in P. Osterman, (ed.), *Internal Labor Markets*. Cambridge, MA: MIT Press, pp. 33–69.

—— (1985). *Employing Bureaucracy*. New York: Columbia University Press.

—— (1991). 'American Exceptionalism Revisited: The Importance of Management', in S. Jacoby (ed.), *Masters to Managers: Historical and Comparative Perspectives on American Employers*. New York: Columbia University Press, pp. 173–200.

—— (1997). *Modern Manors: Welfare Capitalism since the New Deal*. Princeton, NJ: Princeton University Press.

—— (1999). 'Modern Manors: An Overview', *Industrial Relations*, 38(2): 123–7.

—— Nason, E., and Saguchi, K. (2005). 'The Role of the Senior HR Executive in Japan and the United States: Employment Relations, Corporate Governance and Values', *Industrial Relations*, 44(2): 207–41.

Jehn, K., Northcraft, G., and Neale, M. (1999). 'Why Differences Make a Difference: A Field Study of Diversity, Conflict, and Performance in Workgroups', *Administrative Science Quarterly*, 44(4): 741–63.

Johnson, L. and Johnstone, S. (2000). 'The Legislative Framework', in G. Kirton, and A.-M. Greene (eds), *The Dynamics of Managing Diversity*, London: Butterworth/Heinemann, pp. 125–49.

Kahn-Freund, O. (1965). 'Report on the Legal Status of Collective Bargaining and Collective Agreements in Great Britain', in O. Kahn-Freund (ed.), *Labour Relations and the Law: A Comparative Study*, London: Stevens, pp. 21–39.

Kalleberg, A., Knoke, D., Marsden, P., and Spaeth, J. (1996). *Organizations in America: Analyzing Their Structures and Human Resource Practices*. Thousand Oaks, CA: Sage.

Kanter, R. M. (1984). 'Variations in Managerial Career Structure in High-Technology Firms; The Impact of Organizational Characteristics on Internal Labour Market Patterns', in P. Osterman (ed.), *Internal Labour Markets*, Cambridge, MA: MIT Press, pp. 109–32.

Kanter, R. M. (1989). *When Giants Learn to Dance: Mastering the Change of Strategy Management and Careers in the 1990s*. London: Unwin.

Katz, H. and Darbishire, O. (2000). *Converging Divergences: Worldwide Changes in Employment Systems*. Ithaca: Cornell University Press.

—— and Krueger, A. (1991). 'Changes in the Structure of Wages in the Public and Private Sectors.' *Princeton University Working Paper*, no. 282, April.

Katznelson, I. (2003). 'Reflections on Purposive Action in Comparative Historical Social Science', in J. Mahoney and D. Rueschemeyer (eds), *Comparative Historical Analysis in the Social Sciences*, Cambridge: Cambridge University Press, pp. 270–301.

Kaufman, B. (2001). 'The Future of U.S. Private Sector Unionism: Did George Barnett Get It Right After All?', *Journal of Labour Research*, 22(3): 433–58.

Kelly, A. and Brannick, T. (1985). 'Industrial Relations Practices in Multinational Companies in Ireland', *Journal of Irish Business and Administrative Research*, 7: 98–111.

Kerr, C., Dunlop, J., Harbison, F., and Myers, C. (1960). *Industrialism and Industrial Man*. London: Heinemann.

References

Kester, W. (1996). 'American and Japanese Corporate Governance: Convergence to Best Practice?', in S. Berger and R. Dore (eds), *National Diversity and Global Capitalism*, Ithaca: Cornell University Press, pp. 107–37.

Klikauer, T. (2002). 'Stability in Germany's Industrial Relations: A Critique on Hassel's Erosion Thesis', *British Journal of Industrial Relations*, 40(2): 295–308.

Klores, M. (1966). 'Rater Bias in Forced Distribution Performance Ratings', *Personnel Psychology*, 19(4): 411–22.

Knox, B. and Mckinlay, A. (1999). 'Working for the Yankee Dollar: American Inward Investment and Scottish Labour, 1945–1970', *Historical Studies in Industrial Relations*, 7(1): 1–26.

Kochan, T. and Osterman, P. (1994). *The Mutual Gains Enterprise*. Boston, MA: Harvard Business School Press.

—— and Weinstein, M. (1994). 'Recent Developments in U.S. Industrial Relations', *British Journal of Industrial Relations*, 32(4): 483–504.

—— Katz, H., and McKersie, R. (1986). *The Transformation of American Industrial Relations*. New York: Basic Books.

—— —— —— (1994). *The Transformation of American Industrial Relations*, 2nd edn. Ithaca: ILR/Cornell University Press.

—— Bezrukova, K., Ely, R., Jackson, S., Joshi, A., Jehn, K., Leonard, J., Levine, D., and Thomas, D. (2003). 'The Effects of Diversity on Business Performance: Report of the Diversity Research Network', *Human Resource Management*, 42(1): 3–21.

Kohaut, S. and Bellmann, L. (1997). 'Betriebliche Determinanten der Tarifbindung: Eine empirische Analyse auf der Basis des IAB-Betriebspanels 1995', *Industrielle Beziehungen*, 4: 317–34.

—— and Schnabel, C. (2001). *Tarifverträge – nein Danke!? Einflussfaktoren auf der Tarifbindung west- und ostdeutscher Betriebe*, Diskussionspapier 8, Erlangen-Nürnberg: Friedrich-Alexander-Universität.

Konzelmann, S., Forrant, R., and Wilkinson, F. (2004). 'Work Systems, Corporate Strategy and Global Markets: Creative Shop Floors or a "Barge Mentality" ', *Industrial Relations Journal*, 35(3): 216–32.

Kopp, R. (1994). 'International Human Resource Policies and Practices in Japanese, European, and United States Multinationals', *Human Resource Management Journal*, 33(4): 581–99.

Kostova, T. (1999). 'Transnational Transfer of Strategic Organizational Practices: A Contextual Perspective', *Academy of Management Review*, 24(2): 308–24.

—— and Roth, K. (2002). 'Adoption of an Organizational Practice by Subsidiaries of Multinational Corporations: Institutional and Relational Effects', *Academy of Management Journal*, 35(1): 215–33.

—— and Zaheer, S. (1999). 'Organizational Legitimacy Under Conditions of Complexity: The Case of the Multinational Enterprise', *Academy of Management Review*, 24(1): 64–81.

Kotthoff, H. (1981). *Betriebsräte und Betriebliche Herrschaft. Eine Typologie von Partizipationsmustern im Industriebetrieb*. Frankfurt: Campus Verlag.

—— (1994). *Betriebsräte und Bürgerstatus. Wandel und Kontinuität betrieblicher Mitbestimmung*. Munich: Hampp Verlag.

Krell, G. (2001). 'Chancengleichheit durch Personalpolitik: Von "Frauenförderung" zu "Diversity Management" ', in G. Krell (ed.), *Chancengleichheit durch Personalpolitik*, Gabler: Wiesbaden, pp.17–38.

Kristensen, P. H. and Zeitlin, J. (2005). *Local Players in Global Games: The Strategic Constitution of a Multinational Corporation*. Oxford: Oxford University Press.

Kurdelbusch, A. (2002). 'Multinationals and the Rise of Variable Pay In Germany', *European Journal of Industrial Relations*, 8(3): 325–49.

Lam, A. (1997). 'Embedded Firms, Embedded Knowledge', *Organization Studies*, 18(6): 973–96.

Landes, D. (1998). *The Wealth and Poverty of Nations*. London: Abacus.

Lane, C. (1989). *Management and Labour in Europe. The Industrial Enterprise in Germany, Britain and France*. Aldershot: Edward Elgar.

—— (2000). 'Globalization and the German Model of Capitalism: Erosion or Survival?', *British Journal of Sociology*, 51(2): 207–34.

Lawler, E. (2002). 'The Folly of Forced Ranking', *Strategy and Business*, 28(3): 28–32.

Lawrence, P. (1991). 'The Personnel Function: An Anglo-German Comparison', in C. Brewster and S. Tyson (eds.), *International Comparisons in Human Resource Management*, London: Pitman, pp.131–44.

—— (1993). 'Human Resource Management in Germany', in S. Tyson, P. Lawrence, P. Poirson, L. Manzolini, and C. Soler Vicente (eds), *Human Resource Management in Europe: Strategic Issues and Cases*, London: Kogan Page, pp. 25–41.

Lawrence, P. (1993). 'Management development in Europe: a Study in cultural contrasts', *Human Resource Management Journal*, 3, 1, 11–23.

Lawrence, P. (1996). *Management in the USA*. London: Sage.

Lazonick, W. (1998). 'Organizational learning and International Competition', in J. Michie and J. Grieve Smith, (eds), *Globalization, Growth and Governance*, Oxford: Oxford University Press, pp. 204–38.

Lee, G. and Limberg, K. (1995). 'Professional Associations and their Cultural Context: A Comparison of the IPD in Britain and the DGFP in Germany', in H. Wächter and T. Metz (eds), *Professionelle Personalarbeit, Perspektiven der Professionalisierung des Personalwesens*, Sonderband der Zeitschrift für Personalforschung, München: Mering, pp. 13–37.

Lee, T., Fuller, A., Ashton, D., Butler, P., Felstead, A., Unwin, L., and Walters, S. (2004). *Workplace Learning: Main Themes and Perspectives*. Learning as Work Research Paper, no. 2. Leicester: Centre for Labour Market Studies.

Leidner, R. (2002). 'Fast-Food Work in the United States, in T. Royle and B. Towers (eds), *Labour Relations in the Global Fast Food Industry*. London, Routledge, pp. 8–29.

Levine, D. (1995). *Reinventing the Workplace: How Business and Employees can Both Win*. New York: Brookings Institution.

Levy, D. and Egan, D. (2003). 'A Neo-Gramscian Approach to Corporate Political Strategy: Conflict and Accommodation in the Climate Change Negotiations', *Journal of Management Studies*, 40(4): 803–29.

Lichtenstein, N. (2002). *State of the Union: A Century of American Labor*. Princeton: Princeton University Press.

Liff, S. and Wajcman, J. (1996). ' "Sameness" and "Difference" Revisited: Which Way Forward for Equal Opportunity Initiatives?', *Journal of Management Studies*, 33(1): 79–94.

Lipset, S. M. (1962). 'Trade Unions and Social Structure: A Comparative Analysis, II', *Industrial Relations*, 1(2): 75–89.

Locke, R. (1996). *The Collapse of the American Management Mystique*. Oxford: Oxford University Press.

López-Claros, A. (1989). 'Growth-Orientated Adjustment: Spain in the 1980s', *Finance and Development*, 26(1): 38–45.

Lorenz, E. (2000). 'The Transfer of Business Practices to Britain and France', in M. Maurice and A. Sorge (eds), *Embedding Organizations*, Amsterdam: John Benjamins, pp. 241–56.

Lukes, S. (1974). *Power: A Radical View*. London: Macmillan.

McGovern, P. (1989). 'Union Recognition and Union Avoidance in the 1980's', in A. Kelly, T. Murphy, and B. Hillery (eds.), *Industrial Relations in Ireland: Contemporary Issues and Developments*, Dublin: University College Dublin, pp. 61–71.

—— Hope-Hailey, V., and Stiles, P. (1998). 'The Managerial Career after Downsizing: Case Studies from the "Leading Edge" ', *Work, Employment and Society*, 12(5): 457–77.

McLoughlin, I. and Gourlay, S. (1994). *Enterprise Without Unions: Industrial Relations in the Non-Union Firm*. Buckingham: Open University Press.

Mahoney, J. (2001). 'Path-Dependent Explanations of Regime Change: Central America in Comparative Perspective', *Studies in Comparative International Development*, 36(1): 111–40.

—— (2003). 'Strategies of Causal Assessment in Comparative Historical Analysis', in J. Mahoney and D. Rueschemeyer (eds), *Comparative Historical Analysis in the Social Sciences*, Cambridge: Cambridge University Press, pp. 337–72.

—— and Rueschemeyer, D. (2003). *Comparative Historical Analysis in the Social Sciences*, Cambridge: Cambridge University Press.

Mahlmann, M. (2002). 'Anti-discrimination legislation in EU member states', retrieved June 5, 2005, from http://eumc.eu.int/eumc/material/pub/An13/ART13_Germany-en-pdf.

Managham, I. and Silver, M. (1986). *Management Training: Context and Practice*. London: Economic and Social Research Council.

Marginson, P. (2000). 'The Eurocompany and Euro Industrial Relations', *European Journal of Industrial Relations*, 6(1): 9–34.

Marginson, P. and Sisson, K. (1994). 'The Structure of Transnational Capital in Europe: The Emerging Euro-Company and Its Implications for Industrial Relations', in R. Hyman and A. Ferner (eds), *New Frontiers in European Industrial Relations*, Oxford: Blackwell, pp. 15–51.

—— Armstrong, P., Edwards, P., and Purcell, J. (1995). 'Managing Labour in the Global Corporation: A Survey-Based Analysis of Multinationals Operating in the UK', *International Journal of Human Resource Management*, 6(3): 702–19.

Marsden, D. (1999). *A Theory of Employment Systems: Micro-Foundations of Societal Diversity*. Oxford: Oxford University Press.

Martin, G. and Beaumont, P. (1999). 'Co-Ordination and Control of Human Resource Management in Multinational Firms: The Case of CASHCO', *International Journal of Human Resource Management*, 10(1): 21–42.

Martín, A., Romero, F., Valle, C., and Dolan, S. (2001). 'Corporate Business Strategy, Career Management and Recruitment: Do Spanish Firms Adhere to a Contingency Model?', *Career Development International*, 6(3): 149–55.

Martínez Lucio, M. (1998). 'Spain: Regulating Employment and Social Fragmentation', in A. Ferner and R. Hyman (eds.), *Changing Industrial Relations in Europe*, Oxford: Blackwell, pp. 426–58.

Meardi, C., and Tóth, A. (2006). Who is Hybridizing What? Insights on MNC's Employment Practices in Central Europe', in Ferner, A., Quintanilla, J., and Sánchez-Runde, C. (eds). Multinationals, Institutions, and the Construction of Transnational Practices, Basingstoke, Palgrave, 155–83.

Metcalf, D., Hansen, K., and Charlwood, A. (2001). 'Unions and the Sword of Justice: Unions and Pay Systems, Pay Inequality, Pay Discrimination and Low Pay', *National Institute Economic Review*, 176(1): 61–75.

Metz, T. (1999). 'Neuere Konzepte für die Organisation der Personalabteilung', *Das Wirtschaftsstudium*, 12: 1601–4.

Michie, J. (2003). *The Handbook of Globalisation*. Cheltenham: Edward Elgar.

Milkman, R. (1998). 'The New American Workplace: High Road or Low Road?', in P. Thompson, and C. Smith (eds.), *Workplaces of the Future*, Basingstoke: Macmillan, pp. 22–34.

Mills, D. (1985) 'Seniority Versus Ability in Promotion Decisions', *Industrial and Labor Relations Review*, 38(3): 421–6.

Mishel, L., Bernstein, J., and Boushey, H. (2003). *The State of Working America, 2002/2003*. Ithaca: ILR/Cornell University Press.

MitbestG (1976). *Gesetz über die Mitbestimmung der Arbeitnehmer vom 4. Mai 1976* (BGB1. I S. 1153).

Monks, K. (1996). 'Global or Local? HRM in the Multinational Company: The Irish Experience', *The International Journal of Human Resource Management*, 7(3): 721–35.

Mooney, P. (1989). 'The Growth of the Non-Union Sector and Union Counter Strategies in Ireland'. Unpublished PhD thesis. Dublin: Trinity College Dublin.

References

Morgan, G. (2005). 'Institutional Complementarities, Path Dependency and the Dynamics of Firms', in G. Morgan, R. Whitley, and E. Moen (eds), *Changing Capitalisms?* Oxford: Oxford University Press, pp. 415–46.

—— Kelly, B., Sharpe, D., and Whitley, R. (2003). 'Global Managers and Japanese Multinationals: Internationalization and Management in Japanese Financial Institutions', *International Journal of Human Resource Management*, 14(3): 389–408.

Morgan, G., Whitley, R., and Moen, E., (2005). Changing Capitalisms? Oxford: Oxford University Press.

Mueller, F. and Purcell, J. (1992). 'The Europeanization of Manufacturing and the Decentralization of Bargaining: Multinational Management Strategies in the European Automobile Industry', *International Journal of Human Resource Management*, 3(1): 15–34.

Muller, M. (1997). 'Institutional Resilience in a Changing World Economy: The Case of the German Banking and Chemical Industries', *British Journal of Industrial Relations*, 35(4): 609–28.

—— (1998). 'Human Resource and Industrial Relations Practices of UK and US Multinationals in Germany', *International Journal of Human Resource Management*, 9(4): 732–49.

Muller-Camen, M. and Krüger, G. (2004). 'Vielfalt zu fördern bringt viele Vorteile', *Personalmagazin*, 1: 58–60.

—— Almond, P., Gunnigle, P., Quintanilla, J., and Temple, A. (2001). 'Between Home and Host country: Multinationals and Employment Relations in Europe', *Industrial Relations Journal*, 32(5): 435–49.

Murray, S. (1984), *Survey of Employee/Industrial Relations in Irish Private Sector Manufacturing Industry.* Dublin: IDA.

Mylett, T. and Zanko, M. (2002). 'In Through the Door; Critiquing the Internal Labour Market Concept', *Labour and Industry*, 13(2): 145–68.

Negandhi, A. (1983). 'External and Internal Functioning of American, German, and Japanese Multinational Corporations: Decisionmaking and Policy Issues', in M. Casson (ed.), *Multinational Corporations*, Aldershot: Edward Elgar, pp. 557–77.

—— (1986). 'Role and Structure of German Multinationals: A Comparative Profile', in K. Macharzina and W. Staehle (eds), *European Approaches to International Management*, Berlin/New York: Walter de Gruyter, pp. 51–66.

Nicoletti, G., Scarpatta, S., and Boylaud, O. (2000). 'Summary Indicators of Product Market Regulation with an Extension to Employment Protection Legislation', *Economics Department Working Papers*, no. 226. Paris: OECD.

Noble, D. (1977). *America by Design: Science, Technology and the Rise of Corporate Capitalism.* New York: Alfred Knopf.

Nohria, N. and Ghoshal, S. (1997). *The Differentiated Network: Organizing Multinational Companies for Value Creation.* San Francisco, CA: Jossey-Bass.

Nooteboom, J. (1999). 'Voice and Exit-Based Forms of Corporate Control: Anglo-American, European and Japanese', *Journal of Economic Issues*, 33(4): 345–60.

Ó Riain, S. (2000). 'States and Markets in an Era of Globalization', *Annual Review of Sociology*, 26: 187–213.

OECD (Organisation for Economic Coordination and Development) (2004). *Employment Outlook*. Paris: OECD.

O'Higgins, E. R. (2002). 'Government and the Creation of the Celtic Tiger: Can Management Maintain the Momentum?', *Academy of Management Executive*, 16(3): 104–20.

Oliver, C. (1991). 'Strategic Responses to Institutional Processes', *Academy of Management Review*, 16(1): 145–79.

Ortiz, L. (1998). 'Unions' Response to Teamwork: Differences at National and Workplace Level', *Industrial Relations Journal*, 29(1): 42–57.

—— (2002). 'The Resilience of a Company-Level System of Industrial Relations: Union Responses to Teamwork in Renault's Spanish Subsidiary', *European Journal of Industrial Relations*, 8(3): 277–99.

Osterman P. (ed.) (1984a). *Internal Labor Markets*. Cambridge, MA: MIT Press.

—— (1984b). 'The Nature and Importance of Internal Labour Markets', in P. Osterman (ed.), *Internal Labour Markets*. Cambridge, MA: MIT Press, pp. 1–22.

—— (1987). 'Choice of Employment Systems in Internal Labour Markets', *Industrial Relations*, 26(2): 46–67.

—— (1988). *Employment Futures*. New York: Oxford University Press.

—— (1994). 'How Common is Workplace Transformation and How Can We Explain Who Does It?', *Industrial and Labour Relations Review*, 47(2): 173–88.

—— (1996). *Broken Ladders: Managerial Careers in the New Economy*. New York: Oxford University Press.

—— (1999). *Securing Prosperity: The American Labor Market: How it has Changed and What to Do about it*. Princeton, NJ: Princeton University Press.

O'Sullivan, M. (2000). *Contests for Corporate Control: Corporate Governance and Economic Performance in the United States and Germany*. Oxford: Oxford University Press.

Oxenbridge, S., Bram, W., Deadin, S., and Pratten C. (2003) 'Initial responses to the statutary recognition provisions of the Employment Relations Act 1999', *Britsh Journal of Industrial Relations* 41, 2, 315–34.

Palan, R. (ed.) (2000). *Global Political Economy: Contemporary Theories*. London: Routledge.

Pauly, L. and Reich, S. (1997). 'National Structures and Multinational Corporate Behavior: Enduring Differences in the Age of Globalization', *International Organization*, 51(1): 1–30.

Pettigrew, A. (1973). *The Politics of Organizational Decision Making*. London: Tavistock.

—— (1985). *The Awakening Giant: Continuity and Change in ICI*, Oxford: Blackwell.

Pfeffer, J. (1981). *Power in Organizations*. Boston: Pitman.

Pfeffer, J. (1998) *The Human Equation: Putting Peaple First*, Boston, MA: Harvard Business School Press.

References

Pierson, P. (2003). 'Big, Slow-Moving, and . . . Invisible: Macrosocial Processes in the Study of Comparative Politics', in J. Mahoney, and D. Rueschemeyer, (eds.), *Comparative Historical Analysis in the Social Sciences*, Cambridge: Cambridge University Press, pp. 177–207.

Pil, F. and McDuffie, J. (1996). 'The Adoption of High-Involvement Work Practices', *Industrial Relations*, 35(3): 423–55.

Piore, M. (2002). 'Thirty Years Later: Internal Labour Markets: Flexibility and the New Economy', *Journal of Management and Governance*, 6(3): 271–9.

Porter, M. (1990). *The Competitive Advantage of Nations (with a new introduction)*. Basingstoke: Macmillan.

Pruijt, H. (2003). 'Teams between Neo-Taylorism and anti-Taylorism', *Economic and Industrial Democracy*, 24, 1, 77–101.

Pulignano, V. (2006). 'Patterns of Integration in American Multinational Subsidiaries in Europe', in A. Ferner, J. Quintanilla, and C. Sánchez-Runde (eds), *Multinationals, Institutions, and the Construction of Transnational Practices: Convergence and Diversity in the Global Economy*, Basingstoke: Palgrave.

Quinn Mills, D. (1989). *Labor–Management Relations*. New York: McGraw-Hill.

Quintanilla, J. (2001). *Dirección de recursos humanos en empresas multinacionales. Las subsidiarias al descubierto*. Madrid: Financial Times, Prentice Hall

—— Susaeta, L., and López, L. (2004). 'Personalmanagement amerikanischer MNU in spanischen Tochtergesellschaften: vorläufige Ergebnisse der Fallstudien', in H. Wächter, and R. Peters (eds), *Personalpolitik amerikanischer Unternehmen in Europa*, München: Mering, pp. 129–52.

Richard, O. (2000). 'Racial Diversity, Business Strategy, and Firm Performance: A Resource-Based View', *Academy of Management Journal*, 43(2): 164–77.

Rigby, M. and Aledo, M. (2001). 'The Worst Record in Europe? A Comparative Analysis of Industrial Conflict in Spain', *European Journal of Industrial Relations*, 7(3): 287–305.

Roche, W. (1992). 'The Liberal Theory of Industrialism and the Development of Industrial Relations in Ireland', in J. Goldthorpe, and C. Whelan (eds), *The Development of Industrial Society in Ireland*, Oxford: Oxford University Press, pp. 291–327.

—— (1997). 'The Trend of Unionisation', in T. Murphy, and W. Roche (eds), *Irish Industrial Relations in Practice: Revised and Expanded Edition*, Dublin: Oak Tree Press, pp. 41–73.

—— (2001). 'Accounting for the Trend in Union Recognition in Ireland', *Industrial Relations Journal*, 32(1): 37–54.

—— and Geary, J. (1997). 'Multinationals and Industrial Relations Practices', in T. Murphy and W. Roche (eds), *Irish Industrial Relations in Practice: Revised and Expanded Edition*, Dublin: Oak Tree Press, pp. 277–98.

—— and Turner, T. (1998). 'Human Resource Management and Industrial Relations: Substitution, Dualism and Partnership', in W. Roche, K. Monks, and

J. Walsh (eds), *Human Resource Management Strategies: Policy and Practice in Ireland*, Dublin: Oak Tree Press, pp. 67–107.

Romo, O. M. (2005). 'Political Exchange and Bargaining Reform in Italy and Spain', *European Journal of Industrial Relations*, 11(1): 6–26.

Rosenzweig, P. and Nohria, N. (1994). 'Influences on Human Resource Management Practices in Multinational Corporations', *Journal of International Business Studies*, 25(2): 229–51.

Rosenzweig, P. and Singh, J. (1991). 'Organizational Environments and the Multinational Enterprise', *Academy of Management Review*, 16: 340–61.

Roy, D. F. (1980). 'Repression and Incorporation. Fear Stuff, Sweet Stuff and Evil Stuff: Management's Defences Against Unionization in the South', in T. Nichols (ed.), *Capital and Labour: A Marxist Primer*, Glasgow: Fontana, pp. 395–415.

Royle, T. (1998). 'Avoidance Strategies and the German System of Co-Determination', *International Journal of Human Resource Management*, 9(6): 1026–47.

—— (2000). *Working for McDonald's in Europe*. London: Routledge.

Royle, T. (2004). 'Employment practices of multinationals in the Spanish and German quick-food sectors: law-road convergence?', *European Journal of Industrial Relations*, 10, 1: 51–71.

Rubery, J. (1994). 'The British Production Regime: A Societal-Specific System?', *Economy and Society*, 23(3): 335–54.

—— Smith, M., Fagan, C., and Grimshaw, D. (1999). *Women's Employment in Europe: Trends and Prospects*. London: Routledge.

—— Grimshaw, D., and Figueiredo, H. (2005). 'How to Close the Gender Pay Gap in Europe: Towards Gender Mainstreaming of Pay Policy', *Industrial Relations Journal*. 36(3): 184–213.

Rudolph, W. and Wassermann, W. (2002). 'Trendwende zu mehr Stabilität und Respräsentanz des Betriebsrätewesens', *Trendreport Betriebsrätewahlen 2002*, Kassel: Büro für Sozialforschung.

Rugman, A. (2005). *The Regional Multinationals: MNEs and 'Global' Strategic Management*. Cambridge: Cambridge University Press.

Saka, A. (2002). 'Institutional Limits to the Internalization of Work Systems: A Comparative Study of Three Japanese MNCs in the UK', *European Journal of Industrial Relations*, 8(3): 251–75.

Schattschneider, E. (1960). *The Semi-Sovereign People: A Realist's View of Democracy in America*. New York: Holt, Rinehart, & Wilson.

Schmitt, M. and Sadowski, D. (2003). 'A Rationalistic Cost-Minimization Approach to the Transfer of HR/IR Practices: Anglo-Saxon Multinationals in the Federal Republic of Germany', *International Journal of Human Resource Management*, 14(3): 409–30.

Schuler, R. S. (1994). 'World Class Human Resource Departments: Six Critical Issues', *Accounting and Business Review*, 1(1): 43–72.

Scott, W. R. (1995). *Institutions and Organizations*. Thousand Oaks, CA: Sage.

Scott, W. R. (2001). *Institutions and Organizations*, 2nd edn. Thousand Oaks, CA: Sage.

References

Scullion, H. and Starkey, K. (2000). 'In Search of the Changing Role of the Corporate Human Resource Function in the International Firm', *International Journal of Human Resource Management*, 11(6): 1061–81.

Sell, S. K. (2000). 'Big Business and the New Trade Agreements', in R. Stubbs and G. R. D. Underhill (eds), *Political Economy and the Changing Global Order*, Don Mills, Ontario: Oxford University Press, pp. 174–83.

Senge, P. (1991). *The Fifth Dimension: The Art and Practice of the Learning Organisation*. New York: Doubleday.

Shibata, H. (2002). 'Wage and Performance Appraisal in Flux: A Japan–United States Comparison, *Industrial Relations*, 38(2): 192–214.

SHRM (2002). *Diversity Initiative*, [www document] http://www.shrm.org/diversity (accessed 24 July 2003).

Sisson, K. (1987). *The Management of Collective Bargaining: An International Comparison*. Oxford: Blackwell.

Sloan, A. (1986). *My Years with General Motors*. Harmondsworth: Penguin.

Smith, C. and Elger, T. (2000). 'The Societal Effects School and Transnational Transfer: The Case of Japanese Investment in Britain', in M. Maurice, and A. Sorge (eds), *Embedding Organizations: Societal Analysis of Actors, Organizations and Socio-Economic Context*, Amsterdam/Philadelphia: John Benjamins, pp. 225–39.

—— and Meisksins, P. (1995). 'System, Society and Dominance Effects in Cross-National Organisational Analysis', *'Work, Employment and Society*, 9(2): 241–67.

Smith, P. and Maton, G. (1993). 'Union exclusion and the decollectivisation of industrial relations in contemporary britain', *British Journal of Industrial Relations*, 31, 1, 97–114.

Smith, P. and Maton G. (2001). 'New Labour's reform of Britain's employment law: the devil is not only in the details but in the values and policy too', *British Journal of Industrial Relations*, 39, 1, 119–38.

Smith, V. (1999). ' "Postmodern" Manors: Welfare Capitalism at the End of the Century', *Industrial Relations*, 38(2): 135–40.

Sonnenfield, J., Peiperl, M., and Kotter, J. (1988). 'Strategic Determinants of Managerial Labour Markets: A Career Systems View', *Human Resource Management*, 27(4): 369–88.

Sparrow, P. and Hiltrop, J. (1994). *European Human Resource Management in Transition*. New York: Prentice Hall.

Spie, U. and Bahlmann, W. (1978). 'Arbeitsdirektoren in der Eisen- und Stahlindustrie', *Das Mitbestimmungsgespräch*, 10: 245–50.

Storey, J. (ed.) (1995). *Human Resource Management: A Critical Text*. London: Routledge.

—— Edwards, P. and Sisson, K. (1997). *Managers in the Making: Careers, Development and Control in Corporate Britain and Japan*. London: Sage.

Streeck, W. (1997). 'German Capitalism: Does it Exist? Can it Survive?', *New Political Economy* 2(2): 237–57.

324

—— and Thelen, K. (2005). 'Introduction: Institutional Change in Advanced Political Economies', in W. Streeck, and K. Thelen (eds), *Beyond Continuity: Institutional Change in Advanced Political Economies*, Oxford: Oxford University Press, pp. 1–39.

Stubbs, R. and Underhill, G. (eds) (2000). *Political Economy and the Changing Global Order*, 2nd edn. Oxford: Oxford University Press.

Stuber, M. (2003). *Diversity*. Neuwied: Luchterhand.

Sutton, F., Harris, S., Kaysen, C., and Tobin, J. (1956). *The American Business Creed*. New York: Schocken.

Szulanski, G. (1996). 'Exploring Internal Stickiness: Impediments to the Transfer of Best Practice within the Firm', *Strategic Management Journal*, 17 (Winter Special Issue): 27–43.

Tansey, P. (1998). *Ireland at Work: Economic Growth and the Labour Market, 1987–1997*. Dublin: Oak Tree Press.

Taylor, S., Beechler, S., and Napier, N. (1996). 'Toward an Integrative Model of Strategic International Human Resource Management', *Academy of Management Review*, 21(4): 959–85.

Tempel, A. and Walgenbach, P. (forthcoming). 'Global Standardization of Organizational Forms and Management Practices? What New Institutionalism and the Business Systems Approach Can Learn From Each Other', *Journal of Management Studies*.

Tempel, A., Edwards, T., Ferner, A., Muller-Carmen, M., Wächter, H., and Almond, P. (2004). 'Corporate Versus Local Isomorphism? Collective Representation Practices of US MNCs in Britain and Germany'. Paper presented at conference on *Multinationals and the International Diffusion of Organizational Forms and Practices*, 15–17 July, IESE, Barcelona.

Thelen, K. (2003). 'How Institutions Evolve: Insights From Comparative Historical Analysis', in J. Mahoney, and D. Rueschemeyer (eds), *Comparative Historical Analysis in the Social Sciences*, Cambridge: Cambridge University Press, pp. 208–40.

Thompson, A., Mabey, C., Storey, J., Gray, C., and Iles, P. (2001). *Changing Patterns of Management Development*. Oxford: Blackwell.

Towers, B. (1997). *The Representation cap: Change and Reform in the British and American Workplace*. Oxford: OUP.

Tregaskis, O., Ferner, A., and Glover, L. (2005). *The Functions of International HRM Networks in International Companies*. London: C IPD.

Turner, L. (1991). *Democracy at Work: Changing World Markets and the Future of Labor Unions*. Ithaca, NY: Cornell University Press.

Turner, T. and Morley, M. (1995). *Industrial Relations and the New Order*. Dublin: Oak Tree Press.

Turner, T., D'Art, D., and Gunnigle, P. (1997a). 'Pluralism in Retreat: A Comparison of Irish and Multinational Manufacturing Companies', *International Journal of Human Resource Management*, 8(6): 825–40.

References

Turner, T., D'Art, D., and Gunnigle, P. (1997*b*). 'US Multinationals: Changing the Framework of Irish Industrial Relations?', *Industrial Relations Journal*, 28(2): 92–102.

Ulrich, D. (1999). 'Einleitung', in D. Ulrich (ed.), *Strategisches Human Resource Management*. München, Wien: Hanser.

UNCTAD (United Nations Conference on Trade and Development) (1993). *Transnational Corporations and Integrated International Production* (*World Investment Report 1993*). New York: United Nations.

—— (2003). *FDI Policies for Development: National and International Perspectives* (*World Investment Report 2003*). New York/Geneva: United Nations.

—— (2004). *The Shift Towards Services* (*World Investment Report 2004*). New York/Geneva: United Nations.

—— (2005). *Transnational Corporations and the Internationalization of R&D* (*World Investment Report 2005*). New York/Geneva: United Nations.

Underhill, G. (2000). 'Introduction: Conceptualizing the Changing Global Order', in R. Stubbs, and G. Underhill (eds), *Political Economy and the Changing Global Order*, Don Mills, Ontario: Oxford University Press, pp. 3–24.

US Department of Labor (1994). *Commission on the Future of Worker–Management Relations (Dunlop Commission) (1993–1994)*. Washington, DC: US Department of Labor.

Valle, R., Martín, F., and Romero, P. M. (2001). 'Trends and Emerging Values in Human Resource Management: The Spanish Scene', *International Journal of Manpower*, 22(3): 244–51.

Van Ommeren, J. and Brewster, C. (1999). 'The Determinants of the Number of HR Staff in Organisations: Theory and Empirical Evidence'. Cranfield Working Paper, SWP 12/99.

Vickerstaff, S. (1992). 'The Human Resource Management Function', in S. Vickerstaff (ed.), *Human Resource Management in Europe, Text and Cases*, London: Chapman Hall, pp. 1–7.

Visser, J. (1995). 'Trade Unions from a Comparative Perspective', in J. Van Ruysseveldt, R. Huiskamp, and J. Van Hoof (eds), *Comparative Industrial and Employment Relations*, London: Sage, pp. 37–67.

Vogel, D. (1978). 'Why Businessmen Distrust Their State: The Political Consciousness of American Coporate Executives', *British Journal of Political Science*, 8(1): 45–75.

Voos, P. (1996). Review of Bronfenbrenner, K., Friedman, S., Hurd, R., Oswald, R., and Seeber, R. (1998). 'Organizing to Win: New Research on Union Strategies', *British Journal of Industrial Relations*, 37, 3, 511–13.

Wächter, H. (1983). *Mitbestimmung. Politische Forderung und betriebliche Reaktion*. München: Verlag Vahlen.

—— and Muller-Camen, M. (2002). 'Co-determination and Strategic Integration in German Firms', *Human Resource Management Journal*, 12(3): 76–87.

—— and Stengelhofen, T. (1995). 'Germany', in I. Brunstein (ed.), *Human Resource Management in Western Europe*, Berlin, New York: de Gruyter, pp. 89–112.

—— Peters, R., Tempel, A., and Muller-Camen, M. (2003). *The 'Country-of-Origin Effect' in the Cross-National Management of Human Resources: Results and Case Study Evidence of Research on American Multinational Companies in Germany.* Munich/Mering: Rainer Hampp Verlag.

—— Vedder, G., and Führing, M. (eds) (2003). *Personelle Vielfalt in Organisationen.* München: Hampp.

Walker, J. W. (1988). 'How Large Should the HR Staff Be?', *Personnel*, October: 36–42.

Wallace, J., Gunnigle, P., and McMahon, G. (2004). *Industrial Relations in Ireland*, 3rd edn. Dublin: Gill Macmillan.

Walton, R. E. (1982). 'The Topeka Work System: Optimistic Visions, Pessimistic Hypothesis and Reality', in R. Zager, and M. Rosow (eds), *The Innovative Organisation*, New York: Pergamon, pp. 260–87.

Watson, S. and Roth, K. (2003). 'Implementing Lateral Centralization at the Foreign Subsidiary: The Role of Compensation and Reward Systems', in B. McKern, (ed.), *Managing the Global Network Corporation*, London: Routledge, pp. 135–51.

Wentling, R. and Palma-Rivas, N. (2000). 'Current Status of Diversity Initiatives in Selected Multinational Corporations', *Human Resource Development Quarterly*, 11(1): 35–60.

Westney, D. E. (1993). 'Institutionalization Theory and the Multinational Corporation', in S. Ghoshal, and D. E. Westney (eds), *Organization Theory and the Multinational Corporation*, London: Macmillan, pp. 53–76.

Wever, K. (1995). *Negotiating Competitiveness: Employment Relations and Organizational Innovation in Germany and the United States.* Boston, MA: Harvard Business School.

Wheeler, H. and McClendon, J. (1998). 'Employment Relations in the United States', in G. Bamber, and R. Lansbury (eds), *International and Comparative Employment Relations*, 3rd edn. London: Sage, pp. 55–82.

Wheeler, H. N. and McClendon, J. A. (1998). 'Employment Relations in the United States' in G. Bamber and O. R. Lansbury (eds), *International and Comparative Empolyment Relations*, 3rd edn.', London, Sage.

Whitehouse, G. (1992). 'Legislation and Labour Market Gender Inequality: An Analysis of OECD Countries', *Work, Employment and Society*, 6(1): 65–86.

Whitley, R. (1999). *Divergent Capitalisms: The Social Structuring and Change of Business Systems.* Oxford: Oxford University Press.

—— (2001). 'How and Why Are International Firms Different? The Consequences of Cross-Border Managerial Coordination for Firm Characteristics and Behaviour', in G. Morgan, P. H. Kristensen, and R. Whitley (eds), *The Multinational Firm: Organizing Across Institutional and National Divides*, Oxford: Oxford University Press, pp. 27–68.

Windolf, P. and Wood, S. (1988). *Recruitment and Selection in the Labour Market: A Comparative Study of British and West Germany.* Aldershot: Gower.

References

Womack, J., Jones, D., and Roos, D. (1990). *The Machine that Changed the World*. New York/Toronto: Rawson.

Yin, R. (1994). *Case Study Research: Design and Methods*, 2nd edn. Thousand Oaks, CA: Sage.

Yoder, D. (1970). 'Personnel Ratios 1970', *Personnel Administrator*, 15(6): 36–7.

Young, S., Hood, N., Hamill, J. (1985). *Decision-Making in Foreign-Owned Multinational Subsidiaries in the United Kingdom*. ILO working paper, no. 35. Geneva: ILO.

Yuen, E. and Kee, H. T. (1993). 'Headquarters, Host-Culture and Organisational Influences on HRM Policies and Practices', *Management International Review*, 33(4): 361–83.

Zucker, L. G. (1988). *Institutional Patterns and Organizations: Culture and Environment*. Cambridge, MA: Ballinger.

Index